Marie

EQUITY AND EFFICIENCY POLICY IN COMMUNITY CARE

This work was undertaken by the PSSRU, which receives support from the Department of Health; the views expressed in this publication are those of the authors and not necessarily those of the Department of Health.

Equity and Efficiency Policy in Community Care

Needs, service productivities, efficiencies and their implications

BLEDDYN DAVIES
JOSÉ FERNÁNDEZ
with BÜLENT NOMER

Ashgate

Aldershot • Burlington USA • Singapore • Sydney

Published by
Ashgate Publishing Ltd
Gower House
Croft Road
Aldershot
Hants GU11 3HR
England

Ashgate Publishing Company
131 Main Street
Burlington
Vermont 05401
USA

Ashgate website: http://www.ashgate.com

British Library Cataloguing in Publication Data
Davies, Bleddyn, 1936-
   Equity and efficiency policy in community care : needs,
   service productivities, efficiencies and their implications
   1.Public welfare - Great Britain 2.Community health
   services - Great Britain 3.Health care reform - Great
   Britain - Evaluation
   I.Title II.Fernández, José III.Nomer, Bülent
   362.1'068'0941

Library of Congress Control Number: 00-132583

ISBN 0 7546 1281 3

Typeset by Nick Brawn at the PSSRU, University of Kent at Canterbury

Printed in Great Britain by Antony Rowe Ltd.

Contents

List of Tables

List of Figures

Preface

This book focuses on one of the main concerns of analyses of the production of welfare: how variations in service inputs affect outcomes of the kind which justify their public subsidisation and regulation, and how the effects of these variations differ between users and caregivers in different circumstances.

Policy Analytic Context. Chapter 1 describes the context in the evolution of British argument about the production of welfare in British community care. Experiments conducted by the Personal Social Services Research Unit (PSSRU) in budget-devolved care management were finding that the equity and efficiency effects of community care could be greatly improved. In particular, variations in inputs of the standard community services appeared not to have big effects on some of the outcomes most valued by users, caregivers and policy-makers. But the experiments were focused on only some users. Therefore it was important to discover whether the problem of general inequity and inefficiency, especially of low marginal productivities for important outputs, applied to most users; and to understand the problem's causes and develop argument about how to tackle it. For this reason, the PSSRU built into its plan for the quinquennium commencing in 1980 a study of the whole range of elderly users of the community social services.

The general pattern of the findings and of the policy dilemma it raised were discussed in the PSSRU book *Resources, Needs and Outcomes in Community-Based Care* (Davies et al., 1990). Services did indeed have generally low marginal productivities for important outcomes. That is, consumers who received larger amounts of services seemed not to be much better off with respect to the forms of welfare in question as a result of receiving the larger quantities. The diffusion of the innovations then most common was unlikely to correct this, the project showed. So it would be necessary to improve productivities. That would be a more formidable task than to improve targeting, the other prerequisite for improving equity and efficiency.

The findings posed a policy dilemma. Although need priority should be defined in terms of the improvements expected from the use of resources as well as in terms of current state, better targeting would require greater concentration of resources. Were marginal productivities to remain unchanged but resources targeted on fewer recipients, potential users excluded would lose the benefits they gained, while those on whom the resources were concentrated would gain little. Were targeting to be ineffective, pressure would be generated to provide higher cost packages without a reduction in total numbers of recipients, so causing upward pressure on total expenditures, again without big gains in outputs. Hence the dilemma. Should such a high proportion of the reform effort be put into home and community care by ensuring the better performance of care management tasks, in the hope that more effective community care would divert demand away from shelter with care? Or should the effort be divided between improving the productivity of shelter with care and its targeting, and improving the productivity and targeting of home and community care? The government chose the former.

The results presented in this book show the choice to have been correct. It seems that there have been such large productivity gains that the parameters of the production of welfare have been transformed. That is described at the most general level at the beginning of chapter 27, and in more detail in the overview of productivity patterns in chapter 12.

The mapping of the productivities suggests the validity of the key but unstated assumption of the form of new managerialism that is emerging under an energetic and interventionist government committed to the policy area. Much implementation policy since the late 1970s would achieve far less if the assumption were substantially invalid. It is more valid than would have been imagined possible even fifteen years ago. The assumption is that the technology of community care is substantially determinate: that is, the relationship between resource inputs and outcomes of the greatest evaluative importance seem to be statistically describable to a substantial and useful degree. That we realise what are the implications of this substantial technological determinacy is important for policy-making, policy implementation strategy and the development of implementation tools, and for policy analysis. To fail to work through the implications would seriously handicap our efforts. Of course, we must be careful not to let convenience tempt us to overstate the degree of technological determinacy, for reasons explored in chapter 1 and the last section of chapter 27. But a substantial degree of determinacy should now be the working hypothesis for policy analysis and design.

Some of the ways in which a substantial degree of technological determinacy opens new possibilities for policy analysis are explored in the book; for instance, in the discussion of the policy propositions in chapters 23 to 26. Others are not. One example is the potential of the approach developed in the book for providing an important part of the intelligence needed for knowledge-influenced policy design and implementation. A second is the design of indicators for allocating resources between local authorities based on setting output targets, and taking into account area variations in population circumstances and relative prices of service inputs. That was one of the aims of the PSSRU Domiciliary Care Project (DCP) in 1980, unachievable then because of the low degree of technological determinacy at that time.

Interrelationship of ECCEP publications. The PSSRU research programme Evaluating Community Care for Elderly People (ECCEP) has concerns other than mapping the parameters of the production of welfare, the subject of this book. Among them are the pattern of outcomes (in the jargon, 'final outputs'), the pattern of risk factors and other need-related circumstances among users and their informal caregivers, the determinants of who consumes what service in what quantities, and a wide range of questions about processes that influence utilisation and who benefits in what way.

The themes are inter-related. So, therefore, are the publications. Readers of this book will particularly find it useful to interpret this book in the context of three others based on the ECCEP collection of evidence. One is the forthcoming work on utilisation patterns: *Needs-Led or Resource-Driven? Who Gets What in Post-Reform Community Care* (Davies and Fernández, 2000a, forthcoming). A second is *Care Management in Community Care: Structures, Procedures, Assumptive Worlds and Outcomes* (Davies and Fernández, 2000b, forthcoming). The main aim of the third, *Caring for Older People: an Assessment of Community Care in the 1990s* (Bauld, Chesterman, Davies, Judge and Mangalore, 2000) is to describe users' and caregivers' need-related circumstances, changes in state over the six months following assessment, informal caregiving, the receipt of services, and features of care management. Because ECCEP is in part a replication of a project planned in 1980, there is a direct counterpart among earlier publications. *Resources, Needs and Outcomes in Community-Based Care* mapped pre-reform productivities (Davies et al., 1990). Having been written at a time when the pressure to produce quickly was less intense, that and *Care Management, Equity and Efficiency: the International Experience* (Davies, 1992a) contained much more analysis of other literature, particularly about the experience in other countries. The availability of these and other reports and publications allows this to be more an essay, less a self-contained study, and not at all a project report.

Acknowledgements. By far the greater part of the effort of the project has been in design and collection, not the drafting of the final analyses and publications. It is one of the differences between the economics of this and of secondary analyses or most collections by consortia. We could not possibly acknowledge all those who have made important contributions to the ECCEP collection. First, there have been the users, carers, care managers, and the many other managers on whose cooperation we have depended. The design of the study asked a great deal of effort for only a distant and indirect reward. In particular, we made enormous demands on those who were our liaison persons with the collaborating authorities: June Barraclough, Gill Best, Tony Burks, Steve Cody,

Duncan Henderson, Isabelle Houghton, April Lawler, Beverley McCann, Vivian Mellish, Barbara Priestly, Paul Richardson, Pam Satterthwaite, and Sandra Stapely. We cannot acknowledge by name the Directors of Social Services who sat on our Advisory Committee because we have promised the anonymity of their authorities. Neither do conventions allow us to name the twelve members representing the Department of Health. But we can acknowledge Lucianne Sawyer, and Terry Butler (who sat as Chair of the ADSS Service Evaluation Research and Information Committee), as well as the academics Professors Shah Ebrahim, Elaine Murphy, and Claire Wenger.

Then there are those who have been part of the whole ECCEP team at PSSRU. The collection has been complex, vast, and difficult. Many people have contributed since 1995, when the programme's third phase began. Expectations are rising about how quickly research can be completed. This and its companion will appear within five years of the first collection of data on which they are based; a much shorter time than ever before, although the project suffered serious delays and other strains because of an eighteen-month hiatus in mid-project because of recruitment difficulties. The acceleration is due only partly to new technologies for analysis and publication. We should acknowledge that is also due to the greatly increased pressure that research teams withstand.

During the collection period, and until the Department of Health made him an offer he could not refuse, Raymond Warburton was the manager and senior full-time academic member of the team. He brought great policy experience and imagination to the project. He drove us all forward with indefatigable energy and faultless organisation. Without it, there would have been disaster on several occasions, given the extremely tight time framework. Gail Goldstone, Steve Luckham, Alisoun Milne, Steve Carter and Sherrill Stone were involved either full or part-time at various times during that period. Research Services Limited (now IPSOS-RSL Ltd) undertook much of the field interviewing.

During the period between the departure of the collection team and the arrival of the analysis group, progress was made mainly by persuading colleagues to switch projects, and by employing casual and temporary staff. Fortunately, *Community Care in England and France* (Davies, Fernández and colleagues, 1998) had been completed, releasing José Fernández and Robin Saunders. José Fernández first did much to organise the database as well as to undertake the modelling for early analytic papers. Robin Saunders contributed to the production of the early tables and has taken charge of the tracking of resources, needs and outcomes since the second interview with triad members. Sheila Kesby was engaged to fill gaps in our evidence about the utilisation of health services. From the Summer of 1997, the ECCEP team at PSSRU at Kent was complete again, with Ken Judge as project manager. Bleddyn Davies has been principal researcher, designing the project, working with members of the teams at the LSE and Kent, and spending most of his time on the project throughout its entire history.

The book itself is a product of the ECCEP team at the London School of Economics: José Fernández and Bleddyn Davies, with the part-time contribution of Bülent Nomer for a period. This has been an exciting collaboration. Each has contributed acuity, imagination, knowledge, skill and the greatest possible energy, commitment and intellectual excitement. The book has been the product of one of those rare but extraordinarily creative chemistries that make the whole so much more than the sum of what each person could have produced alone, and from which everyone feels enriched. It is hard for the authors to imagine how it could have been the same with a different combination of people.

No book from the PSSRU stable should fail to acknowledge the effort, intelligence, skill and professionalism of the PSSRU's team in its publications office, Nick Brawn and Jane Dennett, who have managed the end-stage of dozens of PSSRU publications, of which more than 20 have been book-length work. The quality of the work at that stage will be evident to all our readers. For this book, Natasha Kemp provided valuable help in editing drafts and assembling the diagrams. We are grateful to Professor Vernon Greene, the pioneer and leading exponent of this kind of analysis in the United States, for carefully reading and enthusiastically discussing the final version of the book with us while he was an academic visitor to the PSSRU at the LSE. Unfortunately, it was too late to extend the draft. However, we were able to rephrase some sentences and so remove unnoticed ambiguities seen by an eye sharpened by years of editing *The Gerontologist*.

On reading the book. We have worked hard to make the messages of the book accessible without over-simplifying important details of our findings. We hope that its accessibility is maximised by its structure, style, and use of figures rather than equations and tables and the full contents lists, glossary and indexes. However, the combination of broad generalisation with detailed reporting makes it sensible for many readers to grasp the approach and broad findings before engaging the detail. For this reason, we suggest reading the intoductory chapter 1 for the context and approach. Then in Part I, read chapters 2 and 3 for their explanation of what is to follow, and chapter 12 for its overviews of productivity patterns and the contributions of services to outputs. Again, in Part II, read the introductory chapter 13 before looking at some of the other chapters. Part II is a necessary bridge between productivity mapping and the policy analysis and discussion in Part III. The policy analysis is as much the main point of the book as the mapping of productivities and efficiencies. Part III depends greatly on allusions to earlier chapters. Chapters 23 to 26 are the most important. The last chapter returns to the implications of the observed degree of technological determinacy.

Inevitably, we often use abbreviations and specialised terms. We have tried to explain these where they are introduced, and the glossary which follows assembles a list of definitions. Throughout the book, we frequently refer to our indicator variables for care outcomes (outputs), such as *length of stay in the com-*

munity, and explanatory variables. To avoid repeating the often long descriptions of these we have used the abbreviated forms which appear as (for example) DAYS in the text. Table 2.1 (page 33) provides a summary of output domains and indicators, and lists of output and explanatory variables with descriptions are given in appendix tables 2.1 (page 415) and 2.2 (page 419).

Glossary

Abbreviations used for output and input indicators

Table 2.1 (page 33) provides a summary of output domains and indicators. A full list and description of the output variables used in the production functions is given in appendix table 2.1 (page 415) and of the explanatory input variables used in the modelling in appendix table 2.2 (page 419).

Abbreviations used in the figures and tables

Behav	behavioural
cog imp	cognitive impairment
CM	care manager
DC	day care
HC	home care
M	home-delivered meals
NRCs	need-related circumstances
NV	nursing visits
PIC	principal informal carer
RE	respite care
Rel pbs	relationship problems
SW	social work, social worker
U	user

continued/...

Other definitions

Term	Explanation
ADL, IADL, PADL	Activities of daily living, instrumental activities of daily living, personal care activities of daily living. See chapters 2 and 6.
Analysis groups or case types	(a) Long interval with PIC (b) Long interval without PIC (c) Short interval with PIC (d) Short interval without PIC (e) Critical interval with PIC (f) Critical interval without PIC Long interval users have at least weekly needs for help with personal care or instrumental activities of daily living; short interval users have daily needs; critical interval needs are for care more than once a day at unpredictable intervals. See chapter 2, section 3. PIC is defined below.
Budgets	
Budget caps	Guideline or mandatory limits in package costs for a user in certain circumstances.
User group budgets	Setting average and aggregate budgets per sub-group of users. Associated with selection of main output goal, and effective arrangements for case-finding and care management applying logics in Davies (1986, 1992), and Davies et al. (1990).
COCA (continuing care) phase	From the end of the set-up period until substantial reassessment and change in plan. *See* SUP (set-up) phase.
Collateral output levels	Levels of other outputs produced by optimising on an output.
Cost function	Equation describing how costs related to outputs and risk factors. See chapters 3 and 11.
Cover of Productivity Proportion (COPP)	Proportion of users of the service(s) affected by the productivity effect(s) in question. See chapter 12.

Term	Explanation
DCP	Domiciliary Care Project (1983-), the first stage of the before-after evaluation of changes in equity and efficiency in community care: principal output, Davies et al. (1990). *See also* MSCEP, ECCEP.
ECCEP	Evaluating Community Care of Elderly People. The third stage of PSSRU research after DCP and MSCEP (q.v.).
Efficiency aspects	See chapter 13 section 2.1.
Input mix	Degree to which inputs so mixed as to maximise outputs given productivities and relative prices.
Output mix	Degree to which outputs so mixed as to maximise overall value of outputs given their relative valuations.
Technical	Degree to which final outputs maximised given input mix and technical efficiency.
Final output	Outcome of service inputs of evaluative significance in its own right rather than because of assumed effects on other outcomes.
IADL	Instrumental activities of daily living. See chapters 2 and 6.
Input	
substitutability	Degree to which one inputs of one resource can be replaced by inputs of another maintaining output constant.
complementarity	Effect of level of an input on the productivity of another input.
Interval need	*See* Analysis groups.
Joint supply	Circumstances in which level of one or more outputs influence the marginal productivity of one or more inputs with respect to another output. See chapter 11.
KCCP	Kent Community Care Project, the first PSSRU evaluation of community care, aimed to develop equity and efficiency theory for a system combining responsiveness to field perceptions of users, carers, and care-managers with higher managerial and policy frameworks. Principal output: Davies and Challis (1986).

Term	Explanation
Marginal cost	
Marginal cost of an output	The additional cost of an increment of an output.
Marginal productivity of a service for an output	The increment of an output associated with an increase in the service by one unit; the slope of the productivity curve given the output level and risk factors.
Diminishing, constant and increasing returns to scale	Marginal productivities falling, constant, or rising given the output and risk factor levels. See chapter 3.
MSCEP	Monitoring Services for the Care of Elderly People (intermediate stage of PSSRU research between DCP and ECCEP). Staff and management interviews and related collections only. Principal output: Gostick et al. (1997). *See also* DCP, ECCEP.
Optimisation scenario	See chapter 13.
'Unconstrained' optimisation	Resources can be shifted between services and user groups without constraints or changing price levels.
'Group-budget-constrained' optimisation	Resources can be moved between services without price differences but the total (and so average) budget for each group is fixed.
'Service-budget-constrained' optimisation	Resources can be reallocated between analysis groups but the total amount of each service commissioned remains constant.
Optimisation	Maximisation of an output by making the best use of resources, subject to the constraints imposed by the 'optimisation scenario'.
Outputs	*See also* Efficiency aspects.
Single output maximand procedure	Procedure for working through consequences of making the best use of resources assuming one output to be the sole goal.
Topic output	The output defined as the output maximand.
PADL	Personal care activities of daily living. See chapters 2 and 6.
PIC	Principal informal carer: principal caregiver, defined in terms of substantial help with tasks of daily living at least weekly.

Term	Explanation
Production function	Equation(s) describing relationships between service inputs, risk factors and final outputs. Frontier (production) functions estimate the maximum produced with the combinations of inputs and risk factors. 'Reduced form' functions have one output as the dependent variable. 'Structural' form functions show also how outputs affect one another. See chapters 3 and 11.
Production of welfare (POW) studies	Studies focused on a set of questions tackling equity and efficiency, utilisation and targeting, the effects of services and other resources on final outputs, allowing for the influence of other types of factor; with associated collations of knowledge, repertoires of techniques for collection and analysis of evidence for description and causal explanation; often applied to the development of argument about policy development. See preface and chapter 1.
Productivities	
average	The average number of units of output associated with a level of input.
marginal	The marginal increase in output to be expected from a marginal increase in input.
Returns to scale	*See* Marginal cost.
Risk factors and production function form	See chapter 3.
Additive risk effects	Effects of risk factors affecting the intercepts of productivity curves but not their slopes; i.e. average but not marginal productivities and costs. See chapter 3, section 1.
Targeting-captured risk effects	Allocation of a service after assessment associated with one or more risk factors present prior to intervention. See chapter 3, section 1.
User group marginal productivity terms	Marginal productivity effects applying only in presence of risk factors. See chapter 3, section 1.
Risk Offset from Productivity Proportion (ROPP)	Proportion of total deleterious effect on outcome offset by contributions of services. See chapter 12.

Term	Explanation
SSD	Social services department.
SUP (set-up phase)	Set-up phase of care-managed community care (from referral to the beginning of the implementation of the complete care plan intended to remain in place until circumstances change). *See also* COCA phase.
Technological determinacy	Degree to which the impacts of service resource inputs predict final outputs and the relationships stable enough for the estimates to provide basis for policy-making: see chap 27 section 2.
Triadic design	Collections containing overlapping evidence from users, their principal informal caregivers and care managers, allowing multiple perspectives and checking of information. See chapter 1, section 4.1.

1   Introduction:
Policy Context and Research Design

The 1990s were distinguished by the effort to reform community and long-term care. At the end of that decade, the signs are that the UK central government intends to pursue reform with still greater vigour for some time to come, deploying ever sharper instruments to promote implementation.

Five years after the reform arrangements were first fully implemented is a good time to take stock. More than in other reforming countries the central focus of the British effort has been the creation at central and local levels of policy systems that are 'self-inventing' (Klein, 1995). It is obvious that doing so has created a capacity for learning and adaptation hitherto unprecedented. But stimuli from outside have been vitally important. By a fortunate accident of history, we have had a new government and a Royal Commission to review progress, raise issues, set some new directions, and energise the system.[1] But they have raised questions that they have not yet been able to analyse in depth this soon.[2] This essay uses the data from the PSSRU's study for the evaluation of post-reform community care of elderly people further to define and discuss some of these issues.

Equity and efficiency are its foci. The issues group themselves around several themes.

- *Maintain, raise or reduce the investment ratio?* The most general issue is whether the achievements of a decade of reform of community and long-term care justified the investment in effort and resources. A decade ago, it was argued that the time was ripe to invest. The message was that the ratio of investment to consumption should increase during the period when a temporary lull in demographic pressure was projected, so that we could enter the period of maximum increase in strain with a well-founded system (Davies et al., 1990, 399-400). It has been argued that there were some areas of the new technology in which investment was insufficient and inconsistently made during the initial period of the reforms (Gostick et al., 1997).

Nevertheless, there have been large investments, and above all an investment orientation: activity to improve the capacity of the system to produce more and more highly valued benefits from the use of the resources, not simply to achieve immediate efficiency improvements. The most general question is whether there is sufficient evidence of success to justify the maintenance of, or increase in, the investment ratio? And if maintaining the investment ratio is justifiable, what should be the aims of the increased investment? On the one hand, the essay fits into a stream from the ECCEP project illuminating the benefits from the reform investments, its special place being to show the effects of these investments on the productivity of services for outputs. On the other hand, it indicates what benefits might be achieved from operating with current efficiencies, as compared with the benefits from alternative strategies for investing in efficiency improvement.

- *Interpretation of 'independence'?* The new government has restated the promotion of 'independence' to be the main goal of community care policy. But 'independence' has many aspects. Therefore, the essay works through the consequences of different interpretations. What are the likely implications for outcomes of making the enhancement of users' feeling of control over their lives the main goal of community care? How would the maximisation of independence in this 'empowerment' sense compare with the maximisation of some of the other broad goals of community care; for instance, user satisfaction with service contributions, or the reduction in the felt burden of caring among principal informal caregivers? How different would these costs and benefits be from a world in which it was the care managers' own evaluations of outcomes for users and caregivers that were optimised?

- *Higher or lower budget levels?* In a world of triennial Comprehensive Spending Reviews and efficiency savings, setting the overall budget in relation to productivities and needs of cases is critical. Given the case-mix, what benefits are foregone because the overall budget is not 10 per cent higher? What benefits would be foregone were the overall budget to be 10 per cent lower?

The policy has also raised narrower issues of prioritisation.

- *Concentration or diffusion of resources across users?* The logic of the 1989 reforms was in several respects a reaction against features of the old system. One element was a reaction against the pre-reform demand-responsiveness in utilisation patterns not balanced by positive targeting policies based on conscious equity policy and the review of the impact of resources on outcomes. The reform logic was to focus resources more on persons for whom the concentration was likely to provide a preferred alternative to unwanted and inappropriately long stays in institutions for long-term care. Since 1995, many have believed that resources are excessively concentrated, and advocate low level services spread across a large number of users. They assert that this would achieve more timely and so more effective prevention. There have been periodic reminders that 'need' can be defined in ways which take into account outcomes and resource costs, outcomes alone or only unacceptable welfare shortfall or 'public sector dependency'; and with these reminders, the argument that prioritisations can apply different bases depending on user circumstances (Culyer et al., 1971; Davies, 1968, 1971, 1977). Rarely have those who put the case for diffusion produced any evidence other than that elderly people above all value the opportunity to continue living at home, and that to a great extent they tend to attribute this to small inputs of household care. They have never attempted the precise mapping of the issue in terms of the trade-off between benefits of different kinds to different users. Has the concentration actually reduced the number of days in institutions among the recipients of costly packages? And if so, would the reduction in the number of days due to services be greater if more of the resources were allocated to those of lower disability?

- The issue is complicated because the outcomes would depend (a) on precisely how the policy is defined and put into effect, and (b) the broader policy scenario set. What would be the differences for outcomes between allocating more resources to the same number of persons of lower disability levels and changing the case-mix so that more persons of lower disability would receive some service, the others remaining similar? What would be the effects of reducing concentration by setting budget caps at levels related to care costs in institutions for long-term care, allowance being made for the assumed superiority of the benefits of remaining at home? And how sensitive would the outcomes be to different assumed levels of the care costs? What would be the effects of making the main goal improvement in the services' contribution to the better performance of core tasks of daily living?

- *Change the mix of services commissioned?* What difference is made to the answers to these questions if it is assumed that making big changes in the quantities of the types of service commissioned could easily be made, and would make little difference to the prices paid for each service?

These are the types of question addressed in Part III. The earlier sections provide the statistical description of the effects of services on policy-relevant outcomes and the mapping of efficiencies for that discussion.

1.   Contemporary policy context

These are not just issues for the moment, though they may be newly recognised in the UK. *Resources, Needs and Outcomes* (Davies et al., 1990) described how a new administration in Wisconsin during the mid-1980s deliberately fostered a debate with representatives of elderly people (thereby increasing the influence of organisations representing them) and focused the discussion on the balance to be struck between offering the option of care at home for the few as against lower level service for the many. Steps recently taken to empower users in the UK may similarly generate a local politics of community care. But because it is rare for this attempt to go so far as substantially to focus the discussion on balancing priorities and on changing the local polity of community care to provide the arena for the debate, as intended in Wisconsin, the articulation of views has overtones of clientelism rather than third way responsibility, however much it may seek to assert the values of 'active citizenship'. Gateshead is not the only authority to be slow to abandon its closed style of policy-making and management, what a joint review called 'cautious and controlling', with dissatisfaction among some user groups and inefficient patterns of service in consequence (Audit Commission and Department of Health, 1999).

The government promotes reform partly as an expression of its broader theme of 'modernisation' (Department of Health, 1998b, chap. 1).[3] The policy framework includes budgeted programmes specifically for *investment* in the modernisation: the allocation of resources to activities now which, though not necessarily producing greater welfare immediately, or, indeed, immediately or directly affecting the current capacity for performance of the system, are designed to do so in the long run.[4] The investment metaphor fits the structure of policies for reform well enough to influence the nature of the argument of this essay.

Three aims may be distinguished, though most of the policies are aimed simultaneously to affect all three:

The first is *(a) making performance consistent by making the less successful package as successful as the most successful without changing the relationships between means and ends.* This can involve changing the balance of aims. Similarly, it can include changing the service mix in the package. But it is not intended to change the mix of outputs the most efficient can produce from any combination of inputs given user and caregiver circumstances.

The second is *(b) making general and pervasive improvement in the relations between means and ends by changing performance-influencing characteristics throughout the mainstream system.* Paraphrased, this means directly or indirectly improving the potential of mainstream technology. Many of the elements in the reform strategy are intended primarily to engage (a), usually by means of (b), reflecting the strength of the belief that new managerialist means are the key to achieving policy goals. *Modernising Social Services* makes greater consistency one of the three main goals for adult care services in targeting. The government proposes various actions to achieve this. The central government is to take a greater role nationally in setting objectives and standards by means of such devices as 'National Service Frameworks', in promoting a common understanding of 'risk-based assessment', and the Long-Term Care Charter, improved transparency and accountability in services. The subject of chapter 7 is improving delivery and efficiency. The means for doing so are various and interdependent. One is to set clear national objectives and priorities through 'National Priorities Guidance' and other means. There are to be new systems of performance monitoring through the 'Best Value' processes. The Best Value regime creates 'the duty to deliver services to clear standards covering both quality and cost by the most effective economical and efficient means available. The aim ... is to secure continuous improvements, and to deliver services which bear comparison to the best'. Additionally authorities are to be subject to five year performance reviews.

(c) Stimulating the development and diffusion of innovatory programmes which potentially have more productive relations between ends and means. Examples are the sponsorship and extension of direct payment schemes, schemes sponsored under the National Carers Strategy, a new grant available subject to the approval of an action plan to stimulate the local development of preventive strategies involving low level service input. The development of special programmes is to be an important method for creating the prioritised 'better preventive services' and 'stronger focus on rehabilitation'. Joint Investment Programmes are encouraged to develop specialist rehabilitation services. The Partnership Grants can be used for improving rehabilitation, but are available only subject to an action plan.

Each of the three elements necessarily has a large investment element; the conscious application of resources in ways which are not necessarily the most efficient for producing better outcomes immediately, but which are designed to improve the system's capacity for performance over a longer period. The importance of investment as a device in the reform strategy makes it useful for policy analysis to be framed to illuminate investment appraisal, albeit in itself, only providing some of the information required for a complete appraisal. Therefore one feature of the essay is that it defines types of investment and attempts to illuminate some of the likely outcomes.

It is less that there are separate devices for each way.[5] There are good reasons why initiatives and programmes defined by their objectives should attempt to work in all three ways simultaneously. A wise reformer realises that whatever else is done, (a), making others perform as successfully as the best within the existing technological constraints, must be an essential part of the reform strategy. On the one hand, fundamentally to change (b) or (c) requires many years. Community care systems are complex, there are many impediments to change, the influence of some devices is only indirect, and the influence of others is narrow not pervasive. Those who work in the system see continuities as well as changes, a perception borne out by the research literature. From the earliest days of reform, the Department talked about 'profound cultural shifts' and, almost a decade later, the policy papers still call for cultural changes, some of them the same as a decade later at the high level of generality in which the exhortations are couched, if not in terms of precisely what is meant. Perhaps what is surprising is how big the changes have been in some areas of activity since 1993, though ECCEP, like other work, illustrates how there are continuities, and wide differences between authorities in the thoroughness of the implementation of the new logic.

The balance between achieving (a), (b) and (c) struck by the reform's architects and builders affects the degree and nature of the usefulness of our results.

- The analysis in this essay most uniquely, directly and fully contributes to a knowledge base for considering what goals to set of type (a), and then for assessing performance in achieving them. Its contributions are to map the 'frontiers' which describe the relations between service inputs and outputs which maximise the latter given the former; to describe the variations in efficiency; to analyse the consequences of improving efficiency given alternative goals and scenarios; to indicate what values implicitly accorded to the patterns of benefits, assuming account is taken of how prices and productivities should influence them.

- The analysis can contribute to achieving aim (b) by helping to evaluate alternative goals for the improvement of the mainstream technological relationships. For instance, it shows for what outputs productivities are low, and beneficiaries who need outputs for the production of which the services are least effectively orientated.

- The analysis of 'technological bias' and of the equity of the existing system suggests what might be the objectives of innovative schemes aimed to contribute to technological development, (c), just as it contributes to improving the technological relationships everywhere, (b). However, ECCEP did not yield data for enough cases to make analysis of the production relations of innovatory schemes with aim (c) worthwhile. In this, it contrasts with the first stage of the before-after evaluation, the Domiciliary Care Project (DCP), which provided enough such data to examine the actual relationships between ends and means achieved by them (Davies et al., 1990, chapter 11).

So the nature of the reforms make the ECCEP evidence relevant to all three foci. But the strongest contribution is to the first: improving equity and efficiency by narrowing the gap between the most efficient and others. That is because the basis of the study is the description of current technological relationships.

2.   The pre-reform productivities challenge

The context is the threat that the pre-reform problem of pervasively low productivities presented to achieving the new policy aims of 1989. Whatever policy means used, continuation of the low productivities would make it unlikely that central goals as defined in the White Paper of 1989 would be achieved. In particular, their continuation would make the policy devices proposed in the White Paper completely ineffective for achieving them. It was clear that the policy system faced a hitherto unrecognised challenge: reform the system to increase productivities, or face an ignominious policy failure. That failure would be the reduction in the number of persons receiving any felt benefit, without compensating improvements in achieving care at home for persons unwillingly forced into institutions for long-term care, the wholesale shift of burdens to informal caregivers without effectively limiting their felt burden to the acceptable, and probably higher costs to public funds. Better targeting, which the PSSRU had argued had been one of the keys to improving equity and efficiency in community care since the 1970s, was also vital — as long as better targeting was subtly enough defined, an issue difficult because of its scientific problems as well as policy dilemmas and practice issues, as was elaborated in a succession of PSSRU books and papers published in the years preceding (and during) the reforms (Bebbington and Davies, 1983, 1993; Davies, 1976, 1981, 1987a,b, 1988, 1992, 1993a,b; Davies and Challis, 1986; Davies et al., 1990).

The productivities argument developed from the PSSRU's Kent Community Care Project (KCCP) (Davies, 1974). From one perspective, it was a set of field arrangements to overcome obstacles to improving equity and efficiency, by putting in place prerequisites for achieving technical progress and the more effective use of resources by substitutions of inputs and of outputs and service development. From another perspective, it was an attempt to work through a model that started from the user and the case manager with concentrated authority, responsibility and accountability for using the resources to achieve ends. The KCCP worked through the consequences upwards and outwards into policy, technologies and practice at other levels and into other parts of the care system, illuminating the issues by drawing on current American experience. The KCCP developed the argument that the nature of community and long-term care and those served by it suggested that arrangements for effectively performing care management tasks were essential mechanisms for achieving effectiveness of service inputs.

The evaluation showed the KCCP to have been conspicuously successful, building as it did, on a wide range of the new ideas of the period.[6] Successful also were its fully-evaluated 'replications' (in Gateshead, Sheppey and Tonbridge), the same basic model for the same group of users applied in different contexts, and applications of the principles and devices of the KCCP to different subgroups of users, evaluated in Darlington and Lewisham.[7]

In particular, the results suggested that the *marginal* productivities of inputs outputs were lower in standard provision than in the KCCP and its replications. From one perspective, the outcomes evaluations demonstrated the merits of the KCCP model and the approach of which it was an example. By the same token, the study of how community care worked in the project and the comparison system demonstrated the weaknesses of the latter. The KCCP and its replications therefore suggested the existence of a service productivities problem.

However, the KCCP was not designed to apply to all elderly persons served by community social services brokered by the social services department. It was a secondary referral model. The service was conceived in the same way as secondary level health care, with its emphasis on matching the needs of a group of users and, the complement of that, targeting only those for whom it was expected to be most appropriate. Users were referred to the programme from standard front-line services if their circumstances suggested that the impact could be much greater given access to intensive and resourceful case management, and/or potentially more costly service packages with flexible filling of gaps left by the services. It was later guesstimated that the KCCP model might be cost-effective for no more than perhaps one fifth of users of community care services (Davies et al., 1990).[8] For others, quite different arrangements for the performance of care management tasks would contribute more, as long as the performance of the tasks received the requisite emphasis.[9]

By 1980, it was clear that there was a need for evaluative research to establish whether the weaknesses in the community care system as they were manifest for the comparison groups of the care management projects applied to users in general. The Depatment of Health supported the inclusion of a project in the PSSRU's proposals for the quinquennium commencing in 1980. The Domiciliary Care Project became the first stage of a study of community care before and after the introduction of the 1990-93 reforms. An important aim was to estimate service productivities, and, unlike the evaluation of the care management experiments, it was designed accordingly.

The productivity estimates were most fully reported in *Resources, Needs and Outcomes* (Davies et al., 1990). They suggested productivities generally to be low; and lowest for types of outputs which were either the goals prioritised in the White Paper of 1989 and related policy statements, or which would be most likely to affect those priority goals. Where there were productivities of services for outputs, many seemed to be subject to fiercely diminishing returns from quite low levels of inputs. Indeed, many amounted almost to threshold effects, with few gains beyond that threshold.[10]

The challenge was clear, it was argued. It was essential to improve the productivities of services. That would be more difficult than the other, and by then better-recognised challenge: to improve targeting. The improvement of targeting required change only at some stages and in some of the functions of the community care system. The improvement of the productivities of individual services required radical changes in assumptions, if not skills, in all stages and functions, over the entire career of the user. It was also argued that targeting and the productivity of services were inter-related. The productivity of a service depends in part on the other elements of the package, and to whom the service is directed: targeting as well as service content and nature.[11]

There was anxiety among those familiar with the findings that at that time, other inferences might be drawn. In particular, if productivities were generally low, indeed too low to be seen through the measurement and specification errors, was there a strong case for maintaining the subsidy to community social services at their existing level? Would not a reduction in the subsidy be more rational than a major increase in service budgets, and a big investment in reform? Such questions were not put in *Resources, Needs and Outcomes*. Neither were they put by those who discussed the results and argument from *Resources, Needs and Outcomes* in other publications.

Evidence since made available provides some clues to what might have been the answers to such questions for the UK during the mid-1980s.

- One source of evidence is a study of cognitively impaired elderly persons by the National Institute for Social Work (Levin et al., 1989, 1994). It suggested that inputs of care did have important benefits for the supporters of elderly dementia sufferers, and they were appreciated by the supporters. However, the effects did not always apply to all the recipients to which they would be expected to be relevant. Also there were some relationships in the opposite direction, though relationships for which plausible explanations were presented in terms of specification or measurement error. However, the study was not mainly focused on service effects. Also, it did not set out to estimate productivity curves or their equivalents: that is, equations showing the effects on outputs of continuous variation in service inputs. Instead, it contained the results of some regression models exploring the effects of whether any, and what combinations, of services were received, making allowance for user circumstances. That is, they handled service inputs as dummy variables, not continuous variables. Related was a study of demented elderly persons (Levin et al., 1994). That too found some impacts on outcomes, but again it did not estimate the effects of variations in inputs on outcomes.

- Another source of evidence was an analysis of the KCCP and its replications. That showed that the ratio of gains of various kinds to costs tended to be higher for those of lower disability, those of lower disability tending to receive less costly packages (Davies et al., 1995). Both are compatible with one of the features of the results reported in *Resources, Needs and Outcomes*. Where productivities were discovered, there were often sharply diminishing returns to scale and threshold effects.

The discourse of that period therefore begs questions for this essay.[12] In post-reform community care, are there substantial productivities for the outputs of greatest policy importance? Are they primarily subject to sharply diminishing returns? Indeed, are there much more than threshold productivity effects for the most important outputs that apply to high proportions of users? Given the nature of the casemix and the relative prices of inputs, what do they imply about what would be the most cost-effective patterns of utilisation of services if one makes various assumptions about policy goals and the scenarios in which managers and other workers are seeking to achieve best value? What light does such analysis throw on the currently controversial manifestations of enduring policy dilemmas? What unrecognised or dimly-perceived policy problems dilemmas do they suggest? And how can these be most constructively tackled and faced?

3.   The essay and the research

The pluralism of policy discussions in community care is mirrored in the variety of evidential bases and concerns in academic analysis and research. With such variety, it is not surprising that there are disagreements about fact, causal inference, and policy conclusions. Undoubtedly variety is strength, if not a prerequisite, for balanced judgement.[13] It is useful to consider what this essay aims to contribute to the variety.

First, this is a 'production of welfare' study. Production of welfare studies focus on equity and efficiency in community care and related areas. They analyse utilisation, but in particular, and more thoroughly than other approaches, the effects of resource inputs on outcomes, taking into account those factors which influence them: user and caregiver circumstances and characteristics of supply systems, for instance.

When the resources for the collection of evidence permit, they study the relations between resource inputs on benefits considered to be of evaluative significance in their own right, not just as proxies believed to be related to these benefits; that is, they study the benefits for *final*, not *intermediate* outputs. Also when resources permit, they both provide statistical estimates of the relationships, and explain them at two levels with evidence and analytic techniques of various kinds. At one of the levels, they describe the processes by which proximate 'causes' affect the outcomes; for example, the processes by which local policy prioritisation affects the case-mix recruited. At the other level, they analyse why some of these proximate causes vary between circumstances; for instance, how historical continuities in general features of the local political culture are still reflected in prioritisation in social services policy. And when resources permit, they analyse the impacts on stakeholders of most concern to the stakeholders in question. So they attempt to describe and explore as well as to test and explain in ways which balance these partially incompatible research objectives.

The production of welfare studies collate argument about causality and techniques for the measurement of key concepts from a variety of subjects (particularly social sciences) but use them in asking questions developed in economics. In doing so, they import arguments about the significance of forms of relationships from economics, and the associated body of modelling techniques from econometrics. And they use the estimates to develop policy argument about issues of current importance (Davies and Knapp, 1981; Davies, 1985). So studies typically start with an argument about performance in the achievement of policy goals, define research questions raised by it, tackle the research questions on the basis of a body of evidence collected for that purpose, and discusses the implications of the answers for the redefinition of policy issues and policy action. Examples of studies which have done this in the stream of studies of community care for elderly people are Davies and Challis (1986) and Davies et al. (1990).

Secondly, this essay is a particular form of production of welfare study. It lays claim to being the most ambitious attempt yet undertaken to use production function modelling to map the effects of variations in services on final outputs; that is, *to map service productivities for outputs.* It then uses the maps to analyse patterns of efficiency; and then, postulating alternative priorities, strategies for improving efficiency, and scenarios about the resource constraints and devices for controlling equity, it considers what would be the likely gains from the alternatives, and what patterns of service commissioning they would entail. Finally, it uses the evidence to discuss a list of policy propositions about how to steer the reforms.

4.   Aims and the research design: collection and analysis

4.1.   Collection design

The design of the collection of data has been described elsewhere, so it is necessary to describe here only the key features of importance to the aims of the essay.

Three aims influenced the design of the ECCEP project: (a) describe patterns of utilisation and the production of welfare covering the whole range of users of community social services, (b) produce argument about how the system might be steered to improve equity and efficiency, and (c) compare equity and efficiency and influences on them pre- and post-reform. This essay is one of the two main studies from it directed at (b), analysis to develop equity and efficiency argument.

The protocol distinguished three types of issue to be tackled in the study: 'what', 'how' and 'why' analysis (Davies, 1985). The 'what' questions are special cases of the general form of the production of welfare question itself. The general form is stated in figure 1.1, which also defines the meaning of 'how' and 'why' questions in the project. The analysis is almost entirely of the 'what' type; and so like the description of patterns of resources, the need-related circumstances of users and caregivers, and 'final outputs' (the impacts of community care on outcomes of value in their own right), and the mapping of the relations between service inputs and final outputs. The purpose of the modelling is more to describe than to illuminate causal processes. The latter is more the purpose of other publications planned for ECCEP.

Figure 1.1 also summarises relevant features of the research design. The focus is the productivity of services for final outcomes for individuals. It was argued that the expectations, assumptions, skills and interactions between three persons greatly influenced not only who gets how much of what service and support, but also the process of the transformation of the resources of all kinds into the final outputs. Our focus is not the 'personal' or 'individual' process of the production of welfare, but a process which during the crucial set-up phase of the care plan establishes the framework for those individual transforma-

Figure 1.1
ECCEP design features

Foci

Who gets how much of what service and informal support at what costs to, and with what effects on, whom. Resources, needs and outcomes, utilisation, productivities and costs.

Description of utilisation propensities, average and marginal productivities and costs, the outcomes and benefits.

How the patterns of needs, resources and outcomes occur; influences of structures and policies, procedures, assumptive worlds perceptions and practice.

Why influences on patterns vary between areas and between cohorts.

Before-after study

Cohorts of new users of community social services in 1984/5 and 1994/5 in 12 areas from 10 authorities in England and Wales.

ECCEP data collections

Interviews with key field level actors for the set-up stage: the triadic design.

- Initial survey firm interviews with 419 community-based users (response rate 82 per cent) and their 238 'principal informal caregivers' (PICs); and in-house team interviews with 425 workers performing the core care management tasks immediately after the conclusion of the set-up phase of care management.
- Follow-up survey firm interviews with 299 users surviving in the community and their 186 PICs, and in-house interviews with 418 persons performing core care management tasks six months after the first interviews.

Other collections include

- Continuous data on service utilisation, changes in need-related circumstances, location
- Interviews with 150 managers at all levels of the SSDs about policy and implementation in policy and practice discussions, with scaling of their perceptions of their authority's priorities for 133 managers. Repeated after six months.
- Interviews with managers of health, housing, independent provider, and other agencies.
- Supplementary collection on health service utilisation and health service organisation and policies.

tions by users and caregivers. During that set-up phase, the processes are dominated, we argue, by a triad: each of the 419 users allocated community services after the set-up phase, their 238 principal informal caregivers, and the 425 'care managers' — whoever most undertook the care management tasks.[14]

indicators of a higher level of generality for argument that does not require such detail.[24] (b) The second element is fully to use the constraints provided by the existing state of knowledge.

(a) *Confining the detailed description to where it matters.* The productivities map must be drawn in as much detail as is compatible with the constraints imposed by good research practice in order to generate hypotheses that other data collections and analysis can investigate. Examples of these constraints are the number of observations and level of statistical significance required for a term to be included in an equation; constraints on the direction of an effect shown in a model based on theoretically-compatible generalisations with much evidential support from social gerontology; and constraints and requirements implicit in production function theory in economics and the associated econometric repertoire.

However, we can draw many of the conclusions we need for policy argument from relationships of an altogether higher level of generality, though the analysis itself uses the same categories as the mapping of efficiency. The analysis of the policy propositions in the concluding section will illustrate that there is a level of discourse at which it is not just a useful contribution to make generalisations using cruder classifications. It would actually create problems to discuss them at the fine level at which productivity effects are described.

So we work at three levels of generality. The productivities are mapped at the most detailed level, revealing many apparently subtle effects. This minimises the danger to internal validity created by using broad-brush indicators. The description and analysis of efficiencies use categories at a more general level. Shifting up the level of generality of the variables defining the framework for the analysis of efficiency reduces the risk that the conclusions about efficiency will reflect associations in the data set due to 'sampling error' (the luck of the sampling process), measurement errors, or specification errors (like the omission of an important causal factor correlated with or affecting the effects of others taken into account in the model). That is, it reduces the danger to external validity. Estimates of the quantitative effects of alternatives are presented, many being quantitative predictions of the consequences of a policy. But the presentation of estimates for end-states is just a heuristic device: more specifically, a device for analysing the general implications of the findings. No one imagines that any of these end-states would be reached. The maps are for a landscape that is changing faster than it can be mapped by the cartographers — indeed, it is an important the aim of policy-makers to change it. The analysis can give general directions, guidance about what changes to prioritise, not a route map that is precise beyond the first few stages of the journey.

(b) *Theoretical and practice requirements and constraints.* We used the constraints on the forms of analysis provided by the current state of knowledge. Economic theory set clear limits to the patterns described, and showed the significance of relationships taking one precise form rather than another. Knowledge about

relationships and causality from gerontology and other subjects defined directions and created expectations about relationships, and these (albeit often general) hypotheses guided the modelling process. Other constraints were set by
the canons of good modelling practice: for instance, careful use of the distinction between exogenous and endogenous; restrictions on the number of cases
on which an equation term could be based; conservative significance levels;
similarity of the value of coefficients among alternative variants of the model
and stability as changes are made; the use of simpler forms where more complicated forms would add little of potential value to the description; and the
restriction of inputs allowed in optimisation to the ranges actually observed.
The reader unfamiliar with the range of theoretical knowledge and analysis
techniques involved will be unable to understand the implication of these
without more precise description. This is provided in chapter 3.

5.   Layout of the book

Part I maps productivities and the contributions which services are estimated
to make to outputs. Chapters 2 and 3 introduce the ideas, the last section of
chapter 3 providing a detailed guide to the nature of the content and presentation of the results chapters. Chapter 12 contains a more general account of the
patterns discovered. Many readers may find it best first to read chapters 2, 3
and 12, and then to follow through by looking at the results in detail.

Part II maps efficiencies as they now are and what they would be were the
most efficient use made of resources, and discusses what equity judgements
are implicit in the observed patterns given prices and productivities. As in Part
I, there is an introductory chapter that explains the approach and provides the
detailed reader's guide to the results.

Finally, Part III discusses propositions based on the types of question posed
in the opening paragraphs of this chapter. The concluding chapter is about the
general nature of the patterns, and what the findings imply for the role of production of welfare studies in policy analysis.

Notes

1   The need was recognised for collating evidence of a wide variety of kinds in the de-
     velopment of the Australian Aged Care Reform Strategy. The quinquennial review
     contributed greatly to steering the reform effort (Commonwealth Department of
     Health Housing and Community Services, 1991). The hopes and expectations of a
     quinquennial review in the UK were argued elsewhere (Davies, 1994).

2   To the former, reform is part of a political as well as policy process, and it is difficult
     to reconcile the time horizons of politics and the development of knowledge-based
     policy and practice. The Royal Commission worked against deadlines that made it
     difficult to work in depth over the whole of its remit.

3   The modernisation theme is reflected in the titles of key policy statement. *Modernising Social Services* was published in November. One month earlier, there was the publication of *Modernising Health and Social Services: National Priorities Guidance*, the year following the publication of a health services White Paper *The New NHS: Modern, Dependable* (Department of Health, 1997b). Also published in 1998 was the White Paper *Modern Public Services for Britain: Investing in Reform* (HM Treasury and Cabinet Office, 1998) and *Modern Local Government: In Touch with the People* (DETR, 1998), about Best Value. *Modernising Social Services* presents a modernisation fund of £1.3 billion additional to current grant levels, describing it as 'a lever for modernisation'. There are five constituents 'grants'; in effect programmes. The elements most relevant for elderly persons are two for the promotion of independence: partnership grant (£647m) and a smaller prevention grant (£100m), the mental health grant (£185m), and training support grant (£20m). (Department of Health, 1998b, para 1.17).

4   The 1998 White Paper set short-term targets, and did not speculate about longer-term time scales: 'the problems cannot be resolved overnight, and will take time and effort to put right ... the proposals in the White Paper look to the future, to the creation of modern social services' (Department of Health, 1998, paras 1.6 and 1.7). The previous administration similarly stressed the length of the time horizons of the reform effort, but implied that what was commencing was a long and continuous process of change, rather than a time-limited reform programme. The government was vague about how long it would take to secure local change and its effects at the beginning of the reform process, though there were those in the central government who clearly did not expect the processes of change to be short-lived. Emphasis was put on the difficulties of changing the culture of the social services. Some documents ascribed to local agencies an 'oral' culture. Perhaps the metaphor implies that operating procedures and assumptive worlds are dominated by tradition, and for that reason had a lower degree of adaptiveness to new conceptual structures than was required by policy change. Time horizons were mentioned later, as the experience of the reform was gained and experience overseas reported; for instance, 'the Government has always said that it would take about a decade for the full benefits of the community care reforms to be realised (Departments of Health and for the Environment, 1995, para. 1.2). The British history will not surprise those who have followed the Australian Aged Care Reform Strategy. By the end of the first quinquennium, there was an expectation that the reforms would take more than a decade to work through (Davies, 1992).

5   The examples illustrate that the three elements are not only heuristically separable, but within implementations using the modernisation programme frameworks at the local level, there is likely to be an organisational level at which (c) a substantial degree organisationally separated. For instance, a special programme for a particular group whose risk assessment suggests a high return from a particular combination of community-based inputs will have its own management and funding at the local level. This is of importance for the development of this essay and for interpreting how its contribution fits into the jigsaw of policy analysis. The essay is primarily directed at (a), improving efficiency within existing technologies; and (b), defining the technological relationships which it should be the focus of policy to improve. The considerable lesser heuristic and structural separation of the three foci (a)-(c) illustrated from the examples help to define the contribution of the essay.

6   For this reason, perceptions of it by outsiders tended to focus on what most pleased or offended the hopes and expectations of beholders. It was one of the most fre-

quently partially or outrageously incorrectly described of social care projects by some, as well as lauded by others.

7   The performance of the KCCP and its three closest evaluated replications have been compared. By the criterion of the costs of outcomes, the KCCP was on the most successful on average, significantly so by the end of the period, showing improving performance throughout its history. The other programmes did not show continuous learning. That may have been partly because in the project whose implementation environment and history was most promising, the authority's policies and values set constraints on the flexibility of input substitutions. It may also have been partly due to the fact that the KCCP was the new venture in which the participants had to learn to apply the principles by doing, with structures like a fortnightly seminar of the care managers and others with the three senior managers of the project: the representative of the Director from headquarters, the local Divisional Director, and principal evaluator. The seminars helped to tease out the implications of experience in attempting to apply the principles. The three second round implementations already had a technology available from the KCCP to apply, and to the degree that they innovated, they did so in ways which less directly affected the impact of resources on outcomes. (Davies and Chesterman, 1996).

8   The Australian Commonwealth government sets uniform guidelines for the provision of care slots for users needing different levels of care. These set the same ratios for the provision for persons of higher and lower care needs irrespective of areas. Even for areas with populations of up to 50 thousand persons, there can be substantial differences in the ratios of persons predicted to have higher care needs to persons with lower care needs. Moreover, the Australian guidelines are for much broader classification of provision, and so are based on much cruder need-related circumstances than would be appropriate for differentiating between those requiring higher and lower levels of care management.

9   The aim should be to provide a range of 'care management arrangements' matched to the circumstances of persons at potential decision points in pathways into and through care systems and policy priorities. The issue was formulated in *Matching Resources to Needs*. There the argument was presented as the rationale of the design of a variety of evaluated schemes each applying the principles and technology of the KCCP, but each with a different combination of care management arrangements. The types of arrangements discussed were targeting and location on pathways into and through care systems, skill mix, the range of services charged to the budget, the average budget per case, the budget cap (Davies and Challis, 1986, chapter 13). The logic for putting together a system of case management teams for an area was later elaborated in *Resources, Needs and Outcomes* and other work (Davies, 1992; Davies et al., 1990). *Care Management, Equity and Efficiency: the International Experience* followed through with a discussion of the user circumstances in which resources allocated to performing care management tasks would be likely to have the highest productivities. The theme has been taken up by others, notably David Challis (Challis, 1994).

10 The PSSRU continued for some time to search for productivity effects in a project developing a social network production of welfare variant of the production of welfare approach. This variant was based on the application of argument based on the approach pioneered by Becker, and applied particularly in the new household economics and labour economics (Becker, 1964; Killingsworth, 1983). It was first applied to social care in work on the motivations, rewards and management of quasi-informal helpers in the Kent Community Care Project (Qureshi et al., 1989). A gen-

eral account of the SPOW perspective was given in Netten and Davies (1991). However, the modelling by Davies and Baines within the framework of this social production of welfare variant of the production of welfare approach did not substantially change the results.

11 For these reasons, care management arrangements and practice would be crucial. For that reason, *Resources, Needs and Outcomes* contained more extensive process analysis of current performance of care management tasks and policy argument about the development of care management in the light of the British and overseas logics and evidence than any work since *Matching Resources to Needs*, and the analysis was further developed in *Case Management, Equity and Efficiency: the International Experience* (Davies, 1992; Davies et al., 1990).

12 The American literature relating to productivities of community social services is also sparse. Only one group appears to have fitted a production function (Greene et al., 1989; Greene, Lovely and Ondrich, 1995). As in the UK, the evidence is only indirect. Partly, this is because the collections have not been designed to be as adequate as possible for production function modelling. Partly, it is because the analysis are not constrained by hypotheses from the economics of production relations using the repertoire of forms and techniques from the associated body of econometrics. Therefore, most are like the British literature because they are more exploratory than production function analysis. Others are theory-based analysis built to estimate relationships and test hypotheses from subjects addressing different fundamental questions.

13 Whether there is balance as well as variety is more questionable. In her paper for the Royal Commission on Long Term Care, Harding comments that too little of the evidence is based on outcomes for users and informal caregivers, and the paper's list of references illustrates the imbalance (Harding, 1999). Others might argue that there are other imbalances: for instance, too little which relates information for large samples with some claim at broad representativeness to insights into how policies, structures, and processes impinge on the way services affect them in everyday life.

14 The target number of interviews was much larger: 760. Recruitment by the SSDs was lower than predicted. The total number of eligible cases actually recruited was 597. Of these, the first interviews were achieved with 492 respondents, a response rate of 82 per cent. Differences between all users eligible for the project and the final sample were tested and the groups found to be similar. Weights were used to correct for variations from equality in the probability of selection and response both for the descriptive reporting and the modelling. The procedures and results of sampling, response, and bias tests were the subject of a technical report (Davies et al., 1996). Users were recruited within a multi-cell sampling framework whose dimensions included interval need, cognitive impairment, and living circumstances. Though it was intended to select quotas from each cell, in fact, all members of most cells were recruited in most authorities. Tests comparing the characteristics of the users interviewed and the group initially recruited by the authorities did not find bias (Fernández, 1997).

15 Dyadic designs are common in collections of quantitative data in psychology. They provide evidence for the triangulation sought in qualitative methods, but looked at from the opposite perspective, they help to define differences in perspectives. They have been useful for both purposes in ECCEP analysis. There were also interviews with the users, principal caregivers (where present) and care managers for 67 users triaged into residential and nursing home care subsequent to assessment. This was intended to illuminate the influence of need-related, other demand circumstances,

and supply factors on the probability of emerging with care at home rather than in a home. They have not been used in this essay, but were one of the databases drawn on in Davies, Fernández and Warburton (1997).

16 Principal informal caregivers were persons undertaking practical tasks to assist with personal or instrumental activities of daily living on a regular basis at least once a week.

17 For users and caregivers, the interviews took place on average 14 weeks after referral, 25 weeks after referral for the care managers. The time lags were longer than had been planned at the design stage, and were due to difficulties which the field teams and organisation undertaking the field interviews had in implementing the agreed procedures. Four levels of interview were conducted with care managers, allocation for each being based on a sampling process increasing the probability of selection for the longest interview among the care managers of more complex cases. Individual variations in the probability of selection for the sample were allowed for in the modelling analysis discussed in the essay by reweighting cases, as in all the project analysis.

18 Proxy interviews were conducted with the principal informal caregiver to provide some of the material otherwise collected in the user interviews in cases of severe cognitive impairment as predicted from the Katzman scale (Katzman et al., 1983) applied in the screening interview.

19 The attempts by the PSSRU MSCEP (monitoring services for the care of elderly people) project authorities are described in *From Vision to Reality in Community Care* (Gostick et al., 1997). MSCEP showed great variation in local attention to the task and the sophistication with which the task was approached, but found evidence of greater attention than was found in their authorities by Lewis and Glennerster (1996). A second reason is that such small samples of authorities are likely not to contain any from the minority whose care management arrangements had anticipated the requirement that they be in place by the appointed day in 1993. A second, is that the MSCEP design interviewed precisely those to whom responsibility had been given for the development of care management policy and practice.

20 Crude comparisons with national databases for a cross-section suggests that the ECCEP's cohort sample differs in the directions which would be predicted (Bauld et al., 1998). That is, the ECCEP cohort appears more disabled at the time of assessment than the national cross-section of users. One reason is that is that the disability distribution of the cohort tends to become progressively more skewed towards those of lower disability through time, as was demonstrated by simulation model with the DCP cohort (Davies and Baines, 1991a, b, 1992). A second reason is that the ECCEP cohort was recruited at the end of a period when progressively fewer users of lower disability were allocated service, the proportion falling rapidly from one cohort to the next, because a cross-section consists of survivors from successive cohorts, and because of the long period of utilisation of a substantial proportion of earlier cohorts still likely to be represented in the cross-section sample. The evidence is striking. Approximately 50 per cent of the 1984/85 DCP cohort remained users of community services after 113 weeks, and by that stage, numbers were falling only slowly. Even post-reform, a decade later, one fifth of the ECCEP cohort remained users after almost five years, despite a higher rate of attrition initially. Again, numbers were falling little between quarters during and later than the third year.

21 Chapter 2 shows the sample to be a cohort of all new users or users starting a new episode of care after a fundamental reassessment of circumstances due to change, and expected to consume services brokered and subsidised by the social services department and expected to do so for two months or longer other than bus passes.

22 Assuming that one describes as productivities effects in which the roles of services are contingent upon particular user or system consequences, including effects in which the role of the service inputs are catalytic.

23 In particular, the emphasis of both is 'productive description' in the context of previous knowledge, the discovery or invention of new phenomena and relationships, the confirmation of previous findings and the support and elaboration of previous hypotheses, and the generation of ideas for further investigation. In both, the starting point is some presumed structure. Both follow 'an open-ended, highly interactive, iterative process, whose actual steps are selected segments of a stubbily-branching treelike pattern of possible actions.' (Tukey and Wild, 1971, 373).

24 The six analysis groups were derived *a priori* on the basis of theoretically-based conventions in the research literature, not from observed covariances in the data. Therefore their use helps the analysis to escape from the quirks of the covariance structure of this one data set.

PART I
MAPPING PRODUCTIVITIES AND SERVICE OUTPUTS

2 Modelling the Impact of Service Inputs on Outputs: Framework and Indicators

The chapter considers the framework for the selection of indicators, the indicators themselves, and the modelling strategy.

1.   Outputs, inputs and risk factors studied

1.1. Outputs

Literature from gerontology and related disciplines, the 'ologies', developed more precise dimensionalities of outputs, and indicators for them. Evaluation studies, including production of welfare evaluations, continuously synthesise and apply them. The ECCEP project attempted to create sufficient continuity with earlier production of welfare studies to permit some comparisons, and to extend cover and incorporate new indicators.

However, the main source for the definition is the policy and practice discourse in the context of the reforms. It has been rich in suggesting dimensions of final output of importance for the evaluation, and to some degree reflects case-level 'theory' and argument of the caring professions and 'ological research-based argument.

Policy discourse includes national and local discussion.

1.1.1. National framework

Key ideas of the 1989 White Paper relating to the choice of outputs to measure for the individual user and caregiver were (a) 'to enable people to live in their own homes wherever feasible and sensible' — including extending the stay in the community prior to admission to institutions for long-term care; (b) to provide support in ways which give 'as much independence as possible' and help in 'reacquiring living skills' — including improvements in users' perceptions of their capacity to cope with the tasks of daily living; (c) 'to give people a greater individual say in how they live their lives' and to procure 'services that respond flexibly and sensitively to the needs of individuals and their carers' — namely felt empowerment over their whole life, and felt empowerment over the processes of service provision; and (d) to provide 'practical support for carers — support for caregivers in undertaking caregiving tasks and in handling problems of their own. Practice guidance spelt these out in more detail, and bridged the assumptive worlds of the policy-makers and care professionals. There are other ideas that relate to general cost-effectiveness.

1.1.2. *Local priorities and interpretations of the national framework*

The ECCEP project undertook a formal collection of evidence about local managers' interpretations of the national framework. First, an analysis of the content of reform documentation was undertaken so as to extract and infer a list of principal goals. That was supplemented with discussions. The final list was therefore based on the White Paper, guidance, and the expressions of views of senior policy-makers, managers and others at national and local levels.

A structured questionnaire was completed at the time of the policy and practice discussions with 150 social services department (SSD) managers at all levels in all the collaborating authorities. The prioritisation questionnaire was actually completed by 133 of the managers. The evidence was about the priority that the managers thought that their authority had implicitly given to each of the list of goals during the period prior to the beginning of the set-up period for the cohort studied, and during the subsequent six months. Those that proved to be of the highest priority during the first period are listed below in order of their ranking.

- *Chance for more users to stay at home rather than enter a care home.* This corresponds to the goal from the White Paper labelled (a) above. The White Paper emphasised this heavily; more concern was expressed with improving the quality of life and care than in the general reform literature and care evaluation. The importance of the goal in part reflects the unpopularity of what is perceived to be the alternative: care in a residential setting. One suspects that the idea 'residential care' carries old images that constrain rational analysis and choice. There is clear evidence that most elderly persons likely to be at risk remain anxious to avoid admission (Peace et al., 1997). The antipathy is deeply rooted historically in the fear of the workhouse (Townsend, 1962). The depth and universality of the negative image suggest more profound reasons than fear of decline and a history of a bad quality of life. Twigg (1998) asks 'how far is residential care the institutional embodiment of ageism, the ultimate expression of the marginalisation of older people in society, in which those who have failed to live up to the dominant ideology of autonomy, independence and self-care are corralled into institutions that we all fear we ourselves will have to enter but we all strive to escape?' Paradoxically, she argues, there has actually been very little in-depth research documenting the day-to-day social life and feelings of residents. For this reason, we have failed to work through Rosalie Kane's type of analysis relating the likely contributions of different forms of shelter-with-care to the circumstances of potential users, as is argued elsewhere (Davies, 1998; Kane, 1995).

This goal clearly had the highest overall score overall: 1.88 as compared with the second highest of 2.53. It was judged to have been the highest priority in eight of the ten authorities. There was a difference between authorities in the ranking which was all but significant at the 1 per cent level. There was a high degree of consensus among managers at different levels: senior managers at headquarters, middle managers, and field and service managers at the facility or field office level. The difference between them was clearly not statistically significant.

- *Empowerment, choice and control over their own lives for users.* This corresponds to the White Paper goal labelled (c). The policy argument linked choice and control to the choice of suppliers and influence on the nature of services and their provision. But the sense of control over life is a central psychological concept linked to well-being, and that is as much so for elderly persons as for others. The dimension became increasingly relevant to caregivers as the new balance of consciousness reflected in the Carers' Act was shifting the perception of caregivers more towards being potential beneficiaries in their own right.

The average ranking the 133 managers gave to this priority was 2.53. The differences in the ranking between areas was clearly not statistically significant. The differences between levels of management were small and not statistically significant.

- *Support for family caregivers.* This corresponds to the White Paper goal labelled (d). The proposition about aims put to the 133 managers was worded so as to reflect the concept as in the Griffiths Report and the White Paper: the provision of practical help for caregivers to enable them to continue. The provisions of the Carers' Act required the separate assessment of caregivers, but remained a step away from treating them as beneficiaries in their own right. But with this new consciousness, it would not be surprising if there were many at the field level who took this step in some circumstances. That was in fact borne out by whom the care managers expected to be the principal beneficiaries of the care plan. In more than one case in ten, the principal informal caregiver was expected to be the sole beneficiary. In three cases in ten, they were expected to share the benefit (Davies, 1997, 341).

Our policy and practice discussions suggested that the managers would have interpreted it in such a way that those thinking that their authority had given priority to achieving a wider range of benefits would have given this a high ranking. The mean value was 3.45. There were differences between authorities that were significant at approximately the 1 per cent level. However, there were no differences between levels of management. This is clearly a policy area in which there was consistency within authorities but substantial differences between them. Those differences were already emerging in the same areas more than a decade before (Davies et al., 1990)

The combination of consensus within, and dissent between, authorities illustrates the power of the new policy precision about ends and means implemented in the context of new managerialist styles and techniques. At first, it appeared to have created a uniform vision within authorities which could reflect either acceptance of the broader national values or strongly nonconformist variants of it.[1] Research illustrates how such effects are most likely when a national policy paradigm confronts a conflicting value which pervades local policy and politics; see for instance, housing policy in Bromley (Young and Kramer, 1978). The feminist and equal opportunities resonances of providing help to caregivers make it precisely the kind of issue where such values are likely to work through. Judging from other areas where local civic values and national commitments were initially in conflict, but the central government was persistent, there could have been a shift through time among the nonconformists (Wistow et al., 1994, 1996).

- *Access to services to users who had previously either done without any help from the SSD or not received appropriate help.* This was not emphasised in the White Paper, but had been discussed in the critiques preceding the reforms, by among other public bodies, the Audit Commission (Audit Commission for England and Wales, 1985, 1986). The priority had a score of 4.03, and the differences between authorities were significant at the 5 per cent level. However, there were no differences between levels of management. Perhaps the issue resonates with the expansiveness of local assumptions about the role of the welfare state, to a lesser degree than support for caregivers with its powerful feminist overtones, partly because the whole period has been one of fiscal austerity for local authorities.

- *Chance to regain as much independence as possible through rehabilitative and skill-enhancing services.* This corresponds to goal (b) in the White Paper. It echoes a value capable of quite different interpretations in the health and social services, as is illustrated in reviews of rehabilitation literatures (and Baldwin, 1998; Sinclair and Dickinson, 1998). We comment elsewhere (page 414) how rarely the ECCEP study suggests there to be arrangements by which the core care management tasks during the set-up period of community care pulled together a range of health professionals involved in active medical and other forms of rehabilitation. What service to help users to regain independence generally means to social service workers and managers is arrangements that are more modest.

The average score was little different from the extension of service to the previously deprived, 4.09. Again, there were big differences between authorities, significant at close to the 1 per cent level. There were small differences between levels of management, significant only at the .07 level. Perhaps field staff more than managers rated this goal to have had high priority.

- *Emphasising welfare gains for users irrespective of cost to the local authority.* This was in opposition to the emphasis on cost-effectiveness in the White Paper. It was asked in this reverse form because agreement with cost-effectiveness would be too easy in the public sector management climate of the times. With a low score of 6.06 and differences between authorities that were not highly significant, this was clearly not considered to be a description that could be claimed for their authorities. Perhaps those who would have been proud to be able to do so would have been too oppressed by the conscious-ness of the harder resource environment. There was no difference between management levels. This is unsurprising given the general environment of fiscal stringency, even in authorities which had the least strategic approach to handling the achievement of goals in conditions of greater fiscal strin-gency.
- *Raising charges in order to generate income, so that services can be extended to those who need subsidised care.* There was a similar mean score of 6.12 and similarly a low degree of variation between authorities. Again, there were no differences between management levels.

It was not that charges were unchanging. Charges were being increased, and systems revised, in several authorities during the first part of the study pe-riod. One authority continued to cling tenaciously to a principle of free service for the elderly its predecessor had put in place immediately after the war (Davies, 1968). Changing the charging system or level was the subject of con-cerned discussion at all levels everywhere.[2] In some places, we had conversa-tions with middle managers who were attempting to use the ineffectiveness of their authorities' systems of policy control to work around the rules of the sys-tem in order to mitigate some of the effects on user demand. Mostly, raising charges was perceived to be a grim necessity, the lesser of evils, not a contribu-tion to improved equity or efficiency.

Arguably, the first five aims, and certainly the first three, catch the most im-portant priorities of the period as seen by authorities. Most imply measurable effects for individual users and caregivers. Because providing support to care-givers is increasingly interpreted as treating caregivers as beneficiaries, sev-eral other dimensions relate to them, as well as to users.

Since the time of the interviews, the importance of reducing the degree of social exclusion and isolation has become a more important general theme in the setting of policy goals.

1.1.3. *Professional and 'ological criteria*

The 'ologies and care professional theory relate some of the general concerns to more precise factors shown or experienced to be important dimensions of quality of life which may be affected by services. Among them are:

- The distinction between satisfaction with the impact of services on some final outcome, and satisfaction with the care process, the manner in which care is brokered and provided. There are findings that suggest that the latter have more influence on overall satisfaction than impacts.

- *General lack of morale and caregivers' perceived stress.* The former has been extensively treated as a final output in evaluation studies, including production of welfare evaluations from the 1970s onwards (Davies and Challis, 1986). The genre has established conventions about measurement. The subdimensionality of the indicators has also been explored, and subdimensions used in evaluations. Likewise, caregivers' subjective sense of general malaise or of burden specifically due to caregiving has been a major focus of research and scales used in evaluations (Davies, 1990; Zarit, 1997).

1.1.4. The dimensions and indicators

Table 2.1 classifies output indicators by broad domains which reflect the main dimensions divined from the content analysis and discussions, and by whether the main beneficiary is the user or the principal informal caregiver (PIC). The indicators for which production functions were fitted are indicated. Production functions were not fitted for the others because numbers were insufficient. Appendix table 2.1 (page 415) shows the derivation of the output variables in greater detail, and gives information about their distributions.

Domain I: User's length of stay in the community. The indicator is the number of days prior to admission to an institution for long-term care, during the period between referral and the tracking collection made during the 22nd month after the median caseload had been referred.[3] The variable is censored, since a proportion of users remained in the community at the end of the period. The implications for modelling are discussed below.

Domain II: Satisfaction with service. There are general indicators of satisfaction with the service and support for both the user and the principal informal caregiver.

Domain III: Perceived improvement in functioning in service-related areas, and unmet needs reported. Production functions have been fitted only for indicators for perceived improvement in functioning for the user.

The use of this dimension is well established in the evaluation literature. It was heavily represented among the evaluations of the American home and day care programmes in the seventies and early eighties, including the evaluations of the projects antecedent to the long-term care channeling experiments, of that project itself, of the contemporaneous evaluations of the Kent Community Care Project (KCCP), its replications and descendants, and the PSSRU Domiciliary Care Project (DCP). Adjusted to take into account of risk factors, it has been shown to be a useful indicator of outcomes for nursing homes (Mukamel, 1997). *Old People's Homes and the Production of Welfare* (Davies and Knapp, 1979) related these to Maslow's arguments about the hierarchical na-

Table 2.1
Output domains and indicators

Domain	Beneficiary/Indicator (in **BOLD**)	
	User	Principal informal caregiver (PIC)
DOMAIN I Length of stay in the community	Number of days living at home prior to admission to an institution for long-term care during period from referral until admission or the tracking collection, conducted during the 22nd month for the median case to be referred **DAYS** Non-subjective *Production function estimated*	
DOMAIN II Satisfaction with service	Degree of satisfaction of user with the level of service being received **USATISF** *Production function estimated*	Caregiver's degree of satisfaction with amount and type of support PIC had from services to help look after user **SATAMSUP** *Production function estimated* Degree to which PIC's experience of the social services was favourable during last six months **PICSSEXP** *Production function estimated*
DOMAIN III Perceived improvement in functioning in service-related areas and reported unmet needs	Improvement in number of states of daily living related to personal care functions ascribed by user to the social services **IMPADL** *Production function estimated* Improvement in number of states of daily living related to household care and other instrumental care functions ascribed by the user to the social services **IMPIADL** *Production function estimated* User's count of unmet needs for help with functional areas covered by community social services **NSF** *Production function estimated*	Degree of satisfaction with amount and type of support PIC had to deal with problems of their own **CSATOWN** *Insufficient cases to estimate production function* Number of aspects of caregiving with which PIC thought that they needed more help **CNBMORE** *Insufficient cases thinking needs unmet to estimate production function*
DOMAIN IV Empowerment, choice and control	User felt control over own life score **IMPEMP** *Production function estimated* User's felt empowerment/influence during set-up stage of care management (scale) **UEMPOW**	

Table 2.1 (continued)

Domain	Beneficiary/Indicator (in **BOLD**)	
	User	Principal informal caregiver (PIC)
DOMAIN V General psychological well-being	Overall lack of morale: PGC score **PGC** *Production function estimated* General dissatisfaction with life score **GDL** *Production function estimated* Dissatisfaction with life development score **DLD** *Production function estimated*	Kosberg carer burden scale **KOSBERG** *Production function estimated*
DOMAIN VI Reduction of social exclusion and improvement of relationships	Degree to which user considered social services to have improved how well user gets on with family and friends **IMPREL** *Production function estimated* Degree of satisfaction of user with chances to socialise and meet people **SATSOC** *Production function estimated*	Employment disadvantage due to caregiving scale **CEMPDIS** *Too few employed caregivers to estimate production function*
DOMAIN VII Worker perception of impact	Worker's rating of the degree to which social services improved the welfare of the user **WKSAT** *Production function estimated*	

ture of needs. In *Matching Resources to Needs in Community Care* (Davies and Challis, 1986), this domain was called *nurturance and compensation for disability*.[4]

Improvements might reflect several causal mechanisms. One is the influence of social services on the will to perform tasks: the Morale effect, called the Heineken effect in the analysis of the KCCP (Davies and Challis, 1986). A second is the influence on the social and material environment. Accounts of good practice are replete with examples of how the combined effect of tiny changes in the latter can have a significant effect on functioning: one type of kettle rather than another, small modifications in room layout. A third is the support and perhaps mobilisation of caregivers around an aspect of enabling hitherto neglected.

We have separate impact indicators for two types of task: (a) adequate assistance for the personal care tasks of daily living, including the provision of supervision to reduce the risks arising from disabilities in terms capacity to perform activities of daily living (ADL), indicated by IMPADL, and (b) assistance and supervision for the 'instrumental' (household and other) tasks of daily living (IADL), indicated by IMPIADL.

Indicators of unmet need have long been used in several countries. Their introduction at a time when efficiency arguments were not highly developed in community care give them importance in the literature, despite theoretical objections. They were used by E.M. Goldberg (1970) in her classic, *Help the Aged*. In the KCCP and its descendants, there were indicators which assessed shortfall in the amount of help required to make the level of care acceptable with respect to personal care and security, and rising and retiring (Challis et al., 1990, 1995; Davies and Challis, 1986; Davies and Chesterman, forthcoming). A similar variable (DESHELP) was an important output in the production functions derived from the DCP, (Davies et al., 1990). Questions about unmet need were asked and analysed in the evaluation of the long-term care channelling project (Mathematica Policy Research, 1982a,b). More widely, the reporting of the number of persons stating that they had needs for service or tasks unmet is one of the long-lasting legacies of the pioneering need surveys of the 1960s and 70s (Harris, 1971; Townsend and Wedderburn, 1965).

The measurement of unmet need using indicators based on questions asking about just that was always open to an objection never developed by the economist critics of the 'needologists' (Williams, 1974). A declaration by potential recipients that there are unmet needs for services is tantamount merely to asserting that these inputs would have positive marginal productivities. Just sub-marginal inputs typically have positive marginal productivities when scarce resources are optimally allocated between their alternative uses, and the price paid by the recipients for the marginal unit consumed is low in relation to its costs. However, it is generally agreed that elderly people have typically made modest demands based on low expectations — though that argument may have diminishing validity at a time when services are being concentrated on only some of those with an expectation that they would have been eligible, and when increasing proportions are expected to be from more demanding generations. Also, questions are now answered in the context of an expectation that a price will have to be paid which is high in relation to the income of the users if not in relation to the real total cost, although users probably distinguish need from what they would demand given the price they would have to pay.

The indicator of unmet needs of the user is a count of unmet needs for help with functional areas covered by community social services, NSF. The indicator is not of unmet needs for individual services, but for help with the tasks for which services provide help or supervision.

The indicator of unmet needs for the principal informal caregiver (PIC) is based on a question about the degree of satisfaction the PIC felt about the amount of support received from the social services to help to care for the user, SATAMSUP. There were too few cases for there to be an analysis of an equivalent indicator for help with the caregiver's own problems.

Domain IV: Empowerment, choice and control. As well as being a theme of the policy discourse, this is an important influence on, and indicator of, general psychological well-being. Felt independence and control over one's own life is a theme of gerontological research and argument as well as being closely linked with the policy objectives of the 1989 White Paper.

The indicator closely reflects Weber's concept: the probability that someone would be in a position to impose their will in the framework of the social relationship in question (Weber, 1971). The impact indicator for users, IMPEMP, is based on three items, and is not identical to the indicator used in the KCCP and its descendants.[5] There is also an indicator of the users' perception of their sense of empowerment by the manner in which the processes were implemented for them during the crucial stages of assessment, care planning, and care arrangement. This process indicator, UEMPOW, was based on the users' views of the influence that they felt they had during the set-up stage of the process.

A production function was estimated for only one of the process indicators for principal informal caregivers: CEMPOW.

Domain V: General psychological well-being. The PGC morale scale (Lawton, 1975) and two of its components were the indicators for users. The Kosberg caregiver burden inventory (Kosberg, 1996; Kosberg and Cairl, 1986; Kosberg et al., 1990) was used for principal informal caregivers. The analysis of the theoretical literature and indicators in *Old People's Homes and the Production of Welfare* (Davies and Knapp, 1979) showed the importance of the concept in American gerontology, and for each of the main indicators. It showed that there was a literature testing the face validity and factor structure of the principal indicators and their psychometric properties for relevant populations, and the appropriateness of the different measures for different purposes.

For users, the PGC morale scale was selected for the evaluation of the Kent Community Care Project because of its suitability for use with disabled elderly persons, and in the descendants of the KCCP and in the DCP and by other evaluation studies partly for comparability (Walker and Warren, 1986). As well as the overall score on the anglicised 17-item form of the PGC morale scale, an indicator of *General Dissatisfaction with Life*, GDL, was derived by adding scores on items 4,6,8,15,16, and 17 (see Davies and Challis, 1986). These items reflected a negative evaluation of the present, lack of family contact, being easily upset, and taking adversity badly. *Dissatisfaction with Life Development*, DLD, based on items 1,2,6, and 10, was a dimension found by factor analyses by several authors, and was related to the idea that life satisfaction diminished with age. Production functions were fitted for the two dimensions, GDL and DLD.

The General Depression Scale was also applied to a sample of users (Yesavage, 1983). The separate measurement of depression was established in the KCCP. Its importance has recently been illustrated by an interventive experiment with the substantial minority of users of community social services in one London borough, an experiment yielding striking results (Banerjee et al., 1996). The data being available for only a sample, no attempt was made to use them in the modelling.

For principal informal caregivers, the DCP used the Rutter Social Malaise Scale. This was an adaptation of the 24 components of an inventory in the Cornell Medical Index Health Questionnaire. The objective was to create 'a useful indicator of emotional disturbance' (Rutter et al., 1970). Analysis of its use with the carers of children with learning disabilities led Bebbington and Quine (1986) 'to give support to the malaise construct and to the inventory', though also concluding that it is an indicator of stress of only moderate validity.[6]

But the Rutter inventory is an indicator of general malaise. Its questions do not link the malaise to caregiving. The Kosberg scale does this. That, too, was designed to help practitioners to diagnose caregiving-related stress, and was based on a general population of elderly persons, not just on those caring for Alzheimer sufferers, the emphasis of some common indicators.[7]

Domain VI: Reduction of social exclusion and improvement of relationships. The reduction of social exclusion is once again[8] argued to be one of the central aims of social policy as a whole. Now the context is a post-modern society which has increasingly strained social cohesion, made economic life more uncertain for the individual, and fostered greater emphasis on individualism than in the traditions of civil society. It is questionable whether integration into the main networks and life chances of society has become that overarching concept which binds together the whole of social policy, as does the French *lutte contre l'exclusion* (Bonoli and Palier, 1995). For social work at the level of the individual, the improvement of relationships has been central both as an end and means.

For the user, the reduction of social exclusion was measured by various indicators in the KCCP and its successors, including indicators of contacts, and self-perceived degrees of loneliness and isolation. The impact indicators for which production functions were fitted include a direct assessment by the user of the degree to which the social services improved the quality of relationships with the family and friends, IMPREL, and more general indicators of satisfaction with the opportunities to socialise, to meet people and to talk about personal and confidential things.

The consequences of intensive long-term caregiving for the social exclusion and deprivation of caregivers is well established. ECCEP measured several. However, numbers were insufficient for the estimation of a production function. In particular, the consequences for work role strain of caregiving has had increasing attention. It was particularly disappointing that too few of the caregivers were in employment and disadvantaged in one or more of these ways for the fitting of models.

Domain VII: Worker perception of impact. Professional workers deny that professional judgement is the opposite of user responsiveness. But another reason for its inclusion was the need for triangulation, *Resources, Needs and Outcomes* (Davies et al, 1990) having shown that CMCURE, an indicator of the number of problems thought by the person mostly undertaking the main care management functions resolved or risks reduced, was not highly correlated with the users' views about the impacts of services. The indicator used here is highly general: how far the care manager considered the community services to have improved the welfare of the user.

1.2. Inputs

Inputs are measured in costs per week. However, the focus is on volume of resource inputs. In the derivation of the input index for each service, the national average costs given by Netten and Dennett (1997) have been used merely as weighting factors for the number of units of inputs variously measured. The broad types of service covered are home care, home-delivered meals, day care, respite care, social work and community nursing. The distributions are described in appendix table 2.2.

1.3. Risk factors, need-related circumstances, and other non-resource inputs affecting the relationships between resource inputs and outputs

The indicators are described in appendix table 2.2 (page 421).

Space does not here allow us to situate the indicators into the rich theoretical argument from the 'ologies and other subjects linking these factors to utilisation and productivities. That literature relates to every domain in which indicators have been tested.

It will be seen that the attempt has been less to test alternative fundamental causes — or rather to estimate their relative importance — than to take into account influences which are causally the most proximate to the influence on the impact of resource inputs on outputs. That is reflected in the balance of the indicators.

Some examples illustrate both the richness of the theory and evidence, and the indirectness of its relevance to our task.

One example is the balance between indicators, which are purely family and network structures, and those that are subjective responses. Both are of proven importance in theory developed by social gerontologists. On *structures*, Freedman (1996), for instance, shows how the presence of a close relative lowers the probability of admission to institutions. Soldo et al. (1990) show an association between the number of surviving daughters is associated with the probability of having a child as a principal informal caregiver. Jette et al. (1992) and Tennstedt et al.(1989) show how sharing a care responsibility can be serial as well as part of the structuring of the week during any one phase, and how that depends on the number of persons in the network. Given the nature of the disability, structures matter.[9]

But in the presence of informal caregivers, more causally immediate to the impact of caregiving is the *subjective response* of the disabled and potential caregivers, and the relationships between them: the sense of burden, the gratifications from caring, individual caregivers' responses to particular features of the caring task or to the behavioural or cognitive consequences of dementia. Argument about the nature of causation of stress and well-being are central. Such established models like that of Pearlin et al. (1990) position the subjective perceptions as near to the effects as objective factors, but the role of coping mechanisms, and of informal systems as buffers mediates these, and in both worlds the subjectivity of broad, long and complex relationships are inescapable.[10]

One coping resource is 'meaning in caregiving' in the sense of 'positive beliefs one holds about oneself and one's caregiving experience such that some benefits or gainful outcomes are construed from it', with the ability to frame caregiving as meaningful and positive explaining significant variation in well-being among caregivers. It is argued (Pearlin et al., 1990) that such factors as meaning, making sense, order or coherence out of existence, is correlated with the broadest of responses, for instance, mental health generally and to successful ageing. The relationships are complicated, and results vary between studies. For some of the well-being outcomes in one analysis, objective stressors explained little, with indicators of how they were perceived and interpreted affecting some (Noonan and Tennstedt, 1997). But for others, including mastery, objective stressors, as well as the coping resources, and strategies had an influence.

These subjective responses themselves then make an independent contribution to the probability of entering a home or making demands for community services (Pruchno et al., 1990; Cohen et al., 1993). The 'ologies likewise show how the structural features and factors influencing the subjective response reflect more fundamental causal processes: for example, the recognition of family obligations and — looser — 'commitments' (Finch, 1995; Qureshi and Walker, 1989); how patterns of social networks reflect much wider aspects of the ways of life, and affect what roles flexible services can play (Wenger, 1992); how caregiving within networks is a reflection of relationships with long histories; how relational propinquity and obligation works through differentially to 'heavy duty caring' and 'support' (Litwak, 1965; Twigg, 1996).

Various arguments interrelate structure and subjective response; for instance, the plausible and important *gender role socialisation hypothesis* put forward by Miller and Cafasso (1992), which explains differences in gender patterns of caregiving, or deleterious consequences for women in the form of stress or burden (Horowitz, 1985; Miller and Cafasso, 1992; Stoller, 1983). Gender had an effect on three out of five measures of caregivers' stress net of other caregiver characteristics, elder characteristics, characteristics of the caregiving situation, and the resources available in the study of employed caregivers by Neal et al. (1997).

Relational propinquity seems to modify the gender and other relationships. Again, there are expectations linked to socialisation. The patterns are clearly different for persons of different relationships. And the caregiving has different effects on the caregivers. For instance, Neal et al. (1997) suggest that caring for a parent is more problematic than caring for persons of other relationships except spouses, for which the problems of caregiving are greatest, as shown by Twigg and Atkin (1994), and others. Neal et al. (1997) suggest that the emotional attachment may increase the likelihood of deleterious consequences.

Evidence about employment and caregiving likewise illustrates these generalisations both about the female performance of care roles and about the effects on work-family conflicts and work strain. For instance, an analysis of data from the National Long-Term Care Survey suggested that employed principal informal caregivers provided fewer hours of help than PICs not in employment (Doty et al., 1996), though a study found small differences in the overall amounts of care provided by employed and other daughters, the former undertook less personal care and cooking but purchased more care (Brody and Schoonover, 1986). But one study found that being employed decreased the hours of caregiving assistance provided by sons, but not by daughters (Stoller, 1983). Most studies show more work-family conflict and work-role strains among women than men (Stone and Short, 1990).

One powerful theme of the sociological argument about informal and formal care is exchange, exchange theory being a point of departure for analysis (Abrams, 1977). Hence, the importance of the history of the relationship for handicapped elderly persons likely to receive community services, because, as Bocquet et al. (1997) suggest for France, the stage at which care is provided and received daily 'probably corresponds to the frontier zone' where one passes from bilateral exchange to unilateral care, and which appears to those involved to be help rather than exchange. Answers to questions about aid in surveys, as in less structured discussion, clearly reflect the ambiguities of the perception of tasks where there has long been a division of labour in a context of bilateral or multilateral exchange, particularly where (as in a form of dementia with gradual onset, rather than an accident causing a fracture) the mutual exchange only slowly changes its balance. They also reflect ambivalences. It is interesting that in France, Attias-Donfut and Rozenkier (1981) found that some 26 per cent more of the children from the pivot generation (aged 49-53) of aged parents stated that they were helping their parents because of health- or disability-related dependence than the parents themselves stated that their children helped.

These are mere illustrations of the richness of the evidence and argument against which must be situated the attempt to predict outputs from risk factors. However, it is not the objective of this part of the study[11] to produce models which show the interrelationship between the causal structures suggested by gerontological theory and production of welfare relationships, merely models that predict outputs as well and simply as possible. Models that concentrate on the latter are likely to bury what is theoretically interesting to the gerontologist in ambiguous indicators and reduced form structures, though the importance of the theory in guiding collection and indicator design remains.

Notes

1 A decade before, we observed much less clarity in the impact of unconformist values. See, for example, the effects on the utilisation functions in chapter 3 of *Resources, Needs and Outcomes* (Davies et al., 1990).

2 Even the authority with that long tradition of free services spoke ominously, perhaps apocalyptically, throughout the period about imminent and major changes, though the changes had not yet occurred two years after the cohort was recruited. What might instigate the change is facing the consequences of diseconomies of scale following local government reorganisation.

3 Arguably, the length of stay in the community is ambiguous as an evaluative criterion, and so as the basis of an indicator of final output. A prolonged length of stay in the community might be due to scarcity in the supply of places in institutions for long-term care rather than the superiority of the quality of life and care in the community. However, the White Paper of 1989 put great emphasis on providing more opportunity to be supported in the community. So a study which is in part an evaluation of the impact of the policy there stated should treat that outcome as final.

4 In the KCCP, the indicators were assessed shortfall in amount of help required to make the level of care acceptable with respect to personal care and security, and rising and retiring. *Old People's Homes and the Production of Welfare* (Davies and Knapp, 1981) distinguished physical from cognitive functioning; and within physical, sensory disabilities from others, because of their prevalence and predictive importance. The KCCP included ratings of the need for help in tasks whose performance was required daily, and tasks whose performance was required weekly. Also included was an indicator of the adequacy of the diet.

5 *Felt degree of control over own life* in the KCCP was based on the sum of five items covering issues of overreliance on others, degree of control in making decisions, whether they felt a burden on others, and reactions to dependence.

6 The evidence about its validity was discussed in an appendix to Davies et al. (1990).

7 The Kosberg scale was applied to all principal informal caregivers. A sample of caregivers were also asked the Rutter scale, so that the relationship between stress due to caregiving and overall psychological malaise and stress could be explored.

8 The idea will not be strange to those familiar with the earlier writings of Titmuss, or Boulding, though the terminology is different.

9 Similar patterns are to be found in other countries. Bocquet et al. show how in the rural areas around Toulouse, famous for its tight-knit families and cohabitation of the elderly with younger family in a primarily peasant rural economy, there is a clear difference between genders in the provision of household and personal care, daughters and daughters-in-law providing household and personal care more than sons, but that there is a less clear difference between husbands and wives, both delivering household and personal care with similar frequency when circumstances are comparable (Bocquet et al., 1996; Le Bras, 1986). That is so more generally in France. When the dependent lives with another elderly person as a couple, the other member of the couple is likely to be the principal informal caregiver, but where the person is widowed, the care is provided by a child in almost one half of the cases (Bouget et al., 1990). So the weight of being the principal personal and household carer falls on women.

10 Buffering reduces the need and demand for formal services. But the caregivers can act as 'reticulists', and so generate demand. Again the effects are common to traditions of gerontology which have not strongly interacted until recently, as well as in different Western societies. Bocquet et al. (1996) define 'le soutien réticulaire' as one of the three types of support given by the network: the mobilisation of social and relational resources, enabling access to others for the provision of services. The same is found in Anglo-Saxon literatures.

3   Estimating Production Functions

This chapter describes the way in which we have used the production function, the econometric tool that handles the study of the impact of service inputs on the measures of outputs. There are four sections. The first summarises the main concepts of production function theory. 'Joint supply' is discussed in chapter 11, which is focused on its estimation. The second section explores the features added to the standard form of the production function to fit it to the needs of the production of welfare approach. The third section discusses important implications of the methodology, and generally provides a 'manual' for the interpretation of the results. The last section outlines the structure of the chapters containing the results for each of the output variables.

1.   Production function theory

The production function is the economist's device to describe the relationship between 'factor' inputs and outputs the 'firm' produces (Koutsoyiannis, 1979). It describes (a) the effects of input level on output levels ('average' productivities), and (b) the marginal gains in outputs that would be achieved by marginal increases in each input ('marginal' productivities).

Production functions can be intricate to estimate empirically for several reasons. First, there are difficulties of measurement and data collection. Perhaps more important, the successful estimation of a production function relies on its ability to describe the complexities of the relationships. Economic theory is built around the significance of certain kinds of difference in the patterns of 'production relations', and shows why it is important to be able to show them. Among other patterns, the estimates must describe:

- *Changes in marginal productivities of inputs at different levels of provision.* How much an output improves following small increases in inputs may depend on the level of provision of the input. Increasing, constant and diminishing returns to scale refer respectively to situations in which the marginal productivities of inputs increase, remain constant and diminish with the input levels. In general, it is assumed that the marginal productivity of a given input will diminish beyond some level of inputs. We shall see the importance of describing these differences throughout the essay; for instance, in the discussion of the effects of concentrating resources on those of greatest disability compared with allocating a higher proportion to persons of lesser disability.

- *Input substitutability*. A targeted level of output may be achieved by various combinations of inputs. The estimation must describe the possible trade-offs between inputs in the production of that output level.
- *Input complementarity*. The rate at which inputs can be substituted in the production of a target output may differ depending on the actual level of the inputs. In other words, the marginal productivity of one input may depend on the level of other inputs.

Different production function forms handle the complexities of such description to varying degrees, and there is a balance to be struck between precision and complexity. The choice between forms depends on which relationships are likely to be important in the field of application and the nature of the questions to be illuminated by the estimates, as well as how well alternate forms fit the data.[1]

2.   Production functions for community care

Estimating the production relations of community care has complications additional to those of more conventional contexts. First, many users receive only one service but outputs are nevertheless achieved. Unless no other combination of services can produce the output, this must mean that there are circumstances in which inputs are perfectly substitutable. The form must allow for such perfect substitutability. Not to do so would be tantamount to assuming that no beneficial effect could be expected from packages providing exclusively home care, though packages consisting only of home care comprise approximately one third of all packages. Secondly, as chapter 1 has argued, community care outputs are affected by many factors in addition to resource inputs, and they can influence average cost without influencing marginal costs, and vice versa. The model form must allow for this also. We explain how this is done in two stages.

2.1. *Many receive only one service*

The core structure of the model is based on an expanded linear form, the quadratic form (Lau, 1974). This convenient production function, of the form

(1) $Y = \alpha + \sum_i \beta_i I_i + \sum_i \sum_j \delta_{ij} I_i I_j$

where Y represents the level of output, and I_i represents the level of input i.[2] It is more flexible than the basic Cobb-Douglas form because it takes into account both the effects of each input on its own (hence allowing for perfect substitutability and the existence of single input packages), non-linear single input effects (through the quadratic terms) as well as the combined effect of the input given the level of other inputs used (thus allowing for input complementarity). With this Lau formulation, the marginal product, $MP(I_i)$, of input i is:

(2) $$MP(I_i) = \beta_i + \Sigma_j \, \delta_{ij} \, I_j \, .$$

Equation 1 establishes the main parameters defining the production function model.

2.2. Impact of risk factors

Chapter 1 argued that decades of research in the human services, particularly schooling, have confirmed that variations in the quantities of the service have a smaller impact on the final outcomes of evaluative importance in their own right than non-resource inputs, particularly the circumstances of the child (Verry and Davies, 1975). For this reason, a 'weak form' of the production of welfare proposition has been preferred to a stronger form (Davies, 1985). The weak form is that 'although other factors are the biggest influences on status and changes of outcomes of evaluative importance, increases in resource inputs are associated with one or more improved outcomes for some ranges of inputs'. The production function modelling must allow for the effects of quasi-inputs, particularly need-related circumstances and other 'risk factors'. This is achieved by the inclusion of three additional sets of terms into the model: (a) appropriate additive terms for risk factors; (b) what we call 'targeting-captured risk effects; and (c) group effects on marginal productivities, a category recognised in *Resources, Needs and Outcomes* (Davies et al., 1990).

Additive terms for risk factors. Risk factors are (hopefully) correlated with service inputs. If their effects were not allowed for, the collinearity would cause the model to be mis-specified, and estimates of average and marginal productivities would be biased, since they would incorporate both the effect of inputs and the effect of the missing factors. Once included, the model functional form becomes

(3) $$Y = \alpha + \Sigma_k \, \gamma_k S_k + \Sigma_i \beta_i I_i + \Sigma_i \, \Sigma_j \, \beta_{ij} \, I_i I_j \, ,$$

where $\Sigma_k \, \gamma_k S_k$ represents relevant need-related circumstances (NRCs) and other risk factors.

Targeting-captured risk effects. It is the task of field-level allocators to take into account need-related circumstances that are not fully (if at all) captured by the broad indicators of need-related circumstances taken into account in the model. This is important in the rationale for employing trained social workers, not merely operatives routinely basing judgement on scores derived from simple standard instruments. Professional training in social work is intended to teach sensitivity to a wide range of sources of case variation, and to the subtlety of need-related circumstances. Therefore, risk factor terms alone may not be precise enough to capture the whole of the non-input effect on outputs. They would omit the risk factors present for only small numbers of users, and the errors in our collection's measurement of risk factors that are more common. Therefore, the modelling must disentangle the positive effect of services from their negative effect on outputs due to their correlation with particular user needs.

The modelling did so by seeking 'targeting-captured risk effects': dummy effects in which selection for a service of a particular kind is associated with one or a combination of need-related circumstances at the first interview. Being risk factors at the first interview, they are almost entirely exogenous with respect to the model. That is, they are unlikely to be to be influenced more than negligibly by the service inputs.[3]

To allow for the targeting-captured need effects, intercept shift dummies are introduced to the model by the addition of the following terms:

$$(4) \qquad Y = \alpha + \sum_k \gamma_k S_k + \sum_i \beta_i I_i + \sum_i \sum_j \beta_{ij} I_i I_j + \sum_i \sum_s \omega_{is} D_i N_s,$$

where D_i is a dummy that takes on the value 1 for positive levels of input i and 0 otherwise, and N_s is a dummy NRC.

Figure 3.1 illustrates how the additive terms for risk factors and targeting-captured need effects correct what would otherwise be biased estimates of productivities. In equation 4, their effects are measured by γ_k and ω_{is} respectively. The two terms between them locate the intercept for the risk groups at points a and c on the output (vertical) axis in figure 3.2. That is, they allow for the share of the output level not due to the service input. Were the terms not to be included, the modelling would assign to the effects of risk factors in output level b on the outputs axis. The consequences would be biased estimates of both average and marginal productivities. The marginal productivities are the slopes of the curves given the input level. Figure 3.2 illustrates how the slope for the curve whose intercept is b is biased. It is, in effect, a weighted average of the true slopes for each of the two risk groups.

User group marginal productivity terms. In addition to their direct effect on outputs, risk factors are likely to affect the relationship between inputs and outputs. In such circumstances, the effects of inputs vary with the circumstances of users. It is therefore necessary to separate the users into homogeneous groups enjoying similar effects from services. This was done by incorporating into the model a set of additional terms:

Figure 3.1
Additive terms for risk factors and targeting-captured need effects

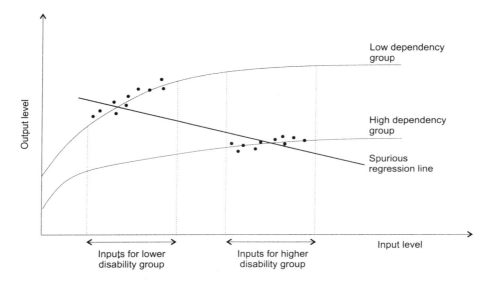

Figure 3.2
User group marginal productivity terms

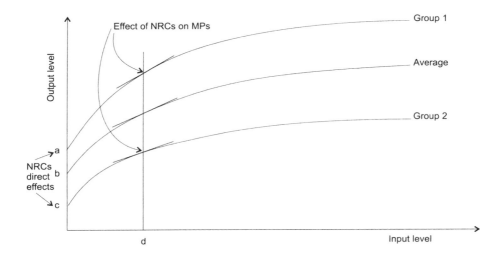

(5) $Y = \alpha + \ldots + \sum_i \sum_s v_{is} I_i N_s,$

where I_i, is the amount of input i, and N_s is the same as above.

Figure 3.2 illustrates how the user group marginal productivity terms correct what would otherwise be a serious bias in the estimation. In this case, the bias would be still more serious. Consider two groups of users. One has on average low service inputs, but services have on average high productivities for its members. The other has high service inputs, but services have on average low productivities for group members. Estimation without the user group marginal productivity terms would produce a spurious productivity curve indicating negative marginal productivity estimates; that is, the slope of the productivity curve would appear to be negative. The result would be a logical absurdity. In a correctly specified model of the world as it is, higher levels of service could not produce lower levels of output over the whole range of variation. The literature yields examples where attempts to fit cost functions have yielded apparently (absurd) negative marginal costs, because the user group marginal cost effects have not been adequately controlled. And there are others where it is likely that estimates of positive marginal costs are likely to be misleadingly over-simple for the same reason. The findings of this section will illustrate just how gross the distortions would be were we to fail to allow for user group marginal productivity effects. They will illustrate that a spurious and absurd negative estimate would be all too probable.

None of these effects — varying returns to scale, perfect elasticity of substitution of inputs, the effects of risk factors on average costs, general and group effects on marginal costs, targeting-captured need effects — are imposed on the models. If they are not there, the modelling is unlikely to show them. The preference in modelling is simplicity, so as to reap the benefits of the vigorous application of Occam's razor. For instance, if there are diminishing returns to scale as well described by the single term of a logarithmic transformation of the service input term, that has been preferred to two terms of a quadratic function in the service input. Also, only exceptionally were terms involving a dummy variable allowed into the models unless at least fifteen cases had the characteristic denoted by the dummy, and additionally had an effect significantly greater than zero in the postulated direction at the 5 per cent level.[4]

Chapter 1 has discussed the general policy of seeking guidance, possible effects and unlikely effects, from the gerontological and related literatures, as well as guidance in the investigation of likely relationships from economics. Similarly, it has listed some of the general rules of good modelling practice applied.[5]

3.   Production functions and causal structures

Chapter 1 described the estimation of productivities and efficiencies as being basically descriptive, although the ECCEP study as a whole also asked the 'how' and 'why' explanatory questions of the production of welfare approach (Davies, 1985). The production function merely maps such 'production of welfare parameters' as productivities. To do that, it must take into account many of the consequences of the structures of causation in the production of welfare. But it is not necessary to map them. In principle, the production function would ideally be the reduced form of a more complex model of causal structure if the aim is to understand the system.[6]

A full model of the causal structures themselves would be more complex. This greater complexity would lead to a discourse that was more refined in terms of need-related circumstances than that of the production function. The indicators of risk factors and need-related circumstances in a production function may be no more than markers of combinations of risks and needs whose influence on productivities are the same. A causal model might distinguish more need-related groups, and might define the risk factors for which the production function includes a marker indicator. The distinction between 'how' and 'why' questions in chapter 1 illustrates how there would be more proximate and more distant causes, with the more distant causes influencing the more proximate ones. A causal model would relate phenomena to one another sequentially as a process through time. A causal model would have quite different boundaries. Some phenomena which would be 'endogenous' in a full causal model, that is influenced by other factors in the model, are 'exogenous' in a production function model. For instance, the quantities and mixes of service inputs received by users would be endogenous in a causal model, but are treated as exogenous in the production function model. The issues were further explored in Davies (1985). Some of the differences between a causal approach and production function modelling are illustrated by a comparison between our analysis and that of Yates et al. (1999).[7]

There are important implications for how the reader interprets the results of our production functions. In particular, it must be remembered that what is discovered for this set to be marker indicators may not turn out in replications to be the most reliable indicator for this purpose. As research evidence accumulates, it may be possible to distinguish the groups with similar risk and need factors in ways that connect still more directly with field assessment concepts and observations. Indeed, some analysis of the ECCEP data with other foci may contribute, though being designed to cover virtually the whole range of users, the ECCEP database may yield less insight than databases for sub-populations, for instance, studies of stroke victims.

4.   Structure of chapters 4-10

The remainder of this section of the book contains a chapter for each of the seven output domains distinguished in table 2.1 (page 33). Within each chapter, the discussion is arranged by the individual output indicators for the domain in question. Then, the discussion of each production function is organised around three sections.

4.1.   *The production function model and the impact of risk factors*

In each chapter, a table summarises the coefficients, goodness of fit, and the proportion of recipients affected by the productivity effects. Two proportions are given. One is the proportion of the recipients of the service in question affected by the productivity effect. The other is the proportion of the entire group of cases on which the equation is based: that is, of the entire ECCEP sample excluding cases for whom the data is missing or the dependent variable is irrelevant (because, for example, the output is for caregivers, and the user is without a caregiver).

The text compares the goodness of fit with that for other production functions, and then discusses the impact of 'need-related circumstances' and other risk factors. There is not much emphasis in the discussion on relating the pattern of influence on risk factors to the results of gerontological research because, as argued earlier, the equations show the effects of marker indicators. However, many of the effects predicted from the gerontological literature are so powerful that the indicators themselves are clearly important phenomena.[8]

4.2.   *Service productivities*

There are one or more diagrams showing the productivity curves for each service input. They show the productivity effects of each of the inputs presented in the table, allowance being made for the other predictor variables in the model.

Each set of curves shows the output level associated with different levels of an input. It depicts two phenomena. One is the input's *average productivities*: the average number of units of output associated with a level of input. The second is the input's *marginal productivities* over some range: that is, the marginal increase in output to be expected from a marginal increase in input at different levels of provision.

Average productivities can be inferred directly from the levels of services and outputs shown by the productivity curve. The marginal productivity at a level is the slope of the curve at that level. Curves depicting increasing or decreasing marginal productivities are characterised by their increasing or decreasing slopes. Average and marginal productivities are invariant with respect to the level of input provided where the 'curve' is a straight line.

The text discusses such scale effects. In particular, it discusses whether the significant productivity effects are primarily found at lower levels of inputs; that is whether the marginal productivities decrease greatly after the provision of low levels of the services. The levels of inputs for which the curves are plotted, in the figures, lie within the range with a significant number of cases for the model in question.

Some productivity effects are general to all recipients of the service. Others show the influence of productivity effects present only for users with some combinations of circumstances. The diagrams show the proportion of the recipients of the service that are affected by the productivity effect.

4.3. Overview

The principal foci of the chapters 4-10 are (a) the overall impact of services given the actual levels allocated compared with risk factors; and (b) how that impact varies between user groups.

4.3.1. Analysis by user type

There are two reasons why it is important to show implications for groups based on the need-related circumstances of users. First, doing so engages some of the choices and dilemmas discussed in chapter 1: for instance, between providing lighter packages for the less dependent compared with heavier packages for the more dependent, or between cases with and without caregivers. Second, it handles the combinations of risk factor and productivity effects. That is important because the equations and productivity curves show individual effects for predictors which can be found in combination, and which are in many cases correlated.

Choice of typology. A vast number of items could form the basis of variables for description. The initial task is much simplified by applying a template based on indicators of two key need-related circumstances: general dependency indicated by interval need, and social support indicated by the presence of someone satisfying the definition for designation as 'principal informal caregiver' (PIC). The categories are the combination of the level on each of the two dimensions. The same categories are used in the ECCEP descriptive book, *Caring for Older People* (Bauld et al., 2000).

Grouping users into such categories has the merit of allowing the most direct comparison across production functions. Also this procedure allows us to base estimates on populations of actual cases. And the analysis can be inclusive because, between them, the categories cover all the cases in the sample.

The disadvantage is the converse of the advantage, in that it reduces the likelihood of building a policy argument on the spurious relationship with a complex indicator, a risk discussed in chapter 1. Basing the analysis that most directly impinges on the policy argument on a crude six-fold typology oversimplifies the argument. It is important not just to find, but to build into the frameworks within which we discuss policy, those of the more complex predictors which replication confirm to be good markers of the influence of risks. This is particularly so at a time when we are attempting to develop a risk management orientation by such means of 'risk-based assessment' (Department of Health, 1998, para. 2.36). The broader the categories and the more general the scales and variables, the cruder must be the policy argument.

Additionally to the interval need by presence of PIC classification, the results are also presented given the levels of cognitive impairment as defined by the Katzman scale (Katzman et al., 1983). Therefore this classification divides the sample into three additional groups: namely, no cognitive impairment, mild cognitive impairment, and severe cognitive impairment.

Diagram showing service impacts for each type. For each production function, there is a diagram which indicates how risk factors as a group, and each service, are predicted by the production function to contribute to the overall score on the outcome indicator. The prediction is derived by multiplying the coefficient for each variable by the level for the variable specified for that user group.

These diagrams differ in form depending on whether the outcome is a negative or positive indicator of welfare. If the indicator is positive, the service contribution increases the score, and so is shown as an addition to the top of the column representing the contribution of the risk factors. If it is a negative indicator, the service contribution reduces the score, and so is shown as a negative value at the bottom of the column. The height of the column without the service contribution shows what would be the outcome predicted in the absence of service. So the overall outcome is shown as the sum of effects of the risk factors and service contributions in the case of positive indicator: the total height of the column. In the case of a negative indicator, the overall outcome is the height of the column due to risk factors with the height beneath the zero subtracted. (That is, in both cases the two components are added, but if the outcome is a negative indicator, the sum is of a positive and negative value.)

4.3.2. *Equity and efficiency comments*

The degree of elaboration of the discussion varies with the extent to which service inputs rather than risk factors affected output levels, and the pattern of variation between user groups. Where service impacts are small, no further evidence is presented or discussed.

Where service impacts are powerful, the degree to which the variations between the user groups reflect marginal productivities and levels of service inputs is discussed. The relative scale of the service impact shown in the diagram discussed in section 4.3.1. is related to information about the average productivities of packages in order to analyse whether big service impacts mainly reflect productivities or equity judgements.

Notes

1   Historically, there have been three main antecedent forms, each having been the basis of a large family of variants. The *input-output production* form was developed by Leontief (1951) in order to map aggregate production relations in the economy as a whole. Its goal was simplicity of form to handle a large number of 'inputs'; in his case, inputs from many 'industries'. So the form assumes that that a unique combination of inputs is required for the production of any particular level of output. Therefore the Leontief production function does not allow for any substitution between the factors of production. The *linear production function* allows for input substitution. It allows for the possibility that one input might produce any quantity of output desired: that is, for perfect substitutability between inputs. But in its simplest form, it does not allow for complementarity between inputs or for varying returns to scale. The range of variants of each of these forms has been expanded over time in order to relax assumptions and constraints. From the Cobb-Douglas form descends variants like the Constant Elasticity of Substitution function and the Translog function, the latter relaxing more assumptions than the former. (A more detailed discussion is included in Intriligator et al. (1996, 284-289).

2   Also, not necessarily implied by the formula, the modelling tested for non-linearities by means of quadratic or log terms in order to test for diminishing or increasing returns. (We did not follow Vernon Greene's example in imposing diminishing returns by using a Gompertz transformation for several reasons. It is true that given optimisation, it would be expected authorities would be operating within the range where diminishing returns would imply. But there are two caveats. One is that the level of inputs observed from the reduced form for one output might be the results of there being one or more other outputs in the objective function. Second, there might be constraints on the supply of certain inputs, preventing the allocators from operating with the optimal mix. Third, contemporary community care is a fiscally constrained if not straitened system. Therefore, most authorities might have to operate in regions of increasing returns on inputs if they were to satisfy reasonable equity criteria. But, fourth, research evidence in general suggests that the allocation processes are such that optimal input mixing is unlikely: the allocators lack information about outcomes and even accurate information about costs, and they lack control over service commissioning, and the like. This last is the nub of our policy argument.

3   A hypothetical example will illustrate the logic. Among long interval need cases with principal informal caregivers, those selected for respite care are almost certain to have in common special combinations of need-related circumstances. It is likely that either these are not fully measured by the indicators, or that each combination applies to insufficient cases for it to emerge with statistical significance in the modelling. However, the effect would be caught by an interaction term defined in terms of 'user received respite care and had long interval needs prior to the period when inputs are made'. The inclusion of such term would not only help to account for differences between users, but would also purge the inputs from their correlation with NRCs.

4   That was lower than was originally planned for the reasons mentioned in chapter 1.

5   The modelling tested for interaction terms between risk factors. The reason was that production of welfare argument creates an expectation that combinations of risk factors would have different effects on the relations between service inputs and outputs than the sum of the effects of the risk factors treated separately. An example is

the way in which studies from several countries have found the level of informal care has affected the marginal productivity of services (Davies, 1992a, appendix 2). Early production of welfare argument postulated that such interaction effects would be pervasive (Davies and Challis, 1986, chapter 4).

6   A reduced form is a simplification of a set of equations describing a causal structure. In a reduced form equation, one variable is treated as dependent on all others in the equation. For instance, the production functions for single outputs discussed in the following chapters are in principle reduced forms of the simultaneous equation production function in chapter 11. The argument in the paragraph above suggests that the production function would ideally be a simplification of a still more complex causal model in which certain variables only were made dependent variables and their dependence on other variables described.

7   That paper also has service inputs as predictors of, at the penultimate stage, caregiver felt burden, though among dyads not triads. But its emphasis is on influences on a sequence of appraisal fields, on process, on revealing relationships that would probably lie behind a term in one of our production functions, whether reduced form or 'structural' (Yates et al., 1999). Indicators that are epiphenomenal could in principle be quite satisfactory marker indicators as long as the subgroups they represent are clear, so that connections can be made with other research linking the indicators to subpopulations evident at assessment and to causal argument.

8   Indicators that are epiphenomenal could in principle be quite satisfactory marker indicators as long as the subgroups they represent are clear, so that connections can be made with other research linking the indicators to sub-populations evident at assessment and to causal argument.

4 Productivities for DAYS Indicator Variable (User's Length of Stay in the Community)

The model is for the number of days living at home prior to admission to an institution for long-term care (DAYS).

The model was fitted using tobit analysis. Chapter 2 explained that the use of tobit analysis was necessary because the distribution of the variable is censored. The variable is censored because the results could not otherwise be produced at this stage without imposing an early cut-off point. The cut-off point was the 22nd month, for the case that was in the median position in the distribution by date of referral.

1. The model and the impact of risk factors

The equation results are summarised in table 4.1.

Goodness of fit. Tobit analysis does not yield a coefficient of variation. The estimate in the table is derived from the estimation of the model through OLS, and is only a crude indicator. The model explains a high proportion of the variance in the dependent variable.

Impact of risk factors. The modelling yielded clearly established effects for variables from each domain.

Reflecting *physical disability,* the big and well-established effect of being *bedbound* is unsurprising. In effect, being *unable to undertake light household tasks* and of long interval need, define thresholds of dependency affecting the output.

From the *mental health* domain, cognitive impairment is well recognised in the literature for the UK and elsewhere as a major risk factor for ceasing to live at home.

Other health problems also contribute. The clarity of the impact of cancer and incontinence impairment as risk factors is again unsurprising. The former

Table 4.1

Production function for days living at home prior to entering institutions[1]

Predictors by domain	Coeff.	Prob.	%[2] Recip- ients	%[3] Users
Risk factors and other need-related circumstances				
General effects				
Physical disability				
User is bed-bound – Cantbed	-202.66	.004		
User cannot do light housework – Cantlhwk	-142.58	.013		
User belongs to long interval need level – Intlong	98.09	.081		
Mental health				
Katzman's cognitive impairment score – Katscore	-8.66	.007		
Other health problems				
User has cancer – Wcancer	-268.40	.016		
User has continence problems – Wincont	-157.36	.009		
Informal care related factors				
Poor PIC/User relationship – Wcupoor	-258.01	.006		
User feels embarrassed by PIC caring – Cupbemb	-547.39	.003		
Other				
User against residential care – Upercent	73.38	.002		
User's age – Age	-10.86	.002		
User is vexed by charging – Vexed	207.08	.044		
User lives alone – Walone	-127.13	.037		
Count of number of user's risk as perceived by CM – Wuserisk	-20.67	.045		
Targeting-captured need effects				
User cognitively impaired targeted for day-care – Dc_cog	-241.28	.009		
User without PIC targeted for day-care – Dc-npic	-286.87	.005		
User living alone targeted for respite care – Re_alon	-123.21	.094		
User in critical interval need targeted for respite care – Re-crit	-209.33	.028		
Productivity effects (£ per week)				
Individual input effects				
Home care				
User cannot do heavy housework tasks – Lhc_hhwk (log)	33.73	.017	93.0	77.8
Day care			100.0	39.8
User has mild/sev cog impairment – Ldc_katm (log)	65.29	.010	43.1	17.3
User not cognitively impaired – Ldc_oth (log)	32.61	.066	56.9	22.5

Table 4.1 (continued)

Predictors by domain	Coeff.	Prob.	%[2] Recipients	%[3] Users
Respite care			80.7	25.7
Users with personal relational problems – Rec_hrel	-6.25	.002	26.1	8.4
Users over-reliant – Rec_reli:	-5.19	.001	15.9	5.1
Users with high no. of problems with IADLs				
– Lre_hiad (log)	67.72	.012	29.5	9.3
Users with behavioural problems – Rec_beha	8.53	.001	23.9	7.6
Users who cannot wash – Lre-wash (log)	55.84	.018	58.0	18.8
Constant	1558.6	.000		

Adj. R[2] .399[4]   Prob. .00000   No. of cases 274

1 Tobit model
2 Proportion of recipients of the service to whom the effect applies
3 Proportion of the sample to whom the effect applies
4 From OLS version

illustrates the rehabilitation of disease information as predictors of utilisation patterns in the work of Manton and others (Manton, 1988; Liu and Manton, 1984; Liu et al., 1990; Manton et al., 1993a,b).

The nature of the significant effects of *informal support* indicators illustrate the importance of incorporating into the analysis subtle measures of *relationships* and attitudes. Here, cases where the user feels *embarrassment* about receiving care or where the care manager perceives the user/carer relationship as poor are associated with a significant decrease in the number of days residing in the community. Relationships were also shown to be important in influencing whether persons immediately entered residential institutions rather than received services at home after first assessment (Davies et al., 1996). The dominant sociological framework for the analysis of caregiving is the structure of exchange relationships into which it fits. Exchange argument is of particular importance for this population. When cases are ranked in descending order of disability, the median user has precisely the number of incapacities to perform personal care ADLs (activities of daily living), which Spector and Fleishman (1998) suggest to be typical of the stage at which the transition from equal to one-sided exchange takes place. In these respects the results closely mirror one strand of argument about what causes variations in the buffering effects of informal support.

The *user's age* often enters equations predicting admission to institutions containing specific dependency indicators, and is likewise one of those variables available in general data sets and sufficiently correlated with utilisation for it to be used in allocations formulae such as the grant standard spending assessments (SSA) (Bebbington et al., 1996). One reason is that it can reflect general frailty.[1] 'Frailty' is reacquiring some status as an epidemiological concept, despite the absence of a consensus about its precise meaning. One definition, 'a broader range of more subtle problems in multiple domains' constituting 'problems and losses of capability which make the individual more vulnerable to environmental challenge', on the one hand separates the concept from gross measures of functioning, but on the other hand makes it too inclusive by including a range of risk, which is broader than would be expected from an idea whose origin lies in the vulnerability arising from uncertainties and weakness in functioning (Strawbridge et al, 1998).[2] The highly significant effect of the count of the *number of risks* reinforces the impression of the importance of general vulnerability.

The direction of the effect for that omnipresent but ambiguous indicator, *living alone*, is interesting. Living alone is powerfully associated with utilisation of community services and with the probability of living in institutions, and for that reason has an important place in the prediction equations used for resource allocations and forecasting (Bebbington and Davies, 1980; Bebbington et al., 1996; Wittenberg et al., 1998). The interesting feature in this equation is its direction. Bivariate analysis of the ECCEP data shows that those living alone tend to be less disabled (Bauld et al., 2000). Once the other factors are taken into account, however, those living alone tend to have a shorter period remaining in the community. That is, controlling for these other characteristics reveals the 'buffering effect' of co-resident support which is so often found in the literature, whatever the range and precision of predictor variables.

User preferences and values count, as well perceptions of objective circumstances. The direction of the influence of the *strength of the user's opposition to the idea of ever entering a home* is what would be predicted. The coefficient is highly significant. The equation predicts that those more strongly against admission stay in the community 350 days longer. Therefore this equation suggests that there has been a change since the mid-1980s. The analysis of the probability of recipients of community social services entering residential care, of the DCP sample, showed that once other influences were controlled, the degree of unwillingness to enter residential care did not have a significant effect on the actual probability, whether during the first six months after referral, or over the subsequent two years (Davies and Baines, 1994). The comparison of the two equations suggests that the degree of user opposition to the idea of admission did not have an effect during the mid-1980s, but that it has gained a clear effect subsequent to the reform. If that is indeed the case, it is an important extension of the user influence and choice. Modelling undertaken using a common pool of variables from the two data sets will constitute an important test of the hypothesis.[3]

Targeting-captured need effects as risk factors. Chapter 2 stated the necessity of separating the need-related elements, embodied in the targeting of services to particular user groups, from the beneficial effects such resources might have on the users' welfare. This is done, it was noted, by including targeting-captured need effects, dummies created by interacting whether users receive a given service with particular need-related circumstances at the time of the first interview.

The model shows how respite care and day care services are targeted to those users at highest risk of institutionalisation. Among the recipients of day care, this is particularly true for those cognitively impaired and/or without principal informal caregivers. Among respite care recipients, those users at particularly high risk of institutionalisation are those living alone and/or with critical interval needs.

All four effects refer to the self-selection or selection for the two services which the parallel analysis of utilisation patterns suggest to be the most carefully-targeted of the services: day care and respite care (Davies and Fernández, 2000).

2.   Service productivities

The results show clear productivities for all or most of the recipients of three services. These are described in figures 4.1 and 4.2.

- Table 4.1 shows a clear marginal productivity of *home care* for 93 per cent of home care recipients. (The last two columns of the table indicate respectively the proportion of service recipients and of users overall to which the productivity term relates.) The productivity for this output exists only for those whose need-related circumstances include physical disability to some degree. Figure 4.1 illustrates the effect, and shows how the marginal productivity diminishes with the scale of the input.
- *Day care* is productive for all recipients, but most strongly and clearly for those who are cognitively impaired (Albert, 1994; Katzman et al., 1983). The patterns are described in figure 4.1. There are diminishing returns to scale: the greater the input, the smaller the increase in output associated with another unit of the input.
- The equation both indicates those for whom *respite care* has the highest and the lowest productivities. Apparently, the biggest effect is for persons with substantial physical disability. This is reflected by the importance of the three variables: many IADLs; behavioural problems; and difficulties with washing — and, still more strongly, combinations of the three found together, as in many cases. The productivity curves are described in figure 4.2. They show how marginal productivities do not fall with the level of input for the 24 per cent of recipients with behavioural problems. For users with many IADL problems and/or who cannot wash, however, marginal productivities from increases in respite care decrease with the level of the service.
- For two risk factors, the input of respite care is inversely correlated with

Figure 4.1
Productivity curves: home care and day care effect on days living at home prior to entering institutions

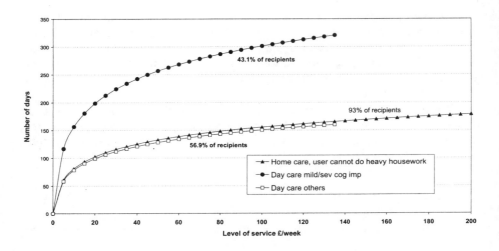

Figure 4.2
Returns to factor: respite care effect on days living at home prior to entering institutions

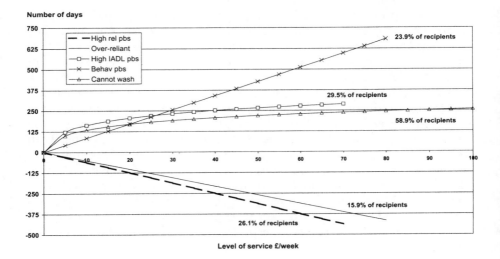

length of stay in the community: bad user-caregiver relationships, and users judged by care managers to be more reliant on others than the average clients in those circumstances. For these, the productivities estimates are negative. In other words, higher levels of respite care are associated with shorter stays in the community, the lines on figure 4.2 sloping downwards. These are characteristics that identify the subgroups that are typically associated with the subsequent breakdown of caregiving.

- The pattern of productivities may reflect what would be good social work practice in some circumstances. In good practice, permanent admission would be preceded by trial periods where circumstances allow. One aspect of the trial is the testing of the consequences of living in a congregate facility. Another is the experience of the congregate facility in which a long-run placement is anticipated. Certainly the former, and in some cases the latter, are reflected in the planned respite care.[4]

3. Overall service impact, impact for groups, and equity and efficiency

Figure 4.3 shows the mean impact, need-related circumstances and the different services have on DAYS, for the average (overall) sample case and for each of the nine groups of users postulated in the analysis. The rationale behind the definition of such groups was presented in the previous chapter.

The figure illustrates the large impact formal services have on DAYS. Al-

Figure 4.3
Contributions of services and risk factors to days living at home prior to entering institutions

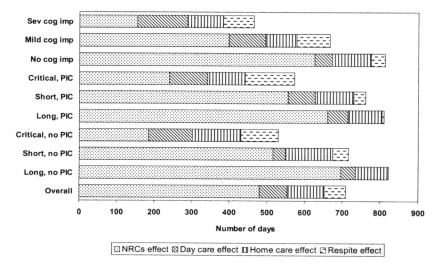

though this is true for all user groups, it is particularly so (both in absolute levels and relative to the effects of the risk factors) the higher the users' level of dependency and/or cognitive impairment. For instance, figure 4.3 suggests, service contributions account for approximately two thirds of the level of DAYS for severely cognitively impaired users and for less than a fifth for users with long interval needs and principal informal caregivers (PICs).

The main service contributions are from respite, home and day care. Although generally home care inputs have the greatest impact, the relative importance of the three services depends greatly on the user's level of needs. Hence, whereas home care contributions remain fairly constant for each of the different user groups, the contributions of day and especially respite care are much greater for users with short and critical interval needs and or cognitive impairment.

Results do not suggest home-delivered meals and nursing visits to have made big impacts on this outcome.

The results reveal significant differences in the levels of outputs achieved by care packages overall and each of the individual services for each of the user groups. The key question is how far are the patterns due to differences in productivities between users, and how far they are due to differences in levels of resources provided, service contributions being the sum of the products of service levels and average service productivities.[5]

This is of key importance because investment strategies concerned primarily with the efficient use of resources would concentrate services on those users that would benefit to the greatest extent from them: that is, on those for whom productivities are highest. This is explored in figure 4.4, which shows the average productivities — the ratios of average gains to costs — for each of the groups.

For each of the groups for which the risk factors predicted big service contributions (see figure 4.3), the average productivity is below that for the sample in general. So overall, the greater service contributions for more dependent user groups are due to larger inputs, not to higher productivities.

4.   Overview

The following are important conclusions:
- *Evidence of service productivity.* There are clear productivity effects for respite, home and day care in a model that works well. Some productivities are high, as the diagrams indicate. Overall, a substantial proportion of the output is associated with the contributions of service packages. Mainly because of the allocation of higher resource inputs, these contributions increase both in absolute terms and relative to the effect of need-related indicators with the level of dependency of the users.
- *User choice.* The degree of rejection of the idea of entering residential care

Figure 4.4
Average productivity for days living at home prior to entering institutions for total package

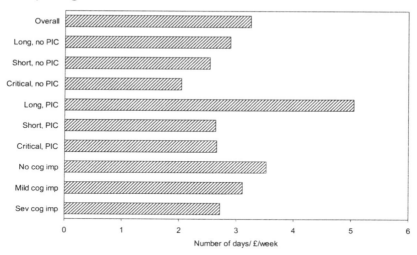

appeared to affect the length of stay in the 1995 cohort, and those least willing to consider admission stayed in the community substantially longer. A similar variable appeared to have no effect for the 1984/85 cohort. That implies an important extension of user influence.

- *Consistency over time in triaging to care at home or in institutions.* The need-related circumstances having effects are the familiar risk factors for admission to institutions for long-term care. The comparison with the results of models predicting triaging of persons to homes or to home care at the end of the set-up stage show important similarities (Davies et al., 1996; Davies and Fernández, 1998). Also there are similarities with the pattern a decade ago described in Davies and Baines (1994). The evidence of these models is encouraging. It seems that similar influences are at work over two different time periods, the set-up and continuing care periods. This reinforces the finding that the utilisation outcomes from the way care managers allocated services between cases are becoming increasing consistent and 'ologically' defensible (Davies et al., 1997; Davies and Fernández, 1998). Of course, both supply and demand factors influence the probability of using institutions rather than community services for care. However, what counts are utilisation patterns, not simply targeting intentions from the supply side.

- *Care managers poured on most water where the fire was fiercest.* They allocated much greater resources on those cases with highest levels of need, although they had the lowest average expected returns. At first sight, it would seem likely that the pattern of productivities and service contributions observed would be defensible only if equity demanded that there should be greatly extended stays in the community for persons with critical interval need or severe cognitive impairment. The pattern might well be inefficient given different equity judgements. But the pattern of productivity variation with scale is complex, as is the influence of risk factors. Therefore, whether or not resources are allocated excessively to those of higher disability will become clear only when we have analysed the results of the optimisation analysis in Part II below. In this respect, the story of the implications of productivities, efficiencies, and input prices has the twists and turns of a Le Carré novel.

Notes

1   This is despite what is almost a fundamental principle of gerontology: that the rates of functional ageing vary greatly between people, so that chronological age is an unreliable measure of functional ageing.

2   Strawbridge et al. (1998) then provide a definition in terms which reflect but extend the geriatricians' emphasis on multiple pathology: 'deficiencies in more than one area or domain of functioning'. The distinction between disability and frailty is then that disability can refer to deficiencies in only one domain. Strawbridge et al. show from longitudinal sets how 'frailty' reflects risk factors operating over the previous three decades, including heavy drinking, cigarette smoking, physical inactivity, depression, social isolation, fair or poor perceived health, prevalence of chronic symptoms, and prevalence of chronic conditions. They refer to some of the studies that show that even late interventions can reduce the probability and degree of frailty.

3   In a study of the carers of confused elderly persons in three areas prior to the reforms, Enid Levin et al. (1994, 137) found that the prior acceptability of residential care to carers was an important predictor of who had entered a residential home within six months. As in the Domiciliary Care Project, the hint of physical violence was a powerful correlate of admission (Davies and Baines, 1994; Levin et al., 1994, 138).

4   The pattern of answers is compatible with some care managers having interpreted the question to be about level of dependency need rather than the psychological propensity to demand more from caregivers given other dependency-generating characteristics. Users in the worst state and most rapid decline are likely to impose the greatest physical and psychological strain on caregivers. The difference between functional capacity and performance is well established in the literature (Jette, 1994; Kelly-Hayes et al., 1992; Patrick et al., 1981; Verbrugge and Jette, 1994; Ziebland et al., 1993). As Glass (1998, 109) puts it, 'functional performance is substantially shaped by the social and cultural context of the home world, and ... functioning cannot be understood in the absence of that context'.

5   Average productivities depend on (a) the degree to which the services are used by persons for whom marginal productivities are highest, (b) the degree to which the users are provided with packages which make the best use of service productivities, (c) levels of service input, and (d) returns to scale.

5 Productivities for USATISF Indicator Variable (Overall Satisfaction with Services)

Of the three indicators for this domain, one relates to users, the others to the principal informal caregivers.

1. Degree of satisfaction of user with the level of service being received (USATISF)

1.1. The model and the impact of risk factors

Goodness of fit. Table 5.1 summarises the equation. The model fits only moderately; less well than other outputs in this domain, and amongst the least-fitting three out of the 17. However, there are statistically highly significant associations both with risk factors and productivities.

Risk factors. The user's level of USATISF seems not to be greatly affected by the precise degree of physical disability other than for the 11 per cent most disabled (who cannot feed themselves), or those with musculo-skeletal problems whose disability causes them to be allocated respite care.

USATISF seems more to reflect low morale (the PGC score being highly significantly correlated) and some causes of it like cancer, the strain on the relationships with caregivers of the kind which leads the social services to offer day care, the isolation and frailty which accompanies extreme old age. Indeed, dissatisfaction with services is likely to be both caused by and a reflection of low morale, just as housing problems are associated with aspects of low morale as cause and effect. The direction of the effect of cognitive impairment probably in part reflects the unreliability of subjective evaluations by those who are confused or demented, though it is partially offset by the opposing effect among those with cognitive impairment receiving home-delivered meals.

Table 5.1
Production function for user satisfaction with level of services

Predictors by domain	Coeff.	Prob.	$\%^1$ Recipients	$\%^2$ Users
Risk factors and other need-related circumstances				
neral effects				
Physical disability				
User has problems with feeding – Canteat	-.584	.031		
Mental health				
Lack of morale score – PGC	-.0467	.000		
Other health problems				
User has cancer – Wcancer	-.472	.032		
User is cognitively impaired – Wcogimp	.396	.002		
Other				
User is over 85 years old – Over85	-.367	.001		
Targeting-captured need effects				
PIC health problems affect caring role, user targeted for day care – Dc_chaf	-.675	.024		
Housing problems, user targeted for home care – Hc_hous	-.235	.045		
Skeletal problems, user targeted for respite care – Re_skel	-.359	.033		
Mild/sev cog imp, user targeted for meals – M-katm	-.362	.047		
Productivity effects (£ per week)				
Individual input effects				
Home care			100.0	84.1
User lives alone – Hcc_wal2 (squared)	.0003	.010	75.9	64.4
User has PIC – Lhc_wpic	.0621	.019	73.3	62.2
Delivered meals				
User cannot shop to buy groceries – Lm_groc (log)	.0865	.066	74.6	25.7
Day care			100.0	32.1
Weekly cost day care – Dc_wcost	.022	.000	100.0	32.1
Day care – Dccst2 (squared)	-.0002	.000	100.0	32.1
Respite care				
User is married – Rec_mar3 (cubed)	9.8.E-7	.038	30.0	6.2
Nursing visits				
User is against entry into residential care – Nvc_prcd	-.0095	.001	67.8	20.7
Constant	2.444	.000		

Adj R^2 .300   Prob. .000   No. of cases 195

1 Proportion of recipients of the service to whom the effect applies
2 Proportion of sample to whom the effect applies

1.2. Service productivities

The productivity curves are shown in figure 5.1.

- The results identify significant productivities for all users of *home care*. Their form depends on two need-related circumstances. For those living alone (75 per cent of home care users and 64 per cent of the sample) home care shows increasing returns to scale. The initial effect of the service is small, and marginal productivities increase significantly with the level of the service provided. For users with principal informal caregivers, the nature of the home care effect is the opposite. Substantial productivities are achieved by the initial units invested, but marginal productivities fall rapidly thereafter. Both effects apply for some 20 per cent of home care recipients, those both living alone and with a principal informal caregiver.

- *Home-delivered meals* are identified to improve users' satisfaction for those recipients who cannot do their grocery shopping (approximately 75 per cent of the recipients of the service). Marginal effects decrease with the service level provided.

- Figure 5.1 suggests *day care* to have a strong productivity effect which reaches its maximum impact at approximately £55 per week. But from that level, the impact on satisfaction diminishes with increases in the service. For users allocated over four attendances per week (over £120 per week), the overall day care effect becomes negative, and is therefore associated

Figure 5.1
Productivity curves: home care, meals, day care, respite care and nursing visits effect on satisfaction with level of services

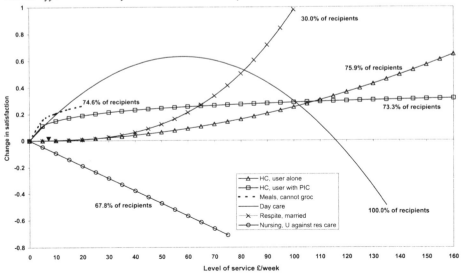

with a reduction in user satisfaction. This may reflect the users' frustration when 'stuck' in day care facilities. Indeed, for cases where the levels of day care consumed are large, the main beneficiary may not be the user but the caregiver. The interests of caregivers and users were considered by care managers to conflict for a substantial proportion of cases (the caregiver being the principal beneficiary of the care package in 12 per cent of cases, and an equal beneficiary with the user in another 35 per cent of cases). So the care plan may deliberately be aiming at, what in the view of the user is an excessive consumption of day care in order to relieve stress on the caregiver, or otherwise to benefit her. Alternatively, such high levels of day care may still be allocated because they contribute to improving other important dimensions of the users' welfare. However, it is also possible that the effect occurs because high levels of day care are allocated to persons with aspects of need and risk not captured by the indicators present in the equation.

The study of the mid-1980s cohort showed that the offer of day care was too often made to clients who did not use it for long; but that for those who continued to use it, some of the productivities were substantial. In particular, there was evidence of a generalised productivity effect on satisfaction with services (SDFAV) which was significant at the 1 per cent level (Davies et al., 1990). On the face of it, there may actually have been an improvement in the strength and clarity of this effect over the decade at lower levels of input, both the terms in the quadratic equation for marginal cost being significant at less than the .000 level.

- *Respite care* has a productivity effect only for users that are married. This may not be surprising, since it is for those that the service is less likely to be employed as a transition towards permanent placement in institution rather than as a tool for providing a break for the caring spouse. However, the effects are negligible unless substantial levels of the service are invested. Beyond such levels, the increasing returns suggest dramatic marginal productivities. The effect is significant at only the 3.8 per cent level, causing the risk of substantial sampling error in the estimate.

- The apparently perverse effect of *community nursing visits* may be a reflection of the greater vulnerability or some other characteristic of those who most resist the possibility of having to enter institutions for long-term care and receive a large nursing input. It is a possibility that will require further modelling to clarify.

1.3.   *Overall service impact, impact for groups, and equity and efficiency*

Figure 5.2 shows service impacts for services and groups. Figure 5.3 shows the average productivities for the overall packages for the different groups.

The pattern has several features.

Figure 5.2
Contributions of services and risk factors to user satisfaction with level of services

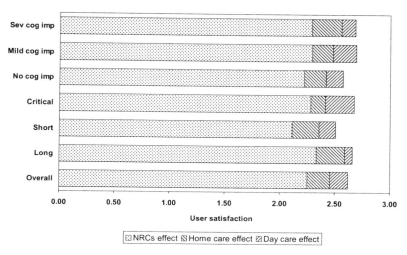

Figure 5.3
Average productivity for user satisfaction with level of services for total package

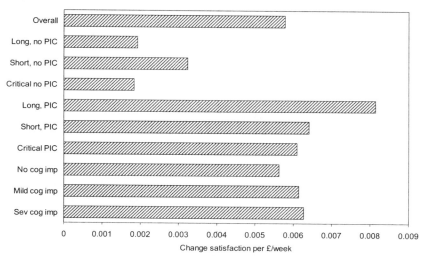

- Even though the variation between groups in the outcome is not large, users with higher interval needs enjoy slightly higher service contributions. There are practically no differences by level of cognitive impairment.

- Risk factors dominate the variation in the dependent variable. But service impacts are substantial for users with principal informal caregivers and for critical interval cases.
- The biggest impacts are made by home care and day care, though home-delivered meals have an effect on short interval cases without principal informal caregivers.

The pattern of service contributions is only partially reflected in the pattern of average productivities. Overall, users without a PIC enjoy significantly higher average productivities, but there are no clear patterns by levels of dependency. Users with long interval needs and PICs enjoy by far the highest average productivities of all the groups. The results show no substantial differences by level of cognitive impairment.

The conclusion is that the highest levels of service contributions for USATISF are partly the result of inputting disproportionately higher levels of services to the groups in order to compensate for the relatively low productivities for the groups. Again, the implication is that the service allocations can only be justified in terms of equity, as they are not fully the result of differences in service productivities.

1.4. Overview

Among the conclusions are that:
- Outcomes do not vary greatly between user groups.
- Overall, service impact is greatest among those with principal informal caregivers and others of critical interval need.
- The higher allocations which are the basis of the bigger service contributions for certain groups must be justified by equity judgements, as they do not fully reflect productivity differences between groups.

2.   Caregivers' degree of satisfaction with amount and type of support obtained by principal informal caregiver from the services to help them look after user (SATAMSUP)

2.1.   The model and the impact of risk factors

Goodness of fit. Table 5.2 shows that the model has few predictors, but that its fit is relatively good. The associations with risk factors are particularly strong, but there are also marginal productivity effects of varying degrees of significance.

Risk factors. The main risk factors are associated with *caregiver problems and worry* (p = .009), *user dependency and frailty* (including a set of targeting-captured influences for bed-bound users and users over 85 years of age attending day care), a *heating variable* which may reflect the unsuitability of the accommodation (p = .000), and *user fears* (p = .003).

Table 5.2
Production function for PIC satisfaction with services' support to help caregiving

Predictors by domain	Coeff.	Prob.	%[1] Recip-ients	%[2] Users
Risk factors and other need-related circumstances				
General effects				
Poverty and material environment				
Heat problems – Wheatpb	-1.988	.000		
Other				
Number of user fears – Ufears	-.122	.003		
Carer problems from caring (worried) – Ccpbwor	-.976	.009		
Targeting-captured need effects				
User is bed-bound and targeted for day care – Dc_bed	-.565	.007		
User is 85 or older – Dc-85	-.365	.052		
Productivity effects (£ per week)				
Individual input effects				
Home care				
User belongs to long interval need – Hcc_long	.007	.047	36.6	27.3
Day care				
User is married – Ldc_marr (log)	.148	.006	35.4	17.6
Respite care				
User has high no of problems with IADLs – Rec_hiad	.005	.039	27.6	8.1
Constant	3.094	.000		

Adj. R^2 .36   Prob. .000   No. of cases 97

1 Proportion of recipients of the service to whom the effect applies
2 Proportion of the sample to whom the effect applies

2.2.   Service productivities

The productivity effect with the highest significance is for *day care where the user is married.* It applied to one third of users of day care, 17 per cent of the sample. Figure 5.4 illustrates the decreasing returns characterising this effect.

The two other effects yield constant marginal productivities irrespective of the level of the input. The higher of the two is for *home care among those of long interval need*, and applies to 29 per cent of the users and 27 per cent of the entire sample.

The lesser of the effects is for *respite care for users with a high number of IADL problems.* This effect, which relates to 27.6 per cent of recipients of respite care, 8 per cent of the sample, was also found in the production function model looking at the length of stay in the community before institutionalisation.

Figure 5.4
*Productivity curves: home care, day care and respite care effect on PIC
satisfaction with level of service provided*

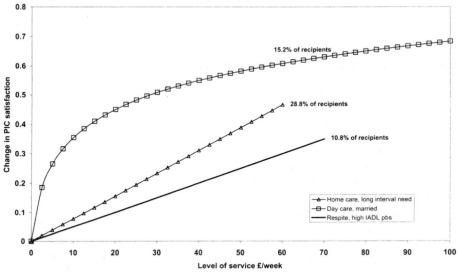

Figure 5.5
*Contributions of services and risk factors to PIC satisfaction with amount
of support to help caregiving*

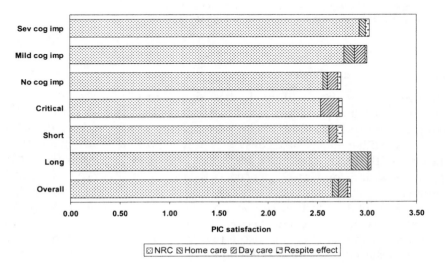

2.3   Overall service impact, impact for groups, and equity and efficiency

Service contributions had little effect compared with the risk factors (see figure 5.5).

Satisfaction did not vary greatly between groups, service contributions appearing somewhat smaller for users with short interval needs or severe cognitive impairment. At the individual service level, the home care effects are concentrated on users with long interval needs, whereas day care contributions are greatest for users with critical interval needs.

In view of the limited relative contributions of the services, issues of equity and efficiency in the group differences are not discussed.

2.4.   Overview

The conclusions are that:
- Satisfaction did not vary greatly between groups.
- Service contributions had little effect compared with the risk factors.

3.   Degree to which the principal informal caregiver's experience of the social services was favourable during the six months of the COCA period (PICSEXP)

This is a process indicator in the sense that it relates to satisfaction with how services were performed rather than the impact of the inputs and how they were used.

3.1.   The model and the impact of risk factors

Goodness of fit. Table 5.3 shows that the model was a much better fit than that for the impact variable in the domain. The correlation of several risk factors with the outcome were highly significant, and so were some productivity effects.

Risk factors. The most important influences include *user dependency* (picking large number of problems with IADLs among those receiving home care, and ulcerated legs or pressure sores among those allocated day care), *caregiver problems* and perhaps *user-caregiver relationships* (including PIC health problems among users allocated day care), *poor housing conditions and level of living* (low income, heating problems, personal environmental problems), and, to a lesser degree and reflecting some of the other factors, *low user morale* (PGC score, vexed by charging).

3.2.   Service productivities

The model identifies significant productivity effects on the PIC's satisfaction with SSD experience for two services. These effects are illustrated in figure 5.6.

Table 5.3

Production function for PIC satisfaction with SSD experience

Predictors by domain	Coeff.	Prob.	%[1] Recipients	%[2] Users
Risk factors and other need-related circumstances				
General effects				
Physical disability				
User cannot do heavy housework tasks – Canthhwk	.590	.000		
Mental health				
Lack of morale score – Pgc	-.018	.049		
Informal care related factors				
Count of user's problems with caring – Cupbnb	-.356	.000		
Poverty and material environment				
Heating problems – Wheatpb	-1.004	.003		
User income – Income	-.336	.009		
Other				
User lives alone – Walone	-.625	.000		
User is vexed by charging – Vexed	-.630	.022		
User previously known to SSD – Current	.272	.002		
Count of personal environmental problems				
– Wpersenv	-.220	.002		
Targeting-captured need effects				
High number of problems with IADLs, & user				
targeted for home care – Hc_hiad	-.631	.000		
Ulcerated legs or pressure sores,				
& user targeted for day care – Dc_ulce	-.496	.029		
PIC health problems affect caring, & user targeted				
for day care – Dc_chaf	-.736	.000		
Productivity effects (£ per week)				
Individual input effects				
Home care			61.9	47.0
User lives alone – Lhc_walo (log)	.120	.012	58.8	44.4
User has high relational problems – Hcc_hrel	.005	.041	7.1	5.6
Day care			76.9	36.0
User lives alone – Dc2_alon	3.6E-5	.028	46.2	21.7
User has high no problems with IADL tasks				
– Ldc_hiad (log)	.223	.000	24.5	11.4
User's PIC is spouse – Dcc_sp	.014	.007	21.2	9.5
Constant	3.280	.000		

Adj. R^2 .578   Prob. .000   No. of cases 105

1 Proportion of recipients of the service to whom the effect applies
2 Proportion of the sample to whom the effect applies

Figure 5.6
Productivity curves: day care and home care effect on PIC satisfaction with SSD experience

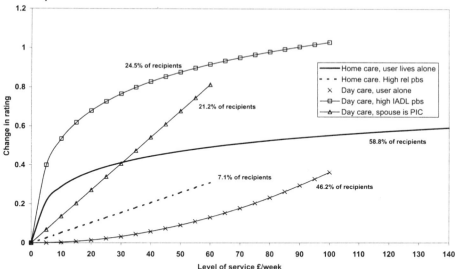

- There are three productivity effects for day care. Two are significant at the 1 per cent level, indeed one at the .000 level.
- The most significant statistically is also the largest, and affects users with a high number of problems with IADL tasks. The effect applies to 24 per cent of recipients, 11 per cent of the entire sample, and is characterised by decreasing returns to scale.
- A second, highly significant, effect is for *day care users whose spouse is the principal informal caregiver*. It applies to 21 per cent of day care users, 9 per cent of the entire sample, and presents constant marginal productivities.
- The third productivity effect is for *day care users who live alone*. The productivity effect is weak, but marginal productivities increase at higher levels of input, reflecting increasing returns to scale. The effect applies to 46 per cent of users of day care.
- There is a substantial minority of day care users who benefit from at least two of the productivity effects.

  The two productivity effects for home care are weaker.

- The effect for *home care among persons living alone* is just short of significance at the 1 per cent level. It applies to 59 per cent of users of home care, a substantial 44 per cent of the entire sample. It is characterised by strongly decreasing returns to scale.

- The second *home care* effect affects only a minority of recipients of the service (7 per cent): those users with high number of relational problems. The effect shows constant returns to scale and is significant only at the 5 per cent level.

3.3.   Overall service impact, impact for groups, and equity and efficiency

Figure 5.7 shows that risk factors make the biggest and a similar contribution to the rating for all nine groups. The service contributions are relatively small, but are also similar across groups.

In the same way as was found for the outcome SATAMSUP, day care contributions are greatest for users with high levels of dependency, whereas home care contributions are concentrated on users with long and short interval needs.

Again, given the limited relative contributions of services, there are no major equity and efficiency considerations to be explored.

Figure 5.7
Contributions of services and risk factors to PIC satisfaction with SSD experience

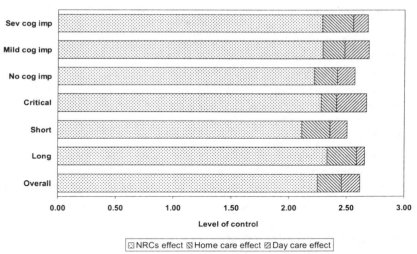

3.4.   Overview

Conclusions are that:
- This well-fitting model yields substantial productivity effects for home and day care.
- Risk factors dominate the dependent variable, and there is little variation in service contribution between groups.

6 Productivities for IMPADL, IMPIADL and NSF Indicator Variables (Perceived Improvement in Functioning in Service-Related Areas and Reported Unmet Needs)

There are production functions for three indicators, all for users.

1. Improvement in number of personal care functions of daily living ascribed by the user to the social services (IMPADL)

1.1. The model and the impact of risk factors

Goodness of fit. The model summarised in table 6.1. accounts for a low proportion of the variance, though its significance is high.

Some might argue that this is unsurprising, since the mechanisms by which social service inputs might impact what the users report to be their functional capacity do not engage all causes of change in it. Indeed, they might argue that functional capacity is not amenable to social service treatment for most users. However, to argue this is to misunderstand, first, important circumstances in which alone or catalytically with other inputs, community service inputs can directly affect capacity in its narrowest and most physiological sense; and secondly, that many social and psychological factors influence perceived functioning (Glass, 1998). Examples of the former are periods of recuperation after a function-enhancing medical procedure or other treatment. The latter is the case because the dependent variable is not derived from a test of functioning, but from the perception of users from their capacity to perform the tasks. The actual physical and mental capacity is mediated by subjective factors. In particular, the low morale or depression suffered by many users, the spill-over effects of declines in perceived health status and the like, affect such perceptions (Spector and Fleishman, 1998).

Table 6.1

Production function for improvement in ADL-related states due to services

Predictors by domain	Coeff.	Prob.	%[1] Recipients	%[2] Users
Risk factors and other need-related circumstances				
General effects				
Physical disability				
User cannot shop to buy groceries – Cantgroc	-1.616	.018		
Mental health				
User is perceived to have low morale – Wlowmora	-1.139	.030		
Pgc lack of morale score – Pgc	-.116	.042		
Informal care related factors				
User has PIC – Wpic	2.971	.000		
PIC is employed – Cemploy	-1.320	.066		
Targeting-captured need effects				
User lives alone, and targeted for day care				
– Dc_walo	-2.992	.000		
PIC is spouse, user targeted for nursing inputs				
– Nv_sp	-4.894	.023		
Productivity effects (£ per week)				
Individual input effects				
Home care				
User lives alone – Lhc_ualo (log)	.330	.033	77.2	66.2
Day care			35.7	14.4
Respite care			81.2	14.4
User discharged from hospital – Rec_fh	.061	.032	31.8	5.5
Nursing visits				
Nursing visits – Lnv (log)	.353	.056	100.0	30.7
Complementarities				
Day care and respite care interaction – Ldr	.345	.007	100.0	14.4
Constant	7.117	.000		

Adj. R^2 .265   Prob. .000   No. of cases 143

1 Proportion of recipients of the service to whom the effect applies
2 Proportion of the sample to whom the effect applies

Impact of risk factors. The most clearly determined relationships are with the presence of a principal informal caregiver (PIC); clearly a buffering effect. The buffering effect of informal caregiving is reduced when the PIC is in paid employment. A targeting-captured risk factor, living alone and receiving day care, reflects the weakening of the buffering protection of informal care. The outcome predicted is negative when the user is of low morale, and the care manager recognises the worker to be of low morale; though the effects are significant only at the 5 per cent level. The importance of these rather than other possible predictors confirms that it is indeed the perception of the capacity rather than the capacity itself that is affected. However, the fact that the receipt of nursing inputs among those whose PIC is a spouse is also a major risk factor also suggests that some are undergoing rapid decline in functioning.

1.2. Service productivities

The model identifies four services which significantly improve the users' perceived capacity to perform ADL tasks. These are:
- *home care* for users living alone, characterised by decreasing returns to scale. This effect affects 77 per cent of the recipients of home care, and 66 per cent of the overall sample.
- *respite care* among persons discharged from hospitals. This effect is constant at the margins for all levels of the service, and only a small proportion (6 per cent) of the overall sample.
- *nursing visits* for all recipients of the service (31 per cent of all users), again marked by decreasing returns to scale.
- *day care* when taken with *respite care*. The marginal productivity of this complementarity effect decreases as the levels of any of the two services increase. Overall approximately 14 per cent of the sample in the model received both respite and day care inputs.

The marginal productivities are subject to wider confidence intervals than in most of the production functions. Figures 6.1 and 6.2 show the productivity curves.

1.3. Overall service impact, impact for groups, and equity and efficiency

Figure 6.3 shows differences between groups in outputs and the impacts of risk factors; but smaller variations in the contributions of services. The two groups for which the contributions of services were greatest were those for whom the risk factors predicted the least improvement; short and critical interval cases without principal informal caregivers. In this respect, the service allocations contributed to a modest reduction in the inequality of the improvement in perceived capacity to perform ADL tasks.

Home care and nursing visits were key for both groups, as to others. Nursing visits, in particular, made a substantial contribution to all but long interval cases, and, to a lesser extent, short interval cases with principal informal caregivers (who presumably contributed to nursing tasks).

The variations in contributions invite questions of equity and efficiency. Figure 6.4 shows the average productivities of packages to decrease significantly with the level of physical disability or cognitive impairment. This is in marked contrast with the homogeneous distribution of service contributions. Again, services seem to have been allocated to the users with greatest needs, in excess of what exclusively efficiency-based criteria would have suggested.

Figure 6.1
Productivity curves: day care and home care effect on improvement in ADL-related states due to services

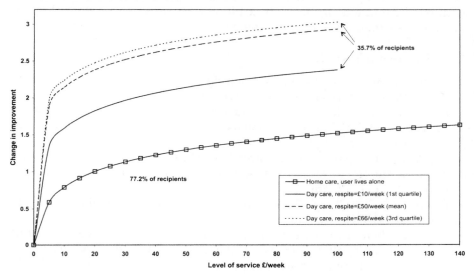

Figure 6.2
Productivity curves: nursing visits and respite care effect on improvement in ADL-related states due to services

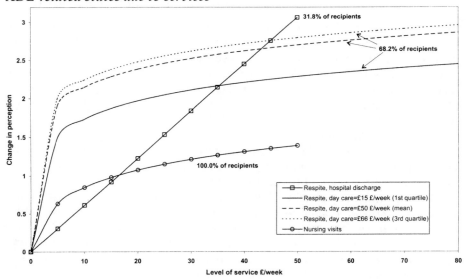

Figure 6.3
Contributions of services and risk factors to improvement in ADL-related states due to services

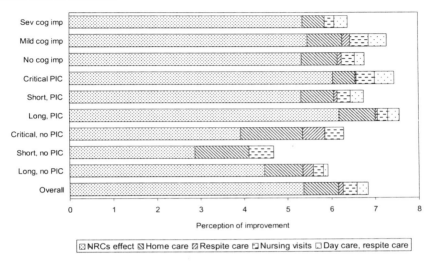

Figure 6.4
Average productivity for improvement in ADL-related states due to services for total package

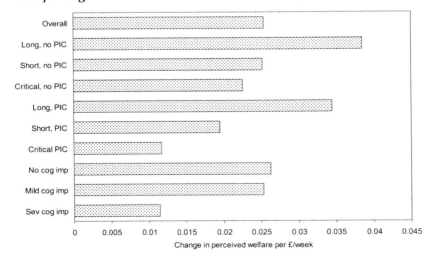

Figure 6.4 also shows the average productivities for users with PICs to be lower than for users without PICs.

1.4. Overview

Conclusions are that:

- There are several productivity effects.
- There were large differences between groups in the final levels of outcomes, but much smaller differences in the contributions to the outcomes made by services.
- The two groups for which the contributions of services were greatest were those for whom the risk factors predicted the least improvement; short and critical interval cases without principal informal caregivers. But this made little difference to inequality of final levels of outcomes between groups.
- The bigger service contributions were not the result of exceptionally high productivities, so the allocations can only be justified on equity grounds.

2.   Improvement in number of household care and other instrumental care functions of daily living ascribed by the user to the social services (IMPIADL)

The dependent variable represents the users' count of improvements in number of states of daily living related to household care and other instrumental care functions ascribed by the user to the social services.

2.1. The model and the impact of risk factors

Table 6.2 shows that the model fits less well than for most of the production functions, but roughly as well as the equivalent variable for personal care activities of daily living. There are nevertheless a small number of risk factors whose associations are clearly significant, and some clearly significant productivity effects.

The indicator of *physical disability* associated with the inability to shop covers 85 per cent of the sample, and so virtually distinguishes the vast majority of those with anything more than the lowest level of incapacity to perform tasks of daily living.

Other important need-related circumstances found by the model to affect the output significantly are related to the user's *social environment*. Hence, whether users live alone and whether PICs have health problems which affect their caring roles are both factors associated with worse perception of capacity to perform IADL tasks, presumably because of a comparative lack of informal support. The targeting-captured circumstances of those allocated day care among those who live alone clearly distinguishes those for whom the social

Table 6.2
Production function for improvement in IADL-related states due to services

Predictors by domain	Coeff.	Prob.	%[1] Recipients	%[2] Users
Risk factors and other need-related circumstances				
General effects				
Physical disability				
User cannot shop to buy groceries – Cantgroc	-3.002	.010		
Informal care related factors				
PIC health problems affect caring – Chaffect	-5.077	.004		
Other				
User is against residential care – Upercent	-.989	.027		
User lives alone – Walone	-2.075	.066		
Targeting-captured need effects				
User lives alone, and targeted for day care – Dc_alon	-5.075	.000		
Productivity effects (£ per week)				
Individual input effects				
Home care			79.1	66.4
User belongs to critical interval need				
– Hc2_crit (squared)	2.0E-4	.014	23.9	20.9
User has PIC – Lhc_wpic (log)	.694	.009	74.1	62.2
Delivered meals				
PIC is close female relative – Mc_clof	.276	.027	35.7	11.9
Day care				
User discharged from hospital – Dcc_fh	.120	.020	20.0	6.0
Nursing visits				
User has PIC – Nvc_upic	.088	.006	72.9	22.2
Constant	19.848	.000		

Adj. R^2 .277   Prob. .000   No. of cases 152

1 Proportion of recipients of the service to whom the effect applies
2 Proportion of the sample to whom the effect applies

services did, and probably could do, most to achieve the outcomes of IADL activities.

2.2. *Service productivities*

Figure 6.5 describes three substantial productivity effects which are invariant with respect to scale, and two smaller effects. The highest marginal productivity appears to be for *home-delivered meals* among users whose principal informal caregiver is a close female relative; that is for 36 per cent of the recipients of

Figure 6.5

Productivity curves: day care, home care, meals and nursing visits effect on improvement in IADL tasks due to services

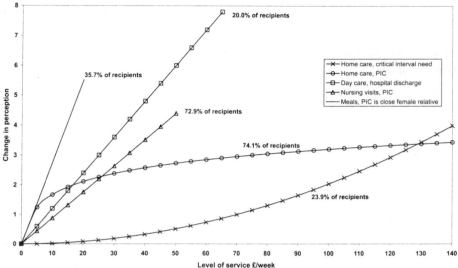

meals, 12 per cent of the entire sample. However, the coefficient is significant at only the 2.7 per cent level. Therefore, the marginal productivity could be substantially different from the best estimate.

Likewise, *day care* for users recently discharged from hospital has a substantial marginal productivity. Presumably, the provision of day care gives the caregiver the opportunity to undertake some of the instrumental activities without distraction. Overall, however, the day care effect affects only a fifth of its recipients and considerably less than a tenth of the sample overall.

The productivity of *home nursing visits* for 72 per cent of its recipients, more than a fifth of the entire sample, may reflect similar causal mechanisms.

The two *home care* productivity effects apply to two-thirds of the entire sample, four recipients of home care out of five.

• The one related to users with PICs presents marked decreasing returns to scale, and comprises 62 per cent of the sample. Nevertheless, it is both significant and large.

• The second affects users with critical interval needs. For those, figure 6.5 shows, the marginal returns from investments in home care increase with the level of input. However, most of the users affected by this effect have PICs and are therefore covered by the first home care effect.

2.3.   *Overall service impact, impact for groups, and equity and efficiency*

Figure 6.6 shows big differences between groups both in the final output levels and in the contribution of service inputs compared with that of the risk factors.

Since only one recipient of community social services in twenty is able to perform all seven of the IADL tasks, it is arguable that for the patterns to reflect equitable interventions, on average, all groups should feel substantial benefit in the outcomes of their performance from the social services, assuming that compensation for the absence of informal support is part of the equity criterion. Yet it is clear that substantial benefits are not felt by users without principal informal caregivers who have short or long interval needs. Can a pattern be equitable in which the services make such a small contribution to either group?

On the one hand, the long interval cases without principal informal caregivers contain many with the lightest degree of dependency, and for whom therefore one would expect a large improvement to be accorded least priority in a fair system. But that is not the case for all. And can it be equitable when the group comprising users with short interval needs and without principal informal caregivers has a contribution from the social services to their welfare no greater than for a group comprising long interval needs and without principal informal caregivers, and when their overall improvement is less? By definition, the short interval cases suffered considerable incapacity to perform IADL functions, and by definition, those without principal informal caregivers were

Figure 6.6
Contributions of services and risk factors to improvement in IADL-related states due to services

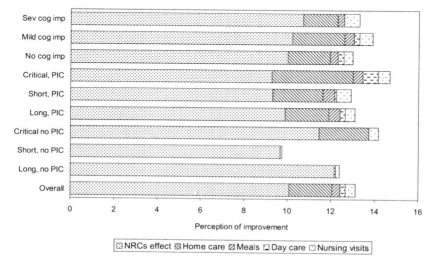

not receiving a substantial amount of informal assistance, at least from any one source.

Figure 6.7 shows how the average productivities of the packages for users without PICs are much lower than for the rest of the groups. This is important in two ways. First, it suggests that the pattern of service contribution, although potentially inequitable, is mainly due to the low productivities of the services rather than to the relative levels of the packages of care. Second, it suggests that the observed allocation of resources to users without PICs is likely to have aimed at the achievement of other outputs. This issue will be tackled in later chapters based on the optimisation analysis.

Figure 6.7
Average productivity for improvement in IADL-related states due to services for overall package

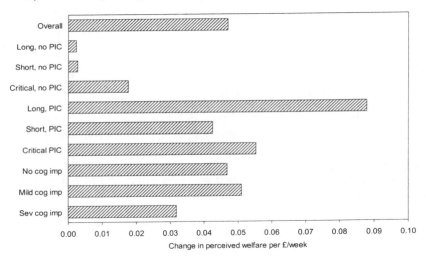

2.4. Overview

Conclusions are that:
- There are clear productivity effects identified for four services: home care, meals on wheels, day care and nursing visits.
- There are big differences between user groups in IADL improvement and the contributions of services to them. Short or long interval cases without principal informal caregivers do not greatly benefit, perhaps a source of inequity.

3   **User's count of unmet needs for help with functional areas covered by community social services (NSF)**

This indicator represents the opinion of the user about the productivities of services for them for that output at the level of service input that they receive.

This type of question has often been used as (a) an inverse indicator of final output (Brown and Phillips, 1986; Davies and Challis, 1986; Davies et al., 1990; Goldberg, 1970; Grannemann et al., 1986). The question has also been used — indeed, was first used — as (b) an indicator of welfare shortfalls which should be met with state-financed or state-subsidised services (Townsend and Wedderburn, 1965). But the question is actually about (c) whether services would have positive productivities. The three concepts are certainly not so closely related in principle that they can be measured with equal validity by one indicator. There is a case for arguing that as it was first used, the information it provides could mislead. The question does not ask whether the benefits for paying for the services for which the need is unmet would be worth the price to the user, or the opportunity cost to society. Moreover, it takes no account of whether there would be more efficient means of achieving the benefits. But there are factors making its use less dangerous in this context. Those being asked it are known to be as modest in their demands as the managers are constrained by resource scarcity or other factors in the allocation of additional services. But it is typically the case that at the optimum, and with constrained budgets, the inputs are allocated at levels for which their marginal productivities are significantly positive.

The argument against the use of need shortfall as an inverse indicator of output is both that it is based on inputs not final outputs, and that persons have productivity curves of very different shapes in the range between the optimum levels and the levels at which the marginal productivities become insignificant.

There are other caveats about the likely reliability of the question. Answers to a question about the likely effects of increases in the input levels are likely to be influenced by many subjective factors. The effectiveness of the services is likely to be difficult to guess at for many users. Defensiveness, denial or the reverse might lead to the under- or overstatement of their dependency.

3.1.   The model and the impact of risk factors

Goodness of fit. Table 6.3 shows the model to be no better-fitting than others in this ill-fitting domain. It nevertheless shows some clear association of the output with risk factors, and some productivity effects. Apparent productivity effects would be expected. Although the question was phrased in terms of the need for more assistance with functional deficits, many would have interpreted the question to be about service shortfalls. So variations in service input are almost tautologically related to shortfalls.

Table 6.3
Production function for count of user-perceived unmet needs

Predictors by domain	Coeff.	Prob.	%[1] Recipients	%[2] Users
Risk factors and other need-related circumstances				
General effects				
Mental health				
Katzman's cognitive impairment score – Katscore	-0.062	0.07		
Informal care related factors				
Carer carer looses leisure time – Ccpblei	1.51	0.04		
PIC's age – Cage	-0.036	0.000		
Targeting-captured need effects				
User lives alone and targeted for meals – M_walo	2.48	0.000		
User is 85 or over and targeted for meals – M_85	2.22	0.005		
User cannot go shopping for groceries & targeted for homecare – HC_groc	0.90	0.065		
Productivity effects				
Individual input effects				
Home care			35.0	27.7
User has severe cognitive impairment – Lhc_kats (log)	-0.53	0.024	31.3	24.6
Delivered meals			54.0	15.1
User belongs to long interval need level – Lm_long (log)	-0.79	0.023	43.4	12.0
Respite care				
PIC is the spouse – Lre_sp (log)	-.081	0.103	18.2	6.3
Social work				
User can't do heavy housework – Lsw_hhwk (log)	-2.76	0.007	85.4	21.3
Nursing visits				
User lives alone – Nv_alon	-0.02	0.031	50.0	21.5
Complementarities				
Home care and meals , user is cognitively impaired – Hmc_wcog	-0.003	0.018	27.6	7.3
Constant	1.526	0.011		
Adj R² (from OLS version) 0.27 Prob. .000 No. of cases	190			

1 Proportion of recipients of the service to whom the effect applies
2 Proportion of the sample to whom the effect applies

Risk factors. The most powerful associations reflect the *buffering effects of informal care*, particularly when the caregiver is a spouse or someone of the same age as the user (p = .000); and for presumably younger caregivers conscious of losing leisure time, (p = 0.04), and the user does not live alone and depends on home-delivered meals (p = .000). The risk is enhanced where the elderly person is very aged and depends on home-delivered meals, and so likely to lack direct informal care for at least much of the day and is frail (p = .005).

3.2. *Service productivities*

Statistically, the most significant productivity effect is for *social work* — that is, social work given independently of care management — among the 85 per cent of social work users who cannot undertake heavy housework. The group comprises 21 per cent of the entire sample. Figure 6.8 illustrates the social work effect, which shows moderate decreasing returns to scale.

There were also productivity effects for home care, home-delivered meals, respite care, and nursing visits, shown in figure 6.9. There were diminishing marginal returns for three recipient groups. One consists of *respite care* recipients among the 18 per cent of users whose caregiver was a spouse. A second consists of *meals* recipients among the 43 per cent of users with long interval needs. The third group comprised *home care* recipients among the 31 per cent of users (and so 24 per cent of the entire sample) whose Katzman score predicted severe cognitive impairment showed decreasing marginal returns.

As can be seen from the productivity curves in figure 6.10, *meals associated with home care* for those with cognitive impairment have significant marginal productivities. The effect relates to some 7 per cent of the sample as a whole.

Figure 6.8
Productivity curves: social work input effect on count of unmet needs

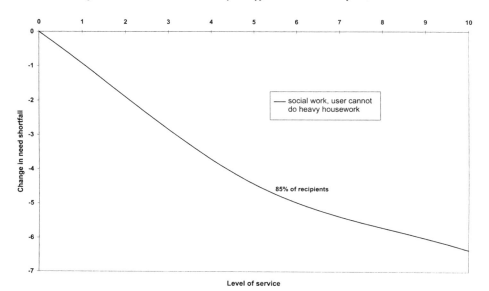

Level of service

Figure 6.9
Productivity curves: home care, respite care and nursing visits effect on count of unmet needs

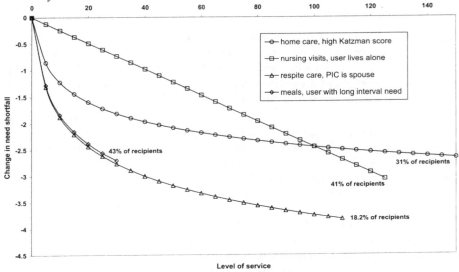

Figure 6.10
Productivity curves: home care and meals complementarity effect on count of unmet needs

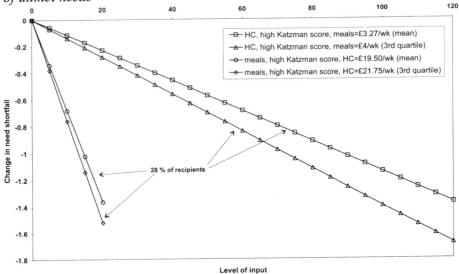

This effect is additional to the other productivity effects of meals and home care for users with both sets of qualifying characteristics; for instance, those predicted to be severely cognitively impaired by the Katzman score and rated to be cognitively impaired by the care manager, or of long interval need and judged by the care manager to be cognitively impaired. Indeed, most of those to whom one home care effect or meals effect applied were also beneficiaries of the other home care or meals effect.

3.3.   *Overall service impact, impact for groups, and equity and efficiency*

Figure 6.11 shows large differences between groups in what the outcomes are predicted to be without service interventions. Excluding the effects of services, unmet needs were predicted to be much higher among those without principal informal caregivers.

The equation predicted service contributions to have a big effect on group differences compared with risk factors.

• The largest service contributions are for users with long and critical interval needs.

• There is a very clear gradient of the service contributions by the user's level of cognitive impairment.

• For users with critical interval needs, figure 6.12 indicates that the average productivity of the package was low compared with the sample as a whole.

Figure 6.11
Contributions of services and risk factors to count of user perceived unmet need

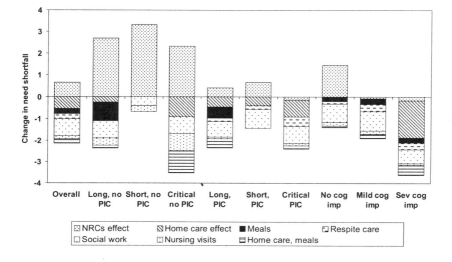

The large service impact was therefore produced by investing levels of service disproportionately large compared with the relative output gains.
- For users with long interval needs, the large service contributions were mainly due to the high average productivities of the package compared with the sample as a whole, as figure 6.12 shows. For those with principal informal caregivers, the question is whether the service inputs produced overkill in relation to the risk.
- The effect of the service contributions far from equalised the average levels of reported need shortfalls, as can be seen if the service contributions are treated as offsets to the column showing the effect of the risk factors.

Figure 6.12
Average productivities for count of user perceived unmet needs for total package

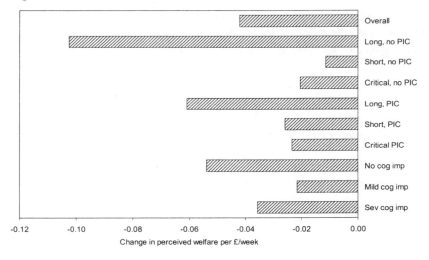

3.4. Overview

Used in some of the most distinguished evaluation studies of community care in the United Kingdom and in other countries, and one of the first types of indicator developed for research for needs-based planning in social welfare of elderly persons, the nature of the question would make it a valid indicator of performance only in what would arguably be untypical situations,[1] and the answers are likely to be made less reliable indicators by many subjective influences on the answers.

Social work inputs additional to care management tasks were highly productive for the 21 per cent of the sample that received it. There were also productivity effects for home care, home-delivered meals, respite care, and nursing visits.

The analysis of variations between groups showed that:

- There were large differences between groups in what the outcomes are predicted to be without service interventions.
- Variations in service inputs were substantial for most groups, perhaps because the question might have been interpreted by many to be about the adequacy of services.
- The effect of the service contributions far from equalised the average levels of reported need shortfalls.

The results raised equity and efficiency questions. (a) There was a big service contribution for persons with critical interval needs which was substantially the result of large service inputs, not typically high service productivities. (b) For persons with long interval needs, the large service contribution was accompanied by high average productivities. These arguments will be taken up again in the discussion of the optimisation models in later chapters.

Note

1   It would be valid only in one or a combination of three situations:
- if the policy goal was to provide inputs up to that level at which there would be no further gains for the output from additional units of the input
- if those who answered the question on which indicator is based would not take into account increments of potential benefit beyond a level falling short of all the potential benefits
- if the shape and position of the productivity curves beyond the level of inputs received were for all users precisely the same.

None of these circumstances is likely.

7 Productivities for IMPEMP, UEMPOW, CEMPOW Indicator Variables (Empowerment, Choice and Control)

Production functions have been fitted for two indicators for users, and one for principal informal caregivers.

1. User felt control over own life score (IMPEMP)

1.1. The model and the impact of risk factors

Goodness of fit. Table 7.1 shows that the goodness of fit is of the same order as the production functions for aspects of morale.

Need-related circumstances and risk factors. The effects of *capacity to perform daily living acts* and of general indicators of *low morale* are clearly significant. As would be expected, the way in which an incapacity to perform activities of daily living, and the kind of condition that causes aspects of incapacity, are extremely good predictors. They work here much better than for morale and its components itself, where the picture is complicated by the associations between these incapacities and other, more psychological, perceptual, and attitudinal need-related and risk factors. The clarity of the relationship survives the time lag of six months between the predictors and the outcome. Unlike the patterns for general morale and its dimensions, the model suggests that *wider environmental problems* restrict the degree to which users feel control over their own lives. There is little sign that *informal care* has buffering effects. Indeed, when caregiver stress is a factor reported by the care manager and (partly no doubt for this reason) users are allocated respite care, users feel that they have less control over their lives.

Table 7.1

Production function for user felt control over own life score

Predictors by domain	Coeff.	Prob.	%[1] Recip-ients	%[2] Users
Risk factors and other need-related circumstances				
General effects				
Physical disability				
Interval need level – Intneed	.379	.000		
User cannot buy groceries – Cantgroc	-.333	.037		
Mental health				
PGC lack of morale score – PGC	-.082	.000		
Other health problems				
Skeletal problems – Wskel	.333	.000		
Poverty and material environment				
Wide environmental problems – Wwidenv	-.222	.045		
Targeting-captured need effects				
User is bed-bound and targeted for respite care – Re_bed	-.978	.042		
PIC is perceived to be stressed and targeted for respite care – Re_cstr	-.502	-.020		
Productivity effects (£ per week)				
Individual input effects				
Home care				
User is critical interval need – Lhc_crit (log)	.119	.015	27.6	23.1
Delivered meals				
User cannot go to toilet – Mc_toil	.067	.014	11.3	3.5
Day care			100.0	
Day care – Ldc (log)	.069	.043	100.0	31.1
Respite care				
User has high no. of ADL problems – Lre_had (log)	.316	.012	29.5	6.9
Nursing visits			64.6	
PIC health problems affect caring – Nvc_chaf	.016	.013	20.0	8.7
Complementarities				
Nursing visits, day care interaction, mild sev cog imp – Ndc_katm	8.7E-4	.016	52.6	5.2
Constant	1.755	.000		

Adj. R^2 .339   Prob.   .000   No. of cases   195

1 Proportion of recipients of the service to whom the effect applies
2 Proportion of the sample to whom the effect applies

1.2. Service productivities

The model yields a group of productivity effects, none of which are significant at the 1 per cent level.

- The biggest marginal productivity is *home-delivered meals* among users who cannot go to the toilet. This effect is described in figure 7.1. The marginal productivity is invariant with respect to scale, and covers 11.3 per cent of recipients (only 3.5 per cent of all users).

- *Respite care* also has a high productivity for 29 per cent of its recipients, those with a large number of ADL problems. For this effect, marginal productivities decrease with the level of the service allocated, as can be seen from the shape of the curve in figure 7.1. Only 6.9 per cent of the entire sample are affected.

- *Home care* also has a substantial productivity for 27.6 per cent of its recipients (23 per cent of the entire sample), shown in figure 7.2. Again, marginal productivities decline with the level of input.

- *Community nursing* inputs significantly improve the outcome among the 20 per cent of the recipients whose principal informal caregivers claim that their own health problems affect their caregiving. Perhaps, some tasks which would otherwise be undertaken by the caregiver are performed by the nurses. Figure 7.1 shows the marginal productivity is constant over the

Figure 7.1
Productivity curves: respite care, nursing and meals effects on user control over life

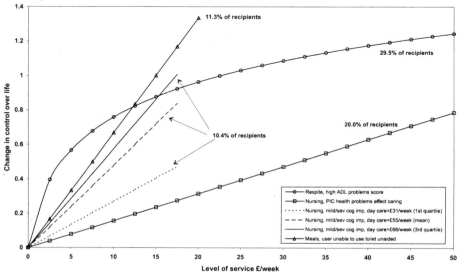

Figure 7.2
Productivity curves: home care and day care effects on user control over life

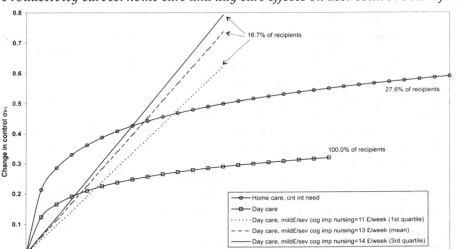

observed range of the service. *Nursing in combination with day care* is a particularly productive combination among cognitively impaired users; for over half of the users receiving both services. The size of the effect is described in different ways in figures 7.1. and 7.2. The former shows the marginal productivity of day care at different levels of nursing input; the latter, the marginal productivity of nursing inputs given various levels of day care.

- In addition to its effect when combined with nursing inputs, *day care* shows a significant effect (at the 5 per cent level) for all its recipients. This general effect, described in figure 7.2, is characterised by decreasing returns to scale: a reduction in its marginal productivity as the level of the service increases. Overall, this effect covers almost a quarter of the users in the sample.

1.3.   *Overall service impact, impact for groups, and equity and efficiency*

Figure 7.3 shows the relative contribution of risk factors and service inputs to the average outcome for each of the groups. For critical interval cases, the service effects are large in relation to the risk factors, particularly for cases with principal informal caregivers. For long and short interval cases, they are small.

Comparison of the total height of the columns in figure 7.3 shows substantial inequality in outcome between groups. Critical interval cases were particularly at risk of feeling a low degree of control over life in the absence of service intervention. The service intervention did close the gap between them and others to a substantial degree: wholly, indeed, compared with short inter-

Figure 7.3

Contributions of services and risk factors to user felt control over own life score

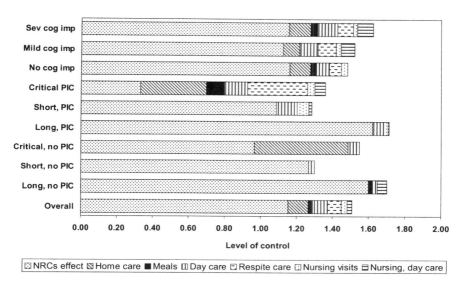

val need cases. But the critical and short interval cases remained feeling less in control of their lives than long interval cases.

Home care makes a big contribution in both groups. For the group with PICs, home and respite care make the biggest contributions.

The degree to which the large inputs reflect marginal productivities can be seen from figures 7.3 and 7.4.

- The average productivity for all services combined is on average extremely high for critical interval cases with PICs, and above average for critical interval cases without PICs.

- Figure 7.4 shows that the overall productivities were low for long and short interval groups. Since these were the groups for which the contribution of services to outputs were lowest, it is clear that high quantities of inputs were not used to compensate for the gap in marginal productivities.

- So the great gains reflected high productivities rather than disproportionately high levels of inputs.

1.4. Overview

Results show that:

- Risk factors are the main influence on variations in the feeling of control over life, but services contribute to it substantially for some groups, particu-

Figure 7.4
Average productivity for user felt control over own life score for total package

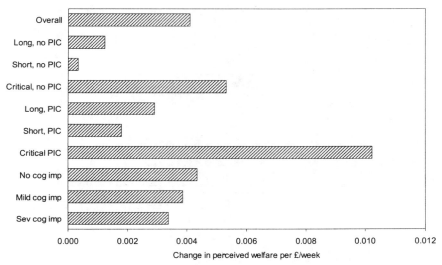

Change in perceived welfare per £/week

larly for those with critical interval needs and principal informal caregivers, for whom the service contributions were the dominant influence.

- There are substantial productivity effects for some users of meals, respite care, home care, and community nursing. Between them, they cover a high proportion of recipients. However, several have marked decreasing returns to scale: for example, the effects for home and respite care.
- The service contributions equalised outcomes considerably compared with the effect of the risk factors taken in isolation. However, the effects were to bring the critical interval cases to approximately the level for short interval cases, not to the higher levels for long interval cases.
- The big effects, concentrated on the critical interval cases, were produced more by the high productivity of services than by the allocation of disproportionately high levels of services.

2.   User's felt empowerment/influence during the set-up stage of care management scale (UEMPOW)

The outcome is focused on how the user felt about one aspect of process, the manner of performance of the core tasks of care management and other tasks during the set-up period. This was the period that preceded the implementation of what was hoped to be a care plan which would continue as long as need-related circumstances remained unchanged. We describe this as a process not an impact outcome.

2.1. The model and the impact of risk factors

Goodness of fit. Table 7.2 shows that the model fits less well than that for IMPEMP, the impact output indicator for the domain. But there are some productivity effects significant at higher than the 5 per cent level, and some clear associations with risk factors.

Need-related circumstances and other risk factors. The principal influences were *dependency- and health-related morale,* and the buffering influence of *informal care* and factors modifying it.

Dependency constrained the degree of empowerment or influence felt by the user to a degree for which the care manager seemed to be unable to compensate. Factors associated with a diminished sense of empowerment included:
- The incapacity to perform personal care ADLs, particularly being unable feed oneself, and being unable to do the shopping.
- The number of risks which the care manager identified for the user.
- Being in the recuperative stage after discharge from hospital.
  It was dependency, rather than the number of health problems itself which diminished the feeling of empowerment. That is understandable, because the process to which the scale relates is focused on dependency, rather than on health treatment, so that the role in the model of the number of health problems is to elaborate the nature of dependency itself.

The *buffering role of informal care* is reflected in various ways. One is the impact of sharing a household with a carer (virtually the converse of living alone). A second is the influence of the user's belief that they had someone in whom they could confide private and intimate thoughts. A third is the targeting of the package by the care manager for the benefit of the caregiver as well as the user. Unsurprisingly, the buffering effect is smaller where the user sees problems in the receipt of the informal care, or the caregiver of users receiving day care perceive a larger number of problems with caregiving.

The impact of *low morale* is similarly unsurprising, since the literature shows control over one's own life to be a predictor and a component of morale.

2.2. Service productivities

One of the mechanisms by which informal care achieves its buffering effect is reflected in the productivity of *home care* among users living alone. This and the other productivity effects are shown in figure 7.5. The role of principal informal caregivers as brokers, advocates and organisers of care is recognised in the gerontological literature and often described in empirical studies (Dechaux, 1994). The effect is significant at the 1 per cent level, and applies to 69 per cent of recipients of home care, and so to 60 per cent of the entire sample.

Table 7.2
Production function for user felt empowerment during set-up phase

Predictors by domain	Coeff.	Prob.	%[1] Recip- ients	%[2] Users
Risk factors and other need-related circumstances				
General effects				
Physical disability				
User cannot eat – Canteat	-1.888	.001		
User cannot go shopping to buy groceries – Cantgroc	-.755	.018		
Mental health				
PGC lack of morale score – PGC	-.089	.003		
User has behavioural problems – Wbehav	-1.005	.053		
Other health problems				
Count user health problems – Wuhlthpb	.170	.072		
Informal care related factors				
User has a confidant – Uconfide	.924	.004		
Count of user problems with caring – Cupbnb	-.601	.006		
PIC is beneficiary on her own of package provided – Wcbenefi	.566	.035		
Other				
Count number of user risks – Wuserisk	-.131	.070		
User discharged from hospital – Fromhosp	-.760	.021		
SUP phase is not finished – Stilset	-1.389	.046		
User lives alone – Walone	-1.131	.009		
Targeting-captured need effects				
PIC has high no of caring problems, user targeted for day care – Dc_cpbh	-.936	.041		
Productivity effects (£ per week)				
Individual input effects				
Home care				
User lives alone – Lhc_alon (log)	.283	.010	69.1	59.8
Day care				
User has high no of problems with IADL tasks – Dcc_hiad	.0247	.026	18.3	5.8
Respite care				
User discharged from hospital – Lre_fh	.320	.050	26.4	6.3
Nursing visits				
PIC is stressed – Lnv_cstr (log)	.251	.035	38.6	15.7
Constant	6.823	.000		

Adj. R^2 .236   Prob. .000   No. of cases 217

1 Proportion of recipients of the service to whom the effect applies
2 Proportion of the sample to whom the effect applies

Figure 7.5

Productivity curves: home care, day care, respite and nursing effects on user empowerment through set-up phase

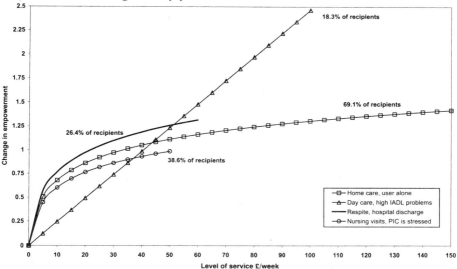

Respite care inputs are associated with improvements in empowerment for users referred to social services after being discharged from hospital, and *community nursing* inputs for users whose PICs are perceived to be stressed. These effects (as the home care effect), are characterised by marked decreasing returns to scale, and cover approximately 26 and 39 per cent of the recipients of the services respectively.

In contrast, *day care* among those with a large number of IADL problems shows constant marginal productivities over a wide range of inputs. The effect applied to 18 per cent of day care recipients, 6 per cent of the entire sample.

2.3. Overall service impact, impact for groups, and equity and efficiency

Figure 7.6 shows the overall outcome to be fairly equal for all groups. So also was the impact of services. The allocations seem to be broadly equitable by two criteria: the final state criterion (the final output level), and the gain contributed by the services. Felt empowerment was least among users with critical interval needs without a principal informal caregiver.

For all groups except the critical interval need and PIC group, the bulk of the package contribution is associated with home care inputs. For that group, the home care contribution is matched by the nursing inputs effect.

However, the contribution of the services was modest relatively to that of the risk factors. Therefore the questions about whether the gains can be pro-

Figure 7.6
Contribution of services and risk factors to user felt empowerment during set-up phase

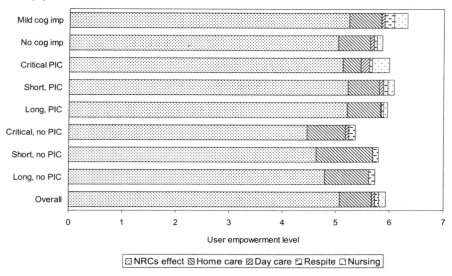

duced more efficiently are less important in this case than whether the level of empowerment felt is adequate.

2.4. Overview

Results include:
- A statistically clear productivity effect for home care influences 60 per cent of the sample. It is, however, subject to significant decreasing marginal productivities. There are also respite and nursing effects, these also being threshold effects. Day care had a constant marginal productivity among those with a large number of IADL problems.
- Both service contributions and the outcome were on average broadly similar between groups. However, users with critical interval needs but without principal informal caregivers appeared to have a low sense of empowerment during the set-up process, service contributions not compensating for the adverse effects of the risk factors.
- Home care was the major contributor to the service effect.

3.   PIC's felt empowerment/influence during set-up stage of care management scale (CEMPOW)

This output variable likewise measures a process rather than an impact outcome, but for informal caregivers.

3.1.   The model and the impact of risk factors

Goodness of fit. Table 7.3 shows that the model fits better than those for the rest of outputs in the domain. There are more and clearer productivity effects, as well as clear associations with risk factors.

The most important risk factors are features of the users' health and dependency, aspects of their relations with informal caregivers, and the subjective feelings of stress felt by the principal informal caregivers.

User *dependency* is of less direct effect in this model because it is mediated through the perception of the PICs of its effects on them. However, there is the targeting-captured need effect associated with musculo-skeletal conditions and the allocation of day care resources, and severe cognitive impairment associated with the allocation of home care.

What is clear about the set of risk factors associated with *informal care and user-carer relationships* is the importance of perceptions and relations rather than the objective circumstances of the caregivers in themselves.

The most powerful dummy effect is the stress of the caregiver role as reported by the caregivers themselves; not, as so often in the care manager-brokered world of post-reform community care, the perception of the care manager. (Both rounds of interviews revealed high proportions of caregivers to have high Rutter stress scores (Davies, 1997a)). Again, the associations between caregiver worry and the allocation of respite care identifies cases with very high level of caregiver stress. Cognitive impairment is well known to add to stress more than physical disability (Twigg, 1992; Twigg and Atkin, 1994). Motivation reflecting love and affection might be associated with the virtual entrapment of the caregiver, thus making it more difficult for them to set limits compatible with protecting themselves from infinite caring demands (Twigg and Atkin, 1995).

3.2.   Service productivities

There were productivity effects for all the main services except for home-delivered meals and social work.

Home care inputs are shown to be effective for two groups.

- The significant effect of *home care* for the caregivers of the 50 per cent of users whose Katzman score predict cognitive impairment is initially weak, but increases with the scale of the input, as can be seen from figure 7.7.

Table 7.3
Production function for PIC felt empowerment during set-up phase

Predictors by domain	Coeff.	Prob.	%[1] Recipients	%[2] Users
Risk factors and other need-related circumstances				
General effects				
Informal care related factors				
User is stressed with PIC caring role – Cupbstr	-4.747	.000		
PIC caring role is motivated by love & affection – Clove	-2.157	.001		
PIC prepares meals – Mcmeal	1.927	.002		
Informal companionship hrs/wk help – Infcomp	-.064	.002		
Other				
User previously known to services – Current	-1.487	.011		
Targeting-captured need effects				
PIC is worried, user targeted for respite care – Re_wor	-3.792	.003		
User has high relational problems & targeted for respite care – Re_hrel	3.9894E-2	.049		
User has skeletal problems & targeted for day care – Dc_skel	-1.991	.019		
User is sev cognitively impaired, & targeted for home care – Hc_kats	-2.456	.002		
Productivity effects (£ per week)				
Individual input effects				
Home care			67.2	45.2
User is severely/mildly cog impaired – Hc2_katm (squared)	7.4E-5	.011	50.0	38.1
User with long interval need – Lhc_long (log)	.519	.037	15.5	11.8
Day care			49.4	25.8
User suffered stroke (log) – Ldc_strk	.451	.027	25.3	13.4
PIC is employed – Ldc_cemp (log)	.412	.026	35.0	18.1
Respite care			38.7	15.8
User has high relational problems – Rec_hrel	.0399	.049	32.3	13.2
User has behavioural problems – Rec_beha	.0674	.008	27.4	11.2
Nursing visits			76.4	36.3
User has skeletal problems – Lnv_skel (log)	.986	.001	32.4	15.3
User has mild/sev cog impairment – Lnv_katm (log)	.414	.069	62.0	29.2
Constant	26.534	.000		

Adj. R^2 .370   Prob. .000   No. of cases 152

1 Proportion of recipients of the service to whom the effect applies
2 Proportion of the sample to whom the effect applies

Figure 7.7
Productivity curves: home care and day care effects on PIC empowerment during set-up phase

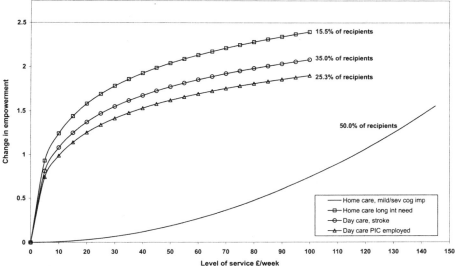

- The productivity effect of home care among the 15 per cent of caregivers with users who are of long interval need presents decreasing returns to scale.
- Between them, the two effects cover 67 per cent of all caregivers of users with home care, and 45 per cent of all caregivers.

Home care inputs are also shown to be effective for two groups of carers, namely those caring for users who have suffered a stroke and those that are in paid employment. Both effects are shown in figure 7.7. The two effects also imply diminishing returns and a threshold beyond which marginal productivities are not high. Again, the effects are widespread. Between them, they cover 49 per cent of the caregivers whose users receive day care, and 25 per cent of all principal informal caregivers in the sample.

The more general of the productivity effects of *respite care*, for relational problems, is also the less powerful, as shown by figure 7.8. The service is also effective for carers with users with behavioural problems. Both effects have constant marginal productivities over a wide range of inputs. Between them, they cover 38.7 per cent of the caregivers of recipients of respite care. Moreover, for more than one fifth of the caregivers, the two effects work in combination. For these, the marginal productivity of respite care is estimated to be the sum of the two coefficients shown in table 7.1.

Nursing visits has a powerful threshold effect for the 32 per cent of the caregivers of recipients with musculo-skeletal problems, and perhaps continuing

Figure 7.8
Productivity curves: respite and nursing effects on PIC empowerment during set-up phase

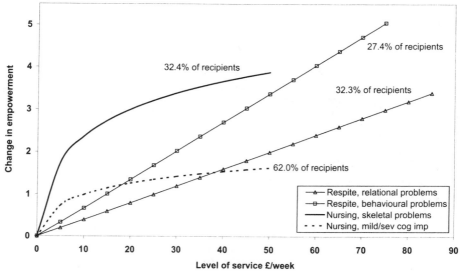

Figure 7.9
Contributions of services and risk factors to PIC empowerment during set-up phase

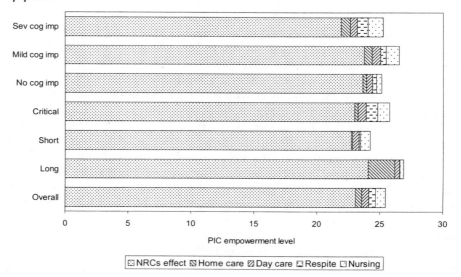

marginal productivity beyond that level. The model identifies a weaker effect, also with decreasing marginal productivities, for the caregivers of the cognitively impaired. The effects are shown in figure 7.8.

3.3. Overall service impact, impact for groups, and equity and efficiency

Figure 7.9 shows that the average level of the final output does not vary greatly between the groups. Neither does the contribution of services. There is perhaps a small positive gradient of service contribution by level of cognitive impairment, which compensates for the differences of empowerment predicted from risk factors. Therefore the pattern is compatible with two equity criteria: equity in criterion state (the output indicator), and equity in welfare gain.

The contribution of the services to the overall state is small compared with the risk factors. Therefore the important question is not whether the gain was produced in the most equitable and efficient way, but whether sufficient was produced. The issue of optimisation and the nature of inequities and inefficiencies is discussed in a later section.

4. Overview

The results show:

- More productivity effects of clear statistical significance than for the other outputs in the domain.
- All the main services had productivity effects, except for home-delivered meals. Home care had two effects, one for the 50 per cent of carers with users whose Katzman score predicted cognitive impairment, the other for the 15 per cent of recipients of long interval need. The other services showing significant productivities are day care respite care and nursing inputs, most of which show significant decreasing returns to scale.
- The effects on the average outcome for groups of service contributions were neither large compared with the effects of risk factors, nor very different.

8   Productivities for PGC, GDL, DLD Indicator Variables (General Psychological Well-being)

Production functions were fitted for three user indicators: overall PGC score (PGC); General Dissatisfaction with Life (GDL), based on a subscale of the PGC scale; and the third, a score on Dissatisfaction with Life Development (DLD). The two subscales are dimensions of overall morale tested using the PGC scale (Lawton, 1975).

1.   Overall lack of morale: the PGC score (PGC)

1.1.   The model and the impact of risk factors

Goodness of fit. Table 8.1 shows that the model fits to much the same degree for the overall scale as for the two components for which the models are discussed below. Like General Dissatisfaction with Life, there are few productivity effects that are as significant as the most clearly determined risk factors.

The risk factors which best predict low morale are related to *dependency*, the buffering effect of *informal care*, and *anxiety*; the same types of factor which influence Dissatisfaction with Life Development and General Dissatisfaction with Life.

- The pattern suggests that dependency as measured by interval need and the users' feeling of being vexed with charging is associated with lower morale.
- Also, users with long interval needs but targeted for receiving social work — often targeted at depressed persons with problems which are more complex than their dependency suggests — are likely to have lower morale.
- A recent discharge from hospital is associated with better morale.
- The number of user fears, users who had been targeted for respite care and who had anxious principal informal caregivers are likely to have lower morale.

Table 8.1
Production function for user overall lack of morale

Predictors by domain	Coeff.	Prob.	%[1] Recip-ients	%[2] Users
Risk factors and other need-related circumstances				
General effects				
Physical disability				
Disability interval need – Intneed (0 Critical, 1 Short, 2 Long)	-2.551	.000		
Mental health				
User has behavioural problems – Wbehav	-5.987	.000		
Informal care related factors				
PIC is employed – Cemploy	1.832	.007		
Informal help hrs/wk with medical care – Infmed	.172	.001		
Personal care hrs/wk (log), User has high no. of ADL problems – Lip_had	-1.882	.002		
Personal care hrs/wk (squared), user short interval need – Ip2_sht	-.038	.035		
Other				
Count of user fears – Ufears	.864	.000		
User discharged from hospital – Fromhosp	-1.834	.002		
User is vexed by charging – Vexed	6.065	.000		
Targeting-captured need effects				
PIC is worried, user targeted for respite care – Re_wor	7.933	.019		
User is long interval need and targeted for social work input – Sw_long	2.020	.017		
Productivity effects (£ per week)				
Individual input effects				
Home care				
PIC is close female relative Hcc_clof	-.027	.001	31.2	25.9
Respite care			43.4	10.9
User discharged from hospital – Re2_fh (squared)	-4.4E-4	.095	24.6	5.7
PIC loses sleep due to worry – Rec_sle	-.115	.020	28.1	6.5
Social work				
User lives alone – Swc_walo	-.877	.038	71.5	11.9
Constant	9.945	.000		

Adj. R^2 .343   Prob. .000   No. of cases 241

1 Proportion of recipients of the service to whom the effect applies
2 Proportion of the sample to whom the effect applies

The model implies that intensity of informal care input buffers the effect of dependency. However, the effect of informal inputs depends on the circumstances of the informal carer and the nature of the tasks they perform.

- Caregiver employment reduces this buffering effect, as it does for the two sub-dimensions of morale examined below.
- Whereas the effect of receiving large amounts of informal help with medical care is to reduce the user's morale, the receipt of informal help with personal care among those with short interval needs and/or with high number of problems with ADL tasks appears to significantly improve morale.

1.2. Service productivities

The nature of the marginal productivity effects are compatible with these patterns and interpretations. The productivity effects for home and respite care are shown in figure 8.1, and those for social work inputs in figure 8.2.

- *Home care* shows a constant productivity effect when there is a principal informal caregiver who is a close female relative. This effect may be compatible with a division of labour between formal and informal care which helps affect relationships. The marginal productivity exists for 31 per cent of users of home care, and so more than one quarter of the sample as a whole.
- *Respite care* inputs show a small productivity effect for users discharged from hospital, affecting approximately 25 per cent of the recipients of the

Figure 8.1
Productivity curves: home care and respite care effect on overall lack of morale

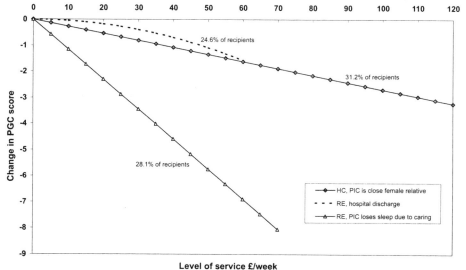

Level of service £/week

Figure 8.2
Productivity curves: social work input effect on overall lack of morale

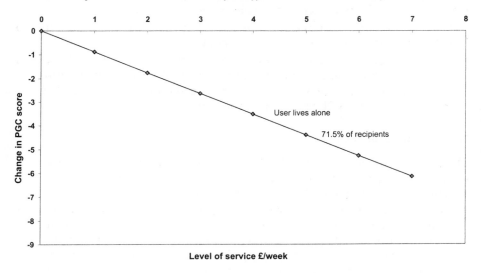

service. They show a constant and much larger marginal productivity when the principal informal caregiver loses sleep with worry, probably a reflection of anxieties of both user and caregivers. This effect covers 28 per cent of users of respite care, but applies to only 6 per cent of the whole sample.

- *Social work* inputs have a similarly large and constant marginal productivity among the 71 per cent of its recipients who live alone. The productivity is probably in part a form of substitution of social worker for relative as a psychological buffer.

1.3. *Overall service impact, impact for groups, and equity and efficiency*

Relative to the predicted levels of the output, the differences in the impact of both risk factors and service inputs between the groups are small, figure 8.3 suggests. There is, however, a positive correlation between the users' lack of morale, their level of cognitive impairment and the size of the service contributions. The outcome variable is unlikely to be reliable for those who are cognitively impaired, so less emphasis should be made of the analysis by that variable.

The most interesting contrasts are between those groups without principal informal caregivers, for which the overall effects of services are small, and users with principal informal caregivers (particularly for those with critical interval needs), groups for which the package contributions are greatest.

Figure 8.3
Contributions of services and risk factors to user overall lack of morale

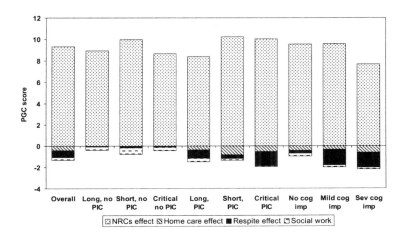

The importance of the services found significantly to improve morale is very different depending on whether users have PICs. For user without PICs, the majority of the contributions come from the effect of social work inputs. In contrast, most of the package contributions in morale for users with PICs is produced by respite care and home care inputs.

Overall, figure 8.4 shows a clear negative correlation between the average productivities of the packages of care and the level of need of the users. From a strictly efficiency point of view, the pattern of final package contributions reveals for this output, a clearly sub-optimal allocation of the resources.

- Users without principal informal caregivers, particularly those with long interval needs, who enjoy the highest package average productivities, receive the smallest package contributions. It is likely that small investments in social work inputs would have improved greatly the outcome for these users, this being by far the input with greatest average productivities.

- Although potentially justifiable in terms of the achievement of other competing goals, the greater package contributions in improvement in morale for users with PICs ars therefore to be explained as a disproportionately great allocation of resources to them, particularly of less productive inputs.

1.4. Overview

Results show that:

- There are fewer clear productivity effects than for other output measures in the domain.

Figure 8.4
Average productivity for user overall lack of morale for total package

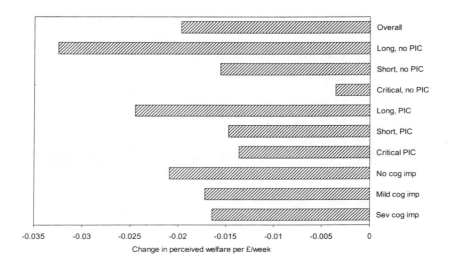

Change in perceived welfare per £/week

- Home and respite care have constant effects, the former applying to more than one in four of all users. Social work inputs have a large and constant marginal productivity for those living alone. It is speculated that part of the effect is that the social worker assumes some of the same buffering properties as the informal caregiver.
- The impact of service contributions is small in relation to that of risk factors.
- Service contributions were even smaller in relation to risk factor effects for those without principal informal caregivers.
- For all groups, social work had high productivities, but made most of the contributions only for users without PICs.

2.   General dissatisfaction with life (GDL)

2.1.   The model and the impact of risk factors

Goodness of fit. Table 8.2 shows that the model predicted the outcome with the same moderate success as the other user indicators in the domain.

Need-related circumstances and other risk factors. The predictors related to (a) physical disability and illness, (b) users anxiety and other attitudes, and (c) the buffering effects of informal care.
- The number of problems the user has performing IADL tasks increased user dissatisfaction significantly at the 1 per cent level. The effects of stroke are still more clearly determined. The targeting-captured effect of the com-

Table 8.2
Production function for user general dissatisfaction with life

Predictors by domain	Coeff.	Prob.	%[1] Recipients	%[2] Users
Risk factors and other need-related circumstances				
General effects				
Physical disability				
Count of problems with IADL – Uiadls	.142	.010		
User cannot wash hands – Cantwhnd	-1.057	.005		
Mental health problems				
User has behavioral problems – Wbehav	-1.617	.000		
Other health problems				
User suffered stroke – Wstroke	.833	.002		
Informal care related factors				
PIC is spouse – Wspouse	-.806	.048		
Informal personal care hrs/wk, high no. of ADL problems – Ipc_had	-.038	.032		
Informal housework care hrs/wk, user lives alone – Ihc_walo	-.242	.003		
Other				
Count of user fears – Ufears	.322	.000		
User is over-reliant – Wurelian	.411	.034		
User is vexed by charging – Vexed	1.224	.011		
User is against entry into residential care – Upercent	.242	.009		
Targeting-captured need effects				
Critical interval need, user targeted for day care – Dc_crit	1.503	.000		
User lives alone and targeted for meals – M_alon	.779	.002		
Productivity effects (£ per week)				
Individual input effects				
Home care				
PIC is close female relative – Hcc_clof	-.0071	.030	31.0	25.6
Meals				
Long interval need – Mc_long	-.0565	.031	42.7	14.6
Day care				38.0	12.4
User discharged from hospital – Ldc_fh (log)	-.248	.042	16.5	5.3
User has high no of problems with ADLs – Dcc_had (log)	-.0176	.066	22.8	7.5
Respite care				
User is married – Re2_marr (squared)	-2.1E-4	.046	25.5	5.9
Constant	1.005	.022		

Adj. R[2] .356   Prob. .000   No. of cases 238

1 Proportion of recipients of the service to whom the effect applies
2 Proportion of the sample to whom the effect applies

bination of day care allocation with critical interval need may reflect both disability and anxiety. The apparently perverse relationship with behavioural problems may reflect the larger measurement error for these cases.

- The buffering effects of informal care are clearly suggested by three predictors: whether the spouse is the PIC; the number of weekly hours of informal help with personal care tasks for users with high number of problems with ADL tasks; the level of informal help with housework for users that live alone. Also, the service targeting-captured effect of users selected for nursing visits with worried PICs is very likely to identify cases near breakdown in caregiving.

- Several predictors suggest the importance of anxiety: most obviously, the number of user fears (of very clear significance) and the care manager's view that the user is more reliant than others in the same circumstances. Perhaps also the strength of the rejection of residential care may reflect the level of users' anxiety.

- The strong association with vexation about charges may also reflect a more general attitude set. An identical effect is present in the other two models relating to users' general psychological well-being.

2.2. Service productivities

The score is a measure of dissatisfaction. The impact of services should be to reduce the score. Therefore the coefficients should have negative values.

In contrast with the more clearly established productivities for another dimension of morale, Dissatisfaction with Life Development, the existence and size of the marginal productivity effects for General Dissatisfaction with Life are established only at the 5 per cent level. The effects are summarised in figures 8.5.

- The marginal productivity for *home care* affects those users whose PIC is a close female relative. It relates to some 31 per cent of recipients of the service, and shows constant marginal returns. Close female relatives acting as PIC thus appear as a buffers whose effects are increased with the catalytic influences of home care.

- *Meals* are estimated to have a high and constant marginal productivity for the 43 per cent of its recipients who are of long interval need.

- *Day care* appears to have a significant effect in reducing DLD scores for two user groups: with a significance level of 6.6. per cent, for those users with a high number of problems performing ADL tasks, and for users recently discharged from hospitals. Together, both effects cover approximately 38 per cent of the recipients of the service. Whereas the effect for users with ADL problems shows constant returns to scale (constant effects of marginal increases in the service), the marginal productivities for users discharged from hospital decrease rapidly as the levels of the service increase.

Figure 8.5

Productivity curves: day care, home care and meals effect on GDL (general dissatisfaction with life)

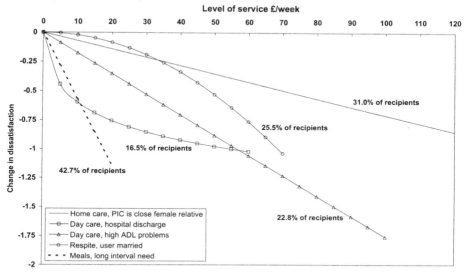

- For the 25 per cent of users who are married, *respite care* has a productivity effect suggesting increasing returns over the range of inputs observed. This is the same effect seen in the model looking at overall satisfaction with the level of services received.

2.3. Overall service impact, impact for groups, and equity and efficiency

Figure 8.6 shows the contributions of the different factors explaining the predicted levels of GDL scores for the groups defined.

- Overall, the contributions made by services are very limited relative to the effect of need-related circumstances.
- Most of the service contributions are for users with PICs, particularly for users with critical interval needs. Among users without PICs, only users with long interval needs enjoy any service contributions at all.
- Even after service contributions, figure 8.6 shows great inequality in the final levels of outputs.

The pattern of average productivities of the total packages in figure 8.7 shows the highest average productivities to be for users with long interval needs and PICs. The observed service contributions are therefore far from those implied by efficiency criteria.

Figure 8.6
Contributions of services and risk factors to user general dissatisfaction with life

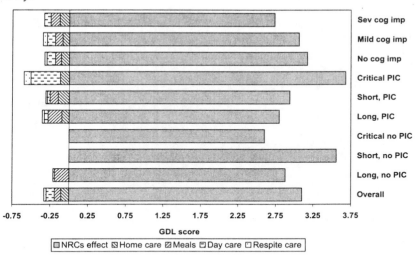

Figure 8.7
Average productivity for user general dissatisfaction with life for total package

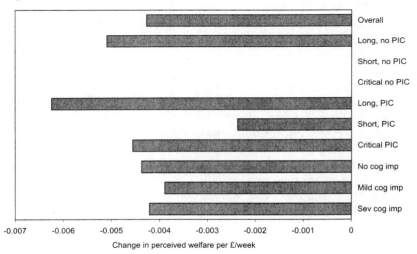

2.4. Overview

The results show that:

- The productivity effects are not highly significant, but of moderately wide coverage. They exist for day care with decreasing returns to scale, for meals and home care with constant marginal productivity, and with increasing returns for respite care.
- There are substantial service contributions only for critical interval cases with principal informal caregivers.

3. Dissatisfaction with life development (DLD)

This dimension corresponds to the dimension called Satisfaction with Life Progression identified by Morris and Sherwood (1975). It more explicitly compares aspects of quality of life with an earlier period than do some of the GDL items, which are focused on the current situation.

3.1. The model and the impact of risk factors

Table 8.3 shows that the model fits comparatively well, to much the same degree as that for General Dissatisfaction with Life. But the productivity effects are more clearly established by their significance levels. So service inputs more influence how the current situation is interpreted in relation to the life span than the nature of the current situation itself.

The model presents the same significant three general sets of risk factors as for General Dissatisfaction with Life: dependency, the buffering effects of informal care and other 'resources', and anxiety, together with the resentment felt about charging.

- *Disability* and *cognitively-related disability* are reflected in well-determined coefficients for interval needs, and in slightly less significant effect for the targeting-captured needs associated with users of day care who cannot buy groceries, and with the receipt of respite care among persons who have had a stroke.
- The buffering effects of *informal care* are caught by the presence of a PIC and by the total input from informal caregivers. The employment of the caregiver reduces this buffering effect, as does the stress of the informal caregivers whose users are 'picked out' for day care.
- Gerontological literature treats informal care as only one 'resource' among several, all likely to be 'buffers'. That is reflected in frameworks and tools for evaluation based most clearly on gerontological argument; for instance, the OARS methodology (Fillenbaum, 1978). Income and assets are other resources. Both income and home ownership — partly reflecting a superior physical environment, tenants being argued by Means (1997) to value life in

Table 8.3
Production function for user dissatisfaction with life development

Predictors by domain	Coeff.	Prob.	$\%^1$ Recipients	$\%^2$ Users
Risk factors and other need-related circumstances				
General effects				
Physical disability				
Interval need level – Intneed	-.318	.000		
Mental health				
User presents behavioural problems – Wbehav	-.688	.019		
Other health problems				
Count user number of health problems – Wuhlthpb	.056	.124		
Informal care related factors				
Presence of PIC – Wpic	-.458	.000		
Informal help hrs/wk all tasks – Inft	-.005	.008		
PIC is employed – Cemploy	.338	.007		
Poverty and material environment				
User income level – Income	-.284	.022		
User owns home (alone or with others) – Uownshs	-.257	.023		
Other				
Count of user fears – Ufears	.153	.000		
User is vexed by charging – Vexed	.694	.003		
Targeting-captured need effects				
User cannot shop to buy groceries, and targeted for day care – Dc_groc	.306	.014		
PIC is stressed, user targeted for home care – Hc_cstr	.217	.059		
User cannot do heavy housework and targeted for respite care – Re_hhwk				
User had stroke and targeted for respite care – Re_strk	.415	.049		
User against admission res care, targeted for social work input – Sw_prcd	.313	.001		
Productivity effects (£ per week)				
Individual input effects				
Home care			58.6	45.2
User has skeletal problems – Lhc_skel (log)	-.0739	.005	48.2	40.2
User cannot go to toilet by himself – Lhc_toil (log)	-.111	.012	24.2	8.3
Delivered meals			26.8	9.2
Day care			50.0	16.5
PIC is close female relative – Dcc_clof	-.0083	.003	44.3	14.4
User has behavioural problems – Ldc_beha (log)	-.162	.071	12.7	4.2
Respite care			64.9	10.7
User is married – Re2_marr (squared)	-1.3E-4	.008	25.5	5.8
User discharged from hospital – Rec_fh	-.0101	.010	25.0	5.7

Table 8.3 (continued)

Predictors by domain	Coeff.	Prob.	%[1] Recipients	%[2] Users
Social work				
User cannot do heavy housework tasks – Swc_hhwk	-.210	.027	87.0	14.5
Complementarities				
Meals and nursing visits interaction, short interval need – Nmc_sht	-7.0E-4	.087	71.0	9.2
Constant	2.253	.000		
Adj. R^2 .349 Prob. .000 No. of cases 218				

1 Proportion of recipients of the service to whom the effect applies
2 Proportion of the sample to whom the effect applies

their own home more often because of allegiance to neighbourhoods than to the home itself — have buffering effects.

- *Anxiety* and the resentment of charging are risk factors for Dissatisfaction with Life Development as for General Dissatisfaction with Life. Perhaps the 'meaning' of the rejection of the residential care alternative among those receiving social work inputs during the continuing care period is partly that the social work is particularly directed at the anxious and demoralised, depression and anxiety being associated; and partly that they are receiving the attention of the social workers because they are at high risk of admission, and so are most anxious about it.

3.2. Service productivities

Five effects are significant at about the 1 per cent level.

- Two effects for *home care* between them cover 59 per cent of home care recipients. The one for users with musculo-skeletal problems itself covers 48 per cent of recipients, but is weaker than the effect for persons unable to go to the toilet unaided, which itself covers 24.2 per cent. Figure 8.8 shows that both effects are characterised by decreasing marginal returns, and so progressively falling average productivities with higher input levels. Both productivity effects apply concurrently to 13.8 per cent of the recipients of home care. The last column in table 8.1 indicates that 45 per cent of the entire sample are affected by one or other of these productivity effects for home care.
- The input of *home-delivered meals* has a productivity effect only in combination with nursing visits, shown in figure 8.9. It affects 26.8 per cent of the recipients of meals. The proportion of the nursing recipients affected is much higher than that of meal recipients: 71 per cent.

Figure 8.8
Productivity curves: day care and home care effect on DLD (dissatisfaction with life development score)

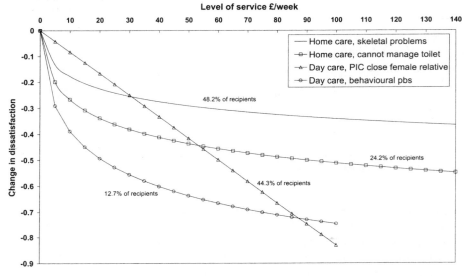

Figure 8.9
Productivity curves: meals and social work input effect on DLD (dissatisfaction with life development score)

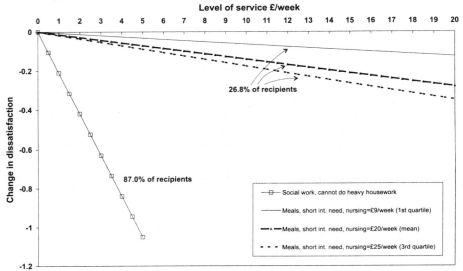

- One of the effects for *day care* shown in figure 8.8 is likewise of high significance: that for the 44 per cent of the service's users whose principal informal caregiver is a close female relative. The effect is substantial and the marginal productivity, and so average productivity, are constant over the observed input range. The other day care effect, for users with behavioural problems, relates to too low a proportion of the sample (4.2 per cent) to be clearly determined and it too appears to be a threshold effect, albeit a large one.

- The two effects for *respite care* shown in figure 8.10 are highly significant, and each relates to approximately one recipient in four of respite recipients. The significance is the more remarkable because only a small minority of the sample are affected, because respite care is narrowly targeted. The factors 'user discharged from hospital' and 'user is married' are also found in the description of respite care effects for a number of other output variables.

- The effect for *social work* shown in figure 8.9 applies to 87 per cent of its recipients, and is by far the largest in the model. The input is best interpreted as counselling/therapeutic social work additional to the tasks performed in care management activity. The relevance to this output would hardly surprise those who have followed the PSSRU community care experiments. It is to the reinterpretation of the present in the context of a life-time perspective: a contribution to the self-actualisation so central to the theory of hu-

Figure 8.10
Productivity curves: nursing visits and respite care effect on DLD
(dissatisfaction with life development score)

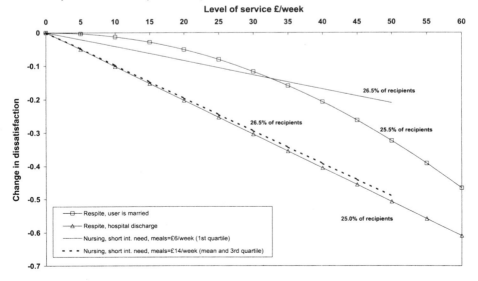

man growth and development for ageing people which is so important to social work curricula. Its importance is to argument about the gains from more intensive, skilled and therapeutic, as distinct from less intensive, administrative care management.

3.3. Overall service impact, impact for groups, and equity and efficiency

As figure 8.11 illustrates, service impacts to some degree offset the effects of risk factors on differences between groups. This contrasts with the picture described for GDL, both in terms of the distribution of the service contributions and their size relative to the need-related circumstances effects.

- There is a clear positive correlation between the users' dependency level, their level of dissatisfaction, and the size of the service contributions. As a result, the effect of the services is to reduce very significantly the differences in the predicted DLD levels. Similar patterns were also found for some of the most important output variables, such as days in the community or carer stress.

- *Home care* shows a significant contribution for all groups, which increases with the user's level of dependency. *Day care* inputs make a greater contribution for users with critical interval needs and users with PICs.

- Even with by far the strongest effect, *social work* inputs only make a significant contribution for users with critical interval needs, and the combination of *meals and nursing inputs* for users with short interval needs.

Figure 8.11
Contributions of services and risk factors to user dissatisfaction with life development

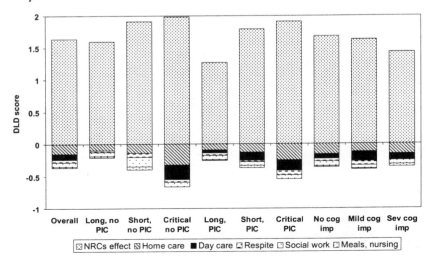

- Figure 8.12 shows the package average productivities to be highest for users with lower levels of needs. This suggests that the pattern of distribution of the service contributions to be against that implied by efficiency criteria, and therefore driven by some other equity-related principles. These could be about particular valuations of users in different circumstances, or about the need for achieving alternative outputs.

Figure 8.12
Average productivity for user dissatisfaction with life development for total package

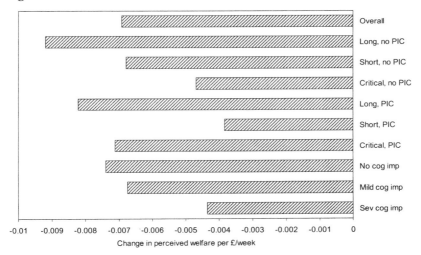

3.4. Overview

Results show that:

- There are more and more highly significant productivity effects for this dimension of morale, rather than for morale in general and for General Dissatisfaction with Life.
- There are substantial threshold effects for home care covering the majority of recipients. Meals have a productivity effect in conjunction with nursing. One of the day care effects influences a high proportion of recipients and suggests a constant marginal productivity over a substantial range of inputs. There are substantial effects for respite and social work.
- The two groups for whom the service contribution is great and the risk factors predict high dissatisfaction are those with critical interval needs. Overall the packages show their highest average productivities for the user groups that enjoy the lowest service contributions.

4.   Kosberg carer burden scale (KOSBERG)

The indicator is an indicator of burden due to caregiving rather than a more general indicator of psychological malaise.

4.1.   *The model and the impact of risk factors*

Goodness of fit. Table 8.4 shows that the model fits well, accounting for more than one half of the variance. There are a substantial number of predictor variables whose effects are well determined and stable.

Impact of risk factors. An indicator of *general dependency level* (the number of IADL disabilities), rather than indicators of physical disability, illness, cognitive impairment and morale separately, has a powerful effect which is clearly established. Relationships between user and caregivers are reflected in the claim of the user to feel stressed because of the inputs of the principal informal caregiver, the extent of the informal caregiving being reflected in the PIC cooking meals, a task mostly done by live-in caregivers, who are well known to suffer greater depression and stress than others (Lieberman and Fisher, 1995; Twigg and Atkin, 1994).

Results for *targeting-captured risk factors* illustrate the big influence of cognitive impairment and caregiver stress, reflected in the association with severe cognitive impairment among recipients of home care; the association of risk to the user among those whose caregivers are under such stress that the user receives respite care; and the association with female (but not male) principal informal caregivers receiving home care, the American gerontological literature suggesting that females are more liable to stress than males, allowance being made for the circumstances (Horowitz, 1985; Stoller, 1983).

Targeting-captured risk factors are better predictors than the risk factors themselves, so they should be included in any assessment system. They combine the information from hands-on assessment with the demand influences which risk factors themselves reflect. The influences captured by the targeting-related group effects closely reflect argument about the causes and nature of caregiver stress.

That the user is the main beneficiary of the package when a recipient of day care may catch those cases in which the care manager is conscious that the package does little to relieve caregiver stress.

The combination of receiving respite care and the paid employment of the principal informal caregiver suggests unusually high caregiver stress due to job and caregiving role conflict.

4.2.   *Service productivities*

A negative sign in table 8.4 indicates a marginal productivity, the Kosberg score being an inverse indicator of final output.

Table 8.4
Production function for Kosberg carer burden scale

Predictors by domain	Coeff.	Prob.	%[1] Recipients	%[2] Users
Risk factors and other need-related circumstances				
General effects				
Physical disability				
Count of number of problems with IADLs – Wiadls	.580	.000		
Informal care related factors				
User is stressed because PIC caring – Cupbstr	3.082	.000		
Main carer cooks meals – Mcmeal	1.610	.001		
Targeting-captured need effects				
User is main beneficiary of package and targeted for daycare – Dc_uben	4.095	.000		
PIC is a close female relative and user targeted for home care – Hc_clof	2.670	.000		
User is severely cognitively impaired and user targeted for home care – Hc_kats	2.473	.001		
User is perceived as at great risk and targeted for respite care – Re-hrsk	5.230	.000		
PIC is employed and user targeted for respite care – Re_cemp	1.590	.066		
Productivity effects (£ per week)				
Individual input effects				
Home care			66.1	48.9
For users with mild or severe cognitive impairment – Hc2_katm (squared)	-1.6E-4	.075	47.1	34.9
For users with mild or severe cognitive impairment – Hc3_katm (cubed)	4.7E-7	.069	47.1	34.9
Delivered meals			38.9	
Day care			85.1	45.6
For employed carers – Ldc_cemp (log)	-.538	.006	39.2	17.8
For users with severe cogn. impairment – Dcc_kats	-.0792	.001	31.1	14.4
Dcc_kats – Dc2_kats (squared)	6.5E-4	.000		
Respite care			65.1	25.3
For over-reliant users – Rec_reli	-.0216	.095	19.0	7.4
For cognitively impaired users – Lre_cog (log)	-.547	.009	54.0	20.9
Social work				
Social work – Sw_wcost	-.655	.008	100.0	18.2
Complementarity				
Day and home care interaction – Dh2 (squared)	-1.4E-8	.060	100.0	27.9
Day care and meals interaction – Ldm (log)	-.317	.020	100.0	12.7
Constant	-.735	.203		

Adj. R^2 .510   Prob. .0000   No. of cases 163

1 Proportion of recipients of the service to whom the effect applies
2 Proportion of the sample to whom the effect applies

The marginal productivities of *home care* among the 47 per cent for whom the Katzman scale predicts mild or severe cognitive impairment are larger, the greater is the level of input. Home care otherwise has a marginal productivity in association with the utilisation of day care for 37 per cent of users. Figure 8.13 shows how great the effect of the level of one service is on the marginal productivity of the other.

Home-delivered meals have an effect only in combination with the receipt of .y care. This effect, described in figure 8.14, applies to 39 per cent of meals' users, approximately 13 per cent of the sample.

Figure 8.15 illustrates the large effect of *day care* for the severely cognitively impaired up to a day care input of approximately £60 per week (approximately two attendances per week). But beyond that, additional day care is associated with negative marginal productivities (although still positive average productivities). It is not surprising that the degree and nature of the strains associated with the highest level of cognitive impairment are such that a community package can make no further impact on caregiver stress; and indeed, higher levels of stress remove the gains possible at low levels. It is to the credit of the departments that there are not many cases on a curve stretching far towards the positive pole of the distribution. It has been observed elsewhere that the average stress of caregivers (measured by the Rutter scale) was actually higher after six months of the continuing care period of community care than at the end of the set-up stage (Davies et al., 1997).

Figure 8.13
Productivity curves: home care effect on Kosberg carer burden scale

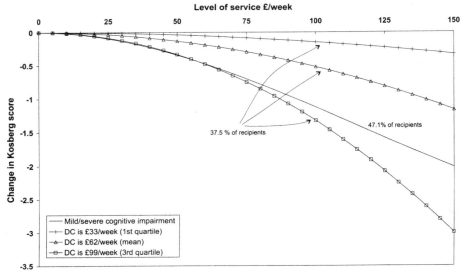

Figure 8.14
Productivity curves: meals and social work effect on Kosberg carer burden scale

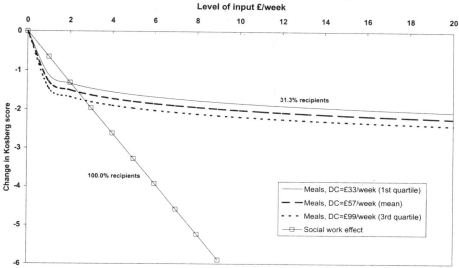

Figure 8.15
Productivity curves: day care effect on Kosberg carer burden scale

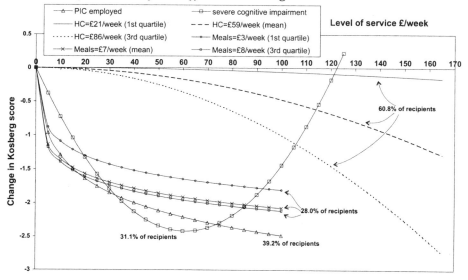

Day care likewise has large and well-established marginal productivities for the 39 per cent of users whose principal informal caregivers are in paid employment, although its marginal impact decreases as the amount of day care provided is increased.

Respite care likewise has substantial marginal productivities for recipients in some circumstances, figure 8.16 shows. The largest (and best established) marginal productivities are for the 54 per cent of users whom the care managers perceive to be cognitively impaired. For the group as a whole, marginal productivities continue to rise slightly at successively higher levels of input, but at a diminishing rate. For the 19 per cent of users whom the care managers considered to be more reliant on caregivers than others in the same circumstances, the marginal productivity is estimated to be substantial, and does not diminish over the whole range of input levels. For them, the confidence interval is large, reflecting the low level of significance with which the effects are established.

Social work inputs during the continuing care phase are predicted to have clear and constant marginal productivities, as can be seen from figure 8.14. These powerful and well-established marginal productivities for long-run intensive social work input are also found in the models looking at some of the users measures of morale.

Figure 8.16
Productivity curves: respite care effect on Kosberg carer burden scale

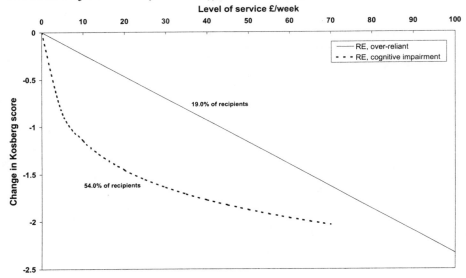

4.3. *Overall service impact, impact for groups, and equity and efficiency*

Figure 8.17 shows the effects of risk factors and service contributions on the user groups. It illustrates:

- The substantial size of the service contributions in relation to the impacts of the risk factors
- The way in which the scale of the service contributions is correlated with dependency, and so with the predicted impact of risk factors. Therefore it equalises the degree of caregiver burden between groups.

The impacts on the caregivers of the cognitively impaired are greater than the impacts on the caregivers of those of critical interval need; that is the benefits to the carers of the cognitively impaired are greater than to those of the physically handicapped.

Service impacts for all groups are large enough to make interesting a discussion of the relative influence of productivities and service levels on the pattern. The overall productivities of resources shown in figure 8.18 reveal different patterns depending on dependency or cognitive impairment.

- The average productivities of the overall packages of care are negatively correlated with dependency, and therefore with service contribution. This is compatible with an attempt to reduce caregiver burden most for cases where the burden is greatest, even though on average such cases enjoy the least benefit per unit of service.

Figure 8.17
Contributions of services and risk factors to Kosberg carer burden scale

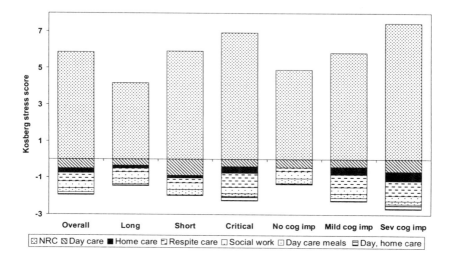

Figure 8.18
Average productivity for Kosberg carer burden scale for total package

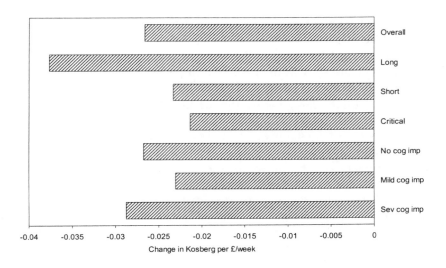

- By level of cognitive impairment, however, the highest average productivity is for users who are severely cognitively impaired. For these users, therefore, services are yielding the highest contributions at least partially because of the higher service productivities.

4.4.   Overview

The results show that:
- The model fits well, and yields several productivity effects which are significant at better than the 1 per cent level.
- Home care improves carer burden for caregivers of users predicted to be cognitively impaired by the Katzman score, and when allocated in conjunction with day care. Meals have an effect only in conjunction with day care. Day care has a large effect for the caregivers of the severely cognitively impaired up to the level of £60 per week, and an effect with increasing marginal productivities as inputs increase for caregivers in paid employment. Respite care likewise has substantial effects for caregivers in some circumstances. Social work has a clear, powerful and constant marginal productivity.
- Service contributions has substantial impacts on groups compared with those of risk factors. The service impacts approached caregiver burden scores between groups, service impacts increasing with the dependency of the user.

- Effects are particularly large for the caregivers of the cognitively impaired.
- The gradient by service contribution is due more to differences in the allocation of services to users, from different groups, than to differences in the productivities of inputs between groups.

9 Productivities for IMPREL and SATSOC Indicator Variables (Reduction in Social Exclusion and Improvement in Relationships)

Production functions were fitted for two outputs for users. One is focused on relationships with family and friends. The other is focused on the chances to socialise and meet people. Too few caregivers were employed to fit a model for the employment disadvantage caregiving scale.

1. Degree to which user considered social services to have improved how well user gets on with family and friends (IMPREL)

1.1. The model and the impact of risk factors

Goodness of fit. Table 9.1 shows that the dependent variable focuses directly on the perceived contribution of the social services. The model explained a low proportion of the variance of the dependent variable.

Impact of risk factors. There are three groups of risk factors affecting the improvement in relationships:

- Apparently influential *mental health indicators* include low morale as measured by the PGC lack of morale score, and the care managers' perception of user depression. Both factors are negatively associated with the output. That there is not a high degree of correspondence between morale scores and the reporting of low morale by the care manager in the ECCEP data has been shown elsewhere (Davies et al., 1997). This fits with results showing a massive under-recognition and treatment of clinical depression among recipients of pre-reform home care services in one authority (Banerjee, 1993; Banerjee and MacDonald, 1996).
- Other *health indicators* include users with cancer associated with less improvement in their relationships with family and friends. The degree of

Table 9.1
Production function for improvement in relationships with family/friends due to services

Predictors by domain	Coeff.	Prob.	%[1] Recip- ients	%[2] Users
Risk factors and other need-related circumstances				
General effects				
Mental health				
PGC lack of morale score – PGC	-.099	.034		
User is perceived to be depressed by CM – Wdepr	-1.449	.014		
Other health problems				
User has cancer – Wcancer	-1.951	.044		
Informal care related factors				
User has PIC – Wpic	1.993	.000		
Targeting-captured need effects				
User lives alone, user attends day care – Dc_alon	-1.798	.004		
Productivity effects (£ per week)				
Individual input effects				
Home care				
User belongs to critical interval need level (squared input) – Hc2_crit	7.23E-5	.087	23.5	19.8
Delivered meals			31.3	13.9
Day care			35.7	13.9
Respite care				
User discharged from hospital – Rec_fh	.069	.003	26.3	5.7
Nursing visits				
User belongs to long interval need level – Nvc_long	.026	.053	35.7	12.3
Complementarities				
Day care meals interaction – Dm_wcost	.003	.051	100	13.9
Constant	7.175	.000		

Adj. R^2 .198   Prob. .000   No. of cases 181

1 Proportion of recipients of the service to whom the effect applies
2 Proportion of the sample to whom the effect applies

physical incapacity of the user itself does not have a major direct effect, the stress caused by the user having cancer probably being more due to other factors than to the physical tending itself.

- *The presence of informal support.* The importance of this effect is further suggested by the targeting captured effect entitled 'user is chosen for day care and lives alone'.

1.2. Service productivities

The model at least hints at productivity effects for all of the principal services. The effect for *home care* for users with critical interval needs is significant only at the 9 per cent level. The marginal productivity is also low, figure 9.1 shows, but increases with the level of home care provided. This may relate to the fact that the construction of a relationship on which to base socialisation is best served by the provision of large and continued inputs. In such cases, formal workers become the very agent of socialisation. The effect was observed over a wide range of the service, and applied to one quarter of users.

The marginal productivity of *respite care* among those discharged from hospital is much greater among the 26 per cent of respite recipients affected: 6 per cent of the sample. The effect of nursing visits on the long interval need users had a lower marginal productivity, but covered a higher proportion of the users (approximately 12 per cent).

The effects of *home-delivered meals* and *day care* are interdependent. The greater the level of meals, the larger is the effect of increments of day care. Likewise, the larger the level of day care used, the higher is the effect of increased levels of meals provision. The effects are described in figure 9.2 and 9.3. The effects are powerful for quite modest packages. The marginal productivity exists for all the recipients of both services: one user of day care in three, one consumer of meals in three; some 14 per cent of the entire sample.

Figure 9.1

Productivity curves: home care, nursing visits and respite care effect on improvement in family/friends relations due to services

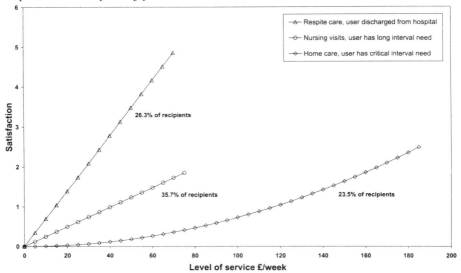

Figure 9.2
Productivity curves: meals effect on improvement in family/friends relations due to services

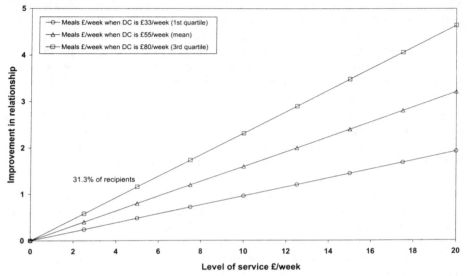

Figure 9.3
Productivity curves: day care effect on improvement in family/friends relations due to services

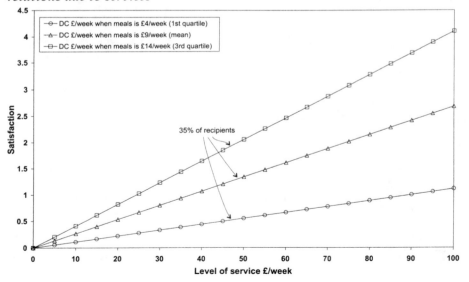

1.3. Overall service impact, impact for groups, and equity and efficiency

Overall, figure 9.4 shows the variation in the levels of services to play only a residual role in explaining the output variable.

- Whereas the service contributions are concentrated on the users with PICs, they are not big enough to compensate for the differences in the levels of outputs predicted by risk factors. Overall, therefore, users with PICs achieve higher levels of the output even after service contributions are taken into account.
- By level of dependency, it is those users with critical interval needs who enjoy the highest service contributions.
- Whereas most of the home care contributions are for users with critical interval needs, respite care inputs make a significant impact only for users with lower levels of needs.

That the overall contribution of the social services is small compared with the effects of the risk factors makes it unnecessary to investigate further the degree to which it is achieved by building on marginal productivities or by inputs of services with low productivities.

The greater improvement among critical interval cases, especially among those with principal informal caregivers, may reflect factors like the adjustment to shock among cases where the onset of disability was a sudden event. Also, for many of those without principal informal caregivers, kinship structures and other social networks may seem to care managers to be unpromising

Figure 9.4

Contributions of services and risk factors to improvement in relationships with family/friends due to services

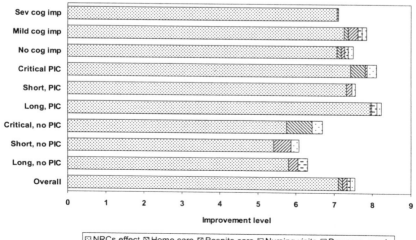

soil in which to achieve substantial gains. However, it is precisely the ground so successfully tilled by the Kent Community Care Project in its creation of quasi-informal care relationships (Davies and Challis, 1986).

1.4. Overview

Results show that:

- The model fits only to a limited extent the variation in the output variable, with all but one of the productivity effects significant at worse than the 1 per cent level. There is a weak productivity effect for home care, but stronger effects for respite care and nursing visits for substantial proportions of the recipients. The joint effect of meals with day care is powerful and applies to all recipients of both services.
- The service contribution is small compared with the impact of risk factors. The service contribution differs little between groups, though it is larger for those in critical interval need or those without PICs.

2.   Degree of satisfaction of user with chances to socialise and to meet people (SATSOC)

2.1. The model and the impact of risk factors

Goodness of fit. Although the model reaches a low coefficient of determination, table 9.2 shows that it is slightly more successful in accounting for the variance of the dependent variable than the alternative model in the present output dimension. Like the model for IMPREL, there are relatively few predictors with a high degree of significance.

Impact of risk factors. The question raised by the pattern of the associations between risk factors and the outcome is the degree to which the outcome is simply their correlate rather than their cause.

- That *physical disability* has little effect is interesting.
- The users who feel this output to be best attained are those initially of *high morale*, and (less clearly) with large amounts of *informal inputs* with housework.
- In contrast, users suffering from a high degree of anxiety (vexed by charging and highly concerned about the risk of institutionalisation) find it more difficult to profit from services in order to improve their chances to socialise and make friends. Alternatively, it may be that the nature of the needs of these users forces services to concentrate on achieving other goals with a relatively higher priority.

Targeting-captured group effects. The model describes two groups who do not score highly on this outcome. One consists of severely cognitively impaired users targeted for the receipt of day care. Clearly, they are unlikely to be able to

Table 9.2
Production function for improvement in chances to socialise and make friends

Predictors by domain	Coeff.	Prob.	%[1] Recipients	%[2] Users
Risk factors and other need-related circumstances				
General effects				
Mental health				
PGC lack of morale score – PGC	-.092	.000		
Informal care related factors				
Informal help with housework hrs/wk – nfhwk	.036	.073		
Other				
User against entry into residential care – Upercent	-.220	.001		
User is vexed by charging – Vexed	-.713	.030		
Targeting-captured need effects				
User is severely cognitively impaired and				
targeted for day care – Dc_kats	-.981	.039		
Number of PIC problems with caring, user targeted				
for day care – Dc_cpnb	-.179	.043		
Productivity effects (£ per week)				
Individual input effects				
Home care				
User in long interval need level – Hc2_long (squared)	5.7E-5	.015	47.4	39.9
Day care				
Day care – Ldc (log)	.091	.029	100.0	30.6
Nursing visits				
User has mild/sev cog impairment – Nvc_katm	.009	.056	29.4	9.7
Constant	5.448	.000		

Adj. R^2 .275   Prob. .000   No. of cases 209

1 Proportion of recipients of the service to whom the effect applies
2 Proportion of the sample to whom the effect applies

cope with life at home for long without much informal care inputs. However, cognitive impairment greatly increases the strain on the caregivers. For people in such circumstances, day care is unlikely to be centred on the achievement of satisfying socialisation. The other group is day care users whose caregivers face a large number of caring problems. Again, the main aim of services for these cases may be the relief of carer burden.

2.2. *Service productivities*

The productivities closely reflect the relationships between the risk factors in the model and the 'outcome'.

- Though significant only at the 1.5 per cent level, *home care* is estimated to have a high productivity for the 47 per cent who have only a low degree of dependency, cases of long interval need, as is illustrated in figure 9.5. The marginal productivities are higher the greater the input. Again, the construction of a relationship on which to base socialisation is not best served by small inputs for short periods of time.

- When the effects of cognitive impairment and the problems of principal informal caregiver are accounted for, *day care* appears to be productive, though the effect is significant at only the 3 per cent level. Figure 9.5 shows how the effects of the marginal increment diminish the higher is the level of input. Indeed, the diminishing returns are strong after the first weekly session (approximately £30 per week).

- Though the effect is less clearly established, *district nurse* visits to cognitively impaired people appear to increase the level of satisfaction with the opportunity to meet people, perhaps by extending the range of contacts by one. The range of inputs is too small for any diminishing returns to become evident.

Figure 9.5
Returns to factor: day care, home care and nursing visits effects on satisfaction with chances to meet people and socialise

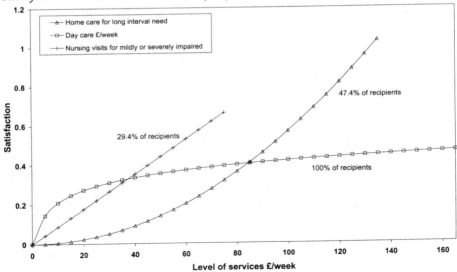

It is interesting that some of the inputs do not have productivities. Productivities for this output would not be expected, though would perhaps be hoped for, from respite care. More interesting is that the inputs of meals appear not to have an effect. Delivery practice is often to spend a minimal amount of time with the user, and to let it be known if the user holds up the process by being slow to answer the door, or prolongs the contact period. There are also the delivery technologies that involve restocking freezers. But it is often argued that one of the major contributions made by home-delivered meals is that they provide frequent social contact and social support.

2.3. Overall service impact, impact for groups, and equity and efficiency

Figure 9.6 shows that the users report their satisfaction with chances to meet people and to socialise to be on average much the same across groups. It is possible that the answers might reflect what is expected of the services as much as what they actually contribute. It also shows that there are only small service effects, save perhaps among the most severely cognitively impaired. Day care often plays a part in these small improvements. But the service effects are too small for an analysis of how it is produced to be worth while.

Figure 9.6
Contributions of services and risk factors to improvement in chances to socialise and confide

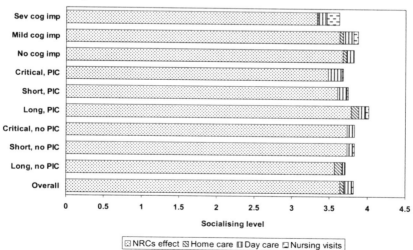

2.4. Overview

The results show that:

- The productivity effects are not highly significant. Home care appears to have high productivities at high service levels among those of long interval needs. Day care, in contrast, shows diminishing returns. There was a community nursing effect.
- Meals do not have a productivity effect. Less surprisingly, neither does respite care.
- The degree of satisfaction predicted is not greatly different between groups. Service contributions do little to equalise them, though perhaps more among the severely cognitively impaired than among others. Day care contributes to most groups.

10 Productivities for WKSAT Indicator Variable (Worker Perception of Impact)

Taking into account the evaluations of outcome of the care managers is important for two reasons: first, because their professional view has a legitimacy which is not removed by the commitment to user responsiveness and empowerment; and because apparent inconsistencies in perception demonstrate a need for the 'triangulation' of evidence — the comparison of results based on independent evidence.

The empirical evidence clearly shows the need to take separate account of care managers' views about outcomes. *Resources, Needs and Outcomes* (Davies et al., 1990) showed that the worker evaluation of the number of problems successfully tackled was not highly correlated with any of the other output indicators. ECCEP is showing how what the care manager described as the problems and circumstances of the case differed quite substantially from what users and caregivers describe (Davies et al., 1990; Davies, 1997; Bauld et al., 2000). The research reinforces other evidence that there is the need for a more standardised, protocol-driven performance of the core care management tasks advocated in *Matching Resources to Needs*, and which is now the basis for much technological development around the world (Davies and Challis, 1986; Davies, 1992a).

The indicator is 'care manager's perception of the degree of improvement in user's welfare due to social services help received' (WKSAT).

1. The model and the impact of risk factors

Goodness of fit. Table 10.1 shows that the model is highly significant although it explains only 24 per cent of the variance.

Impact of risk factors. The results shown in table 10.1 show a wide number of need-related circumstances and other risk factors to influence, in the care managers' view, the scope for improvements in the users' welfare.

Table 10.1
Production function for case manager's perception of the impact of services on user welfare

Predictors by domain	Coeff.	Prob.	%[1] Recipients	%[2] Users
Risk factors and other need-related circumstances				
General effects				
Physical disability				
User cannot prepare meals – Cantmeal	-.203	.056		
User is bedbound – Cantbed	-.364	.010		
Health problems				
Number of health problems – Whealth	.065	.028		
User suffers from cancer – Wcancer	-.346	.064		
Informal care related factors				
PIC is perceived to be stressed by CM – Wcstress	-.210	.050		
PIC's caring is due to love and affection – Clove	.406	.000		
PIC is employed – Cemploy	-.340	.008		
Other				
User's NRCs require short SSD intervention – Shortint	-.466	.024		
User is vexed by charging – Vexed	-.330	.091		
User receives palliative carePallcare	-1.460	.065		
Targeting-captured need effects				
Mild/sev cog impairment, user targeted for day care – Dc_Katm	-.624	.000		
User is over-reliant and targeted for day care – Dc_reli	-.518	.037		
User is perceived as high-risk and targeted for respite care – Re_hrsk	-.336	.054		
User lives alone and targeted for respite care – Re_walo	-.393	.009		
Productivity effects (£ per week)				
Individual input effects				
Home care				
Home care – Hc_wcost	.003	.001	100.0	85.5
Delivered meals			11.9	
Day care			80.7	33.7
PIC health pbs affect caringDcc_chaf	.014	.000	33.4	12.5
User lives alone – Ldc_ualo (log)	.090	.008	52.9	19.6
Respite care			65.3	24.2
Mild/severe cognitive impairment – Rec_katm	.006	.007	54.3	16.0
PIC is employed – Rec_cemp	.005	.070	22.1	7.5

Table 10.1 (continued)

Predictors by domain	Coeff.	Prob.	%[1] Recipients	%[2] Users
Complementarities				
Day care, respite care interaction, user cannot wash				
– Drc_wash	1.9 E-4	.000	56.3	11.5
Home care, meals interaction, high number of				
relational problems – Hmc_hrel	4.5 E-4	.057	11.9	4.2
Constant	2.672	.000		

Adj. R[2] .243   Prob. .000   No. of cases 319

1 Proportion of recipients of the service to whom the effect applies
2 Proportion of sample to whom the effect applies

- In the care manager's view, improvements in the welfare of users in the top of the distribution by physical *disability*, the bed-bound, and those unable to prepare meals.
- However, welfare improvements are more likely to be achieved by the services on average for users with health problems (apart from cancer): that is, the higher the degree of 'frailty' in the sense used by Strawbridge et al. (1998).
- The aspects of *informal caregiving* which are most associated with gain in welfare are relational and affective, rather than simply the presence of the informal caregiver, or the structure of the network. That the caregiver is in employment is in part a structural indicator, but reflects conflicting roles as caregiver and employee.

Targeting-captured group effects. Again, it is the two services that are most carefully targeted for which the effects exist.
- The effects pick out two groups of day care recipients for whom the benefits are likely to be enjoyed substantially, if not mainly, by principal informal caregivers: users who are predicted by the Katzman score to be cognitively impaired, and those who are thought by care managers to be more reliant than others in similar circumstances.
- The two groups of recipients of respite care are those without the buffering protection of having informal caregivers or others living with them, and those earlier judged by the care manager to be at high risk.

2.   Service productivities

The results show care managers to identify all the main social services with improvements in the welfare of most of the recipients of the inputs. The effects are shown in figures 10.1 to 10.4.

- Figure 10.1. shows care managers to consider increments of *home care* to have a small but clear effect on the welfare of user, with a constant marginal productivity over the entire range observed in the sample.

- *Home care and meals* inputs complement each other and yield significant improvements in welfare for users with relationship problems with their caregivers. Figures 10.1 and 10.2 describes the pattern.

- *Day care* inputs alone are shown by figure 10.3 to have a significant impact on the users welfare for users of high level of disability, those who cannot wash, and users who live alone. Whereas the former effect exhibits constant returns to scale, the latter is characterised by decreasing returns, that is a reduction in the marginal effect of additional inputs.

- The productivities for respite care are described in figure 10.4. Respite care appear to the care managers to have marginal productivities among those who are cognitively impaired, and among those whose principal informal caregiver is in paid employment. The marginal productivities are little different for these two groups, as is also illustrated in figure 10.4.

- As for home care and meal input, the marginal productivity of day care increases when provided with another input, respite care, among the 56 per cent of users of both services together who are unable to wash themselves.

Figure 10.1
Productivity curves: home care effect on care manager's perception of services' impact on user welfare

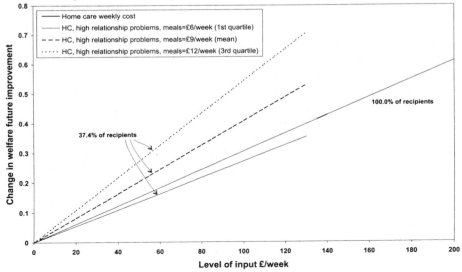

Figure 10.2
Productivity curves: meals effect on care manager's perception of services'
impact on user welfare

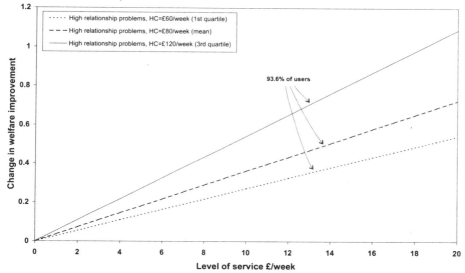

Figure 10.3
Productivity curves: day care effect on care manager's perception of
services' impact on user welfare

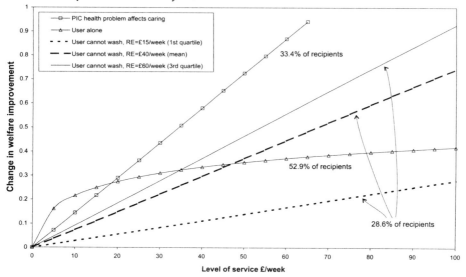

Figure 10.4
Productivity curves: respite care effect on care manager's perception of services' impact on user welfare

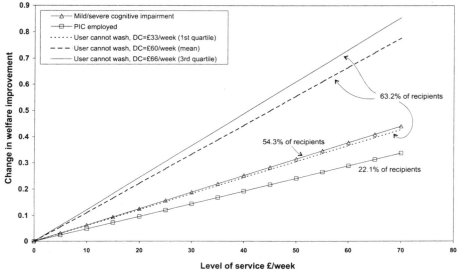

3.   **Overall service impact, impact for groups, and equity and efficiency**

Figure 10.5 shows that service impact is for some groups substantial in relation to the effects of risk factors.

- The service contributions increase with the level of dependency and/or cognitive impairment, and are greater for those with principal informal caregivers.

- Figure 10.6 shows that for overall packages, the average productivities are negatively correlated with the users' level of dependency and so with the level of service contributions.

- So the pattern of service contributions is produced by the greater concentration of services on the more dependent users than would be suggested by criteria based exclusively on efficiency grounds. In other words, the differences in service contributions cannot be due to the relative efficiencies of services between groups, but must be explained in terms of an equity prioritisation.

- On the other hand, figure 10.6 also shows that the productivities of services taken together are greater for users with principal informal caregivers, those for whom the service contributions are greater. So some of this difference in service contributions could be due to productivities, not to differences in service levels.

Figure 10.5
Contributions of services and risk factors to care manager's perception of services' impact on user welfare

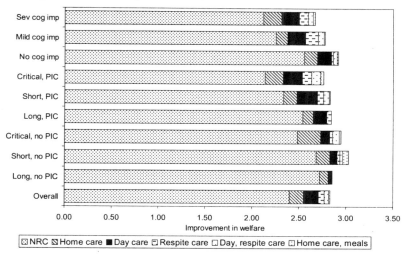

Figure 10.6
Average productivity for care manager's perception of services' impact on user welfare for total package

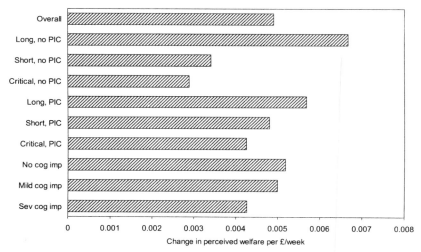

4.   Overview

Results show that:
- There are a number of productivity effects of high statistical significance, though the equation does not explain a high proportion of the overall variance.
- Home care has a small but clear effect for all recipients, and also an effect jointly with meals. There are several day and respite care effects, one when provided together.
- Service contributions to group averages are substantial compared with risk factors.
- Service contributions increase with dependency. This is due mainly to the concentration of progressively greater quantities of services as dependency is increased. However, service contributions are greater for those with principal informal caregivers. This difference is in part due to differences in service productivities.

11 Joint Supply in the Production System

The previous chapters have explored overall service productivities based on reduced form production function models, one output at a time. Potentially, however, gains in the levels of a given output may be affected by the levels of the remaining outputs. Therefore this chapter attempts to show the degree to which 'joint supply' takes place: that is, the extent to which the resources required to produce an increment in one output depends on the level of other outputs.

The study of joint supply further illuminates the path by which services affect outputs. Whereas some services may affect an output directly, others may do so indirectly through their effect on other variables. This is illustrated in figure 11.1, where inputs I_1, I_2 and I_3 and need-related circumstances (NRCs) are hypothesised to affect the levels of two output measures, O_1 and O_2. Although I_1 and I_3 have both direct effects on O_1 and O_2, I_2 only has a direct impact on O_1. However, because O_1 affects O_2, increases in the levels of I_2 will improve levels of O_2 through its direct effect on O_1. I_2 therefore has an indirect effect on O_2.

The practical importance of understanding joint supply is obvious. Whether and how outputs interrelate with each other influences the nature of strategies aiming to improve equity and efficiency. For instance the existence

Figure 11.1
Joint supply

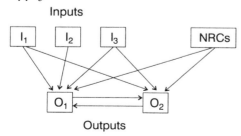

Inputs

I_1 I_2 I_3 NRCs

O_1 O_2

Outputs

of clear links between one output and several others may make it useful to designate it to be the central aim of the system. It is possible that packages of care designed in such a way as to maximise one output might produce high levels of other outputs also, because of the contributions made by the first output to producing the others.

What makes joint supply particularly important in a social care context is the multiplicity of potential objectives and their likely interrelation. Empirical estimation has frequently demonstrated their existence when the analyses have used model forms that allow them to be evident (Davies and Challis, 1986).

The contents of the remainder of the chapter are as follows:

- Section 1 describes the two alternative tools used for the analysis of joint supply, that is the cost function and the simultaneous production function. Section 1.1 relates the cost function and the production models of the kind used in chapters 4 to 10, and explains how it is often more convenient to diagnose joint supply by estimating the cost functions implicit in the underlying production function. Section 1.2 discusses the use of the more elaborate simultaneous equation production function.
- Section 2 exposes the results derived from both models. The results of the cost function and simultaneous production model are summarised in tables 11.1 and 11.2 respectively. Figure 11.2 summarises the main relations between service inputs and outputs, and between outputs themselves, given the simultaneous production function.
- Section 3 provides a short summary of the main results.

1.   Handling joint supply: cost function versus simultaneous production function

Reduced form production function models of the kind so far presented do not provide evidence about the nature of joint supply. For instance, following the example proposed in figure 11.1, a reduced form model for output O_2 would show significant productivities for I_2, and estimates of the effects of I_1 and I_3 would include their direct and indirect effects. If what we aim at is distinguishing the effects of individual services, and estimating the interrelationships between outputs, the analysis needs to treat all output variables in one single model. The present section describes two alternative ways of doing so: the cost function model and the simultaneous production function model.

1.1.   Cost function and joint supply

Cost functions are derived from the technological relationships implied by the production functions (Koutsoyiannis, 1979). In fact, duality theory in microeconomics shows that under particular assumptions (profit maximisa-

Table 11.1
Cost function model parameter estimates and significances

Predictors by domain	Coeff.	Prob.
Risk factors and other need-related circumstances		
General effects		
Physical disability		
Count of problems with ADL and IADL – WADL_IAD	3.221	0.007
Other health problems		
User has ulcerated legs or pressure sores – WULCER	27.068	0.007
Informal care related factors		
Total number user and PIC risks – WTOTRISK	5.350	0.000
Count of problems because PIC caring – CUPBNB	20.961	0.000
Balancing conflict between user and PIC is a problem – WCUCONFL	33.453	0.006
Outputs		
Individual output effects		
Days living at home prior to entering institutions squared – (DAYS)^2	0.0001	0.001
Improvement in ADL related states due to services – IMPADL	26.980	0.000
Improvement in IADL related states due to services squared – (IMPADL)^2	0.361	0.000
KOSBERG carer burden scale squared – (KOSBERG)^2	1.744	0.000
User felt control over own life score – IMPEMP	15.469	0.026
Dissatisfaction with life development squared – (DLD)^2	24.754	0.012
Satisfaction with level of services squared – (USATISF)^2	73.120	0.000
Joint supply effects		
Improvement in ADL related states due to services and dissatisfaction with life development – IMPADLDLD	-17.891	0.000
Improvement in user felt control over own life and improvement in IADL related states due to services – IMPIADL	-2.170	0.057
Days living at home prior to entering institutions and Kosberg carer burden score – DAYSKOSBERG	-0.011	0.071
Kosberg carer burden scale and satisfaction with level of services – KOSBERGUSATISF	-10.754	0.003
Constant	-32.869	0.000

Adj. R^2 0.738   Prob. 0.000

Table 11.2
Joint supply effects from simultaneous equations production function

	Dependent variables													
	DAYS		DLD		KOSBERG		USATISF		IMPADL		IMPIADL		IMPEMP	
Predictors	coeff	sig.	coeff	sig.	coeff	sig.	coeff	sig.	coeff	sig.	coeff	sig.	coeff	sig.
DAYS														
DLD									0.38	0.00				
KOSBERG	0.11*	0.01												
USATISF					0.46**	0.05								
IMPADL			0.00	0.01										
IMPIADL														
IMPEMP														

* Kosberg carer stress squared
**Log of USATISF

Figure 11.2
Simultaneous equations production function: productivities and joint supply

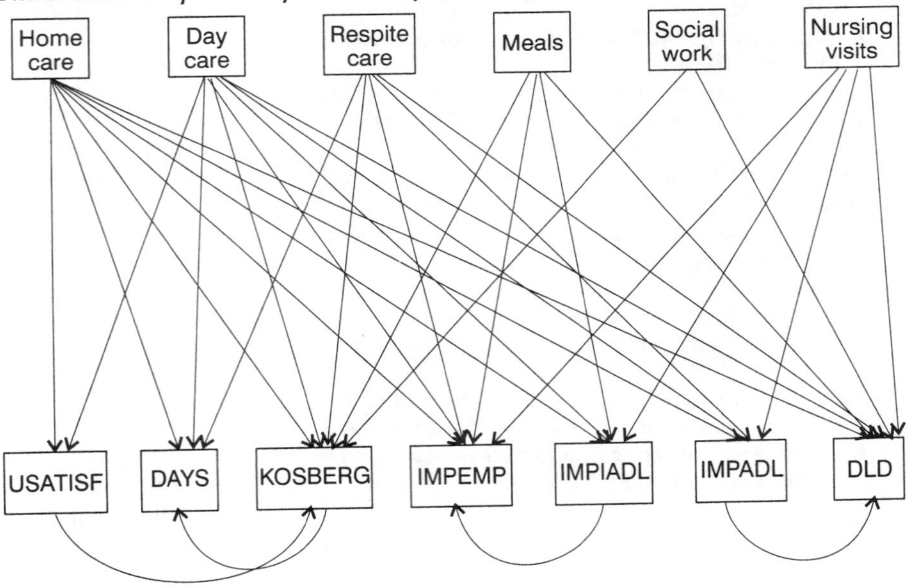

tion or cost minimisation), the estimates of production and costs functions can be derived from one another (Shephard, 1970; Fuss and McFadden, 1978).

Given their similarities, it is not surprising that both cost and production functions are able to reveal many of the features of the production process. For instance, increasing or decreasing returns to scale in production functions (increasing or decreasing marginal productivities of inputs) are equivalent to, respectively, decreasing or increasing marginal costs of outputs in cost functions. Differences in the productivities of inputs will be reflected in the cost function, but as differences in the costs of outputs. Like good production functions, cost functions need to account for the impact that NRCs have both directly on costs, and indirectly through their effect on the cost of outputs. This is because the cost of achieving particular outputs is likely to be higher; for instance, for those that are most disabled. However, cost functions do not need to include terms to control the targeting-captured need effects mentioned in chapter 3 because they deal with the sum of all service input costs.

In mathematical notation, the cost function to be estimated is of the form:

$$C = \alpha + \Sigma i\ \beta i\ Si + \Sigma j\ \delta j\ O_j + \Sigma_j \Sigma_k\ \lambda_{ik}\ O_j\ O_k$$

where C represents overall cost of package; O_j represents the level of output j; and S_j represents the need-related circumstance j. The presence of joint supply effects is revealed by the existence of significant effects of the $O_j\ O_k$ terms.

Despite the similarities between production and cost functions, their foci are different. Cost functions specifically map the relationship between resources and each and every output in one single model, and are therefore a convenient device for discovering the existence of joint supply.

However, and even though they reveal the existence of joint supply, they do not provide the complete information about it that is required for our argument. In particular, they do not reveal the direction of the influence of the level of one output on the costs of another. For instance, they do not show whether the production of a high level of users' morale makes it cheaper to produce improvements in their ability to perform ADL tasks; on the contrary, the production of a high level of ability to perform ADL tasks reduces the additional cost of an improvement in morale; or both, a higher level of each output reducing the cost of increasing the other.

1.2. *Simultaneous production function models and joint supply*

A simultaneous production function model differs from the reduced form production functions explored, so far in that outputs are hypothesised also to depend on other measures of outputs. Like cost functions, a simultaneous production function treats all output variables in one single model, and is therefore able to detect the presence of joint supply. In contrast to the cost function, the simultaneous equation production function fully reveals the joint supply effects. In other words, it not only reveals the presence of joint supply effects between pairs of outputs, but also the direction of the effects.

In the present case, the production function model constructed has the following general specification.

$$O_1 = f(DC,HC,M,RE,SW,NV,O_2,O_3,\ldots,O_7,e_1)$$
$$O_2 = f(DC,HC,M,RE,SW,NV,O_1,O_3,\ldots,O_7,e_2)$$

....

$$O_6 = f(DC,HC,M,RE,SW,NV,O_1,O_2,\ldots,O_7, e_6)$$
$$O_7 = f(DC,HC,M,RE,SW,NV,O_1,O_2,\ldots,O_6, e_7)$$

where O_1 to O_7 represent seven output measures, DC, HC, M, RE, SW and NV represent respectively the levels of day care, home care, meals, respite care, social work, and nursing visits and e_1 to e_7 represent the error terms in the seven equations.[1]

However, such models are notoriously difficult to estimate, as they handle simultaneously a necessarily substantial number of equations relating to a set of important objectives.

Given the easier estimation of the cost function, and the fact that it allows us to identify more readily the existence of joint supply, the estimation will therefore use the results implied by the cost function in the specification of the simultaneous production model.

2.   Analysis of results

2.1. *Joint supply relationships reflected in the cost function*

There are choices to be made in the model description of the system. Like painters, modellers have to balance figurative detail (with its dangers of leaving the reader unable to see the wood for the trees), and abstraction (with its danger of leaving the reader with a characterisation so general, as to have little relationship to the reality which it is the purpose to understand and manage). A description based on the 17 outputs would be too complex to be of most help. There would be little gain to the policy-making reader for the description to include outputs for which the production function did not work well, and for which the service contributions offset little of the effect of risk factors. The choice made has been to describe the system in terms of a handful of outputs for which the risk offset proportions (the extent to which the effects of services offset the effect of the need-related circumstances) shown in chapter 12 (below) are highest, but which are also broadly representative of the broad domains of outcomes shown in table 2.1 (page 33).

The seven output variables used in the estimation of the cost function were therefore: days living at home prior to entering institutions (DAYS), improvement in ADL-related states due to services (IMPADL), improvement in IADL-related states due to services (IMPIADL), the scale measuring the felt burden of caregiving (KOSBERG), user felt control over own life score (IMPEMP), dissatisfaction with life development score (DLD), and satisfaction with the level of services provided score (USATISF). Worker satisfaction has not been included. It was felt that only user- and PIC-related output measures should be used.

The output measures used in the cost function modelling are restricted to the share of the variance in the original output measure that is attributed (by the reduced form production functions) to the effect of the services. For instance, the measure of the length of stay in the community employed in the cost function is not the total observed length of stay in the community, but the share that is imputable to the effect of the packages of care provided. This device allows an easier interpretation of the results, since the output measures are net of the influence that NRCs and other risk factors have on them, but nevertheless represent the overall effect of inputs, that is, the sum of direct and effects.

The results of the estimation of the cost function model are summarised in table 11.1. The model fits well.

Joint supply effects. A main aim in fitting a cost function is to suggest what joint supply effects exist.

- There is a clearly determined joint supply effect between improvement in the performance of personal care activities of daily living (IMPADL) and the dimension of morale indicating dissatisfaction with life development (DLD). That is, high levels of IMPADL and of DLD are associated with lower costs of (further) improving either.
- The joint supply effect between DAYS and the indicator for felt burden of caregiving is significantly greater than zero at the .071 level, but there is a more clearly determined joint supply effect between the indicator for the field burden of caregiving and USATISF, the indicator of user satisfaction. This suggests that reducing the sense of burden among caregivers is more likely to lower the cost of additional days spent in their own homes by users with PICs than the opposite. It also raises the possibility that a strategy directed at reducing the caregivers' sense of burden might also yield both an extension in the length of stay of users in their own homes and improve users' satisfaction with services. This result is therefore important.
- High levels of improvement in the performance of household and other instrumental activities (IMPIADL) and high levels of improvement in users' sense of control over their own lives (IMPEMP) are associated with cheaper improvements in either.
- During the modelling another two pairs of variables nearly entered the model: improvement in ADL-related states and dissatisfaction with life development and days living at home prior to entering institutions; and days living at home prior to entering institutions and dissatisfaction with life development score.

Main marginal cost effects. The importance of these terms is (a) that they demonstrate whether there are separable marginal costs for all the outputs or whether there is such collinearity between them that this is not possible; and (b) they take a still broader view of returns to scale than do the reduced form production functions so far considered.

- Marginal cost estimates are yielded for all the topic outputs used in the efficiency analysis of chapters 13 to 20, with all but one of the seven main effects significant in excess of zero at the 1 per cent level, and all significant at the 5 per cent level.
- Five of the main output effects, the main marginal cost terms, have a quadratic (squared) form, reflecting the diminishing returns shown by the reduced form production functions of earlier chapters.
  These results are however not altogether surprising, given that the output estimates are derived from the results of the reduced form production functions.

Risk factors and need-related circumstances

- As with the reduced form production functions, the results imply that the perceptions and circumstances of caregivers are more important than that oft-quoted surrogate for stress and excessive input, informal caregiving hours. Modelling has shown informal caregiving hours to predict outcomes in studies in France and the USA; most recently by Davies, Fernández and Saunders, 1998, 129; and Benjamin et al., 1998, II, appendix D, tables D-2, D-5, and D-14). But as has generally been the case in British production of welfare studies where indicators of hours compete as predictors of utilisation or outcomes with the more direct indicators of circumstances, feelings and relationships, the latter prove more powerful predictors (Davies et al., 1990).

2.2. *Results of the simultaneous equation model*

The model is estimated using the 3SLS estimation technique (see Greene, 1993, p.611). This is firstly because the model needs to be estimated simultaneously as a system of seven equations, given the presence of endogenous explanatory variables and the potential non-recursivity of the model (see Koutsoyiannis 1977, 331); and secondly, because the error terms of the equations in the model (e_1 to e_7) are likely to be correlated. For instance, users with higher morale than average may also have a higher functional capacity.

As in the case of the cost function, the 3SLS model uses as measures of output only the proportions of the variance in the observed output measures that are attributable to the effect of the packages of care.

The results are too complicated to state fully in a text table, because the form of the simultaneous model reflects the forms discovered in estimating the reduced form functions as well as the cost function. However, the results are summarised in figure 11.2 and the coefficients describing the strength of joint supply effects are stated in table 11.2.

The figure illustrates two sets of features. One is the pattern of joint supply. However, it also indicates the directions of causality underlying the joint supply.

- The simultaneous equation model confirms the pattern of joint supply revealed by the cost function model.
- In no case did arrows connecting outputs point in both directions. That is, there are no examples of reciprocal causation between outputs. The direction of the arrows is of obvious policy importance.

The other feature is the pattern of direct productivity effects of service inputs. The overall effects are captured by the reduced form models and so have already been reported. The indirect effects can be seen in the figure by following arrows from the service inputs through one output to other outputs.

- In the full structural simultaneous equation model, two service inputs, home care and day care, affect all the seven outputs.
- At the other extreme, social work has direct productivity effects only for the reduction in felt burden of caregiving, and dissatisfaction with life development. Other effects described in the reduced form functions are indirect. Because social work inputs have a productivity for the reduction of caregiver stress, it is possible for it indirectly to affect DAYS also. However, this effect is not strong enough for the reduced form model to capture it.
- Home-delivered meals do not have productivity effects for DAYS, USATISF, and IMPADL, but do for DLD, a dimension of morale. This kind of effect has long been claimed for the service.

The importance of table 11.2 is that it shows the relative clarity and strength of the joint supply effects shown in the figure. The most intriguing set of effects are those connecting user satisfaction with services (USATISF) with the reduction in caregiver's felt burden (KOSBERG), and KOSBERG with longer stays by users in their own homes (DAYS). The coefficient for the effect of KOSBERG on DAYS is well determined, much better determined than in the cost function, where the measure is of the net influence of effects in either direction and so more ambiguous. The effect of USATISF on KOSBERG is less well determined than the more ambiguous estimate from the cost function, but nevertheless significantly greater than zero at about the 5 per cent level.

Other joint supply effects are well determined.

3.   Summary

For simplicity's sake, the analysis of joint supply has been restricted to seven outputs with high service contributions relative to the effects of need-related circumstances. Among them they cover most of the output dimensions listed in chapter 2.

The estimation of the cost function and of the simultaneous equation production function model identifies significant evidence of joint supply effects between the following pairs of output variables:

- user satisfaction with the level of services on carer burden score
- carer burden score on days spent in the community

- user perceived level of improvement in IADL tasks due to services on user level of control over own life
- user perceived level of improvement in ADL tasks due to services on user level of morale

Although none of the seven outputs postulated reveals itself as central to the achievement of most of the others, the results nevertheless raise important questions.

First, they identify the link between improvements in functioning (IADL and ADL tasks) and subsequent improvements in morale: perception of control over own life and reduction in dissatisfaction with life development.

Second, they raise the possibility that improvements on the user length of stay in the community may be achieved through interventions aiming to reduce the level of PIC caring burden. This result is particularly important given that improvements in PICs' and users' welfare may be perceived as conflicting objectives, the attainment of one objective being thought to be, for most families, at the expense of one another. That the opposite is on average the case raises the question whether with investment, the two outputs could be made even more complementary.

However, the importance of the direct service effects is clear even in the simultaneous production function. Given that the overall effect of services are the sum of their direct and direct effects, whether outputs such as DAYS and KOSBERG should be perceived as complementary or conflicting still depends on the extent to which the direct effects of services offset the interrelation between the two outputs.

This constitutes one of the main themes of Part II of the book.

Note

1   Each equation in the simultaneous equation system was over-identified by the rank and order criteria. Not all indicators of service inputs and other endogenous variables appeared in all models, and most of the selected indicators referred to subgroups, with different subgroups being relevant for equations for different outputs.

12 Service Productivities: the Main Patterns

Chapter 1 stated that one of the most important purposes of estimating a production function is to derive what amount to hypotheses, by detailed description of the effects of service inputs and markers for risk factors, alone and in combination with one another. The first section of this chapter shifts up the level of generality of the discussion by outlining the main patterns with respect to input scale effects, the evidence of complementarity and substitutability between services, and differences in productivities between users.

The second section also generalises more broadly. It does so by summarising the pattern of service contributions: the impact of services, given productivities and the distribution of inputs. The analysis focuses on (a) the overall success of packages in improving outputs, (b) the relative merit of the different services in explaining the overall output gains, and (c) how the distribution of service contributions between analysis groups relate to average productivities of services for members of the groups.

1. Productivity patterns

1.1. Scale effects

Table 12.1 contains a count of the number of productivity effects for each of the broad services for all 17 outputs. The three forms of variation in returns to scale distinguished earlier are the focus: diminishing, constant, and increasing returns. Joint effects, reflecting the complementarity of services in the production of an outcome, are attributed to (and counted for) both services.[1] The small number of terms implying negative productivities has not been counted. The table shows that:

- Home, day and respite care have the largest number of effects. Overall, home care inputs are found to improve the outcome for all 17 output measures, day care inputs for 15 and respite care inputs for 13. Then follow meals on wheels, nursing visits and social work inputs, which affect nine, eight and four out of the 17 output measures respectively.

Table 12.1
Number and nature of service productivity effects

Service	Equations affected	Increasing returns		Constant returns		Diminishing returns	
	Number	Number	Per cent	Number	Per cent	Number	Per cent
Home care	17	7	28	7	28	11	44
Meals	9		0	7	70	3	30
Day care	15	2	7	9	33	16	59
Respite care	13	3	12	15	60	7	28
Social work	4		0	3	75	1	25
Nursing visit	8		0	7	64	4	36
Total		12	12	48	47	42	41

- By far the most common types of effects are those showing either diminishing or constant returns to scale. But their prevalence differs between services. Whereas diminishing returns to scale effects account for the highest proportion of day care and home care productivities, over half of the effects for the rest of the services show constant returns to scale. This should be unsurprising for services such as meals on wheels or social work inputs, allocated over limited ranges and therefore less likely to show more intricate productivity patterns.
- Only 12 per cent of the effects show some signs of increasing returns. Though many of the effects for home care suggest diminishing returns, it is also the case that home care has the majority of effects with increasing returns. That most of them refer to home care is not surprising. Home care has been traditionally allocated as the core input for most care packages, only to be complemented by other services such as day or respite care. In the current sample, for instance, home care was provided as the only service for approximately one third of cases, and made up on its own almost half the care package cost of the average case. Being the core service in many packages of care, it may well be necessary for home care inputs to be allocated in large quantities for them to produce improvements in outputs such as for example the reduction of carer stress or user satisfaction with services. The provision of high quantities of home care inputs may for instance encourage stronger emotional and affective links between the home care worker and the user of the services, hence decreasing isolation and improving morale.

1.2. *Complementarity and substitutability*

It has been argued that the potential substitutability of service inputs is one of the defining characteristics of community and long-term care compared with many acute interventions. The question has always been whether this substitution potential has been realised in managing service content and mix (Davies, 1995; Davies and Challis, 1986). As predicted from that theory, our evidence suggests a very high degree of substitutability between services. For instance, that many care packages for persons of quite different circumstances consist of only one service suggests that allocators believe that each can produce a variety of outputs. The questions are (a) what range and levels of outputs can be produced from a single service as well as (b) what combinations can be produced from what input mixes. The former question is interesting because having fewer workers with wider spans of output goals from a single service offers potential benefits as well as potential economies.

Table 12.2 reports that in all equations, at least two services have significant productivities when inputted on their own. Moreover, the effects are most often general enough for them simultaneously to affect many users. Only seven out of the 17 equations included any sign of complementarity between services. The evidence is summarised in table 12.2.

Table 12.2
Presence of complementarity effects

	Meals	Day care	Respite care	Social work	Nursing visit	Total
Home care	2	1				3
Meals		2			1	5
Day care			2		1	6
Respite care						2
Social work						0
Nursing visit						2

Table 12.2 presents a count of the complementarity effects between the six services investigated and shows that:

- Day care and meals on wheels are the two inputs most usually showing complementarity with other services. In fact, all nine complementarity effects involve one or other of the two services.
- Day care inputs show evidence of complementarity with all services but social work inputs. The evidence of complementarity is particularly strong for meals and respite care.
- Meals on wheels inputs show evidence of complementarity predominantly with day care and home care inputs, but also with nursing visits.
- None of the complementarity effects affects social work inputs. However, this may be due to their much smaller range of provision.

To conclude: (a) the productivity effects of services tend to be independent of the input levels for other services; (b) the issue is whether simple care packages would also be the most efficient, given the potential gains from avoiding care packages with too many workers and services.

1.3. Differences in marginal productivities between user groups

Table 12.3 lists all the factors found to have differentiated marginal productivity effects. The numbers inside it represent the count of the times that the factors are found to alter productivities for a given service. The last column sums the total number of effects per factor.

General patterns. Table 12.3 shows that most of the service productivities are best described as being specific to subgroups. Overall, only 14 per cent of the effects are common to all recipients of the service. That supports the arguments of chapter 1.

Chapters 1 and 3 described how the analysis strategy was to use the modelling to describe the production relations in detail, restricting the range of risk factors only for theoretical or statistical reasons. Appendix table 2.2 (page 421) presents a substantial list of potential markers whose effects were explored.

In spite of this, table 12.3 shows that it is actually a small number of factor types that are the markers of the groups to which the productivity effects apply.

One aspect of the existence of a fuzzy underlying pattern which is simpler than our more precise statistical description is that most of the markers were found to be the best discriminants in several equations. (a) Most of the variables found to differentiate marginal productivities between users are found to do so in several equations or for several services. (b) Overall, only 7 per cent of the effects are not found repeated, the others recurring on average almost four times. (c) Seven out of the 22 factors recur at least five times, with variables such as 'user lives alone' recurring seven times, and 'interval need' or 'cognitive impairment' recurring 11 and 13 times respectively.

Additionally, most of the factors affect several of the service inputs. (a) Only six of the 22 factors affect the productivities for only one of the services. (b) Six factors affect the marginal productivities of at least three out of the six services, despite the few effects found for meals and social work inputs. (c) The two factors whose effects are most widespread are 'user lives alone' and 'user is cognitively impaired', which affect respectively the marginal productivities of four and five of the six services.

Also, what distinguishes the disability-related discriminants is the threshold which is statistically most efficient in discriminating population groups. They are not different in kind, merely in degree. And *natura non facit saltum*: the variation in the productivity effects are likely to differ in degree between disability levels rather than to be actually restricted to the group to which the productivity is attributed.

Table 12.3
Differences in marginal productivities: discriminating factors

Nature of indicator	Home care	Meals	Day care	Respite care	Social work	Nursing inputs	Total
Dependency							
High number of problems with ADL tasks			3	3			6
Interval need	6	3				2	11
User cannot buy groceries on their own		1					1
User cannot do heavy housework tasks	1				2		3
User cannot go to toilet on their own	1	1					2
User cannot wash on their own			1	2			3
Mental health							
Behavioural problems			1	2			3
Cognitive impairment	4	1	3	2		3	13
Health problems							
Skeletal muscular problems	1					1	2
User discharged from hospital			2	5			7
User had stroke			1				1
Informal care / informal networks							
Presence of PIC	2					1	3
PIC is close female relative	2	1	1				4
PIC is employed			2	1			3
User is married			2	4			6
PIC health affects caring role			1			1	2
PIC is stressed						1	1
PIC loses sleep due to worry				1			1
Relational problems	2	1		2			5
Mediating							
User is heavily reliant on others				1			1
User lives alone	4		1		1	1	7
User against entry into residential care						1	1
Common effect for all recipients	2	2	7	1	1	1	14

Pattern across services. Table 12.3 shows that:

• For some services, differences in productivities are clearly associated with few factors. For instance, for home care and respite care (two of the services with greatest number of productivities), most of the differences in productivities are linked with three factors. For home care, they are interval

need, cognitive impairment and living alone. For respite care, they are a high number of problems with ADL tasks, user discharged from hospital, and user is married.
- There are important similarities in the variation of marginal productivities for two pairs of services: home care and meals (the more 'traditional' services), and day and respite care (the 'newer' ones). That is, most of the factors influencing productivities for home care also do so for meals, and most that affect productivities for day care productivities also affect them for respite care.

2.   Pattern of contribution given observed allocations

2.1. Package contributions across outputs

The modelling identified marginal productivity effects for all final outputs. Between them, they spanned many of the principal domains and effects for which users, caregivers and society value the public subsidy to community care. Comparisons of service contributions are made with two new performance indicators: *Risk Offset Proportion from Productivity effects (ROPPs)* and *Cover of Productivity Proportions (COPPs)*.

Risk Offset Proportion from Productivity effects. A ROPP measures the degree to which the effects of risk factors are offset by service impacts. It is the proportion of the total effect of risk factors and service inputs predicted by each of the production function models that are offset by the service contributions.[2]

Though a ROPP is an important measure of performance, we lack the evidence to interpret its value.
- Exactly what order of magnitude of ROPP constitutes good performance is difficult to specify. It is likely to vary between outputs. We do not know of other applications of an indicator equivalent to the ROPP, and so of a literature with which to compare our results. The judgement about the adequacy of performance should depend on the degree of irremovability or irresistibility of the risks. The lower the degree to which the factors are resistible or removable, the better the performance implied by an offset proportion of a given magnitude.
- The ROPP is an average. The effect of service contributions is often likely to be great on a minority of beneficiaries, much smaller for the majority.
- The ROPP is not the only indicator of the effect of services, and should be interpreted in the context of the others.

Cover of Productivity Proportion. COPPs measure the proportion of the entire sample affected by the productivity effects. Targeting questions would be raised if service contributions, however large, were limited to small minorities of users and caregivers.

Figure 12.1 summarises ROPPs and COPPs for the 17 output measures. The outputs are arranged from left to right in descending order of ROPP. One can distinguish between three groups.

Figure 12.1
Proportional contribution of formal care and proportion of users affected

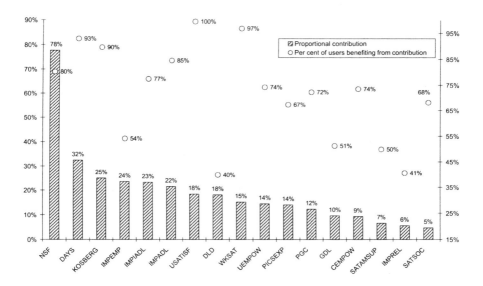

2.1.1. Outputs with high and medium offset proportions

The first consists of the single variable labelled NSF: the *user's count of unmet needs for help with functional areas covered by community social services.* Chapter 6 expressed misgivings about the meaning that could be attached to shortfall judgements as the basis of output indicators, despite the distinguished provenance of the approach. Some of the interpretative difficulties explain the extremely high offset proportion. But the big service contribution cannot be considered irrelevant to the evaluation of post-reform productivities.

The second group consisted of seven outputs (DAYS, KOSBERG, IMPEMP, IMPADL, IMPIADL, USATISF, DLD) for which the offset proportions varied between 32 and 18 per cent. In this group there were representatives of all domains except for the one about care manager judgements about service contributions.

Among the seven outputs, it was for DAYS, *the number of days living at home prior to admission to an institution for long-term care,* that the service contributions had the highest ROPP. An effect that accounts for 32 per cent of the predicted variable level suggests substantial success, since no one can doubt the power and uncontrollability of many of the medical and social factors causing admission to institutions. There were productivity effects for 93 per cent of users: a very high COPP, given the diversity in the goals of provision. The apparent success by this criterion is particularly important because, as chapter 2 showed, the commitment to this goal implicit in chapter 1 of the 1989 White Paper was matched by the high priority which managers at all levels in all authorities had attached to it during the period which most affected the study cohort. Therefore these high ROPPs and COPPs are of great evaluative importance.

The indicator with the second greatest ROPP was KOSBERG, *the indicator of reduction in the felt burden of caregiving.* A ROPP of 25 per cent would seem creditable, given the irresistibility and immovability of some of those risk-generating factors. The COPP was 90 per cent. Success by this criterion too is of obvious importance in the policy context. Without it, there would be serious misgivings about one of the most fundamental aspects by which the equity of the system would be judged. Again, the estimated values for ROPP and COPP appear to be of great evaluative significance.

Empowerment, choice and control (IMPEMP) were important themes of the reform policy in the age of Griffiths and the White Paper. They had long been important canons of the values of the caring professions. It was on average ranked second by the 133 ECCEP managers. There was a lower cover of 90 per cent, and a substantial offset effect of 24 per cent. Whether 24 per cent for this output is equivalent in performance for the same scale proportion for such variables as DAYS depends on the judgement about the irresistibility and irremovability of the factors depressing the sense of empowerment. (The variable was based on control over the whole of life, not just over areas at which the services are most directly aimed.) Perhaps there might be more cause for concern about the cover than about the offset proportion.

Two other output indicators measure *improvements in areas of functioning related to what the community services do ascribed by the user to the social services.* One related to personal care functions, IMPADL; the other to instrumental activities, IMPIADL. The offset proportions were similar and substantial: 22 and 23 per cent. The cover proportions were high, particularly for IMPADL. Chapters 2 and 6 discussed how the variables are likely to reflect subjective interpretations and small environmental changes as well as changes in actual capacity, and how the former were more likely to be directly influenced by community social services themselves. So both the offset and cover proportions may well be judged creditable, though for these as for other indicators, it would be important to have evidence allowing a comparison of performance for similar indicators.

The productivity effects for USATISF, the *degree of satisfaction of user with the level of service being received,* covers the entire sample. At first sight, it would seem arguable that with adequate resourcing, authorities could set higher target offsets for the output than 18 per cent. However, chapter 5 argued that the risk factors seemed to be related to low morale, and the perception of service adequacy could well be depressed among the demoralised. And in Parts III and IV, we shall see that such policy propositions must take other factors into account.

Dissatisfaction with life development, DLD, had a cover proportion of 40 per cent, much lower than for the other models. Combined with a substantial overall offset effect, the service contribution was large for those who benefited. Chapters 2 and 8 discussed the context of DLD, the converse of self-actualisation, in social work literature and values. The results showed the productivity of social work inputs. Perhaps the cover proportion directly reflects the extensiveness in provision of qualified social work inputs.

2.1.2. Outputs with low offset and cover proportions

Care managers believed that the services benefited almost everyone. However, it is not obvious that the offset proportion for WKSAT, the *care manager's perceptions of the degree of improvement in user's welfare due to social services help received*, is high. Chapter 10 shows how the bigger service effects are for groups for whom the productivities of services are judged by the care managers to be least, no doubt because concentrating more resources on the more dependent underlies the equity judgements reflected in allocations. The offset proportion is low, partly because equity judgements cause services to be allocated to those for whom productivities are judged to be low.

Perhaps at first sight, higher offset and cover proportions could be expected from *users' felt empowerment/influence during the set-up stage of care management*, UEMPOW. Chapter 7 showed how the risk factors reflect general morale, informal care and support, and dependency. Respondents' answers seemed to have been affected by the immovable and irreversible, as well as by social services process. Perhaps the cover rather than the offset proportion might be the focus for improvement.

The results reported in chapters 5 and 7 suggest that the same may be true for CEMPOW, *principal informal caregivers' felt empowerment/influence during the set-up stage of care management*, and PICSEXP, the *degree to which the principal informal caregiver's experience of the social services was favourable during the six months of the COCA period*. Caregivers' degree of satisfaction with amount and type of support from the services to help them look after the user, SATAMSUP, likewise had a low offset ratio. Again, the answers are coloured by risk factors that are not likely to be greatly affected by the services. But its cover ratio was much lower. The low ratios for this and for CEMPOW qualifies the interpretation we should put on the ratios for the Kosberg carer burden score.

The ratios for the indicator of *overall lack of morale*, the PGC score, have the opposite pattern from DLD, discussed above. The model for the PGC score produced a high cover but a low offset proportion. A low offset proportion is not surprising. The discussion of risk factors in chapter 8 illustrated the intractability of the factors that influence scores. General morale is sometimes affected by services, as in the intensive Kent Community Care Project and some of its replications. But often it is not. DLD is arguably more closely related to the objectives of good counselling and casework, and more amenable to influence by it, since it invites the evaluative reinterpretation of how one relates to reality rather than the evaluation of a deeply dissatisfying reality itself. *General dissatisfaction with life*, GDL, has much the same offset proportion, but a much lower cover proportion. The same comments apply as to the comparison of the results for general morale with Dissatisfaction with Life Development.

The two equations with the lowest offset ratios are from the same domain: reduction of social exclusion and improvement in socialisation and relationships. The proportions for SATSOC, *users' degree of satisfaction with chances to socialise and to meet people*, may not be disappointing. Perhaps, also, the low proportions for IMPREL, the *degree to which the user considered social services to have improved how the user gets on with family and friends*, are not surprising. For many, the relationships with family and friends are already too good to be greatly bettered, and some of the risk factors described in chapter 9 could not easily be offset by services.

2.1.3. Overview

The services achieve high offset and cover ratios for some of the outputs whose policy importance is central to the reforms. These include the number of days supported in the community prior to residential admission, the reduction of carer stress score, the perceived impact of social services on functioning in areas related to services' tasks, and general satisfaction with services. There are others of great importance for which the cover proportion is only slightly lower. An examination of the risk factors suggests their intractability for many users. Examples are the indicator of the sense of control over life, and dissatisfaction with life development. However, there are others for which the ratios are less satisfactory. The results for some of these qualify the impression derived from the proportions for the outputs with the highest offset and cover proportions. Overall, however, the results reported in this section are certainly incompatible with the impression of community services that are failing to produce benefits of central policy relevance for high proportions of users.

2.2. Service contributions across outputs

Figure 12.2 shows the shares of the overall service contributions attributed to the different inputs. For clarity, the diagram simplifies the exposition in several ways. First, it distinguishes groups only by the interval need of the user. Secondly, the analysis is for the seven outputs in the second category distinguished in the last section. These seven combine substantial offset and cover ratios. Between them they are from a broad span of the domains defined in chapter 2.

Figure 12.2
Service share to overall package contribution for different measures of output

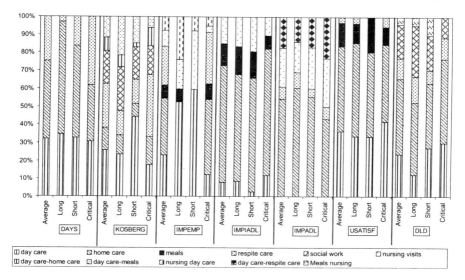

The figure illustrates that *home care* remains the foundation of the contribution of care packages. It makes an important contribution to all outputs whatever the level of dependency. There are two exceptions, firstly for the sense of empowerment among users. They are for those long and short interval needs. Second, the contributions made by home care are large in relation to other services. Again, there are two exceptions. The home care inputs by themselves contribute less to the relief of caregiver burden compared with other services. That is so when one also takes into account the joint effect of home care taken with day care, separately shown in the diagram. And there are the two lighter dependency groups for which home care is estimated to make a negligible contribution, either on its own or in combination with another service.

For most of the outputs, *day care* makes a contribution that is second only to home care. For important outputs like days before admission to institutions, its contribution is greater. Day care makes big contributions also to user satisfaction, the reduction of caregiver stress, sense of empowerment, reduced sense of dissatisfaction with life development among users with short and critical interval needs; and, with respite care, to users' perceived improvement in personal care (ADL) functioning. In their pre-reform study, Davies et al. (1990) also showed productivities for day care. But it was not then, as now, to the same degree, the foundations of many packages, and did not make such large and pervasive contributions to outputs.

Compared with pre-reform community care, one of the new features is the importance of the contribution of *respite care*. It impacts substantially on days prior to admission to institutions, to the relief of caregivers' stress, to the sense of empowerment of users, to the reduction of dissatisfaction with life development; and alone and in combination with day care, to the users' perception of their capacity to perform personal care functions. For most, the contribution is particularly great where it would be most expected, among those with critical interval needs. That contribution is made in spite of shortages and variations in supply between areas.

The big and low-cost contributions of *'social work'* on the relief of caregiver stress and the reduction of dissatisfaction with life development is one of the most interesting of the results. Indeed, it suggests that small investments in qualified social work inputs may potentially yield very substantial returns, for a limited number of outputs. This may be achievable through the provision of more therapeutically-focused care management inputs, at least for some carefully targeted users.

Community nursing makes contributions primarily to two outputs: users' perception of control over their lives, where there is an effect when consumed with day care as well as a direct effect; and users' perceptions of improved capacity to perform personal care and instrumental activities (for both ADLs and IADLs). The last may in part reflect the allocation of nurses to those in the recovery phase after an illness or accident. In combination with meals, there is also estimated to be a small contribution to the reduction of dissatisfaction with life development.

Home-delivered meals make smaller contributions than other services, and to four outputs. They cannot be expected to have the big contributions of the broader long-established services. The interesting feature of the results is therefore that meals do contribute substantially to user satisfaction (USATISF), to users' perceptions that social services improved their IADL functioning, and to the sense of control of life among users of lower dependency; and, in packages with day care, to the relief of caregiver burden. Perhaps these tend to be cases with the greatest variety of inputs.

2.3. *Service contributions and average productivities across outputs*

So far the evidence has shown significant gains from social service inputs for a wide range of outputs. This section outlines the distribution of those output gains between user groups, and investigates whether the distribution is mainly due to differences in the productivities of services between users or to differences in the allocation of budgets.

Figure 12.3 summarises the output gains and the average productivities of the packages of care. For simplicity, the results are stated only for the seven outputs with substantial offset and cover ratios mentioned above. Again, users are grouped exclusively by interval need category.

The overall pattern is clear. Service contributions in all cases increase with the level of dependency. However, for all outputs but IMPEMP, the gradient for

Figure 12.3
Output gains and average productivities by interval need category

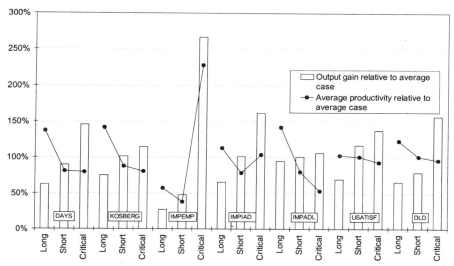

productivities is in the opposite direction, the productivities for long interval (light dependency) cases exceeding the productivities for critical interval cases.

By the criterion of their contributions to outputs, the inputs of services to cases of high dependency have been greater than would be the case were they merely to reflect variations in marginal productivities in relation to prices. There are both user differences in service productivities and diminishing returns to scale. That is, much higher service inputs are being made to users in the higher need categories although the inputs produce significantly lower improvements in welfare than for less dependent users. One would predict from the combination of high inputs and low productivities that the average productivities of the packages of more dependent people would be lower. The diagrams show that to be the case.

This consistent negative correlation between service contributions and average productivities suggests both equity and efficiency questions. The subtle relationship between efficient responses to productivities and the equity judgements implicit in the patterns of utilisation and productivities constitute one of the main themes of the next part of the book.

Notes

1   This count of effects is only a crude indicator of the productivity of services, as it takes no account of the magnitude of the effects.

2   With this definition, the ROPP can vary between between 0 and 100 per cent.

PART II
EQUITY AND EFFICIENCY:
ACTUAL AND OPTIMAL

13 Equity and Efficiency Analysis: Assumptions and Methods

Discussion of policy issues requires evidence about more than fundamental relationships and processes, and this is well illustrated by PSSRU studies. Knowledge of fundamental properties in itself can mislead unless it is combined with additional information and is presented in another format (Davies, 1978). How that is illustrated by this study will also become clear when the discussion of policy propositions is compared with evidence about productivities alone. Meanwhile Part II makes the transition from the fundamental knowledge about the production relations of welfare to the factual basis and analytic framework for the discussion of policy issues, by providing the tailor-made empirical estimates for the policy propositions discussed in the last chapter of the book. The purpose of this chapter is to describe features of the analysis whose results are presented in the rest of the section.

First, there is the general aim of the section. It is to provide information about what potential benefits there might be from alternative *investment foci*. By 'investment foci' we mean is the focus of the effort and resources diverted from short-run benefits to create long-lasting benefit streams: more generally the diversion of resources from direct service consumption in order to improve productivities, efficiency in exploiting them, and the capacity of the system to balance outputs and who benefits from them most fairly. Much efficiency improvement can best be seen as an investment activity, whether a special programme with its own resources (like projects financed from grants under the Social Services Modernisation Programme), or an orientation of one component of general management effort (Department of Health, 1998b). The features of the investment foci discussed here are the choice of outputs, the prioritisation of analysis groups, and the focus on the relaxation of supply constraints on services.

Second, there are some of the *technical concepts*, often discussed but not hitherto used with the same thoroughness in empirical production of welfare analyses: particularly two of POW's repertoire of efficiency concepts, technical and input mix efficiency.

Third, there are *key assumptions*. Such assumptions are necessary to conduct the analysis, but their nature will not necessarily be intuitively obvious, even to those most familiar with production of welfare research and discourse about equity and efficiency in community care. The choice of two of the assumptive features of the analysis is made necessary because the analysis is intended to be a direct contribution to policy discourse, rather than an indirect contribution of the kind made by the mapping of productivities in earlier chapters. To make it relevant for policy, the analysis is built partly on assumptions about how the world of post-reform community care actually works, and how it might work better.

One assumption is that the policy-makers specify only one goal for users in similar circumstances, and this they attempt to achieve to the highest degree compatible with the best use of available resources. This heuristic device we call the *single output maximand* procedure. We shall see that the procedure dictates useful analytic aims, forms and content for this part of the study, and is a simple and powerful way of illuminating the implications of a potentially large number of alternative sets of prioritisations. For instance, applying the procedure, the aim becomes to illuminate the choice of the output to maximise.

A second assumption is about the constraints on making the best use of resources: the *optimisation scenario* assumption. Alternative assumptions are made about the flexibility with which service supply can be increased, and about the use of user group budgets as a device to help to manage equity from above, without unduly constraining field level responsiveness to individual user circumstances. The optimisation scenario procedure also allows us to examine the outcome consequences of focusing exclusively on only one of the two kinds of substitution that optimisation could entail given the choice of the output maximand: redistribution of benefits between groups of users, and redistribution of spending across service types. That illuminates the nature of current productivities and efficiencies, as well as choices about how to focus investment in improving consistency in efficiency levels.

The third assumption arises from the nature of our evidence. This forces us to attribute patterns, the evidence for the explanation of which is incomplete, either to equity or inefficiency: the *inequity/inefficiency interpretation* assumption.

The first three sections of the chapter are organised around these topics. The fourth outlines the common structure used in the remaining chapters on efficiency.

1.   Optimisation scenario assumptions

Optimisation is undertaken because it produces evidence of much more direct applicability to the discussion of policy alternatives than knowledge about productivities and prices and current output patterns themselves. Productivities provide clues. But the clues can mislead unless interpreted in the context of information about relative prices, and assumptions about the context in which the alternatives would be implemented.[1] The optimisation analysis sketches the hypothetical world that would be produced given the efficient use of resources, and so suggests directions for change.

The assumptions made in this section are of three kinds: about what output to maximise; about flexibility with respect to service supply and prices/costs; and about whether spending budgets for user subgroups are used for 'equity control'. The second and third scenarios are interesting because in part they can be created by policy action, and are policy outcomes worth discussion in their own right. Their definition reflects the observation and study of the ECCEP authorities over two decades, and the national discourse about efficiency improvement. But partly their interest is that the contrast between one of the scenarios and each of the others illuminates the degree to which current shortfalls from perfect efficiency are due to each of two forms of bias. One is bias in the mixing of service inputs. The other is bias in 'favouring' users in some analysis groups at the expense of others. They show what proportion of the overall gain potentially available would be achieved from eliminating first only one of the biases, and then from eliminating only the other.

1.1.   The single output optimand

Optimisation analysis requires us to specify what it is we wish to maximise. We have not followed what would be the most obvious of procedures. Economic theory, like operations research, handles the issue of what to maximise by postulating an 'objective function' that attaches weights to all the relevant outputs, making the values of the weights depend on such circumstances as the levels of the output and other circumstances.[2] The most obvious procedure would be to simulate the effects of one or a small number of objective functions, of one or a small number of alternative sets of weights for outputs. The single output optimand procedure seems to be an odd choice. Why make it?

Absence of valid weighting system. This argument is decisive. There is no source providing the weights for our outputs, subtly differentiating the weighting systems by combinations of levels of our seventeen outputs (or even the most important half a dozen), and predicting them from user and caregiver circumstances of the wide range used in this analysis.[3] That there is no alternative other than speculative sensitivity analysis is intellectually an unappealing basis for policy discourse. However, there are more appealing arguments for the single maximand output procedure.

Need for clear and simple goals. An important theme of the pre-reform critique was vagueness about means and ends.[4] Prioritisation is essentially the simplification and clarification of goals. This is illustrated by the reforms. As they unfold, documents further clarify and so simplify goals as well as strengthen the other elements of the reforms thought to be prerequisites for success; for instance, structures and procedures providing mechanisms for action (Davies, 1997).

This theme of the critique caught the attention of policy-makers with the growing influence of the new managerialist belief in performance management partly because policy processes have the tendency to proliferate and complicate goals. It is always easier to commit policy to yet another goal than to drop an established one. Moreover, local policy statements and guidelines to field staff do not generally express this complexity in a single verbal or numerical formula neatly attaching quantitative weights to the competing objectives even where the goals are at their simplest; and for what are for most circumstances, good reasons. The organisational control of prioritisation is generally left to personal judgements and the mysteries of front-line management and supervision. But there are tight cognitive and appreciational constraints to the degree to which managers can grasp the streams of costs and benefits from complex combinations of goals each with weightings conditional on many circumstances (Lindblom, 1965; Simon, 1955). In such circumstances, the single maximand procedure is a powerful way of revealing how acute are the dilemmas of policy choice.

So one argument for fixing a single maximand for a period is that it simplifies the setting and monitoring of goal achievement and, by doing so, allows policies about objectives meaning and a better chance of succeeding. There can be fewer rationalisations and alibis to justify failure to adapt in order to shift performance in the desired direction.

New consensus about goals. A second argument is based on the high degree of consensus about priorities between managers within and between authorities. It will be remembered from chapter 2 that managers at all levels were asked to assess the ranking of priorities implicit in the behaviour of their departments. That pattern suggests that there has been agreement about some goals to an extent that would have amazed pre-reform observers. There were three which ranked highly, the first being clearly more highly ranked than the other two: the chance for more users to stay at home rather than enter a home; user empowerment, choice and control over their own lives; and support for family caregivers. For many users, the three goals may not be in fierce competition. It is an aim of this analysis to establish the degree to which dedicating the system to any one of them produces results similar to the results when the others are chosen.

That is not to say that other goals are considered invalid. They are acknowledged by the analytic framework for the handling of evidence presented below. They dominate in some cases. At least some are taken into account in almost all. There is little short-run danger that they will be flagrantly over-ridden in circumstances where the consequences would be a real loss of welfare to the stakeholders, although they are not the single clearest goal of the system as a whole. As soon as that becomes a danger, the specification of the maximand can be changed. But there is the real danger that if presented with a list of goals without clearly specifying their relative importance, the criteria will be applied with great inconsistency.

Compatibility with national priorities. As the reform process has advanced, successive attempts to set national priorities have become increasingly compatible with using the single maximand procedure as a heuristic device.

What is important for usefulness of the single output maximand procedure is how compatible it is with the nature of the clarification and simplification now being undertaken. Priorities and objectives are certainly clearly stated in *Modernising Social Services* (Department of Health, 1998b). The immediate national priority is to promote independence. The national objectives reiterated the promotion of independence; and added, inter alia, 'to enable adults … to live as safe, full and normal a life as possible, in their own home wherever possible', 'to enable informal carers to care or continue to care for as long as they and the service user wish', and allow for choice and different responses for different needs and circumstances' (para. 7.6).[5]

At first sight, this statement of objectives appears to be much more complex than setting a single maximand. However, (a) some of the objectives (like 'choice' and the matching of interventions to needs and desires) are about processes and mechanisms: that is, they are about constraints on how to achieve maximands, rather than maximands themselves (such as the life being full, safe, normal, and allowing choice). (b) Some are worded to imply that the rationale of including them is to a great extent that they are instruments for the attainment of other more general objectives. By implication, support for caregivers was originally provided in order to achieve longer stays in the community and other facets of 'independence'. The definition of eligibility criteria has the same purpose. (c) Some refer primarily to mutually exclusive groups. Different single output maximands can be set for groups with and without caregivers under great strain. Therefore, there need be no conflict between making the provision of support for caregivers the maximand for some groups, while making the extension of the period when users can be supported at home the maximand for others.

Goals are redefinable. A fourth argument is that the focus of policy-makers and managers should be to secure the direction of change, not doggedly to attain a precise goal specified a decade in advance. The specification of the goal is useful only because it allows the measurement of change in that direction. The general lessons of policy and organisational analysis and features of this context make it important that any maximand outcome chosen would (and should) change through time. In particular, priorities can be expected to alter. Indeed, they should: the higher the production of one output, the less value is likely to be attached to further increments of it compared with improvements in other outputs. Collateral effects on other outcomes are likely to change, as personnel respond to the incentives set by new managerialist systems to achieve them with increasingly ruthless efficiency. Also, evidence about what the collateral effects are will become fuller and clearer through time. That they should not be revised frequently and without deliberation is in practice no difficulty, because actually approaching their attainment would require great effort over a very long period.

The usefulness of the procedure is increased by acknowledging that *the maximand output chosen can and should differ between groups*. For instance, the reduction of intolerable caregiver stress might be set as the maximand for some user groups with caregivers making large inputs. It might make little sense for users whose circumstances are unlikely to generate much stress for their principal caregivers.

The single output maximand procedure best contributes to the definition and analysis of clear policy propositions. The aim of the analysis is to contribute to policy discourse. Any contribution made to the advancement of basic knowledge is a means to that end. The mapping of the social service productivities is in itself basic research. Its connection with policy discourse is indirect. As explained in chapter 2, the device used to apply the basic science to policy discourse is the discussion of policy propositions. The single output maximand procedure contributes to this in a particularly revealing way.

So the choice of the single output maximand procedure is driven as much by its positive virtues as by the lack of information. It is certainly more supportable than the arbitrary choice of weights for objective and welfare functions, perhaps together with equally arbitrary procedures to illuminate the sensitivity of the estimates to alternative weights. Is a virtue that it makes the illumination of the implications of choosing one single output optimand than another a key theme of the section and of the book as a whole. The story will be seen to have many complex twists and turns, new revelations of importance for policy choice and implementation at every stage, like a Le Carré novel. Dealt with in any other way, it would either have raced away into complete incomprehensibility, or would have forced simplifications that would have been indefensible for the analysis of current policy issues in the current institutional context.

1.2. *Flexibility of service supply*

The analysis contrasts two opposing assumptions:
- *Absolute flexibility of the quantity supplied at the current price/cost.* That is, the assumption is of infinitely elastic supply curves. The optimisation issues

are about the changes in benefits between users, the changes in the package costs of these benefits, and the changes in the quantities of individual services commissioned.

• *Unadjustability of the expenditure on each service and the prices paid for the services.* In this scenario, the optimisation issue is how to distribute it across persons in the way that maximises the output being discussed. The optimisation issues are about the gains for each group and their costs. By definition, there can be no change in the total quantity of individual services commissioned.

1.2.1. Optimisation subject only to the overall budget: 'unconstrained optimisation'

This scenario has been chosen to reflect the 'ideal-type' for an authority that has successfully applied the policy by seeking greater value by fostering flexibility in supply. Only the total of expenditure is fixed. The mix of service inputs, the mix of outputs, the allocation of the budget between cases, and who benefits to what extent in what way, can be balanced subject to only one constraint: the total level of expenditure on the entire caseload from the entire budget of the social services department. The key issue is whether the quantity of each service can be increased or reduced to the degree suggested by the optimisation without substantial changes in price.[6]

The question is how far this scenario would be attainable by policy effort were the policy investment in it to be highly successful. If the success were partial everywhere, studying its implications would still suggest the benefits likely from effective policies designed to make reality more like the ideal-type. How closely it already corresponds to reality, and whether it will be attainable in the future, proves to be of great policy importance. Therefore the analysis of evidence about it is deferred until why it is important becomes clearest, in the final section of the book.

1.2.2. 'Service-budget-constrained optimisation'

Along one dimension, that of the flexibility of the supply system, the opposing assumption to 'unconstrained' optimisation is optimisation within a fixed total budget for each service: expenditure on each service (and its price) is assumed to be fixed. The rigidity assumed is solely on the supply side. The scenario allows flexibility in redistributing across user types in order to maximise the output given the budget, productivities and prices.

The significance of this optimisation scenario is that it assumes a form of rigidity important in the authorities whose behaviour has been least affected by the reforms.

This scenario is well grounded in the historic characteristics of British local government.[7] The community care White Paper of 1989 diagrammatically contrasted the pre-reform system with the new policy intention. In the pre-reform system, the total budget was divided between services covering a wide geographical area, and filtered down within services to service production units. The effect was incremental change in service supply of the kind described for a wide range of local government expenditures in such studies as that by Greenwood and Hining (1976), Greenwood et al. (1977) and Kelly (1989). From this would be predicted a permanent imbalance in the same direction: the excessive supply of the services with the longest history over which to build the budget base, and the under-supply of the relatively new services. Also predictable would be compartmentalisation of thinking: and so restricted inventiveness in developing new ways of achieving ends, of fitting means to new or untypical mixes of ends after more holistic assessment, of generating and tapping new sources and of inputs associated with them.[8] In the post-reform system, the budget was to be allocated from a high level to the care management team who would then buy in services already bulk-contracted at set prices, or spot purchase services. There was to be a more general emphasis on aspects of entrepreneurial behaviour associated with innovation at all levels. The entrepreneurial behaviour of local champions was a theme of the Audit Commission (1996). The concept 'entrepreneurial case management' has been adopted from academic studies in some Social Services Inspectorate publications (Department of Health, 1991).

Most authorities are working with a hybrid between the 1989 White Paper's old and new models for the flow of purchasing power. The best recent evidence is indirect — from the joint reviews by the Audit Commission and the Social Services Inspectorate. On occasion, the reports define a general problem. An example is from a report on one of the ECCEP authorities: planning is 'service rather than needs led', adding that 'care management doesn't inform planning', and that 'analysis of need ... consists of monitoring vacancies and waiting lists, and measuring pressure on budgets' (Audit Commission and SSI, 1999, para. 4.4). The same report argued that the authority 'remains essentially traditional and resistant to change', and that was 'perhaps why decisions have been made to retain many services in council control, such as elderly persons' homes, day centres and home care', although, 'in common with the national picture, the in-house service is less flexible and more expensive than externally provided services' (ibid., paras 1.3 and 3.5.6). The report of the joint review on another of the ECCEP authorities pointed to the 'historical budget allocations' as an area for development, and commented on the 'different and uncoordinated systems in place for managing in-house services and one for the purchase of external services' while being 'not yet able to make reliable quality and cost comparisons between internal and external services' (Audit Commission and SSI 1997, para. 6.2, 6.5.1). So the theme of inflexibility in the adjustment of service budgets in general is more clearly defined as a general issue than was the generally low levels of marginal productivities during the mid-1980s. Indeed, the specific issue of incrementalism in the budgetary process is seen as a symptom of a number of specific diseases, some with common causes in the general ethos of particular authorities — and, since similar comments occur in reports on different authorities, the general ethos of authorities in general.

1.2.3. 'Group-budget-constrained optimisation'

It was an essential element of the incentive structure of the early British experiments in budget-devolved care management to require care management teams to operate within an overall service budget calculated as the product of an average spend per case and the number of cases. The incentives affected all cases and all trade-offs involving equity and efficiency, within the range of items charged to the budgets and goals taken into account in the holistic social assessments. Accompanying the average budget was the budget cap, intended to provide an incentive to avoid spending an inequitably high proportion of public funds on cases whose costs exceeded that of care in alternative settings, and whose opportunity cost was reflected in the exclusion of many cases of median or lower package cost.[9]

The same devices were found in some of the earliest American experiments established contemporaneously with the Kent Community Care Project, notably ACCESS (Eggert, 1990). In 1980, it was part of the design of one variant of what Rosalie Kane later called the 'noblest experiment of them all', the long-term care channelling demonstration. The rationale was the same: the provision of incentives to improve equity and efficiency (Davies and Challis, 1986, 87-94; Department of Health, Education and Welfare, 1980; Mathematica Policy Research, 1980, 9). These devices were on the shortlist of discriminants between care management models picked out for their implications for the equity and efficiency logics of the world's foremost evaluated community care programmes with care management in the early 1990s (Davies, 1992a, 50).

The related device of fixing differential budgets for subgroups of users, and then inviting care management teams and managers at other levels to optimise within them is found in programmes in America and elsewhere, as *Matching Resources to Needs in Community Care* (Davies and Challis, 1986), *Resources, Needs and Outcomes* (Davies et al., 1990) and *Care Management, Equity and Efficiency: the International Experience* (Davies, 1992a) described. It has been used in other than care management projects, albeit projects conscious of equity and efficiency goals (Coopers and Lybrand, 1994; Pruger, 1977; Pruger et al., 1977). Some British authorities, for example Cheshire, fix different budget caps for users in different circumstances, or users on the caseload of workers of differing degrees of professional status. Average budgets and budget caps can serve purposes of both equity and efficiency control and improvement.

Fixing budgets for target subgroups is a technique well adapted to the post-reform devolution of responsibility and an invitation to optimise flexibly to care management teams and others. As well as assumptions about the resources required to produce the targeted level of output for the group, these group budgets implicitly embody equity judgements; that is, they are statements of the relative priorities to be accorded to benefits for each group. Such a mechanism would create equity for output distributions as long as group budgets take into account variations in marginal productivities and prices, the relations between service inputs and outputs for cases in different circumstances, and the prioritisation of goals.[9]

The assumptions about the relations between service inputs and outputs are not what are of interest in the current pattern of allocations in this study, because productivities are directly estimated and yield more precise knowledge than would be available to managers. The significance of this scenario is that its comparison with the unconstrained optimisation shows the degree to which the latter results in redistribution between case types, and the loss of overall output that would occur were equity to be controlled by setting group shares in the budget similar to current actual allocations. Comparing these with service-budget-constrained optimisation helps to put the effects of that into perspective. Also, were one to assume that actual allocations take into account efficiency shortfalls, actual observed group averages would reflect the equity judgements implicit in the allocations.

The scenario makes the assumption that the current allocations between groups would be equitable given optimisation with respect to service mix. That assumption can be interpreted as having two component assumptions, both equally heroic. One is that allocations between groups are on average equitable in this unfair and inefficient world. The other is that these same allocations would remain equitable were the unfair and inefficient world to be transformed into one that is perfectly fair and efficient, although the relative improvement in efficiency entailed would be different between analysis groups. The assumptions are made *faute de mieux*. Comparisons of optimisation between this and other allocations of the budget between groups are feasible but have not been undertaken.

2.   Equity or inefficiency interpretation assumption

The optimisations map differences between how resource inputs and outputs actually do vary between groups, and how they would vary given an allocation of resources which mixed and allocated services in the way which would maximise the chosen output, given the pattern of productivities and relative service prices. But are these differences due solely, or indeed at all, to variations in efficiency? Or are they due partly or wholly to differences in what emerges as 'fair' from the interactions and negotiations between triad members: the care managers, users, and principal informal caregivers? In other words, are the observed patterns wholly a reflection of inefficiency, wholly a reflection of implicit equity judgements, or a mix of both? And if both are mixed, are they mixed in the same proportions for users in different circumstances?

ECCEP analysis may provide some circumstantial evidence that might narrow the range of judgements possible. But as in our consideration of the single output maximand assumption, we see that ultimately our strategy is dictated by the absence of a weighting system embodied in objective and social welfare functions based on a process and evidence which gives them legitimacy.

What we do is first to assume that the differences are wholly due to input mix, otherwise called 'allocative', efficiency. Then, in the final chapter of the section, we perform a complete gestalt switch, and attribute them entirely to the implicit equity judgements.

2.1. Aspects of efficiency

Following earlier PSSRU work, for example *Matching Resources to Needs in Community Care* (Davies and Challis, 1986), *Resources, Needs and Outcomes* (Davies et al., 1990) and *Care Management, Equity and Efficiency: the International Experience* (Davies, 1992a) the analysis distinguishes two kinds of inefficiency in production: *'technical'* and *'input mix'*.

- By *technical efficiency*, we mean the quantity of outputs produced from the level and mix of inputs: the greater the output from the inputs, the higher the degree of efficiency.

- By *input mix efficiency*, we mean how effectively the relative productivities and prices of inputs are exploited to create the targeted outputs at the least cost: the more closely does the input mix correspond to what is required to balance the ratios of the marginal productivities of inputs to their relative prices at the margin, the higher is input mix efficiency.

Figure 13.1 explains the concept and shows how they are related. It is based on the pioneering paper by Farrell (1957).

2.2. Utilitarianism and the equity assumption

The procedure for optimisation is to maximise the sum of outputs. In the case of two of the optimising scenarios, it involves redistributing resources across users and caregivers irrespective of the degree of their shortfall of welfare. This is nakedly utilitarian. However, the group budgets scenario constrains the allocation across groups. That is a significant departure from a purely utilitarian approach.

The analysis groups to which the group budgets relate are those described and used in Part I (see table 2.1, page 33). However, the calculations are for cases with mean levels of the predictor variables for the members of the groups. The results are more correctly described as for case types than for analysis groups.

Figure 13.1
Technical and input mix efficiencies

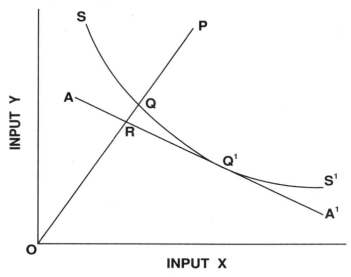

Technical efficiency is the maximisation of the quanta of outputs from the chosen
   levels and mix of inputs.
P describes a producer which makes each unit of output with a certain input mix. The
   curve SS^1 describes the substitutability of x and y at the production frontier: the
   combinations of x and y which the perfectly efficient producer could use to make the
   unit of output.
Q is a perfectly efficient producer making the unit of output with the same combination
   as P. The perfectly efficient producer makes OP/OQ as much output as P from the
   same inputs. So OQ/OP is a measure of the technical efficiency of firm P.
Input mix efficiency is the adjustment of the mix of inputs to their relative prices and
   technical substitutability so as to produce the chosen outputs at least cost given the
   degree of technical efficiency.
Substitution opportunities for the perfectly technically efficient firm is represented by
   SS^1. The relative prices of inputs x and y are indicated by the slope of the line AA^1.
Working with the input combination Q^1, a firm of perfect technical efficiency would
   make the unit of output at OR/OO times the cost of a perfectly efficient producer
   working with input mix Q, assuming that input prices are invariant with respect to
   the quantities purchased. Also, if producer P changed its input mix to that of Q^1, its
   costs would be reduced by OQ/OR. So OR/OQ measures input mix efficiency.
The diagram is taken from Farrell's classic paper (1957). It assumes constant returns
   to scale; that the 'efficient production function', the true frontier production function,
   is known; and that input prices are invariant with respect to input quantities purchased. Relaxation of these assumptions complicates but does not basically
   change the argument.

3. Common structure of efficiency chapters (14-21)

The argument of this chapter is the basis of the structure and contents of each subsequent chapter in this section.

The single output optimand assumption makes the central issue the choice of output to maximise. The focus of each chapter is the case for adopting one (or one of a domain) of the main outputs for which productivities were presented in the last section. Outputs from the same domain are discussed in the same chapter. The abbreviated titles for outputs are as described in table 1 of chapter 2. The output being discussed is called the *'topic output'* of the chapter or its part.

The second level headings distinguish the two types of efficiency: *'technical'* and *'input mix'* efficiencies.[11] Efficiency differences are analysed for the six 'analysis groups' used in Part I. They are combinations of 'interval need' and whether the user has a principal informal caregiver as defined by the ECCEP project. For each type of efficiency, the results are presented using standard diagrams.

Technical efficiency. The standard diagrams for technical efficiency show for each analysis group the percentage shortfall in technical efficiency compared with the estimated frontier (for concave functions); or residuals around the average (for the other functions).

There is only one description for technical efficiency. However, for all the chapters for which it was technically possible to estimate a frontier function, there are two figures, each showing the consequences of putting in varying levels of input into one of two *strategies for investing in efficiency improvement*. The diagrams show the implications of different levels of effort for (a) output gains, and (b), as an alternative, cost savings. The first strategy of efficiency improvement suggested is to raise the efficiency level of the least efficient to a higher *floor level*. The figure shows the consequences of setting floors at different levels. The nature of the estimates are described in more detail in section 2.1 of chapter 15 in the context of the discussion of the results for USATISF. The second investment strategy is *the improvement of the efficiency of each of the least efficient 33 per cent of units by the same percentage*. The results show the consequences of setting the percentage improvement at different levels.

Input mix efficiency. For input mix efficiency, there is a description for each of the three *optimisation scenarios* described above: (a) *'unconstrained optimisation'* — resources can be shifted between services and user groups without constraints or changing price levels; (b) *'group-budget-constrained optimisation'* — resources can be moved between services without price differences but the total (and so average) budget for each group is fixed; and (c) *'service-budget-constrained optimisation'* — resources can be reallocated between analysis groups but the total amount of each service commissioned remains constant.

The standard diagrams for input mix efficiencies compare pairs of results for each analysis group. The first of the pair describes estimates for the actual pattern observed. It is juxtaposed against the equivalent estimates given the optimisation under discussion.

There are two standard diagrams for input mix efficiencies.

The first shows three estimates for each pair. (a) One is the level of output for a case with the mean values of the predictors for the analysis group.[12] The ale is on the right of the diagram. The advantage of assuming mean values is 1at it is less affected by outliers. The disadvantage is that it does not describe the pattern of variation within analysis groups. (b) The second estimate is the gross cost of the package for the 'average case' for the analysis group. That is indicated by the height of the bar, the scale being on the left of the diagram. (c) The third is the gross cost of each of the main services in the package for the average case. Some package components for some case types are too small to be shown on the diagram.

There is a diagram for each optimisation scenario for each output. The text discusses the result of each diagram and makes allusions across diagrams. There are two foci: (a) inefficiencies in observed service balance and the reallocations which optimisation would entail; and (b) differences between user groups and the reallocations that the optimisations would create.

A second standard diagram is shown for the outputs that the first diagram suggests might be a candidate to be chosen as the maximand. It focuses on the levels and mixes of what we call *'collateral outputs'* caused by the choice of the topic output given optimisation and the scenario in questions. The concept 'collateral output' is used by analogy with 'collateral damage' in war studies. Given the single maximand assumption, the optimisation is based on maximising the level of the topic output subject to the constraints of the scenario. None of the other outputs is taken into account in this optimisation process. However, the structures of inputs determined by the optimisation has effects for the production of other outputs also. Given the single optimisation assumption, these effects are unintended. These are the effects which are called 'collateral outputs'.

The diagrams for collateral outputs are organised around analysis groups. For each analysis group, bars for the observed and collateral outputs are juxtaposed. The height of the bars indicate the level of output compared with that would be achieved if the collateral output in question were the maximand output instead.

The text accompanying the figures for collateral outputs discusses: (a) collateral compared with the maximum output achievable for each output — almost always, the output that would occur if that output were to be the overall maximand;[13] (b) actual output compared with the maximum achievable for the topic output; (c) collateral compared with actual outputs; (d) major differences in pattern between optimisations with or without user group budgets; and (e) major differences in pattern between optimisations with or without the maintenance of service budgets. Particular attention is paid to whether reallocations created by an optimisation would leave some users worse off than currently. The reason is that a reallocation between levels of outputs implies a redistribution between the stakeholders, and stakeholders value these outputs differently. Because, therefore, a deterioriation in certain benefits implies a deterioration in the welfare of some stakeholders, such a deterioration makes it unlikely that the change would satisfy the criterion for a 'Pareto improvement', a fundamental criterion suggested by theoretical welfare economics for evaluation (Pareto, 1971, chap. 6 and appendix, para. 89). That criterion is in practice too rigorous for practical use. It greatly reduced the capacity of economists to identify improvements. Attempting to extend the range of cases on which the economist could unambiguously pronounce some change to be a gain or otherwise, there were efforts by Hicks, Kaldor, Little, Samuelson and Scitovsky to formulate criteria around the gainers compensating, or being able to compensate, losers (Graaf, 1957, 84-90). Our discussion is about evidence at least twice removed from that needed to apply the Pareto or compensation criteria, and so supports even less definitive judgement. Deterioration in one of our dimensions of welfare compared with current levels does not necessarily implies a loss of welfare for stakeholders. Stakeholders may attach no value to the higher level of that current benefit than the lower post-change level. Neither would higher post-change than pre-change levels of all benefits (observed and unobserved) for all users and caregivers necessarily demonstrate a Pareto improvement. There are other stakeholders who would certainly lose by the change; notably, general taxpayers financing most of the investment required to improve efficiency.

The contents are illustrated by the heads and subheads of each chapter. The first level head distinguishes technical efficiency, input mix efficiency, and overview. The greater part of the text is in the second section discussing input mix efficiency. Section 2 is subdivided by optimisation scenario: 2.1 dealing with 'unconstrained' optimisation; 2.2 with group-budget-constrained optimisation; and 2.3 with service-budget-constrained optimisation. Within these, there is a third level consisting of two headings: topic output levels, package costs, service mixes and analysis group variations; and collateral output levels.

Notes

1   For instance, many of the marginal productivity effects affecting the output DAYS were found to be subject to diminishing returns. Were the unconstrained optimisation not to redistribute from critical interval cases to long interval cases, it would be important to know whether the gains it produced were due to reallocation between users (suggesting equity questions) or reallocation between services (purely an efficiency matter). Contrasting optimal solutions for the three supply-focused scenarios would illuminate this.

2   Apparently, operations researchers tend to use the concept 'objective function' to include more than simply the valuation weights and outputs, the usage in economic theory (Henderson and Quandt, 1971, 338-9, 341).

3   No doubt, improved weighting systems based on average user valuations will become available in time. However, it is likely that there are great and systematic variations of valuations around averages. They are likely to reflect national and group cultures. Compare the implicit evaluation of the importance of the quality of home-delivered meals in England and France found by Davies et al., 1998. But, if there were not a temptation to argue that the average weights should be applied in individual care planning, it would seem too obvious for it to be necessary to argue (a) that valuations are likely to vary greatly in response to many factors, (b) that, as psychologists' studies of valuations of life of elderly people suggest, such valuations are likely to be the outcome of 'a complex intrapsychic process' affected by a wide range of cultural social and psychological factors (Lawton et al., 1999), and (c) that the factors are of a kind that should be taken into account in handling equity issues in individual care planning in a policy system that sets user-responsiveness as one of its most important goals.

     Moreover, there are at least three stakeholders: frail elderly 'users', principal informal caregivers, and those responsible for making the most cost-effective use of public resources. That there are three views makes it necessary to weight the valuations of each. Clearly, we could not use the evaluations implicit in system allocations derived later in the section without complete circularity of argument. So we lack evidence of a degree of validity that would justify putting it into a position in which it would dominate our subsequent statistical argument.

4   First it was argued by the academics; most famously, Matilda Goldberg (Goldberg and Connelly, 1982; Davies, 1981; Davies and Challis, 1986). Then it was adopted by the Department and the Audit Commission (Audit Commission, 1985, 1986; DHSS, 1987). The effect was to be seen in the much greater clarity of the 1989 White Paper and its associated documentation, and arguably still greater clarity in the 1998 White Paper (DHSS, 1989; Department of Health, 1998b).

5   We refer below to some other White Paper topics, which the analyses inform. These include some devices which in some places in the White Paper are treated as instrumental objectives. One example is a set of eligibility criteria of practical use to the field, but whose language allows the prioritisation to reflect judgements from higher policy-makers, managers and elected politicians with monitoring, rewards and sanctions to secure compliance. A second is the re-invention of needs-based planning around the assumptions of the new community care. A third is the demonstration of the effectiveness and value for money of the care and support provided. The issue being discussed here is the usefulness of the single maximand assumption.

6   Even though the optimum aggregate service levels can extend beyond what is observed in the sample, the allocation to any of the user groups is bound by the maximum allocation observed for the service. This condition, pertinent for all optimisation scenarios, is set in order to maximise the reliability of the inferences derived from the analysis.

7   And perhaps of local government in other parts of the world too. See for instance the contrasts between Australian Community Options projects auspiced by local authorities and other agencies (Department of Health, Housing and Community Services, 1992).

8　An overview of joint reviews comments how 'the most substantial changes' in the proportion of home care purchased from the private sector 'have been found in councils that take a holistic approach to planning' (Audit Commission et al., 1999, 22).The holistic approach to planning starts 'with a well-informed strategic overview that takes into account internal and external pressures and resource shifts and draws messages from both the front-line and the strategies of other key players. This is then translated into a business plan, with specified targets and time scales, which is itself tightly linked to the council's commissioning and performance frameworks.' (Audit Commission et al., 1999, 22.)

9　*Resources, Needs and Outcomes* estimated that seven cases at the lower level of package costs would be excluded for every one high package cost case served (Davies et al., 1990).

10　But it has usually been operated in contexts in which none of these have been known. In these circumstances, the agency policy-makers have tended to define equity in terms of inputs. Pruger, for instance, justified this on the grounds that community services were more people processing than people changing, in the sense that inputs themselves, not their consequences for what we are calling outputs, are the basis of equity criteria (Pruger, 1977). (That is a use of the two concepts in ways which conveys a different meaning from that their inventor had intended; Hasenfeld, 1983.)

11　Economists now more commonly call input mix efficiency 'allocative efficiency'. Farrell originally called it 'price efficiency' (Farrell, 1957).

12　Save for the results for optimisations testing the effects of alternative budget caps for care costs. Those are based on the application of the optimisation to each and every case.

13　But not necessarily. The collateral for an analysis group might be larger for another maximand output because of redistributions between analysis groups.

14 Efficiencies for DAYS Indicator Variable (Users' Length of Stay in the Community)

Arguably, users' length of stay in the community (DAYS) is the output that reflects the most important goal of the 1989 White Paper. Chapter 11 showed an additional reason for the significance of this output. Three of the most important general outputs for the two main beneficiary stakeholders appear to be causally linked and, arguably, they are the three most important outputs. (a) The higher the level of user satisfaction produced by the services, the fewer resources are required to reduce (b) caregivers' sense of burden to a targeted degree. The lower the level of caregivers' sense of burden, the fewer resources are required to achieve (c) a targeted reduction in the number of days spent at home rather than in institutions for long-term care. To paraphrase: for many, user satisfaction contributes to, and is associated with reduced sense of caregiver burden; and a feeling that the burden is less contributes to increased length of stay in the community. So the choice of increased length of stay in the community might also secure the relief of caregiver stress as a means to that end, and enhance user satisfaction. That will be tested below.

The dependent variable is defined in table 1 of chapter 2 (page 33). The average production function is described in table 4.1 and the productivity effects in figures 4.1 and 4.2.

1. Technical efficiency

The dependent variable was censored after two years, so that it was not possible to estimate a frontier production function version. Therefore, the estimates of variations in technical efficiency are based on the analysis of residuals around the estimates predicted from the 'average' version of the production function; the version described in chapter 4.

Figure 14.1 shows the patterns of residuals. Without being able to estimate the position of a frontier, inferences about the implications of improvement

Figure 14.1
Technical efficiency index* for users' length of stay in the community

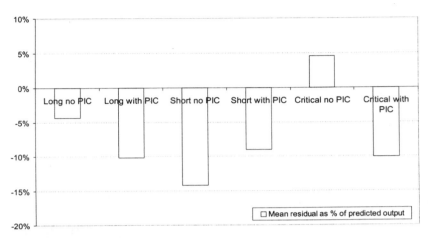

* ratio of residuals over the average output for given sub-group

are more indirect. The pattern of results is clear. There is little difference on average between those with principal informal caregivers. Among others, the degree of efficiency seemed to be greatest for those of critical interval need, least for those with short interval needs.

2.   'Input mix' efficiency

It will be remembered that the analysis will illuminate the degree of divergence of the actual 'input', in this case service, mix from that in which the ratios of the quantities inputted are proportional to the ratios of their marginal productivities to prices, and that therefore yields highest levels of the output considered.

The degree of variation in inefficiency between user groups is described for each of the optimisation scenarios summarised in chapter 13.

2.1.   *Assumption (a): Resources can be shifted subject only to a total budget constraint: 'unconstrained optimisation' (figure 14.2)*

2.1.1.   *Outputs, package costs, service mixes, and analysis group variations*

The case allows optimisation by the redistribution of resources both across users and services with constant service prices.

As described in chapter 13, figure 14.2 shows:

Figure 14.2
Input mix efficiency for length of stay in the community (DAYS):
'unconstrained' optimisation

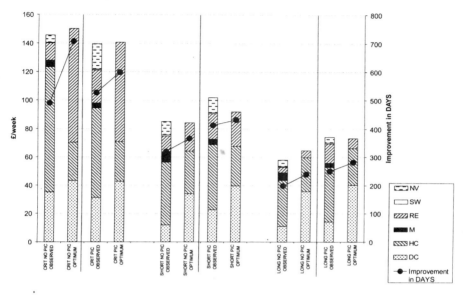

- The average quantities of services actually allocated, measured in terms of gross costs, in the first of each pair of columns.
- The average quantities that would be allocated were inputs to be mixed perfectly efficiently, in the second of each pair of columns.
- The total cost of packages, measured by the height of the column.
- The average level of output observed for the group (in the first column), and the average level of output derived from the efficient allocation of resources.
- The absolute increase in output made possible by achieving not observed but perfect efficiency, indicated by the difference in output levels and the slope of the line connecting them.

The units for input quantities are labelled in the left-hand margin of the figure. The units for output levels are labelled in the right-hand margin. The results are shown for each combination of interval need and caregiver support.

The patterns revealed are important. They are about the differences in service balance between current allocations and what is predicted to be most efficient; and differences between groups.

Inefficiencies in service balance

- For each of the six groups postulated, the optimal input mix requires a reduction in the inputs of home care. This was a conclusion also reached by an optimisation analysis of the long-term channeling project taking a some-what similar output as the sole criterion, the probability of transition to nursing homes as an outcome (Greene et al., 1993).

- Indeed, the optimal mix requires much the same home care input on average for members of all groups; an input costing about £20 per week in 1996 prices. One cannot conclude from this that were inputs to be mixed in the best way, all individual users should receive much the same inputs of home care. However, the crude need correlates from which the groups are defined clearly do not discriminate those users requiring more or less home care. The discriminants are subtler; perhaps, much subtler, table 4.1 and figure 4.1 suggest. There is a productivity effect for home care that applies to 93 per cent of users, but the marginal productivities are small beyond a low threshold.

Home care developed as the foundation stone of the community services. It is more easily varied in quantity within a certain range with respect to times and tasks. The growth of independent supply undertaking a wider range of task with greater flexibility of timing may change the productivity curve, and so make this finding out-dated.

- Home-delivered meals account for a small proportion of the observed input mix. But it does not feature in an optimal allocation. The result is consonant with table 4.1, where there was no productivity effect for meals.

Like home help, home-delivered meals is one of the oldest-established services. It is possible that it captured a clientele and established a delivery techno-structure that provides it with a larger share in packages than its usefulness for the current clientele would justify.

But in interpreting the result, one must bear in mind several factors. (a) The models are general. There are likely to be cases for which there are important productivities. (b) One must also bear in mind that charging policies can cause meals to have a very low subsidy.

- In contrast, the optimal mix would include more day care than is actually provided for all user groups; and in all groups, day care comprises a higher proportion of package costs than home care. The differences in the optimal utilisation between groups would be much smaller than the differences in amounts actually consumed. That is because, as table 4.1 and figure 4.1 show, (a) the day care effect is subject to diminishing returns, and (b), the bigger productivity effects are for those who are cognitively impaired. The productivity curve for day care for other than the cognitively impaired is similar in its position, slope and shape to that for home care. Greater disparities between the optimum allocation of day care for the different groups may therefore not be apparent in figure 14.2 because of the presence of cognitively impaired users in all the groups defined in the analysis. This is confirmed by figure 14.3, which carries out the optimisation with two different groups: those presenting cognitive impairment and/or behavioural

Figure 14.3
*Input mix efficiency for length of stay in the community (DAYS) for people
who are/are not cognitively impaired or have behavioural difficulties:
'unconstrained' optimisation*

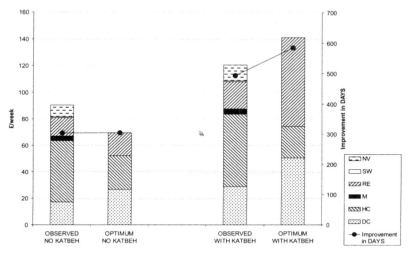

Note
KATBEH: cognitive impairment and/or behavioural disturbance

disturbance and those not. Although figure 14.3 shows how the optimum allocation for both groups entails an increase in the levels of days care, such increase is more than twice as big for those users cognitively impaired and/or with behavioural disturbances.

Day care provision has been growing over many years. But it is regarded not as a fundamental building block for most packages, but as a service to be carefully targeted on only some. There are some good reasons. *Resources, Needs and Outcomes* found that the prescription of day care for those for whom it was not appropriate but for which there were few alternatives resulted in a high rate of attrition of disillusioned users. However, it is also the case that day care could offer attractive and useful types of care with economies of concentration that outweigh the transport costs that are particularly valuable for those at most risk of admission to institutions. It is quite plausible that it is being under-supplied in relation to other services, and might appear to be more under-supplied were the range of services typically provided under its roof to cover a wider range of the needs of the users.

- For all but those with long interval need with principal informal caregivers, the best input mix would on average include more respite care. The larger increases would be suggested for the more disabled; those with short or critical interval need.

Table 4.1 and figure 4.2 showed several risk factors to affect the productivity curves for respite care. None were at the level of generality of interval need. Nevertheless, the interval need classification does pick out those for whom the greatest gains would be made by the provision of more respite care. The strongest predictor of high productivity is behavioural problems, and its effect is constant irrespective of the level of outcome. This is associated with cognitive impairment, particularly with severe cognitive impairment. It is likely that the gains from inputting more into those with behavioural problems might be greater than for any group shown in figure 14.2. That is indeed shown by figure 14.3, which shows substantial gains from the large increase in respite care for those with cognitive impairment and behavioural disturbance, though associated with the already mentioned increase in day care.

However, figure 4.2 also showed how there were those for whom respite care was planned to be a precursor to admission for long-stay care in institutions, and/or a predictor of such admission. What the optimisation model strongly suggests is that the preventive effect much outweighed the others.

Differences between user groups
- For those with short or long interval need, the absolute gains from perfectly efficient rather than actual service mixes were similar and substantial; between 15 and 50 days. The percentage increase in days would be greater for those of long interval need. The gains would be due to increasing the use of day care and diminishing the inputs of home care.
- The biggest effects are for those with critical interval needs, particularly those with critical interval needs but without principal informal caregivers (more than 200 days). That is associated with the increased use of day and respite care and reduction in home care inputs.
- The optimal solution leaves the budget for every single one of the six groups practically unchanged. Figure 14.2 only implies very limited transfers of resources from the short interval need users with PICs to the long and critical interval need users without PICs. This is even though the 'unconstrained' optimisation scenario allows for free resource transfers between all users and services.

2.1.2. 'Collateral outputs': the consequences for other outputs of optimising on DAYS

The results are summarised in figure 14.4. Their analysis focuses on the following three main elements:
- Comparison for each of the analysis groups of the actual output levels for the target output variable against the levels that would be achieved with the optimum mixes of resources. This is shown in the figures by the distance between the white columns and the 100 per cent line, and illuminates the room for potential improvement in the given target variable.
- Comparison of the collateral output levels against the actual levels. This, shown in the figures by the distance between the heights of the white (ac-

Figure 14.4
Collateral output levels for optimisation on DAYS with 'unconstrained'
optimisation

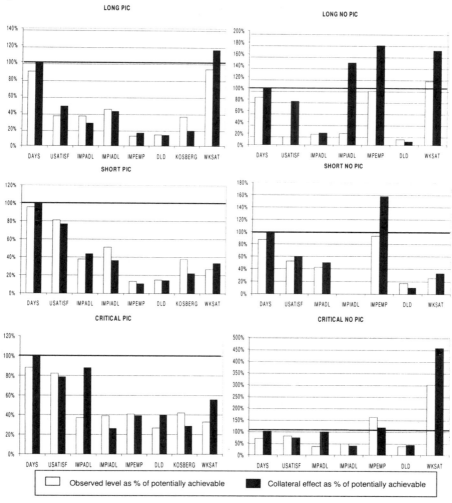

tual) and black (collateral) columns, reveals the extent to which improvements in the target output would deteriorate or ameliorate the levels of the other outputs. This is key when applying, for instance, equity improvement criteria such as the Pareto improvement criterion.

- Comparison of the collateral levels against the maximum levels achievable given optimisation on each of the collateral outputs. This is shown in the figures by the distance between the black (collateral) columns and the 100 per cent line. It is important to consider not only whether optimisation with respect to the target variable increases the collateral levels of the rest of outputs, but also whether even after such improvements the levels achieved would be distant from what could be attained. In order to do so, the analysis will divide between high collateral outputs, those achieving 80 per cent or above of their maximum attainable, and low collateral levels, those that lay at 40 per cent or below of their maximum attainable.

Actual output compared with the maximum achievable
- Actual DAYS is 80 per cent or more of what is achievable for all six groups. Part I has described how managers at all levels everywhere describe this as having been the highest priority of their department, and how the pattern of service contributions suggests that the services are indeed 'tooled up' to deliver this type of benefit for users. These high proportions of the maximum achievable actually delivered for the six groups reflect the same phenomenon.
- Additionally, the productivity patterns for DAYS describe marked decreasing returns to scale. This means that the cost of additional units of DAYS increases exponentially, and therefore that there is a level beyond which significant increases in inputs, even optimally mixed, will not yield noticeable increases in DAYS. This fact reduces somewhat the opportunity for the realisation of very significant improvements in DAYS.

Collateral compared with actual outputs
- Overall, the collateral level exceeds the current level for approximately 21 outputs in the different groups: in 21 cases the black column is higher than the white column. This is more than twice the number of cases in which the collateral output is notably inferior to the current output.

  Collateral output losses:
- The significant deterioration in collateral outputs is concentrated on the user groups with PICs. Notably, the unconstrained optimisation on DAYS is associated with a significant deterioration in the levels of reduction in perceived carer burden (KOSBERG). This is true for all the three relevant groups. Even though chapter 12 demonstrated KOSBERG and DAYS to be causally linked, it appears that the differences in the direct effects of the services on the two outputs would be big enough to overcompensate for their interrelationship.
- All user groups with PICs experience, after unconstrained optimisation on DAYS, a deterioration in their IMPIADL levels.

  Collateral output gains:
- For two outputs, DAYS and WKSAT, the collateral levels would be higher for all groups. This is important in two ways. Firstly, it implies that 'unconstrained' optimisation on DAYS does not require transfers in resources such that any of the groups would have to 'give away' days for other groups to

enjoy. On the contrary, the optimum service-mix yields an increase of up to 20 per cent in the level of DAYS for every single one of the six groups postulated. Secondly, the fact that optimisation on DAYS increases WKSAT levels for all groups corroborates the importance that extending the users' length of stay in the community has in the care managers' ranking of priorities.

- For five out of the six user groups, the unconstrained optimisation on DAYS is associated with a significant increase in IMPADL levels. This effect is more important the higher the level of dependency of the user.

- The greatest relative improvements in collateral levels would be experienced by users in the long and short interval without PICs categories, for whom only DLD collateral levels would be lower than the actual levels.

Collateral outputs compared with the maximum achievable for each output

Low collateral output levels:

- Again, most of the outputs with low collateral levels would be concentrated on the user groups with PICs. For such groups, the unconstrained optimisation on DAYS leaves the collateral levels for KOSBERG, IMPEMP and IMPIADL at between 10 and 40 per cent of their maximum attainable.

- For all groups, the collateral levels of DLD would be below 40 per cent of their maximum attainable. This is more so the lower the user's level of dependency. This effect should be interpreted together with the low collateral rates for KOSBERG. Indeed, chapters in an earlier section of this study showed the dramatically strong effect that social work input had on the two outputs. However, social work was not found significantly to increase the levels of DAYS, and hence is not in the DAYS optimum service mix (see figure 14.2). Since social work represents a relatively small part of the package of care, a slight departure from the optimum input mix that invested a limited additional amount of social work would be likely to improve very significantly the collateral levels for DLD and KOSBERG without hindering seriously the levels achieved for DAYS.

- The two long interval category groups experience IMPADL collaterals of approximately 20 per cent of their attainable maxima.

High collateral output levels:

- Which outputs have the high collateral scores differ between the majority of analysis groups. However, most of the outputs for which the collateral effects would be more than 80 per cent of the maximum achievable would be concentrated on two user groups. For these groups, succeeding in maximising days would also produce high levels of another four outputs: WKSAT, IMPADL, USATISF and IMPEMP for critical interval cases without PICs, and WKSAT, IMPIADL, USATISF and IMPEMP for long interval cases without PICs. For both groups, the collateral levels of WKSAT would be actually far above the levels that would produce the unconstrained optimisation that maximises WKSAT.

- For IMPADL, the collateral output exceeds 80 per cent of the maximum attainable also for critical interval cases with PICs. It makes good sense that it should be for users of great dependency because it is for them that the difficulty for all concerned in handling ADLs is likely to break down the will to remain at home and the willingness to provide the necessary support.
- Overall, there would be high collateral levels for USATISF for four out of the six groups postulated, and high collaterals for IMPEMP for all users without PICs.

2.2.   Assumption (b): Optimisation subject to user group average budgets: 'group-budget-constrained optimisation' (figure 14.5)

2.2.1.   Outputs, package costs, service mixes, and analysis group variations

The scenario allows for the transfer of resources only between service inputs, not between broad types of user. The scenario could have particular significance in two cases, the first more interesting than the second.

- It would be appropriate for a situation in which the prioritisation between groups is achieved by securing adherence to a mean budget for each group. Chapter 13 has described how this technique has already been used and how it balances the top-down control of overall patterns with discretion to reflect the detailed understanding and particular and idiosyncratic nature of what discriminates between cases.
- Alternatively, or additionally, it could reflect a compromise between the maximisation only of the topic output and taking some account of collateral outputs.
- However, it is useful to postulate this case for another reason also. It shows how far the gains shown in figure 14.2 would be the result of redistributing across groups as well as services. In one respect, therefore, it indicates the effect of input mix inefficiency itself more precisely.

The results are shown in figure 14.5.

Patterns of service reallocations
Section 2.1.1 mentioned how the 'unconstrained' DAYS optimisation would not significantly transfer resources between the analysis groups. Consequently, many of the conclusions of the previous section are directly applicable here too.

Inefficiencies in service balance
The patterns include the following features.

- Again, the input of home care is absolutely and relatively smaller in every group when the user group budget is accompanied by efficient mixing of services. It is the productivities pattern discussed above which most counts, not differences in prioritisations between groups.

Figure 14.5
Input mix efficiency for length of stay in the community (DAYS): group-budget-constrained optimisation

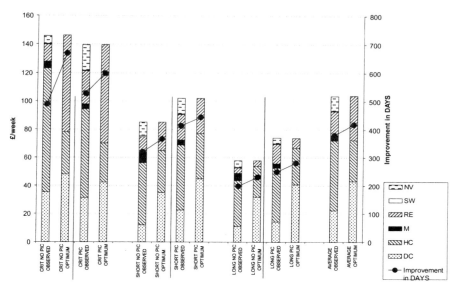

- Again, where service inputs would be used most efficiently, home-delivered meals do not feature.
- Again, day care inputs would be increased when inputs would be mixed most efficiently. Again, the more dramatic increases would be for short and long interval cases.
- Again, respite care inputs would be increased when inputs are most efficiently mixed for most groups. The biggest increases would be for critical interval cases, the least for short interval cases; for those without PICs more than those with them.

Differences between user groups
The gains in output would be practically identical to the ones implied by the optimisation scenarios of figures 14.2 and 14.5. Neither does the hypothecating of a budget share to each group cause the outputs for some groups to be much higher, protected as they would be by the fixing of the group budget.

The only group that the hypothecation of budgets would disadvantage to some extent, compared with overall optimisation of figure 14.2, are persons with critical interval needs and no PIC, even though they still benefit from an increase in DAYS of almost 200.

2.2.2. 'Collateral outputs': the consequences for other outputs of optimising on DAYS

It will be remembered that the significance of this scenario is that it postulates the use of a mechanism for controlling equity in a way that allows care managers to respond to complex variations in individuals' needs. Therefore, it is a mechanism that is both compatible with the principles of the reforms, and the assumptions of many senior managers about the importance of balancing clear priorities set by the centre with leaving an adequate degree of discretion to those actually dealing with the case.

Generally, the patterns of changes in collateral outputs for this optimisation scenario would be likely to appear more even than for the 'unconstrained' scenario. This is because the benchmark against which each of the seven collateral output levels are measured, their maximum attainable, is calculated with a fixed budget for each user group, thus preventing the concentration of resources in one group for one output and in different groups for the others.

Consequently, it is important to remember when interpreting the results that the 100 per cent lines refer to different absolute maximum attainable levels of outputs for each of the optimisation scenarios. Indeed, collateral output levels of 20 per cent in one optimisation scenario might in fact allude to higher absolute levels than 90 per cent collateral levels in a different optimisation case.

Results are summarised in figure 14.6.

Again, because the 'unconstrained' optimisation implied almost identical user group budgets than the present scenario, most of the inferences drawn from the analysis of the 'unconstrained' optimisation would be directly applicable to the present case.

Actual output compared with the maximum achievable
- After optimisation subject to user group average budgets, as in the 'unconstrained' scenario, actual DAYS is 75 per cent or more of what is achievable for all six groups.
- The greatest room for improvement is for critical interval users with PICs; the smallest for short interval users without PICs.

Collateral compared with actual outputs
- Overall, the collateral level exceeds the current level for approximately 27 outputs in the different groups, against 13 cases for which the collateral level is significantly lower than the current level.

Collateral output losses:
- Of the 13 losses in collateral output, 10 would be related to users with PICs. As in the case of the 'unconstrained' optimisation, there is a significant deterioration in the levels of KOSBERG for the three user groups with PICs.
- There is a notable deterioration in the collateral IMPIADL levels for all user groups with PICs.

Figure 14.6
Collateral output levels for optimisation on DAYS with group-budget-constrained optimisation

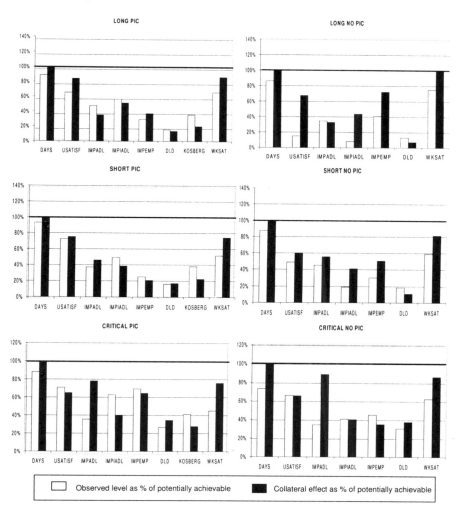

- Both user groups in the critical interval category and those in the short interval category with PICs experience a reduction in their IMPEMP levels.

  Collateral output gains:
- There would be gains in the collateral levels for all groups for DAYS and WKSAT.

- For all groups in the short and critical interval categories, the optimisation on DAYS is associated with a significant increase in IMPADL levels. Again this effect is more important the higher the level of dependency of the user.
- The greatest relative improvements in collateral levels would be experienced by users in the long and short interval without PICs categories. For these, only DLD collateral levels would be lower than the actual levels.
- All users in the long and short interval categories experience gains in their collateral levels of USATISF.

Collateral outputs compared with the maximum achievable for each output

Low collateral output levels:

- For user groups with PICs, the optimisation leaves the collateral levels for KOSBERG at approximately 20 per cent.
- For all groups, the collateral levels of DLD would be below 40 per cent of their maximum attainable. This is more so the lower the user's level of dependency.
- There would be low collateral levels for IMPIADL for the short and critical interval user groups.

High collateral output levels:

- As is the case for the 'unconstrained' scenario, most of the outputs for which the collateral effects would be more than 80 per cent of the maximum achievable would be concentrated on critical interval cases without PICs and long interval cases without PICs.
- For IMPADL, the collateral output approaches or exceeds 80 per cent of the maximum attainable for the critical interval cases.
- Overall, there would be collateral levels for USATISF above the 60 per cent of the attainable for all six groups postulated.

2.3.   Assumption (c): Total expenditure on each service maintained: 'Service-budget-constrained optimisation' (figures 14.7 and 14.8)

This postulates a world where the supply of each service is fixed in total. In such circumstances, the task is to so distribute the services between users as to maximise the output for the cost. We also learn more about the potential gains from mixing services optimally from the comparison of this world with the world of optimisation by transfers across groups and services whose implications are shown in figure 14.2

2.3.1.   *Outputs, package costs, service mixes, and analysis group variations*

The results are shown in figure 14.7.

Figure 14.7
Input mix efficiency for length of stay in the community (DAYS): service-budget-constrained optimisation

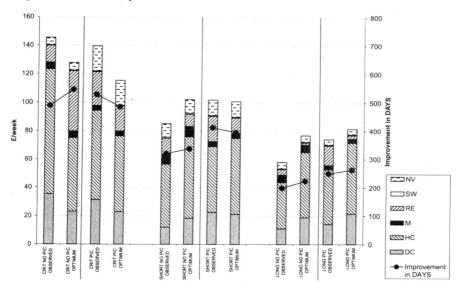

Inefficiencies in the service balance

Although the total quantum of services remains unchanged, the services can be redistributed across groups in response to marginal productivity differences among the groups' populations.

The patterns include:

- The reduction of home care inputs for critical interval users, particularly critical interval users without PICs. The residual supply of the quota of home care would be better used, the model implies, by increasing inputs for short and long interval need cases, evening out the differences in the home care levels between the different groups.

- The reallocation of the stock of day care from persons of critical interval need to those of long interval need and those of short interval need without PICs.

- The reallocation of respite care greatly to increase the input of users with critical interval needs and without PICs and away from others, particularly from long interval cases with PICs.

- Since they do not affect DAYS, the budgets for the rest of the inputs (social work, nursing visits and meals) would be distributed in the optimum allocation as in the observed input mix.

Differences between user groups
- In both of the other scenarios, optimisation increased the level of output for every one of the user groups.[1] Mixing inputs optimally given the restriction that the total volumes of each service could not be varied would not have this property. The level of output would actually fall for users with critical or short interval need and a principal informal caregiver. The loss to critical interval cases with PICs is estimated to be on average as much as 40 days.
- Compared with the actual differences in the total package costs, the optimal differences under this scenario are substantially reduced, although the gradient by interval need remains. The difference made to total package costs for each group is greater than with unrestricted optimisation.
- Optimising given total service consumption would cause the total package costs of those with principal informal caregivers and critical interval needs to be reduced more than those of critical interval cases without informal caregivers. Among the other groups, the presence of a PIC is associated with a smaller increase in package costs. So in all cases, optimisation would increase the cost-reducing effect of having a principal informal caregiver.

2.3.2. 'Collateral outputs': the consequences for other outputs of optimising on DAYS

In chapter 13 it was hypothesised that the effect is to allocate excessive shares of SSD budgets to older-established services like home-delivered meals and home care. In many areas, home care services still direct much of their effort on housekeeping for those of low dependency and risk of admission to institutions, and allocate an insufficient share to the new services and to social work. Whereas a scenario with group budgets would reflect the amalgam of ideas and technology found in the more advanced programmes around the world, the fixed service budget scenario reflects a feature of the pre-reform system. It was already beginning to break down by the late 1980s, but as the litany of complaints about these features from the SSI and Audit Commission illustrate (and ECCEP confirms), some of the structures and procedures which reinforced it remain to varying extents in most areas.

The results are shown in figure 14.8.

Actual output compared with the maximum achievable
- In contrast with what the previous two optimising scenarios showed, the service-budget-constrained optimisation implies the reduction in DAYS for some of the user groups. In fact, figure 14.8 shows, the optimum input mix for the fixed input budgets case produces a transfer of DAYS from users in the short and critical interval groups with PICs to the rest of the groups, specially the critical interval users without PICs.

Figure 14.8
*Collateral output levels for optimisation on DAYS with service-budget-
constrained optimisation*

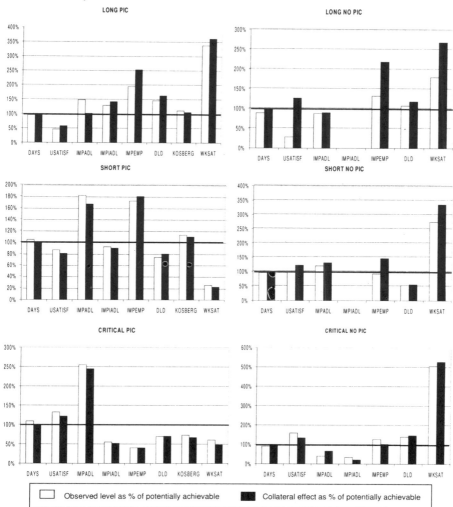

Collateral compared with actual outputs

Collateral output losses:

- Most of the collateral output losses would be concentrated on short and critical interval users with PICs, for whom DAYS, USATISF, IMPADL, IMPIADL, KOSBERG and WKSAT all have collateral levels below their actual level. In the previous optimisation scenarios, and for the same two user groups, the collateral levels of IMPADL would have been greater than the actual levels. At least partly, this is related to the reduction in the budget for these two groups implied by the service-budget-constrained optimisation.

- As in the first two optimisation scenarios, the collateral levels of KOSBERG would be lower than the actual levels for the three applicable groups.
- As already mentioned, and in contrast with what was shown for the 'unconstrained' and the group-budget-constrained cases, the service-budget-constrained optimisation for DAYS yields a decrease in the collateral levels of WKSAT for two groups.

Collateral output gains:

- The significant gains in the collateral outputs would be concentrated on four groups: the three user groups with PICs (as in the previous two optimisations) and the long interval group with PICs.
- Two groups, the long and short interval groups without PICs, would not suffer from any reduction in their collateral output levels following the service-budget-constrained optimisation. In the previous optimisation scenarios, both would have suffered a significant deterioration in their DLD levels.
- In fact, DLD levels would increase for all groups after optimisation on DAYS, especially for users in the long interval categories and the critical interval category without PICs.
- All users but those in the critical interval category without PICs enjoy collateral IMPEMP outputs that would be greater than the actual levels. This is more so the lower the user's level of dependency.

Collateral outputs compared with the maximum achievable for each output

- The service-budget-constrained scenario shows many more collateral levels reaching more than 80 per cent and even 100 per cent of what could be achievable than the previous two optimisation scenarios. In fact, a total of 26 collateral levels would be above 80 per cent of the maximum achievable, against only 5 collateral levels below 40 per cent of their potentially achievable. As was previously argued, caution is required when interpreting this phenomenon, since it does not necessarily indicate that the absolute collateral levels would be higher for the service-budget-constrained optimisation.[2] In fact, since the optimisation on any of the collateral outputs would inevitably achieve greater overall output levels than the ones achieved through the optimisation for DAYS, this should be interpreted as the sign of substantial losses in the collateral output for the user groups for which the collateral level stands below the 100 per cent line.

Low collateral output levels:

- As was mentioned above, the service-budget-constrained optimisation would present very few collateral output levels that lay below 40 per cent of their achievable maximum. These would be: IMPIADL for those users in the critical interval without PICs (as was found in the previous two scenarios); WKSAT for short interval users with PICs (contrarily to what was found in the previous two optimisations) and IMPEMP for the critical interval cases with PICs (as found for the unconstrained optimisation).

High collateral output levels:

- For four user groups, those without PICs or in the long interval category, the collateral levels of WKSAT and IMPEMP would be well above the 100 per cent level. This would be so also with the 'unconstrained' optimisation, although to a lower degree. It reveals significant differences in the optimum allocation of resources implied by the service-budget-constrained optimisation of DAYS and the two other variables. Placed under either of the two scenarios (unconstrained or service-budget-constrained optimisations), a manager wishing to optimise DAYS would have therefore to forego significant levels of the WKSAT and UEMPOW.

- Given the constraint on service budgets, the levels of collateral outputs achieved for IMPADL would be higher than 80 per cent of their maximum for all the six user groups postulated. In fact, the collateral levels of IMPADL would be well above 100 per cent of their maximum attainable for all users with PICs and the users in the short interval category without PICs. The same argument stated for WKSAT and IMPEMP would therefore be valid for IMPADL also.

- The collaterals for KOSBERG and for DLD would be higher with fixed than with adjustable service budgets. The actual output would also be higher in relation to the maximum achievable with the optimisation scenario in question for the long and short interval groups. This would be due to a combination of factors. First, since the amount of social work would be limited to its observed total budget, the optimisations with respect to KOSBERG and DLD would yield much lower maximum attainable levels than for the other two scenarios. Second, even though not effective in the production of DAYS, services such as social work inputs, meals or nursing visits would still be allocated in the present optimisation, following their observed pattern of distribution, hence boosting the collateral levels of KOSBERG and DLD.

- Given either optimisation scenario, maximisation of days would cause fairly high levels of collateral outputs for USATISF.

3.   Overview

Technical efficiency

Because of the truncation in DAYS, it has not been possible to estimate a production frontier function. The inferences about technical efficiency must therefore be very limited. Nevertheless, the analysis of residuals shows small differences between the different user groups.

Input mix efficiency: the 'unconstrained' optimisation

• The 'unconstrained' optimisation would cause the concentration of the resources on three services: home care, day care and respite care.

• Of those three, home care levels would be substantially reduced, and similar quantities of the service would be allocated to all user groups. But both day care and respite care levels would be significantly increased, particularly for those users of higher dependency, cognitively impaired or with behavioural problems.

• Even though the unconstrained optimisation implies important shifts in resources between inputs, it would leave practically unaltered the levels of budgets associated with each of the six analysis groups.

• Given the optimum input mix, each of the six types of user postulated in the analysis would enjoy higher levels of DAYS. In other words, the unconstrained optimisation would not require output transfers between user groups.

• Overall, the unconstrained optimisation would achieve levels for DAYS 19 per cent higher than those observed.

The different optimising scenarios: how binding are the constraints?

• We have argued that unconstrained optimisation would not substantially alter user group budgets. Consequently, the optimum allocation of resources and levels of output derived from the group-budget fixed optimisation would be practically identical to those obtained from the 'unconstrained' optimising scenario. In that sense, fixing the user group budgets to their observed levels would not represent a binding constraint for the optimisation of DAYS.

• Overall, the group-budget-constrained optimisation would attain 99 per cent of the DAYS reached by the unconstrained optimisation.

• In contrast, fixing the service supply levels would cause considerable changes to the optimum input mixes and levels of output achieved.

    – The optimum solution would reduce differences in the allocation of budgets between user groups, and would imply lower budgets for the critical interval users and higher for the long interval groups. Consequently, the levels of DAYS achieved for critical and short interval users with PICs would be reduced.

    – Day and home care budgets would be evenly distributed among the six user groups, whereas respite care would be concentrated on those in the critical interval without PICs.

    – The overall gains from the optimisation would be much lower than for the previous optimising scenarios.

• Overall, the service-budget-constrained optimisation would attain 86 per cent of the DAYS reached by the unconstrained optimisation.

Collateral effects

- Optimising on DAYS would achieve low collateral levels mainly for KOSBERG (even though the structural model shows them to be inter-related), DLD and IMPIADL.
- Optimising on DAYS would achieve high collateral levels for WKSAT, USATISF and IMPADL for those users with high levels of dependency.

Notes

1   There are likely to be definitions of more refined and smaller user groups for which this would not be so.

2   In fact this could never be the case, at least for the total sum of user groups outcomes, since by definition the more constraining the optimisation scenario, the less freedom there is for optimisation, and the lower the absolute levels of the outputs that can be achieved.

15 Efficiencies for USATISF Indicator Variable (Degree of Satisfaction of User with the Overall Level of Service Received)

We have mentioned the double significance of USATISF. It is the most general of the output indicators of user satisfaction. And, chapter 12 showed, it contributes directly to the reduction in caregivers' sense of burden, and so indirectly to the increase in the length of users' stays in the community. The production function for USATISF is discussed in section 1 of chapter 5. It is summarised in table 5.1. Figure 5.1 shows the productivity curves.

1. Technical efficiency (figures 15.1 to 15.3)

The form of the production function was concave, allowing the fitting of a 'frontier function' compatible with the average production function shown in chapter 5. Figure 15.1 shows the variation in technical efficiency between the six user groups.

Variations between user groups
The main findings are that:
- The degree of technical inefficiency overall is approximately 24 per cent.
- There is little variation between groups with principal informal caregivers.
- Efficiency is greater among those with critical interval needs than others; 21 per cent compared with 27-28 per cent.

Gains from alternative strategies for efficiency improvement among the efficiency tail
One strategy of efficiency improvement suggested in chapter 13 was to attempt to raise the efficiency level of the least efficient to a higher *floor level*.

The nature of the improvement postulated can be illustrated from figure 15.2, which shows the results. The diagram reports the results of five assumptions which constitute variants of the general strategy. One assumption is that

Figure 15.1
Technical efficiency index* for user satisfaction with level of services

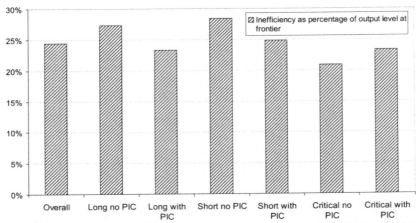

* ratio of difference between outputs achieved given service levels and mix to inputs predicted
for the user and output predicted given maximum technical efficiency given service levels and
mix to the actual output achieved

Figure 15.2
*Average output gain or cost saving from postulated improvement in
technical efficiency in the production of USATISF*

*Efficiency improvement strategy: the least efficient are made as efficient as units at a
prescribed higher percentile in the distribution ordered from least to most efficient*

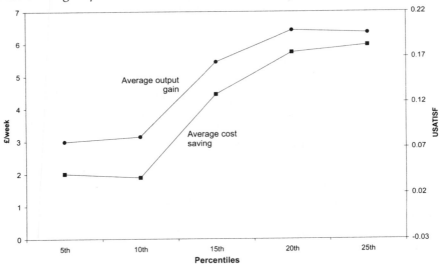

those with efficiencies lower than the unit which is at the fifth percentile point on the distribution of inefficiency would have their efficiency raised to the level of a unit at the fifth percentile. A second assumption is that all the units with inefficiencies lower than the level of the unit at the tenth percentile would be made as efficient as the unit at that tenth percentile level. And so on. That is, the efficiencies of the least efficient units would be improved to a prescribed semi-decile quantile (a percentile divisible by five) level higher than their current position in the ranking of units from the least to the most efficient. The results of these assumptions shown in the diagram illustrate the implications of choosing one of them rather than the others, and allow a comparison of this general strategy for improving efficiency with other strategies.

The results shown in figure 15.2 suggest that average output gains or its alternative, the average cost savings, would be greatest for improvements to a floor set at the 20th percentile point. However, the total gains would be greatest if the highest of the floors postulated were to be set, the 25th percentile point.

Chapter 13 postulated an alternative goal for the improvement of efficiency: the improvement of the efficiency of each of the least efficient 33 per cent of units by the same percentage. Figure 15.3 shows:

Figure 15.3
Average output gain or cost saving from postulated improvement in technical efficiency in the production of USATISF

Efficiency improvement strategy: prescribed percentage increase in efficiency for each of the 33 per cent most inefficient units

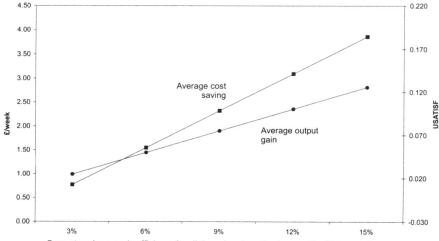

Percentage increase in efficiency for all those for whom the degree of inefficiency is lower than the most efficient 33%

- Gains in output and reduced costs from efficiency improvements would be in the range between 3 and 15 per cent. It follows from the nature of the change postulated that a linear relationship is predicted between cost savings and the percentage improvement in efficiency postulated, and the increase in output and the percentage improvement postulated. So the marginal gains would be the same for each of the alternative benefits for the same proportional improvements whatever the starting point: from 3 to 6 per cent, just as from 12 to 15 per cent.
- Average gains per case would be of approximately 27 pence per week per percentage improvement in efficiency among the third of units that are least efficient.

2.   Input mix efficiency

2.1.   *Assumption (a): Optimisation subject only to the overall budget: 'unconstrained optimisation' (figures 15.4 and 15.5)*

2.1.1. *Outputs, package costs, service mixes, and analysis group variations*

The results are shown in figure 15.4.

Figure 15.4
Input mix efficiency for user satisfaction with level of services (USATISF): 'unconstrained' optimisation

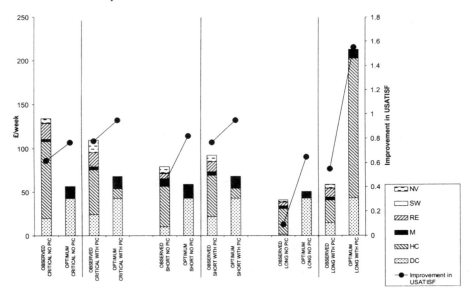

Inefficiencies in service balance

For all groups other than long interval need cases with principal informal care-givers, unrestricted optimisation of the total budget would cause large reductions in home care inputs. However, there would be an increase in the allocation of meals among all groups because of the very high productivity of small inputs shown in figure 5.1. But the cost of the increased meals would be a fraction of the reduction in the cost of the home care.

- There would be big increases in the inputs of day care. Figure 5.1 shows very high productivities from low spending, but rapidly diminishing returns. It is likely that large utilisation of conventional day care could be boring. There are two caveats. (a) Recent work has commended greater ingenuity in day care arrangements: more programmed activities elsewhere and the like. These might shift to a higher level the input at which returns rapidly diminish and become negative. (b) The results reflect the experience of those now provided with service. A large change in targeting might have different results. *Resources, Needs and Outcomes* showed how day care was often allocated *faute de mieux*. Many allocated it would consume it only for a short period. But among those for whom it was suitable, it was highly productive. It is not yet clear whether the first of these remains. If it does, the results of the optimisation model would have to be treated more cautiously.

- There would also be big reductions in the allocation of respite care. Though respite care would be used by individuals within groups, the case with circumstances that are average for the group would be insufficiently likely to use it for utilisation to appear on the figure. The circumstances in which respite care is most likely are also the most demoralising for users. The respite is more often for the caregiver than for the user. Heavy consumption of it is unlikely to increase user satisfaction with services. The productivity effect shown in figure 5.1 is as low as that of home care over much of the range of inputs.

- The total cost of the package would be substantially reduced for all groups save those with long interval needs. Long interval cases with principal informal caregivers would have much more costly packages, made up largely of home care. The biggest reductions in package costs would be for users with critical interval needs and no informal caregivers. Again, the results must be interpreted carefully. General morale is most likely to give a rosy glow to perceived satisfaction with the services among long interval need users with PICs, and most likely to depress the satisfaction among those without PICs and with critical interval needs.

Differences between user groups

- Optimisation is accompanied by improved outcomes for all groups. But the greatest gainers would be long interval cases (particularly those with PICs) and short interval cases without PICs. So the manager choosing this output as the sole maximand might be tempted to require the reallocation of resources to the more lightly dependent. However, the manager would be well advised to recall that in most of the ECCEP authorities, those of light dependency chosen to receive services are a small proportion of all those at that level of disability. The results are for a highly targeted subgroup of those of such dependency. Extending the group substantially might change the productivities.

The reduction of home care would be less for persons with PICs, because of the higher productivity for those shown in figure 5.1. In fact, the optimum home care allocation for long interval users with PICs would be many times greater than the observed level.

2.1.2. 'Collateral outputs': the consequences for other outputs of optimising on USATISF

The results are summarised in figure 15.5.

The actual output compared with the maximum achievable

- Figure 15.5 shows how the unconstrained optimisation of USATISF would achieve substantial relative improvements for all the six user groups postulated. In fact, for only two groups is USATISF more than 80 per cent of what would be achieved if it were the maximand of an optimisation. Consequently, USATISF can be seen as a less clear product of the current system than some of the other White Paper goals, particularly DAYS.
- Following optimisation, the greater relative improvements would be for those users in the long interval categories.

Collateral compared with actual outputs

Collateral output losses:
- Due to the significant decrease in their budgets implied by the optimisation, all the collateral output levels for the critical interval groups would be lower than the observed levels.
- There would be important losses in collateral DAYS and DLD for all but the long interval with PIC group. Furthermore, the losses would be greater, the higher the user's level of dependency.
- Optimising on USATISF brings about decreases in collateral IMPADL levels for all user groups.
- There is a negative gradient between the collateral levels for several outputs (KOSBERG, WKSAT, IMPIADL, IMPEMP) and the users' level of dependency: whereas users of lower dependency would enjoy higher collateral levels than observed, users of higher dependency reach collateral levels that would be lower than the actual levels.

Collateral output gains:
- There would be relatively few gains in collateral levels, these being concentrated on the users of relative low dependency.

Figure 15.5
Collateral output levels for optimisation on USATISF with 'unconstrained' optimisation

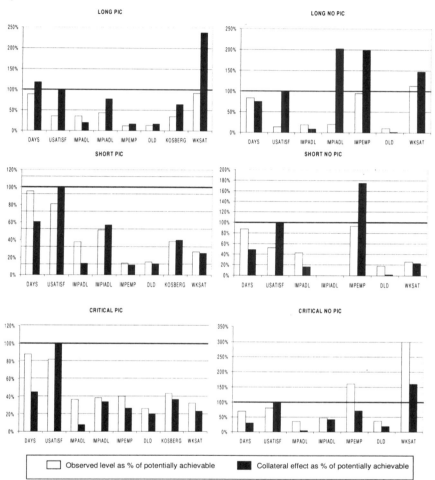

Collateral outputs compared with the maximum achievable for each output

Low collateral output levels:

- Given unconstrained optimisation on USATISF, a very substantial number of collateral levels would not reach 40 per cent of the potentially achievable. Therefore, USATISF would not be a good choice of maximand were the goal also to produce a range of other benefits.

- Most of these low collateral levels would be concentrated on the users of higher disability or with PICs. For users in the critical interval with PIC group, all collateral levels excepting DAYS would lie below the 40 per cent benchmark. Even for DAYS, the collateral level for the group would be just above 40 per cent of the maximum attainable.

High collateral output levels:
- Only users in the long interval groups achieve a significant amount (three each) of collateral outputs above 80 per cent of the potentially achievable. These would be DAYS, IMPIADL and WKSAT for the long interval users with PICs, and IMPIADL, IMPEMP and WKSAT for the long interval users without PICs, DAYS lying just below the 80 per cent level.
- The collateral levels of WKSAT would be well above the 100 per cent line for three user groups, namely the two groups, long interval and critical interval users without PICs. This finding reveals how the 'unconstrained' optimisation on USATISF would attribute much higher levels of resources to those three user groups than what is implied by the equivalent optimisation on WKSAT. The same conclusion would apply to long and short interval users without PICs for IMPEMP, and to long interval users without PICs for IMPIADL.

2.2. Assumption (b): Optimisation subject to user group average budgets: 'group-budget-constrained optimisation' (figures 15.6 and 15.7)

2.2.1. Outputs, package costs, service mixes, and analysis group variations

The results are shown in figure 15.6.

Inefficiencies in service balance
- The restriction that each group should have the same overall level of expenditure prevents the concentration of home care on long interval cases with PICs. There would be nevertheless large reductions, and the virtual removal of home care from two groups (long and short interval without PICs).
- As in the 'unconstrained' scenario, the optimum service mix would result in a significant increase of inputs of day care and meals.
- There would still be such large reductions in the utilisation of respite care that the average over each group would be too small to be represented on the figure.
- The constraint on the optimisation would prevent the big redistribution of average package costs towards those of long interval need.

Differences between user groups
- Again, as in the 'unconstrained' optimisation, all the groups postulated in the analysis experience an increase in levels of USATISF.
- The greatest gains would be for short and long interval cases without PICs,

Figure 15.6
Input mix efficiency for user satisfaction with level of services (USATISF):
group-budget-constrained optimisation

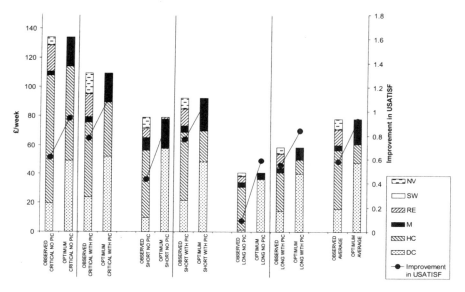

but no group would gain to the extent that long interval cases without PICs
would gain with unrestricted optimisation.

2.2.2. *'Collateral outputs': the consequences for other outputs of optimising on*
USATISF

The results are summarised in figure 15.7.

The actual output compared with the maximum achievable

- The group-budget-constrained optimisation yields significant relative improvements for all six user groups. These would be particularly high for the
  users without PICs.

Collateral compared with actual outputs

- The group-budget-constrained optimisation would yield equivalent number of significant gains and losses in collateral outputs.
- Moreover, losses and gains would be scattered among the different user
  groups.

  Collateral output losses:

- Optimising USATISF while holding the group budgets constant produces
  consistent lower collateral levels for all groups for IMPADL, DLD, and for

Figure 15.7
Collateral output levels for optimisation on USATISF with group-budget-constrained optimisation

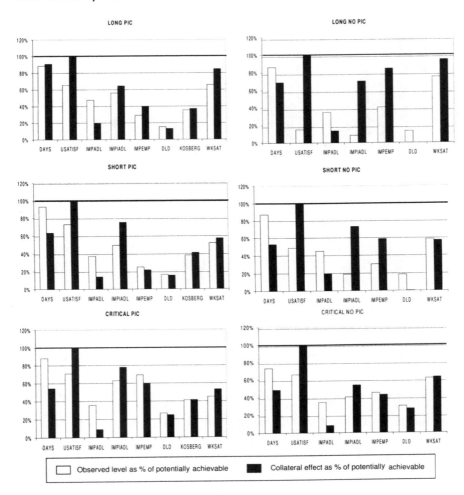

DAYS for all users but those in the long interval category with PICs. For DAYS, the loss would be of at least 20 percentage points.

- There is a small fall in IMPEMP collateral levels for users in the critical interval categories and in the short interval category with PICs.

Collateral output gains:

- The optimum input mix generates gains for all users in collateral levels for

IMPIADL and for all users but those in the short interval category without PICs for WKSAT.

- Three user groups, the long interval categories and the short interval group without PICs would enjoy very significant relative improvements in collateral levels for IMPEMP.
- The collateral levels of KOSBERG would remain very close to their observed values. Compared with the optimisation of DAYS, optimising on USATISF would therefore confer greater benefits in the form of reduced felt burden of caregiving.

Collateral outputs compared with the maximum achievable for each output
- Although the optimisation on USATISF with constrained user groups yields a number of increases in collateral levels, there remain many more collateral levels below 40 per cent than above 80 per cent of their maximum achievable.

Low collateral output levels:
- For all groups, the collateral levels of IMPADL, DLD and KOSBERG (even though levels of KOSBERG would not experience significant decreases after optimisation) remain at approximately 40 per cent or below their potentially achievable.

High collateral output levels:
- After optimisation on USATISF, the collateral levels of WKSAT would be higher than 80 per cent of their maximum attainable for users in the long interval groups, and near 60 per cent for the rest of the groups.
- For all user groups but those in the critical interval category without PICs, the collateral levels of IMPIADL reach levels above 60 per cent of their potentially achievable.

2.3. Assumption (c): Total expenditure on each service maintained: 'service-budget-constrained' optimisation (figures15.8 and 15.9)

2.3.1. Outputs, package costs, service mixes, and analysis group variations

The results are shown in figure 15.8.

Inefficiencies in service balance
- The big redistribution of home care to users with long interval needs and PICs that would follow from unconstrained optimisation of the budget would also occur with fixed total quantities of each service, but there would also be a redistribution towards persons in short interval need with PICs. Home care costs would on average be too small to be shown on the figure for users without PICs.
- Changes in day care distributions would be much smaller than with any of the previous two optimisation scenarios, all groups receiving similar quantities of the service.

Figure 15.8
Input mix efficiency for user satisfaction with level of services (USATISF):
service-budget-constrained optimisation

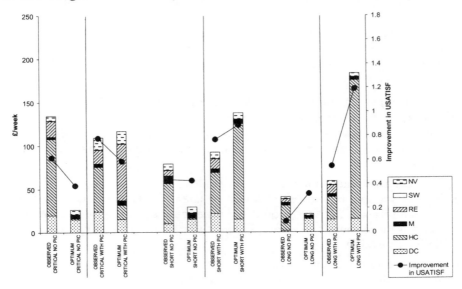

- Respite care would be concentrated on critical interval cases with PICs.

- Package costs would differ much more between groups than in the other two optimisations. Users with PICs would receive much higher budgets.

Differences between user groups

The welfare of critical interval users would be reduced. Only long interval need cases, especially those without PICs, would have an improvement in welfare comparable to that under unconstrained optimisation.

2.3.2. *'Collateral outputs': the consequences for other outputs of optimising on USATISF*

The results are shown in figure 15.9.

The actual output compared with the maximum achievable

- In contrast to the first two scenarios, the service-budget-constrained optimisation implies transfers in the levels of outputs between the user groups.

- Hence, the optimum input mix implies that users with critical interval needs would forego significant levels of USATISF, reallocated mainly to users in the long interval need categories.

Figure 15.9
Collateral output levels for optimisation on USATISF with service-budget-constrained optimisation

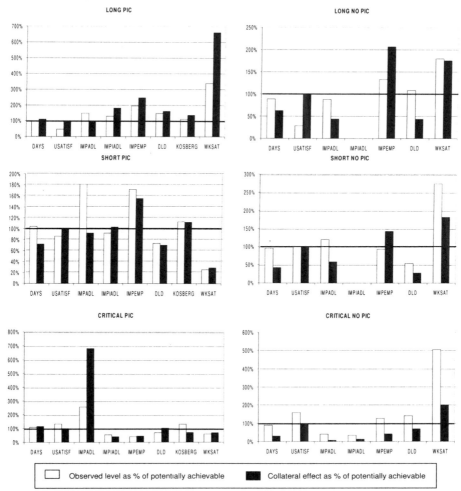

Collateral compared with actual outputs

- Overall, optimising USATISF with fixed service budgets produces more collateral losses (20) than gains (14).
- Although generally users with PICs enjoy more gains than users without PICs, most of the gains and losses in collateral output levels would be concentrated on two groups.

Collateral output losses:

- For one group, the critical interval without PICs, all of the collateral output levels would be lower than the actual levels. Optimising on USATISF with fixed input budgets would therefore yield for this group a reduction in all the dimensions of welfare (including USATISF itself) explored in the analysis.
- Collateral levels of WKSAT would be lower than the actual levels for all users without PICs. This is more accentuated the higher the level of need of the users.
- There is a negative gradient between KOSBERG collateral levels and levels of dependency, so that whereas for long interval users collateral KOSBERG levels would be notably above the actual levels, there would be a clear deterioration in KOSBERG collateral levels for users with critical interval needs.
- There would be substantial decreases in collateral levels for IMPADL for all users but those with critical interval needs and PICs.
- For DAYS and DLD, all users without PICs or in the short interval category with PICs would suffer collateral output losses.

Collateral output gains:

- Most of the output gains would be concentrated on the users with long interval needs and PICs For those, all collateral output levels except for IMPADL would be above the actual levels. This would clearly be due to the high budget allocated to the group by the optimisation.
- Collateral levels of WKSAT would be higher than the actual levels for all users with PICs This would be more accentuated the lower the level of need of the users. This is the opposite effect to the one described for users without PICs.

Collateral outputs compared with the maximum achievable for each output

- Even though after optimisation there would be more losses in collateral outputs than gains, a significant number of collateral levels remain at relatively high levels, this being particularly so for the users with PICs.

Low collateral output levels:

- Users with critical interval needs and no PICs observed the highest number (four out of six) of outputs with low collateral levels. These would be DAYS, IMPIADL, IMPADL and IMPEMP.
- DAYS collateral levels lay at 40 per cent or less of their maximum achievable for two user groups: those with critical or short interval needs without PICs.
- Both IMPIADL and IMPEMP collateral levels would be below 40 per cent of their maximum achievable for users with critical interval needs.

High collateral output levels:

- All collateral KOSBERG levels would be above 80 per cent of their maximum achievable.
- Collateral WKSAT levels for all users but those with short interval needs and PICs would be above 80 per cent of their maximum attainable.

- A majority of collateral output levels would be above 80 per cent of their maximum achievable for users in the short interval category with PICs.
- All collateral output levels for users in the long interval category with PICs would be higher than 80 per cent of their maximum achievable.
- In fact, the majority of them (WKSAT, KOSBERG, DLD, IMPEMP, IMPIADL and DAYS) would reach levels above the 100 per cent line. This reveals that with respect to such outputs and in a world that is constrained in the overall supply of individual services, users in the long interval need category with PICs would be 'over assisted' by the optimisation on USATISF.
- The same reasoning can be applied to:
  - users with PICs for WKSAT,
  - users with long or short interval needs for IMPEMP,
  - users with critical interval needs and PICs for IMPADL,
  - users with long or critical interval needs with PICs for DAYS and DLD.

3.   Overview

Technical efficiency
- The level of inefficiency was on average 24 per cent.
- There was little variation between the six groups postulated in the analysis.
- Average cost savings or output gains from improvements in the least efficient units would increase as the inefficiency of higher proportions of the least efficient cases were raised up to the level of the 20th percentile unit.

Input mix efficiency: the 'unconstrained' optimisation
- The unconstrained optimisation of USATISF would reduce to three the number of services to be allocated: home care, day care and meals.
- Levels of home care would be greatly reduced but for users with long interval needs and with PICs, for whom they would be very significantly increased.
- Levels of day care and meals would be increased for all user groups, and allocated to each of them in similar quantities.
- As a consequence, the optimum mix would cause a large redistribution in the budgets from users with critical and short interval needs towards users in the long interval groups.
- Levels of USATISF for all groups would be noticeably increased for all user groups, but particularly for users in the long interval need groups.
- Overall, the unconstrained optimisation would achieve levels of USATISF 76 per cent higher than the ones observed.

The different optimising scenarios: how binding would be the constraints?
- Compared with the unconstrained case, fixing the group budgets causes a redistribution of the budgets (and consequently of benefits) from users with long interval needs with PICs towards users in higher levels of dependency.

- There is also a redistribution of the levels of home care in the same direction.
- Overall, the group-constrained optimisation achieves 95 per cent of the levels of USATISF achieved by the unconstrained optimisation.
- As in DAYS optimisation, it would be the service budget constraint that would cause most changes with respect to the unconstrained solution. Services would shift towards those users with PICs, particularly of lower dependency.
- Respite care would be concentrated on users with critical interval needs and PICs, and home care on users with long and short interval needs and PICs.
- The service-budget constraint optimum input mixes would yield lower collateral levels for users in the higher levels of need, therefore concentrating even more than the unconstrained scenario most of the output gains on users with long interval needs.
- Overall, the service-constrained optimisation achieves 67 per cent of the levels of USATISF achieved by the unconstrained optimisation.

The collateral effects
- Discounting user group resource transfers, the optimisation of USATISF would increase levels of IMPIADL for all users, reaching collateral levels above 80 per cent of the potentially achievable for all users but those in the critical interval need group with no PICs.
- Considerable collateral gains would also be achieved for WKSAT for all groups but those in the short interval need group with no PICs.
- Optimising USATISF brings, however, low levels of collateral outputs for IMPADL and DLD, leaving KOSBERG unaltered and decreasing significantly DAYS for all users but those with long interval needs and PICs.

16 Efficiencies for IMPADL Indicator Variable (Degree of Improvement in Personal Care Functions of Daily Living Ascribed by User to Social Services)

One could envisage two contexts providing a rationale for the choice of the improvement in personal care functioning ascribed to services as the sole objective.

- The improvement of functioning in these activities of daily living is at the core of home care. It could be argued that the other influences on the attainment of other goals are complex.
- The search for consistency through similarity in the criteria for matching services to needs and qualifying criteria used for establishing eligibility for insurance benefits might suggest that one would consider the maximisation of IMPADL. This could arise in a financing system based on a national funding pool with standard criteria administered by local authority care management teams as fiscal intermediaries; one scenario compatible with, for instance, the recommendations of the JRF Inquiry (Joseph Rowntree Foundation, 1995).

The dependent variable is defined in table 1 of chapter 2. The average production function is described in table 6.1 and the productivity effects in figures 6.1 and 6.2.

1. Technical efficiency (figures 16.1 to 16.3)

Variations between user groups. The form of the average production function allowed the fitting of a frontier production function. The pattern of variations between user groups shown in figure 16.1 implied by the frontier function shows:

- On average, a degree of inefficiency of about 24 per cent. Allowing for risk

Figure 16.1
Technical efficiency index* for improvement in ADL-related states due to services

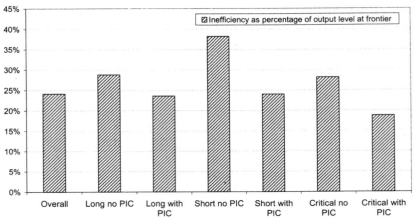

* ratio of difference between outputs achieved given service levels and mix to inputs predicted for the user and output predicted given maximum technical efficiency given service levels and mix to the actual output achieved

Figure 16.2
Average output gain or cost saving from postulated improvement in technical efficiency in the production of IMPADL

Efficiency improvement strategy: the least efficient are made as efficient as units at a prescribed higher percentile in the distribution ordered from least to most efficient

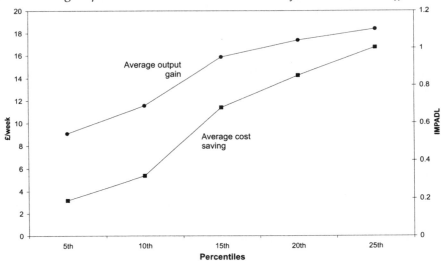

Figure 16.3
Average output gain or cost saving from postulated improvement in technical efficiency in the production of IMPADL

Efficiency improvement strategy: prescribed percentage increase in efficiency for each of the 33 per cent most inefficient units

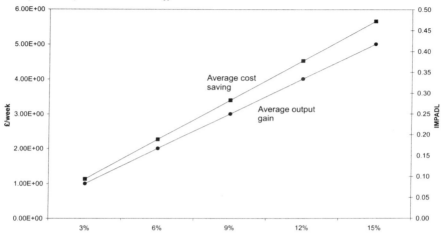

Percentage increase in efficiency for all those for whom the degree of inefficiency is lower
than the most efficient 33%

factors, were all cases to produce the outcomes achieved from the input mix as efficiently as for the case for whom the production was most efficient, the output would be 24 per cent greater.

- Large differences in the average degree of efficiency between groups. The efficiency was particularly low for short interval cases without principal informal caregivers. Were the services for them to be fully technically efficient, the model implies, there would be a 38 per cent higher level of the output. In contrast, the potential increase in outputs from fully efficient transformation of the mix of services into outputs would be only 19 per cent among users with principal informal caregivers with critical interval needs.

The gains from the alternative investment strategies. Consider the two hypothetical strategies for efficiency improvement: the improvement of efficiency of the least efficient to a higher floor level, and similar proportionate improvements in efficiency for each unit in the least efficient third of units. (Fuller explanations are provided in chapters 13 and 15.)

Figure 16.2 shows that the average gains made would be sensitive to the floor set. The marginal gains would be greatest if the floor were set at the fifteenth percentile. However, the average gain would increase as higher proportions of users were included. Therefore, for the percentiles postulated, the average gain per unit would be greatest for the 25th percentile. That would be so either for IMPADL or for its alternative, the cost saving.

The alternative strategy is to raise the efficiency of the most inefficient 33 per cent by the same proportion, the analysis examining also the effects of choosing one from a range of relative increases. Figure 16.3 shows that the average gains would be of approximately 33 pence per week per percentage point improvement in efficiency for the third least efficient.

2.   Input mix efficiency

2.1.   Assumption (a): Optimisation subject only to the overall budget: 'unconstrained optimisation' (figures 16.4 and 16.5)

2.1.1.   Outputs, package costs, service mixes, and analysis group variations

The results are shown in figure 16.4.

Inefficiencies in service balance
- The optimum solution for the unconstrained optimisation of IMPADL entails almost identical packages of care for all user groups.
- Packages with an efficient input mix would on average contain less home

Figure 16.4
Input mix efficiency for improvement in ADL-related states due to services (IMPADL): 'unconstrained' optimisation

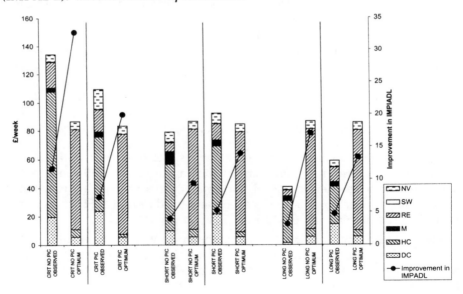

care and fewer meals, irrespective of the user group, despite the productivity of home care for 77 per cent of its recipients shown in figure 6.1.
• Packages would also contain less day care despite a productivity effect when day care is combined with respite care.
• Respite care would be greatly increased for all groups, which would now receive approximately 70 pence per week, the maximum allowed in the model.
• Nursing visits would constitute a larger share of the packages and would be allocated in the same levels to all users, reflecting the productivity effect shown in figure 6.2.
• Social work and meals would not form part of the optimum package.
• There would be significant output gains for all groups.

Differences between user groups
• As was mentioned above, the unconstrained optimisation of IMPADL yields almost identical packages of care for all users.
• The main output gainers from optimisation would be critical interval cases without PICs, though all groups would gain considerably.
• Package costs would on average be substantially lower for critical interval cases and higher for long interval cases. The redistribution would be particularly large for critical and long interval cases without PICs.

2.1.2. 'Collateral outputs': the consequences for other outputs of optimising on IMPADL

The case for the optimisation of IMPADL as the sole criterion seems weak. It could only be argued as the system goal if its production yielded high levels of other variables, particularly the crucial and interdependent variables such as DAYS, KOSBERG and USATISF, and so if the collateral output levels associated with IMPADL were to be high.

The results are summarised in figure 16.5.

The actual output compared with the maximum achievable
• After 'unconstrained' optimisation, all user groups enjoy great relative increases in their levels of IMPADL.
• There is therefore no transfer in outputs implied by the optimum input mix.

Collateral compared with actual outputs
A large number (26) of collateral outputs would be lower than the actual levels, with the few improvements concentrated in one single user group.

There would be losses in collateral levels of:
• DAYS for all users but those with critical needs and no PICs.
• KOSBERG for all three applicable groups.
• USATISF, IMPIADL and IMPEMP for all users but those with long interval needs without PICs.
• WKSAT for users with short or critical interval needs.

Figure 16.5
Collateral output levels for optimisation on IMPADL with 'unconstrained'
optimisation

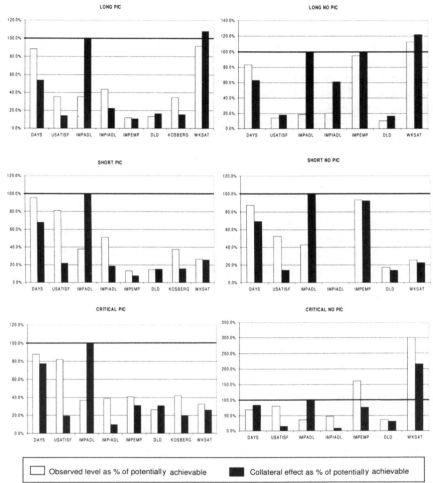

There would be gains in collateral levels of:

- DLD for users with long interval needs or users without PICs.
- All output variables but DAYS for users with long interval needs and no PIC.

Collateral outputs compared with the maximum achievable for each output

- The unconstrained optimisation leaves many more collateral output levels
  below 40 per cent than above 80 per cent of the maximum attainable levels.

- Though there would be no clear 'winners', most of the high collateral levels correspond to users without PICs.

Collateral output levels lay below 40 per cent of the maximum achievable for:

- USATISF, DLD, KOSBERG for all applicable user groups.
- IMPEMP for all users with PICs.
- IMPIADL for all users but those with long interval needs and no PICs.

Collateral output levels reach 80 per cent or above of the maximum achievable for:

- IMPEMP for all users without PICs.
- WKSAT for users with long interval needs and users with critical interval needs and without PIC.
- DAYS only for users with critical interval needs and no PICs.

2.2. Assumption (b): Optimisation subject to user group average budgets: 'group-budget-constrained optimisation' (figures 16.6 and 16.7)

2.2.1. Outputs, package costs, service mixes, and analysis group variations

The results are shown in figure 16.6.

Figure 16.6
Input mix efficiency for improvement in ADL-related states due to services (IMPADL): group-budget-constrained optimisation

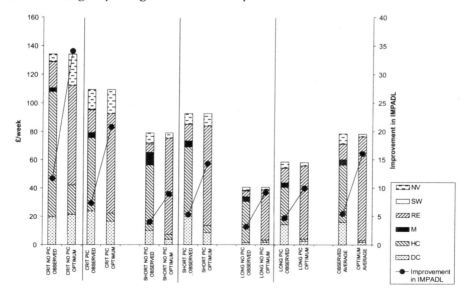

Inefficiencies in service balance
- As with unconstrained optimisation, group-budget-constrained optimisa-tion would shift resources to the newer services. It would much reduce the inputs of home care, and cease altogether the provision of meals and social work inputs. Again, there would be big increases in the utilisation of respite care. The utilisation of day care would not be decreased for users in the criti-cal interval need category, although it would only be residual for users with lower levels of need.
- The increase in community nurse visits would be focused more on those of critical interval need.

Differences between user groups
- All groups gain with group-budget-constrained optimisation also. For most groups, output gains would be similar given either scenario, and somewhat lower for the long interval cases.
- Package costs are by definition fixed given group budgets, and therefore still present a marked gradient by levels of dependency.

2.2.2. 'Collateral outputs': the consequences for other outputs of optimising on IMPADL

Results are summarised in figure 16.7.

The actual output compared with the maximum achievable
- As in the previous scenario, all users enjoy gains in IMPADL following group-budget optimisation, with relative improvements of approximately 60 per cent.

Collateral compared with actual outputs
- The optimisation leaves far many more losses than gains in collateral levels: collateral levels would be below actual levels for 31 outputs, the reverse be-ing true for only six outputs.
- Although very few, the collateral gains would be concentrated on users of critical interval needs.

There would be losses in collateral levels of:
- USATISF, IMPIADL and IMPEMP for the six groups defined in the analysis.
- DLD and DAYS for all users with long or short interval needs.
- KOSBERG for the three applicable groups.
- WKSAT for users with long interval needs and with short interval needs and no PICs.

There would be gains in collateral levels of:
- DAYS and DLD for users with critical interval needs. As was mentioned in the DAYS optimisation section, it makes sense for improvements in IMPADL to be associated with extending the length of stay in the community for users in

Figure 16.7
Collateral output levels for optimisation on IMPADL with group-budget-constrained optimisation

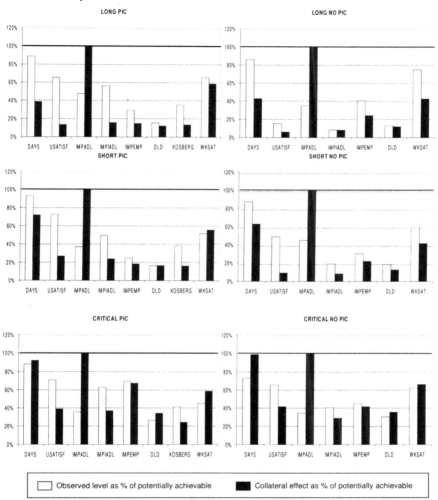

the critical interval need category. Probably the same argument is applicable to DLD.

- WKSAT for users in the critical interval need category and users with short interval needs and PIC, maybe reflecting the importance in the care managers' priorities that achieving improvements in the ability to undertake ADL tasks has for critical interval need cases.

Collateral outputs compared with the maximum achievable for each output

- As in the previous optimisation scenario, most of the collateral outputs remain at very low levels.
- In fact, there would be only two collateral output levels reaching more than 80 per cent of their potentially achievable level. As in the 'unconstrained' optimisation, they correspond to users with critical interval needs.

Collateral output levels lay below 40 per cent of the maximum achievable for:
- USATISF, IMPIADL, KOSBERG and DLD for all applicable user groups.
- IMPEMP for all users except those with critical interval needs and with PICs.
- DAYS for users with long interval needs.

Collateral output levels reach 80 per cent or above of the maximum achievable for:
- DAYS for users in the critical interval need groups.

2.3. Assumption (c): Total expenditure on each service maintained: 'service-budget-constrained' optimisation (figures 16.8 and 16.9)

2.3.1. Outputs, package costs, service mixes, and analysis group variations

The results are shown in figure 16.8.

Figure 16.8
Input mix efficiency for improvement in ADL-related states due to services (IMPADL): service-budget-constrained optimisation

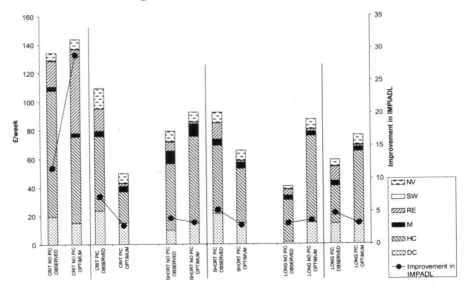

Inefficiencies in service balance
- In contrast with the unconstrained maximisation, there would be important inputs of home care and meals for all users.
- The pattern for day care would be broadly similar to that with unconstrained optimisation. There would be a large increase for long interval users without PICs.
- There would be an increase in respite care for critical interval users without PICs at the expense of reductions in respite care for all other cases, particularly critical and short interval cases with PICs. This contrasts with big increases in respite allocation to all case types given unconstrained optimisation.
- Nursing visits would be reduced for users with critical interval needs and PICs, but there would be small increases for other critical interval need cases and for long interval cases. Under either unconstrained or group-budget-constrained optimisation, long interval cases would be allocated more nurse visits.

Differences between user groups
- As with unconstrained optimisation, the package costs would be increased for long interval cases, but the increases would be used to finance extra home care not respite care.
- Critical interval need users with PICs would receive significantly lower budgets than in the unconstrained optimisation case. This lower package would consist mainly of nursing inputs, home and day care, instead of respite care.
- Critical interval need users without PICs would receive much higher budgets than in the unconstrained optimisation case. The additional expenditure would finance much more home care input.
- The gain in ADL functioning would be concentrated almost exclusively on users with critical interval needs and no PICs, leaving the rest of the users with either the same or lower levels of IMPADL.
- Although the package costs for short interval and long interval cases would be much the same as those from unconstrained optimisation, again the budgets would be used for home care, not respite care, and the output would actually fall for the two short interval case types, not rise substantially.

2.3.2. *'Collateral outputs': the consequences for other outputs of optimising on IMPADL*

The results are shown in figure 16.9.

The actual output compared with the maximum achievable
In contrast with the first two optimisation scenarios, the service-budget-constrained optimisation requires some users to 'give up' IMPADL in order to increase its overall levels. In fact, the optimum input mix produces very sub-

Figure 16.9
Collateral output levels for optimisation on IMPADL with service-budget-constrained optimisation

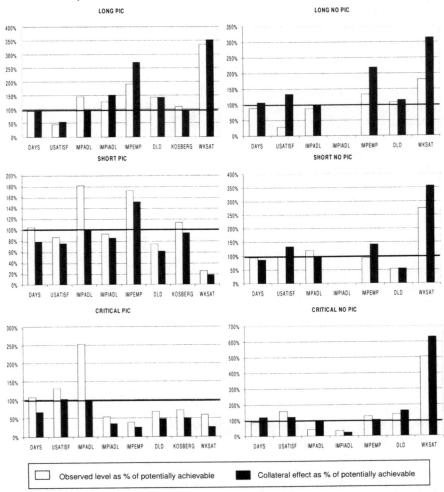

stantial reductions in IMPADL levels for four user groups (those with PICs and those with short interval need without PICs).

Collateral compared with actual outputs

- Although to a lesser degree, the majority of changes in collateral outputs imply a reduction from the actual levels (for 20 outputs, against 15 increases).

- Most of the gains in collateral outputs would be for users without PICs, and users with long interval needs.

There would be losses in collateral levels of:
- All collateral outputs for users with short and critical interval need with PICs.
- KOSBERG for the three applicable groups.
- DLD for all users with PICs.
- DAYS for users with short interval needs and users with critical interval needs and PICs.
- IMPIADL, USATISF and IMPEMP for users in the critical interval group or with short interval needs and PICs.

There would be gains in collateral levels of:
- USATISF and IMPEMP for users with long interval needs and short interval needs without PICs.
- DAYS for users with long interval needs or with critical interval needs without PICs.
- WKSAT for users without PICs and users with long interval needs.
- DLD for users without PICs.

Collateral outputs compared with the maximum achievable for each output
Given the constraints on the allocation of the different services, and hence the lower potentially achievable levels of collateral outputs, the service-budget-constrained optimisation reaches a much greater number of high collateral relative outputs than the two precedent optimisation scenarios. Therefore there are 25 collateral levels above 80 per cent of their maximum achievable, against only 5 below 40 per cent.

Collateral output levels lay below 40 per cent of the maximum achievable for:
- IMPIADL, IMPEMP and WKSAT for users with critical interval needs and PICs.
- IMPIADL for users with critical interval needs and no PICs.
- WKSAT for user with short interval need and PICs.

Collateral output levels reach 80 per cent or above of the maximum achievable for:
- DAYS and IMPEMP for all users except those with critical interval needs and PICs. Many critical interval cases with PICs could be expected to remain in their current situation for a shorter period than most other groups, making lower levels of IMPEMP less unacceptable.
- KOSBERG for users with long and short interval needs.
- For several user groups and variables, the collateral levels reach significantly over the 100 per cent line. As mentioned before, this indicates, in terms of each of the collateral outputs, the 'over-allocation' of resources to such user groups. There is evidence of this for:
- WKSAT for users with long interval needs and users without PICs.

- IMPEMP for users with long and short interval needs.
- USATISF for users without PICs.
- IMPIADL for users with long interval needs and PICs.
- DLD for users with long interval needs or with critical interval needs without PICs.

3.   Overview

Technical efficiency
- The average inefficiency rate for IMPADL is 24 per cent, the lowest being for the packages of users with critical interval needs and PICs, and the highest for users with short interval needs and no PICs.
- Average cost savings or output gains from improvements in the least efficient units would rise as larger proportions of the least efficient cases were included.

Input mix efficiency: the 'unconstrained' optimisation
- The unconstrained optimisation for IMPADL would concentrate the resources on one input (respite care), providing residual amounts of another three (day care, home care and nursing inputs).
- After optimisation the packages of care for the six groups in the analysis are almost identical. The differences in the observed budgets therefore disappear.
- Although the six groups significantly increase their levels of IMPADL, users with critical interval needs and no PICs enjoy the greatest gains.
- Overall, the unconstrained optimisation increases the levels of IMPADL to almost 300 per cent of their observed levels.

The different optimising scenarios: how binding would be the constraints?
- Compared with the unconstrained case, the group-budget constraint optimisation implies very similar proportional mixes of the four inputs mentioned above. There is however a slight bias for the concentration of nursing and home care inputs on the users with highest levels of need.
- Because of the fixation of the resources destined to the different users, the group-budget-constrained optimisation implies higher IMPADL output levels for users with critical interval needs and lower for the users of lower dependency than in the unconstrained case.
- Overall, the group-budget-constrained optimisation reaches 91 per cent of the output levels achieved in the 'unconstrained' optimisation.
- Again, fixing the supply levels of the different services alters more severely the distribution of services and outputs.
- Resources would be concentrated on those users with PICs, particularly those with critical interval needs.

- Users in the long interval need category receive higher budgets than the observed.
- Home care inputs would be spread evenly between the different groups.
- Respite care would be concentrated mainly on users with critical interval need and PICs.
- As a consequence, only one group, critical interval need without PICs, reaches substantial improvements in IMPADL, with the rest of the groups enjoying the same or lower levels.
- Overall, service-budget-constrained optimisation reaches 42 per cent of the levels attained by the unconstrained optimisation.

The collateral effects
- For both the 'unconstrained' and the group-budget-constrained optimisations, the collateral output levels would be typically worse than the observed and lower than 40 per cent of their achievable maximum.
- When fixing group-budgets, IMPADL as a maximand brings about high collateral levels only for DAYS, and only for critical interval need users.
- On the other hand, even though much lower absolute levels of IMPADL would be achieved, its maximisation in a system with fixed service supply reaches high collateral levels for a significant number of outputs. Therefore, if the system is doomed to an excessive incrementalism in the determination of service budget shares, optimisation by IMPADL would not have disastrous results for some of the main outputs.

17 Efficiencies for IMPIADL Indicator Variable (Degree of Improvement in Household Care and Other Instrumental Care Functions of Daily Living Ascribed by User to Social Services)

The rationale for the choice of such an indicator is that this broader indicator of dependency, relating to instrumental activities of daily living, is focused on the levels at which community social services have traditionally directed their tasks. The choice would have been more appropriate given the divisions of labour and service tasks of the early 1980s, before the reform critique was developed. IMPIADL might be a suitable goal to set for an agency subsidising provision in a financing system in which tasks to compensate for ADLs were financed by another agency. However, the production function for IADLs alone would not be ideal for the purpose because the performance of tasks related to the one tend to make the use of resources for the production of the other more effective. That is, there are joint supply effects between IMPADL and IMPIADL, as has been seen in chapter 12. In this case, inefficiencies for the production of the two outputs together may be overstated by a production function for one of the products only.

The production function is described in table 6.2 and the productivity curves in figure 6.9.

1. Technical efficiency (figures 17.1 to 17.3)

Efficiency variation between groups. The frontier function yielded the pattern of variations between user groups described in figure 17.1. The main features of the pattern are:
- The average level of efficiency is higher — that is, inefficiency is less — than for IMPADL, of the order of 19 per cent rather than 24 per cent.

Figure 17.1
Technical efficiency index* for improvement in IADL-related states due to services

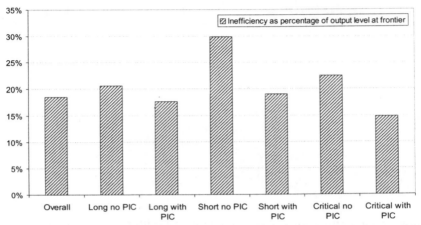

* ratio of difference between outputs achieved given service levels and mix to inputs predicted for the user and output predicted given maximum technical efficiency given service levels and mix to the actual output achieved

Figure 17.2
Average output gain or cost saving from postulated improvement in technical efficiency in the production of IMPIADL

Efficiency improvement strategy: the least efficient are made as efficient as units at a prescribed higher percentile in the distribution ordered from least to most efficient

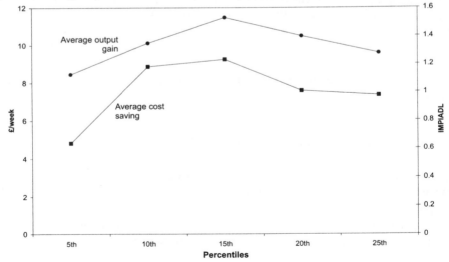

Figure 17.3

Average output gain or cost saving from postulated improvement in technical efficiency in the production of IMPIADL

Efficiency improvement strategy: prescribed percentage increase in efficiency for each of the 33 per cent most inefficient units

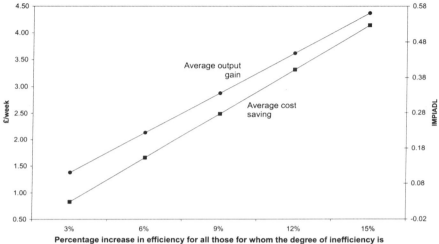

Percentage increase in efficiency for all those for whom the degree of inefficiency is lower than the most efficient 33%

- The pattern of variation between user groups is similar for IMPADL and IMPIADL. Inefficiency is highest for short interval users without PICs (30 per cent inefficient). It is lowest for critical interval users with a PIC (15 per cent inefficient).

Gains from alternative strategies for efficiency improvement. The first strategy postulated is to improve the standards in the tail to a selected efficiency floor. Figure 17.2 shows that the floor which captures the greatest overall gain is at the 25th percentile. But the greatest average gain among gainers would be obtained setting a floor at the 15th percentile.

The results of the alternative efficiency improvement strategy, raising each unit among the least efficient third by the same percentage, are reported in figure 17.3. The average cost saving per percentage point improvement in efficiency for the third least efficient is 28 pence per week.

2.   Input mix efficiency

The same three sets of assumptions about the constraints on optimisation are considered as for the other variables. Their rationales have been discussed above.

2.1.   Assumption (a): Optimisation subject only to the overall budget: 'unconstrained optimisation' (figures 17.4 and 17.5)

2.1.1.   Outputs, package costs, service mixes, and analysis group variations

The results are shown in figure 17.4.

Figure 17.4
Input mix efficiency for improvement in IADL-related states due to services (IMPIADL): 'unconstrained' optimisation

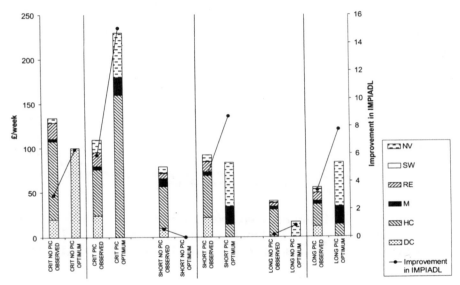

Inefficiencies in service balance

Unconstrained optimisation has the following effects, the figure implies:

*   As for other important outcomes, the shift of resources from home care for five user groups. For users in the critical interval need group, however, a very substantial increase in the level of home care, reaping the benefits of the increasing returns to scale for home care shown in figure 6.9.
*   The shift of resources into community nursing for all users with PICs, and for users in the long interval category.
*   The shift of resources into day care for users with critical interval needs and no PICs though, unlike for other outputs, not for the other user groups.
*   The reduction in the inputs of respite care, reflecting the absence of a productivity effect in figure 6.9. This is in complete contrast with the pattern for some other outputs, like IMPADL or DAYS.

Differences between user groups

- Considerable redistribution of the total costs of packages between the users in the six groups. Although resources increase with levels of dependency, users with PICs in each of the need interval categories receive much higher levels of resources.
- The model suggests the virtual cessation of service for short interval cases without PICs.
- The 'unconstrained' optimisation increases significantly levels of IMPIADL for users with critical interval needs and users with PICs.
- The absolute increase for users with long interval needs and no PICs is small, and there is a loss in IMPIADL for users with short interval needs and no PICs.

The changes following from the unconstrained optimisation of IMPIADL are dramatic. They are quite different from those required for optimising some other outputs. They involve redistribution between groups of users as well as between service inputs. They involve substantial expansions and contractions of types of service in total.

2.1.2. 'Collateral outputs': the consequences for other outputs of optimising on IMPIADL

This too is not one of the small number of the most general impacts that between them cover the main choices of priorities for the services. Setting a strategy for efficiency improvement to maximise it would make sense only if doing so produced high collateral outputs for the shorter list of outputs: DAYS, reduction in felt caregiver burden, USATISF, and perhaps IMPEMP and WKSAT. The structural production function model plausibly suggested a non-reciprocal joint supply relationship between IMPIADL and IMPEMP. Also IMPIADL is closely related to the traditional goals of home care, and the contribution to cost-effectiveness of the policy of some authorities from as early as the 1980s not to provide general household care has been extensively questioned (Davies et al., 1990; Joseph Rowntree Foundation, 1995). It is therefore possible that there might be cases in which it would make good sense to maximise on IMPIADL.

The results are summarised in figure 17.5.

The actual output compared with the maximum achievable

- As was mentioned above, the unconstrained optimisation for IMPIADL implies the non-allocation of resources to users with short interval needs and no PICs, clearly a non-defensible option. Consequently optimum IMPIADL levels for this group are equal to zero.
- The rest of the groups enjoy high relative increases in IMPIADL.

Collateral compared with actual outputs

Optimising IMPIADL with no constraints on the supply of services or user group budgets has disastrous consequences for the collateral outputs defined

Figure 17.5
Collateral output levels for optimisation on IMPIADL with 'unconstrained'
optimisation

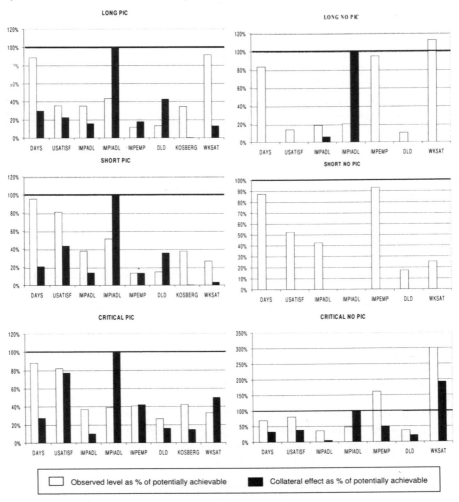

in the analysis. Indeed, only four collateral output levels increase with respect
to their observed levels, and a remarkable 33 deteriorate.

There are losses in collateral levels of:

* All output variables for users without PICs.
* DAYS, USATISF, IMPADL and KOSBERG for users with PICs.
* DLD for all users but those with long or short interval needs with PICs.

- WKSAT for all users but those with critical interval needs and PICs.

There are gains in collateral levels of:
- DLD for users with long or short interval needs and PICs.
- WKSAT for users with critical interval needs and PICs.
- IMPEMP for users with long interval needs and PICs.

Collateral outputs compared with the maximum achievable for each output
Together with the falls in collateral levels for the vast majority of outputs, figure 17.5 shows final collateral output levels below 40 per cent of their potentially achievable for most indicators, and almost none above 80 per cent.

Collateral output levels lay below 40 per cent of the maximum achievable for:
- All collateral outputs for long and short interval need cases.
- All collateral outputs for critical interval need cases except for USATISF and WKSAT for users with PICs, and IMPEMP and WKSAT for users without PICs.

Collateral output levels reach 80 per cent or above of the maximum achievable for:
- Only one collateral output, WKSAT, and this only for users with critical interval needs without PICs.
- However, WKSAT collateral level for this group is well above the 100 per cent line, thus suggesting the over-provision to the group with respect to WKSAT.

It might be argued that there are some groups for which the maximisation of IMPIADL might be considered. For instance, this is implied by the advocates of spreading lower levels of services to a wider clientele, suggesting that this might prevent deterioration. However, given an 'unconstrained' optimisation, there is no group shown in figure 17.5 for which this would appear to be valid.

2.2. Assumption (b): Optimisation subject to user group average budgets: 'group-budget-constrained optimisation' (figures 17.6 and 17.7)

2.2.1. Outputs, package costs, service mixes, and analysis group variations

It will be remembered that this is the case in which it is assumed that prioritisation rules for allocation between groups are fixed as budget averages for the group, and/or in which the manager makes some allowance for the differential production relations between the groups for other outputs.

The optimisation affects both service patterns and output gains by groups. The results are shown in figure 17.6.

Inefficiencies in service balance
- Paradoxically, very large reductions in the inputs of home care are implied. This is a paradox because it is tasks for coping with IADLs which have been the traditional mainstay of the British home help tradition. The explanation

Figure 17.6
Input mix efficiency for improvement in IADL-related states due to services (IMPIADL): group-budget-constrained optimisation

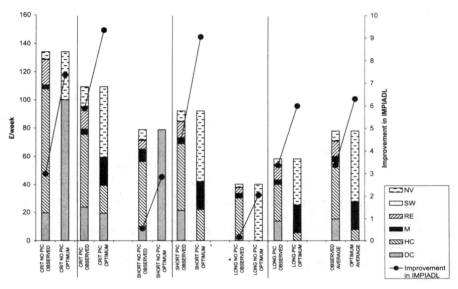

is that the input of nursing visits are much greater for all groups. Given joint supply in the production of IMPIADL and IMPADL, perhaps more of the inputs come better from someone able to undertake a wider range of the tasks, the nursing assistant. Greene et al. found that optimisation required a bigger input of skilled nursing, but their output was the reduction of transitions to nursing homes, not all institutions for long-term care (1993), and so the result is not strictly comparable. The optimisation solution emerging from this model is that the large input of nursing would be complemented by more home-delivered meals for several groups (those with PICs) as well by the reduced level of home care.

- The optimal solution suggests greater utilisation of day care for users of critical and short interval need cases without PICs, but less use by other groups. This reflects the high productivity for persons discharged from hospital shown in figure 6.9. This result again illustrates how the revision of service mixes is sensitive to the output chosen, because it contrasts with the implications of some of the models for other important outputs.
- As in the previous optimisation scenario, respite care has no place in the optimisation for this output variable when group budget shares are fixed.

Differences between user groups

Fixing budget shares creates different patterns of output gains and losses on average for group members.

- All user groups substantially improve their levels of IMPIADL.
- Hence, not allowing for user group budget transfers improves dramatically the levels of IMPIADL achieved for users without PICs, at the expense of a reduction in the levels of IMPIADL for users with PICs (relative to the unconstrained case).

2.2.2. *'Collateral outputs': the consequences for other outputs of optimising on IMPIADL*

Results are summarised in figure 17.7. With very few exceptions, the picture is almost identical to the one described in figure 17.5: a great deal more reductions than increases in collateral levels, and final collateral levels well below their maximum attainable for most user groups and variables.

The actual output compared with the maximum achievable

- Fixing user group budgets allows users in the short interval need category with PICs to enjoy substantial increases in their levels of IMPIADL.
- As in the previous scenario, the rest of the groups enjoy high relative increases in IMPIADL.

Collateral compared with actual outputs

There are losses in collateral levels of:

- All output variables for users without long interval needs.
- DAYS, IMPADL, KOSBERG at WKSAT for all applicable users.
- DLD for all users without PICs or users with critical interval needs.
- USATISF for users with long interval needs, users with short interval needs and PICs, and users with critical interval needs and no PICs.
- IMPEMP for users with long interval needs and users with short interval needs and PICs.

There are gains in collateral levels of:

- DLD for users with long or short interval needs and PICs. This effect was also found in the unconstrained optimisation.
- USATISF for users with short interval needs and no PICs.
- IMPEMP for users with critical interval needs and short interval needs and no PICs.

Collateral outputs compared with the maximum achievable for each output

As for the 'unconstrained' optimisation, figure 17.7 shows final collateral output levels below 40 per cent of their potentially achievable for most indicators, and almost none above 80 per cent.

Figure 17.7
Collateral output levels for optimisation on IMPIADL with group-budget-constrained optimisation

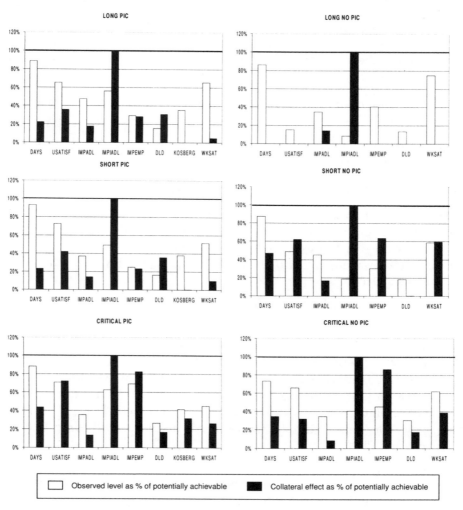

Collateral output levels lay below 40 per cent of the maximum achievable for:
- All collateral outputs for long interval need cases.
- All collateral outputs for short interval need cases with PICs.
- KOSBERG, DLD and IMPADL for all applicable users.
- WKSAT for all users except those with short interval needs without PICs.

- DAYS and USATISF for users with long interval needs, short interval needs and PICs, and critical interval needs without PICs.
- IMPEMP for users with long interval needs and short interval needs and PICs.

Collateral output levels reach 80 per cent or above of the maximum achievable for:

- Again only one collateral output, this time IMPEMP, and this only for users with critical interval needs. This might be the consequence of the interrelationship between IMPEMP and IMPIADL implied by the simultaneous model in chapter 12.

In neither the unconstrained nor group-budget-constrained scenarios does there seem to be a case for maximising on IMPIADL. Moreover, were the optimisation scenario to be fixed group budgets, and given the current resources allocated to each of the groups, none of the groups defined in the analysis would clearly benefit from such a maximisation. The bottom line is surely the universally low levels of DAYS and reduction in caregiver burden: lower levels than currently obtained.

2.3. Assumption (c): Total expenditure on each service maintained: 'service-budget-constrained' optimisation (figures 17.8 and 17.9)

2.3.1. Outputs, package costs, service mixes, and analysis group variations

The results are shown in figure 17.8.

Inefficiencies in service balance

The patterns are quite different from either of the other cases.

- Home care is redistributed to both critical interval need groups and away from others.
- Community nursing visits are concentrated on those users with critical interval needs and PICs.
- Day care is redistributed to users with critical interval needs but no PICs.

Differences between user groups

- As for the unconstrained case, the optimum allocation of resources focuses resources on those users with higher levels of need.
- Among the long and short interval categories, users without PICs receive trivial amounts of resources. In fact, their packages of care are composed of the services without significant impacts on IMPIADL. Because of the service-budget constraint, such services remain at their observed levels for each of the user groups.
- The pattern of output gains follows the allocations of the resources, the significant gains being for users with critical interval needs.

Figure 17.8
*Input mix efficiency for improvement in IADL-related states due to services
(IMPIADL): service-budget-constrained optimisation*

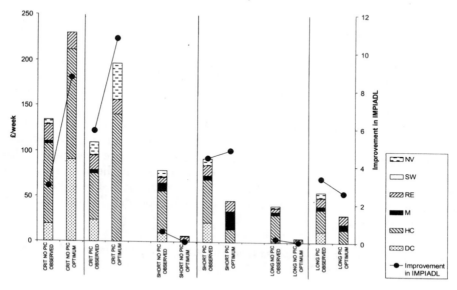

- Contrarily to the unconstrained case, the service-budget-constrained optimisation for IMPIADL does not produce significant absolute improvements
  for any of the long and short interval groups.

2.3.2. *'Collateral outputs': the consequences for other outputs of optimising on IMPIADL*

The results are shown in figure 17.9.

Although clearly not enough to postulate IMPIADL as a maximand for systems bound by rigidities in the supply of services, figure 17.9 shows many
more collateral output levels above 80 per cent of their attainable levels, and
fewer below 40 per cent than for the first two scenarios. Nevertheless, the picture is of contrasts between groups, with critical interval need users much
better off than those in lower need categories, particularly those without PICs.

The actual output compared with the maximum achievable

- The service-budget optimum allocation produces transfers of IMPIADL
  levels between users.
- It implies zero levels of IMPIADL for two groups, namely the long and short
  interval groups without PICs.
- The rest of the groups enjoy high relative increases in IMPIADL.

Figure 17.9
Collateral output levels for optimisation on IMPIADL with service-budget-constrained optimisation

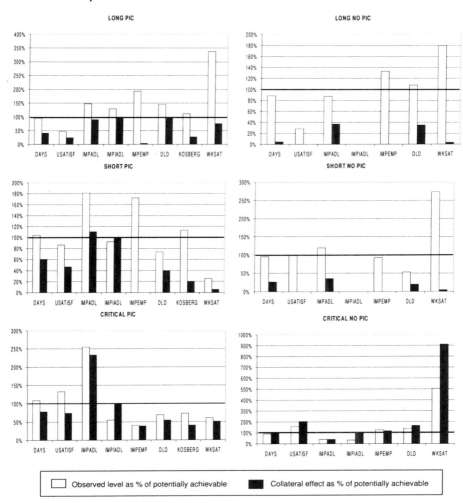

Collateral compared with actual outputs
- There are losses in collateral levels for all outputs for all users but those with critical interval needs without PICs.
- For those, only the collateral output for IMPEMP is below the observed levels, whereas the rest of collateral output levels are above them.

Collateral outputs compared with the maximum achievable for each output

Collateral output levels lay below 40 per cent of the maximum achievable for:

- All output variables for users with long and short interval needs and no PICs. These two groups are the clear losers to emerge from the service-budget-constrained optimisation.
- KOSBERG for all users with PICs.
- DAYS and USATISF for users with long interval needs and users with short interval needs and no PICs.
- IMPADL for all users without PICs.
- IMPEMP for all users except those with critical interval needs and no PICs.
- DLD for users with short interval needs.

Collateral output levels reach 80 per cent or above of the maximum achievable for:

- All collateral outputs for users with critical interval needs and no PICs. These users are by far the 'winners' from the service-budget-constrained optimisation of IMPIADL.
- IMPADL for all users with PICs.
- DLD and WKSAT for users with long interval needs and PICs.

Clearly, for the service-budget-constrained case also, there is little case for adopting IMPIADL as the general maximand.

3.   Overview

Technical efficiency
- The average inefficiency rate for IMPIADL was 19 per cent, the lowest being for the packages of users with critical interval needs and PICs, and the highest for users with short interval needs and no PICs.
- Average cost savings or output gains from improvements in the least efficient units rise as larger proportions of the least efficient cases are included until the 15th percentile.

Input mix efficiency: the 'unconstrained' optimisation
- The optimisation of IMPIADL brings many changes to the allocation of resources, with great diversity in budgets and input mixes.
- Overall, resources are concentrated on critical interval need users.
- For each interval group, users with PICs receive far greater budgets.
- Users with PICs receive high levels of home care, meals and nursing visits, and critical interval users without PICs exclusively day care.
- Only users with PICs or with critical interval needs enjoy significant increases in their levels of IMPIADL.
- Overall, unconstrained optimisation increases the levels of IMPIADL to more than 200 per cent of their observed levels.

The different optimising scenarios: how binding are the constraints?
- Compared with the unconstrained case, the group-budget constraint optimisation implies much greater budgets for users with long and short interval needs and no PICs, together with a notable reduction in the budget for users with critical interval needs and PICs.
- Higher levels of nursing inputs and day care would be used, at the expense of a reduction in home care inputs.
- Because of the constraints on the resources destined to the different users, the group-budget-constrained optimisation implies more general and similar IMPIADL gains.
- Overall, the group-budget-constrained optimisation reaches 95 per cent of the output levels achieved in the 'unconstrained' optimisation.
- Fixing the supply levels of the different services focuses even more resources on users with critical interval needs, who now receive the bulk of the home care inputs.
- As a consequence, only users with critical interval needs reach substantial improvements in IMPIADL, with the rest of the groups enjoying similar or lower levels.
- Overall service-budget-constrained optimisation reaches 70 per cent of the levels attained by the unconstrained optimisation.

The collateral effects
For all scenarios, the collateral output levels achieved by optimisation on IMPIADL are typically worse than the observed and lower than 40 per cent of their achievable maximum. Overall, IMPIADL is not a suitable maximand.

18 Efficiencies for IMPEMP Indicator Variable (User Felt Control Over Own Life Score)

The average production function is summarised in table 7.1, and the productivity curves are shown in figures 7.1 and 7.2.

1. Technical efficiency (figures 18.1 to 18.3)

Variations in average inefficiencies between groups. The frontier function illustrated in figure 18.1 implies:

- A high degree of efficiency in production, with inefficiency being on average only 18 per cent.

- Substantial relative variation in efficiency. Production is least technically efficient for short interval cases generally, particularly short interval cases without PICs, for whom the degree of inefficiency is on average 26 per cent. It is most efficient for long interval cases, for whom the degree of inefficiency is approximately 16 per cent.

- On average, production for those with or without a PIC is of similar efficiency. That is interesting because some have argued that care managers respond more to the PIC's than to the user's perceptions of user needs. If anything, the presence of a PIC appears to diminish efficiency for users with critical interval needs, and to increase it for short interval users. Therefore, these small differences are in opposing directions for the two groups for whom one would expect it to be most valid to argue that care managers lean on the judgements of the PICs more than on those of the users. However, the differences are small. This may in part be because care plans are likely to respond to PIC needs as well as user needs, so making it misleading to base a judgement about efficiency based on the empowerment only of one of the parties.

Figure 18.1
Technical efficiency index* for user felt control over own life score

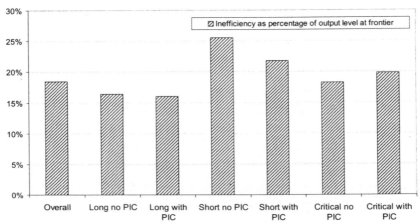

* ratio of difference between outputs achieved given service levels and mix to inputs predicted for the user and output predicted given maximum technical efficiency given service levels and mix to the actual output achieved

Figure 18.2
Average output gain or cost saving from postulated improvement in technical efficiency in the production of IMPEMP

Efficiency improvement strategy: the least efficient are made as efficient as units at a prescribed higher percentile in the distribution ordered from least to most efficient

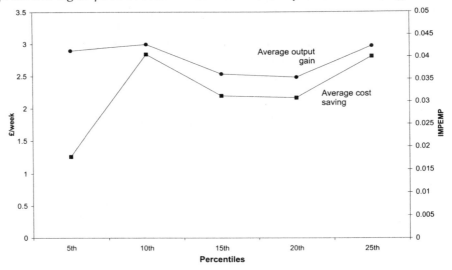

Figure 18.3
*Average output gain or cost saving from postulated improvement in
technical efficiency in the production of IMPEMP*

*Efficiency improvement strategy: prescribed percentage increase in efficiency for
each of the 33 per cent most inefficient units*

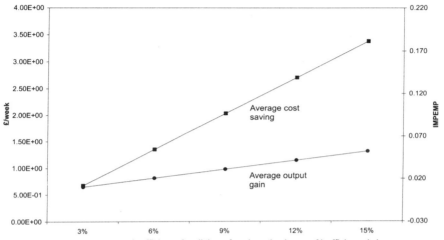

Gains from alternative strategies for efficiency improvement. One simulation is to
raise the level of the tail to a certain floor. The results shown in figure 18.2 suggest:
- The average output gain per case would be substantial given the removal of
  the end of the tail of the distribution by setting the floor at the first decile.
  The greatest improvement would be among those between the fifth and
  tenth percentiles. But the average gain per unit would be less for higher
  floors.
- There would be a greater relative gain in the form of cost saving than in the
  form of IMPEMP if the floor level were set at the first decile.

The other strategy simulated was to increase efficiency of each unit in the
tail by the same proportionate amount. Figure 18.3 suggests savings of approximately 22 pence per week per percentage point gain in efficiency for the
third least efficient.

2.   Input mix efficiency

2.1.   *Assumption (a): Optimisation subject only to the overall budget: 'unconstrained optimisation' (figures 18.4 and 18.5)*

2.1.1.   *Outputs, package costs, service mixes, and analysis group variations*

The results are shown in figure 18.4.

Figure 18.4
Input mix efficiency for user felt control over own life score (IMPEMP): 'unconstrained' optimisation

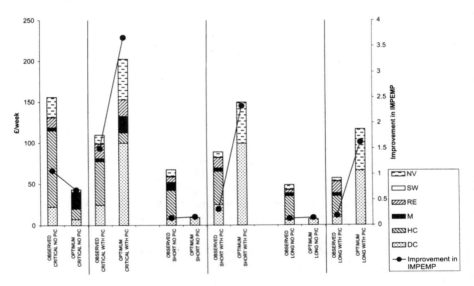

Inefficiencies in service balance
Patterns have similar features to those of other outputs.

- Less spending on home care, despite the productivity effect for critical interval need users shown in figure 7.1; and less spending on meals for most groups, but not critical interval cases, reflecting the productivity effect for users unable to use the toilet unaided.
- Nursing visits and day care inputs would be reallocated from users without to users with PICs. Figure 7.1 shows the consumption of nursing and day care to be interdependent among those with cognitive impairment.
- Respite care would be reduced for all cases but those with critical interval needs and PICs.

User group differences
- Overall, budgets would be greatly increased for those with PICs but reduced for those without. Particularly substantial is the fall in budget for critical interval cases without PICs.
- Consequently, there are big increases in IMPEMP for those with PICs, but either constant or lower levels for those without PICs.

2.1.2. *'Collateral outputs': the consequences for other outputs of optimising on IMPEMP*

IMPEMP would only be a contender for maximisation were its collateral outputs for the most important dimensions to be high. The results of the structural production function model did not find any interrelation with other output measures.

The results are summarised in figure 18.5.

The actual output compared with the maximum achievable
- Users without PICs either enjoy very small relative improvements in IMPEMP or a significant fall.
- On the other hand, there is a significant potential for relative gains following optimisation for users with PICs.

Collateral compared with actual outputs
There is a majority of collateral output losses, with most of the gains focused on users with PICs. This only reflects the concentration of resources on users with PICs involved in the 'unconstrained' optimisation.

There are losses in collateral levels of:
- DAYS and IMPADL for all users but those with critical interval needs and no PICs.
- KOSBERG and USATISF for users with short or critical needs.
- DLD and WKSAT for users without PICs.

There are gains in collateral levels of:
- IMPIADL for users with long interval needs and users with PICs.
- USATISF for users with long interval needs.
- WKSAT for users with PICs.
- DLD for users with short or critical interval needs and PICs.
- DAYS only for users with critical interval needs and PICs. For this group, all collateral outputs but USATISF were higher than the observed values.

Collateral outputs compared with the maximum achievable for each output
There are more collateral outputs below 40 per cent of their attainable level than above 80 per cent. The high collateral outputs are mainly related to one user group (critical interval with PIC) and one variable (WKSAT).

Figure 18.5
Collateral output levels for optimisation on IMPEMP with 'unconstrained'
optimisation

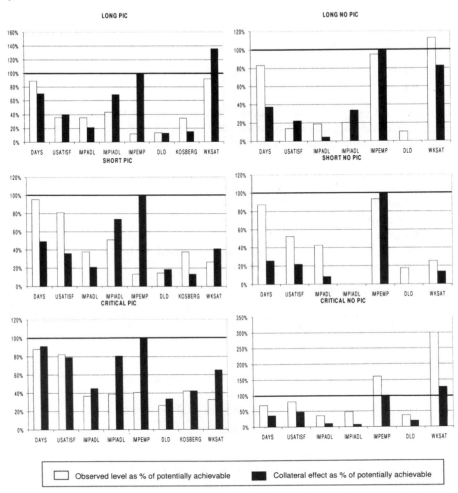

Collateral output levels lay below 40 per cent of the maximum achievable for:

- DAYS for all users without PICs.
- KOSBERG, IMPADL and DLD for all applicable groups.
- USATISF for users with long and short interval needs.
- WKSAT for users with short interval needs.

Collateral output levels reach 80 per cent or above of the maximum achievable for:

- DAYS, USATISF and IMPIADL for users with critical interval needs and PICs.
- WKSAT for users with long interval needs and users with critical interval needs and no PICs.

There is therefore little case for the adoption of IMPEMP as a maximand.

2.2. Assumption (b): Optimisation subject to user group average budgets: 'group-budget-constrained optimisation' (figures 18.6 and 18.7)

2.2.1. Outputs, package costs, service mixes, and analysis group variations

The results are shown in figure 18.6.

Figure 18.6
Input mix efficiency for user felt control over own life score (IMPEMP): group-budget-constrained optimisation

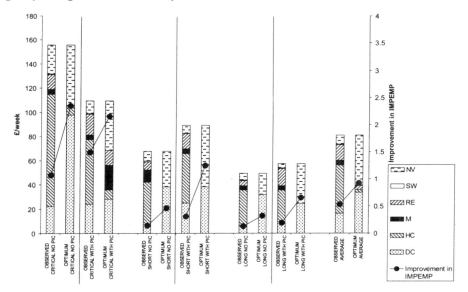

Inefficiencies in service balance
- Again, there are big reductions in the utilisation of home care.
- There are big increases in the utilisation of day care for those in all groups without PICs.

Output differences between user groups
- Compared with the unconstrained redistribution of the overall budget in assumption (a), the big gains to those with PICs are not made.

- All users enjoy increases in their levels of IMPEMP.

2.2.2. 'Collateral outputs': the consequences for other outputs of optimising on IMPEMP

Results are summarised in figure 18.7.

The actual output compared with the maximum achievable
There are very significant relative gains in IMPEMP to be made by all groups through the optimisation with fixed group budgets.

Collateral compared with actual outputs
Optimising keeping the observed group-budgets produces fewer increases in collateral output levels than the unconstrained case, most of the gains focusing on two variables.

There are losses in collateral levels of: .
- All outputs for users with long interval needs and PICs.
- DAYS, IMPADL and DLD for all user groups.
- WKSAT for all users except those with long interval needs and no PICs.
- USATISF for users with long and short interval needs with PICs, and for users with critical interval needs and no PICs.

There are gains in collateral levels of:
- IMPIADL for all user groups but the long interval with PIC category.
- USATISF for users with long and short interval needs without PICs, and for users with critical interval needs and PICs.
- WKSAT for users with long interval needs and no PICs.

Collateral outputs compared with the maximum achievable for each output
Although the group-budget-constrained optimisation yields more collateral outputs below 40 per cent than above 80 per cent of their potentially achievable levels, a significant number remain between the two thresholds. Moreover, four out of the five collateral levels above 80 per cent correspond to one output.

Collateral output levels lay below 40 per cent of the maximum achievable for:
- KOSBERG, DLD and IMPADL for all user types.
- DAYS for users with short interval needs.
- WKSAT for users with short and critical interval needs and PICs.

Collateral output levels reach 80 per cent or above of the maximum achievable for:
- IMPIADL for users without PICs or users with critical interval needs.
- WKSAT for users with long interval needs and no PICs.

These low collateral levels for the key output indicators make IMPEMP an unsuitable maximand.

Figure 18.7
Collateral output levels for optimisation on IMPEMP with group-budget-constrained optimisation

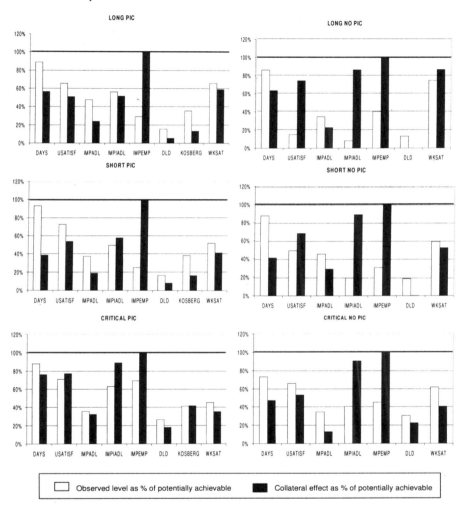

2.3. Assumption (c): Total expenditure on each service maintained: 'service-budget-constrained' optimisation (figures 18.8 and 18.9)

2.3.1. *Outputs, package costs, service mixes, and analysis group variations*

The results are summarised in figure 18.8.

Figure 18.8
Input mix efficiency for user felt control over own life score (IMPEMP):
service-budget-constrained optimisation

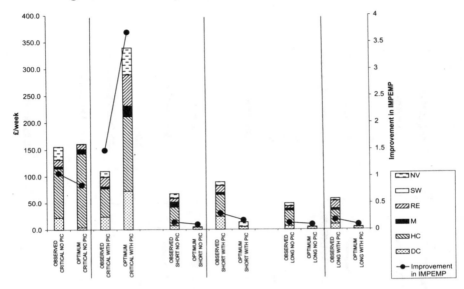

Inefficiencies in service balance

- Due to the constraint on the supply of services, the optimum input mixes
  differ very substantially from the ones derived from the previous two
  optimisations.
- Fixing the budget shares of individual services causes an increase in home
  care inputs to critical interval users.

Differences between user groups

- Whereas the unconstrained optimisation mainly transferred resources from
  users without PICs to users with, the service-budget optimisation allocates
  almost the entirety of the overall budget to users in the critical interval category. Among those, however, users with PICs still receive higher budgets.
- Following the new optimum allocation of resources, only users with critical
  interval needs and with PIC enjoy gains in IMPEMP. This finding on its own
  disqualifies the use of IMPEMP as a maximand for systems with constraints
  on the supply levels of the different services.

2.3.2. '*Collateral outputs': the consequences for other outputs of optimising on
  IMPEMP*

The results are shown in figure 18.9.

Figure 18.9
Collateral output levels for optimisation on IMPEMP with service-budget-constrained optimisation

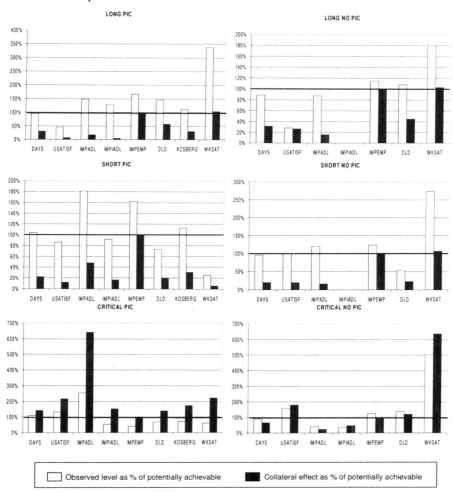

The actual output compared with the maximum achievable

As mentioned above, five out of the six user groups defined in the analysis would suffer losses in IMPEMP following optimisation, and only users with critical interval needs and PICs would enjoy significant increases.

Collateral compared with actual outputs
Given the optimum budget shares of the different groups, it is not surprising to find that all collateral levels for users with long and short interval needs lay below the observed values. Even users with critical needs and no PICs experience losses after optimisation in collateral levels for three output measures. Nor it is surprising that all collateral outputs are above their observed levels for users with critical interval needs and PICs.

Collateral outputs compared with the maximum achievable for each output
The analysis of final levels of collateral outputs only confirms the findings mentioned above. Almost all collateral outputs for users in the long and short interval need categories fall below 40 per cent of their maximum attainable, and the vast majority of outputs above the 80 per cent threshold correspond to critical interval need users. Among them, all collateral output levels for users with PICs exceed the 100 per cent line.

3.   Overview

Technical efficiency
- The average inefficiency rate for IMPEMP was 18 per cent, the lowest being for the packages for users with long interval needs, and the highest for users with short interval needs.
- Average cost savings or output gains from improvements in the least efficient units reach their peak when the 10 per cent least efficient are targeted.

Input mix efficiency: the 'unconstrained' optimisation.
- The optimisation of IMPEMP brings many changes to the allocation of resources, with clearly different patterns for users with and without PICs.
- Overall, resources are concentrated on users with PICs, although there is still a gradient by dependency: for each interval group, users with PICs would receive far greater budgets.
- Users with PICs would receive high levels of day care and nursing visits.
- Additionally, critical interval users would receive meals and respite care.
- Only users with PICs would enjoy significant increases in their levels of IMPEMP.
- Overall, the unconstrained optimisation would increase the levels of IMPEMP to more than 250 per cent of their observed levels.

The different optimising scenarios: how binding are the constraints?
- Compared with the unconstrained case, the group-budget-constrained optimisation implies greater budgets for users without PICs, together with a notable reduction in the budget for users with critical interval needs and PICs.
- Higher levels of nursing inputs and day care would be used, at the expense of a reduction in home care inputs.

- In contrast with the unconstrained scenario, the group-budget-constrained optimisation would produce significant IMPEMP gains for all users.
- Overall, the group-budget-constrained optimisation would reach 83 per cent of the output levels achieved in the 'unconstrained' optimisation.
- Compared with the unconstrained case, the service-budget constraint optimisation implies greater budgets for users with critical needs, and the allocation of relatively insignificant packages of care to the other groups. Among users with critical interval needs, those with PICs would receive twice the level of resources.
- As a consequence, only users with critical interval needs and PICs would attain substantial improvements in IMPEMP, with the rest of the groups enjoying the same or lower levels.
- Overall service-budget-constrained optimisation would reach 58 per cent of the levels attained by the unconstrained optimisation.

The collateral effects
For all scenarios, the collateral output levels achieved by optimisation on IMPEMP are typically worse than the actual levels observed and lower than 40 per cent of their achievable maximum. Overall, IMPEMP is not therefore a suitable maximand.

19 Efficiencies for DLD Indicator Variable (User Dissatisfaction with Life Development Score)

1. Technical efficiency

The conditions were not satisfied for the fitting of a frontier model. Therefore figure 19.1 is based on the analysis of residuals. Variations between groups are small, save that the efficiency is substantially less for users with critical interval needs but no PIC. Perhaps to be in critical interval need and without a prin-

Figure 19.1
Technical efficiency index* for user dissatisfaction with life development score

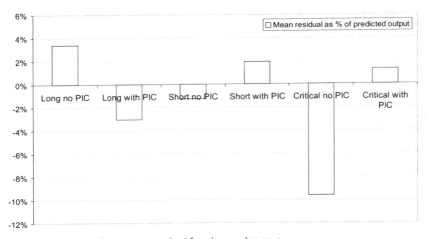

* ratio of residuals over the average output for given sub-group

cipal informal caregiver (and so probably lacking in intimates) is likely to create morale problems at the more immovable end of the spectrum.

2.   Input mix efficiency

2.1.   *Assumption (a): Optimisation subject only to the overall budget: 'unconstrained optimisation' (figures 19.2 and 19.3)*

2.1.1.   *Outputs, package costs, service mixes, and analysis group variations*

Unconstrained optimisation within the budget would result in big increases in the output. However, the increases would be small were the supply of social work to be constrained. As might be expected, the input of social work is a crucial variable for this output. The results are shown in figure 19.2.

Inefficiencies in service balance
Optimisation would:
- Increase the inputs of social work for all groups. But though the relative increase would be large, the share of social work in the overall package costs would remain small.[1]
- Reduce the utilisation of home care in all groups.

Figure 19.2
Input mix efficiency for user dissatisfaction with life development score (DLD): 'unconstrained' optimisation

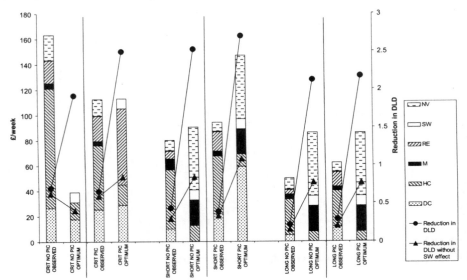

- Increase the utilisation of meals for short and long interval cases.
- Greatly increase the utilisation of day care among short interval cases with PICs.
- Greatly increase the inputs of respite care among critical interval groups, but reduce them among other groups.
- Reduce the inputs of home nursing visits among those with critical interval need, but greatly increase them for other groups.

Differences between user groups
- The optimum budgets for the different user groups are acutely different from the observed.
- Among users with short and critical interval needs, there is a general shift of resources towards those users with PICs, so that for both categories those users with PICs receive substantially more resources.
- Contrarily, users with and without PICs in the long interval need category receive identical care packages.
- In contrast with any of the previous output optimisations, the unconstrained optimisation for DLD allocates the higher budget levels to users in the short interval need category.
- Increases in outputs would be of much the same extent for all groups.

2.1.2. 'Collateral outputs': the consequences for other outputs of optimising on DLD

Results are described in figure 19.3.

The actual output compared with the maximum achievable
- The unconstrained optimisation of DLD achieves very substantial increases in the relative levels of DLD for all user groups.
- It therefore does not require any transfers of DLD levels between users.

Collateral compared with actual outputs
Although there is a majority of collateral outputs below the observed levels, the optimisation of DLD also yields a substantial number of increases in collateral outputs. However, these relate only to users with PICs and users with long interval needs.

There are losses in collateral levels of:
- All outputs for users with short or critical interval needs with PICs.
- DAYS and IMPADL for all users but those with critical interval needs and PICs.
- WKSAT for all users with long interval needs or without PICs.
- IMPEMP for all users with critical interval needs or without PICs.
- IMPIADL for users with critical interval needs.
- USATISF for users with critical interval needs, long interval needs and PICs, and short interval needs without PICs.

Figure 19.3
Collateral output levels for optimisation on DLD with 'unconstrained'
optimisation

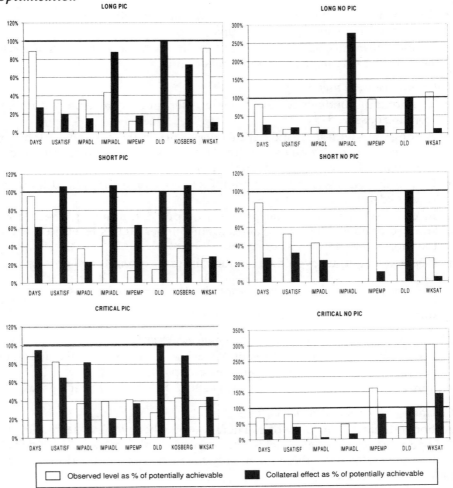

There are gains in collateral levels of:

- KOSBERG for the three applicable groups.
- IMPIADL for users with long interval needs and users with short interval needs and PICs.
- WKSAT for users with short and critical interval needs with PICs.
- USATISF for users with long interval needs and no PICs and users with short interval needs and PICs.

- IMPEMP for users with long and short interval needs with PICs.

Collateral outputs compared with the maximum achievable for each output
- Again, there are a majority of low collateral output levels, concentrated principally on users without PICs.

Collateral output levels lay below 40 per cent of the maximum achievable for:
- DAYS and USATISF for users with long interval needs and users without PICs.
- IMPADL for all users but those with critical interval needs and PICs.
- WKSAT for users with long and short interval needs.
- IMPEMP for users with long interval needs, users with short interval needs and no PICs, and users with critical interval needs and PICs.
- IMPIADL for users with critical interval needs

Collateral output levels reach 80 per cent or above of the maximum achievable for:
- All users only for KOSBERG. This is not surprising however because of the very substantial effect that social work inputs have on both outputs.
- IMPIADL for users with long interval needs, and users with short interval need and PICs.
- DAYS and IMPADL for users with critical interval needs and PICs.

2.2. Assumption (b): Optimisation subject to user group average budgets: 'group-budget-constrained optimisation' (figures 19.4 and 19.5)

2.2.1. Outputs, package costs, service mixes, and analysis group variations

The results are shown in figure 19.4.

Inefficiencies in service balance
- Relative to the unconstrained optimum, fixing user group budgets increases the resources allocated to users with critical interval needs without PICs, decreasing those allocated to long interval need users and particularly short interval need cases with PIC.
- Again, there would be large increases in social work, and large reductions in home care inputs.
- There would be an increase in day care and a big increase in respite care for critical interval cases without as well as with principal informal caregivers.
- Some of the other patterns would remain: for instance, the patterns for community nursing inputs and meals.

Differences between user groups
- There would be much the same pattern and extent of increase in outputs as with unconstrained optimisation
- With constraints on the supply of social work, the group share constraint

Figure 19.4
Input mix efficiency for user dissatisfaction with life development score
(DLD): group-budget-constrained optimisation

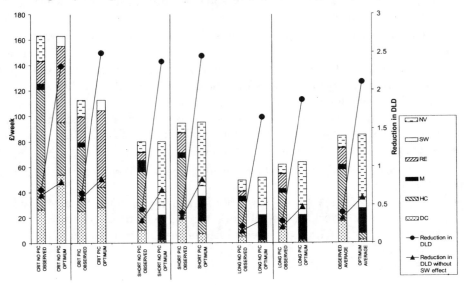

causes the improvement to be greatest for those of short not critical interval
needs.

2.2.2. *'Collateral outputs': the consequences for other outputs of optimising on DLD*

The results are shown in figure 19.5.

The actual output compared with the maximum achievable
* As for the unconstrained case, the group-budget-constrained optimisation
  achieves very substantial increases in the relative levels of DLD for all user
  groups.

Collateral compared with actual outputs
* Although again there is a majority of collateral outputs below the observed
  levels, the optimisation of DLD with fixed group-budgets yields increases in
  collateral levels for higher numbers of outputs than the unconstrained case.
* Overall, many of the changes generated by the unconstrained optimisation
  are also present in the fixed group budget scenario.

  There are losses in collateral levels of:
* DAYS, IMPADL and WKSAT for users with long and short interval needs.
* IMPEMP for all users with critical interval needs or without PICs.
* IMPIADL for users with critical interval needs.

Figure 19.5
Collateral output levels for optimisation on DLD with group-budget-constrained optimisation

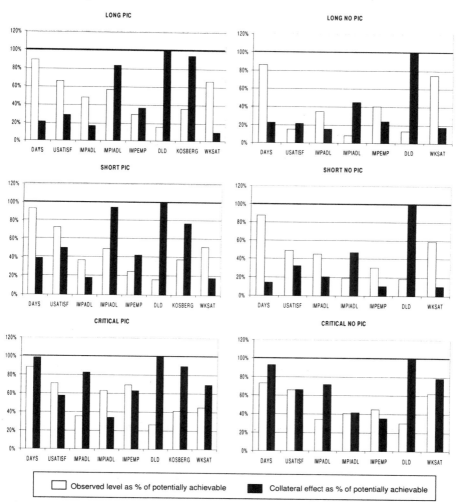

- USATISF for users without PICs or with short interval needs.

  There are gains in collateral levels of:
- KOSBERG for the three applicable groups.
- DAYS, IMPADL and WKSAT for users with critical interval needs.
- IMPIADL for users with long or short interval needs and users without PICs.
- WKSAT for users with short and critical interval needs with PICs.

- USATISF for users with long interval needs and no PICs and users with short interval needs and PICs.
- IMPEMP for users with long and short interval needs with PICs.

Collateral outputs compared with the maximum achievable for each output
- Again, there are a majority of low collateral output levels, concentrated on users without PICs and low dependency.

Collateral output levels lay at or below 40 per cent of the maximum achievable for:
- DAYS, USATISF, IMPADL and WKSAT for users with long and short interval needs.
- IMPEMP for users with long and short interval needs, and users with critical interval needs without PICs.
- IMPIADL for users with critical interval needs

Collateral output levels reach 80 per cent or above of the maximum achievable for:
- Again, for all users only for KOSBERG.
- IMPIADL for users with long and short interval need and PICs.
- DAYS, IMPADL and WKSAT for users with critical interval needs. For such cases, therefore, the optimisation of DLD with current budgets achieves very high collateral levels for some of the key outputs. This makes DLD a potential candidate as maximand for them.

2.3. Assumption (c): Total expenditure on each service maintained: 'service-budget-constrained' optimisation (figures 19.6 and 19.7)

2.3.1. Outputs, package costs, service mixes, and analysis group variations

The results are summarised in figure 19.6.

Inefficiencies in service balance
- Only a redistribution of the home care input is possible under this scenario. The redistribution would be strongly away from critical interval cases without PICs, and substantially towards critical interval cases with PICs.
- Meals are redistributed towards the less dependent, and away from the most dependent.
- There is a large redistribution of day care towards short interval cases with PICs.

Differences between user groups
- Even though the service mix is significantly different, the budget shares of each of the groups are similar than those implied by the unconstrained optimisation.
- Users with critical and short interval needs with PICs benefit from the highest budgets.

Figure 19.6
Input mix efficiency for user dissatisfaction with life development score
(DLD): service-budget-constrained optimisation

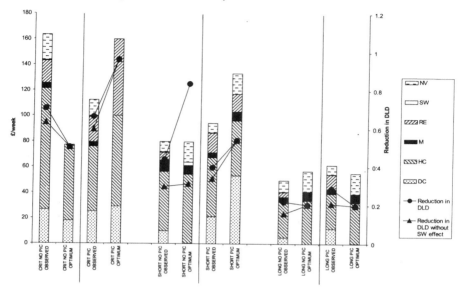

- Again, long interval need cases have identical care packages.
- Not all groups would benefit from higher DLD levels, as with the other optimisation scenarios. Groups on average losing would be the long interval groups, and particularly, critical interval users without PICs. The gains for the others would on average be greater than the losses to these groups, but the gains would not be comparable to those under the other optimising scenarios.

2.3.2. 'Collateral outputs': the consequences for other outputs of optimising on DLD

Figure 19.7 summarises the results.

The actual output compared with the maximum achievable
In contrast with the first two, the service-budget-constrained optimisation achieves substantial increases in the relative levels of DLD for only three user groups.

Collateral compared with actual outputs
- Optimising DLD with fixed service-budgets produces the lowest number of improvements in collateral output levels out of the three hypothesised optimisations.
- Moreover, the vast majority of improvements relate to one group of users,

Figure 19.7
Collateral output levels for optimisation on DLD with service-budget-constrained optimisation

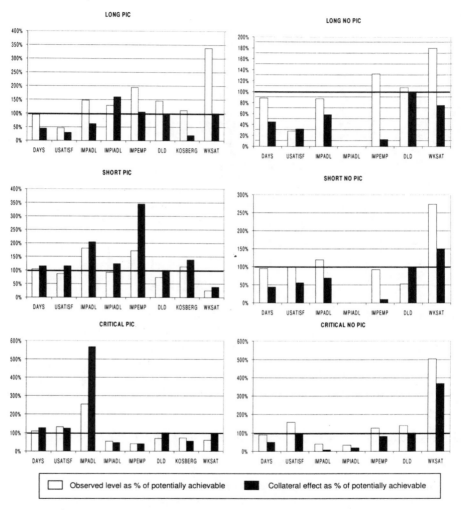

those with short interval needs and PICs. Indeed, all collateral output levels for this group are higher than the observed values.

- Users with critical interval needs and PICs also enjoy increases in collateral outputs for DAYS, IMPADL and WKSAT.

  There are losses in collateral levels of:

- All outputs for all users without PICs.

- KOSBERG for users with long and critical interval needs. This is in marked contrast with the first two optimisations, which yielded higher collateral levels for KOSBERG for all applicable groups.
- All outputs but IMPIADL for users with long interval needs and PICs.

Collateral outputs compared with the maximum achievable for each output
- As for the previous optimisations, there are a majority of low collateral output levels, concentrated on users without PICs.

Collateral output levels lay at or below 40 per cent of the maximum achievable for:
- DAYS for users without PICs.
- USATISF for users with long interval needs.
- IMPIADL for users with critical interval needs.
- IMPEMP for users with long and short interval needs without PICs, and users with critical interval needs with PICs.

Collateral output levels reach 80 per cent or above of the maximum achievable for:
- KOSBERG only for users with short interval needs. In fact, all collateral output levels for this group apart from WKSAT are above their observed levels.
- WKSAT for all users but those with short interval needs and PICs.
- IMPEMP for users with long and short interval needs with PICs, and users with critical interval needs without PICs.
- USATISF for users with critical interval needs and users with short interval needs and PICs.
- DAYS for users with short and critical interval needs and PICs.
- IMPADL for users with short and critical interval needs and PICs.
- IMPIADL for users with long and short interval needs and PICs.

3.   Overview

Input mix efficiency: the 'unconstrained' optimisation
- The optimisation of DLD implies significant changes in the allocation of services.
- Among short and critical interval need groups, users with PICs receive significantly higher resources, whereas all users with long interval needs receive identical packages of care.
- Overall, resources are highest for users with short interval needs and PICs.
- Users with long and short interval needs receive higher levels of social work, nursing inputs, and meals.
- Additionally, significant levels of respite care are allocated to critical interval users with PICs.
- All user groups enjoy very significant increases in their levels of DLD, most of the effect being related to the increase in social work inputs.

- Overall, the unconstrained optimisation increases the levels of DLD to more than 200 per cent of their observed levels.

The different optimising scenarios: how binding are the constraints?
- Compared with the unconstrained case, the group-budget constraint optimisation implies greater budgets mainly for critical interval need users without PICs, together with a notable reduction in the budget for users with short interval needs and PICs.
- Higher levels of home, day and respite care are allocated to users with critical interval needs and no PICs.
- The group-budget-constrained optimisation also produces significant DLD gains for all users.
- Overall, the group-budget-constrained optimisation reaches 84 per cent of the output levels achieved in the 'unconstrained' optimisation.
- Compared with the unconstrained case, the service-budget-constrained optimisation implies greater budgets for users with critical needs, and the allocation of significant levels of home care to all user groups.
- Among users with critical interval needs, those with PICs receive twice the level of resources.
- In contrast with the first two scenarios, three user groups lose DLD levels following optimisation.
- Overall service-budget-constrained optimisation reaches 57 per cent of the levels attained by the unconstrained optimisation.

The collateral effects
- For users with critical interval needs, and for the group-budget-constrained case, DLD optimisation yields significant improvements in important collateral outputs.
- DLD could therefore be seen as a potential maximand for critical interval need users, if current budget allocations were to be preserved.

Note

1   This is because services are constrained in the analysis not to exceed the maximum levels observed in the sample in sufficient numbers. The level of social work was therefore capped to £8 per week.

20 Efficiencies for KOSBERG Indicator Variable (Felt Burden of Caregiving)

The production function is summarised in table 8.4 and the productivity curves shown in figures 8.25-8.28. This is one of the key outputs. First, it is the most general of the measures of the outputs of community care for one stakeholder in the 'triad' (the informal carer) with important concerns with community care outcomes. Secondly, its importance is enhanced, it will be remembered from chapter 12, because of its complementary relationship with user satisfaction and days at home rather than institutions. Current discourse would attach great importance to this output, even though its precise prioritisation differs between authorities, as was shown by the results of managers' ratings of their authorities' prioritisations (Department of Health, 1998; 1999).

1. Technical efficiency (figures 20.1 to 20.3)

The output is relevant for only three of the six groups.

Group differences in average inefficiency. Figure 20.1 shows a high degree of inefficiency, approximately 40 per cent. This suggests that social services have not been tooled up to produce this output alone. Inefficiency levels reduce with the users' disability, so that the packages of care for users with critical interval needs have on average a 35 per cent technical inefficiency rate against a 47 per cent rate for users with long interval needs.

Gains from alternative strategies for efficiency improvement. Figure 20.2 shows the estimated improvements made by setting the 'efficiency floor' at different levels. Untypically, the results suggest a different pattern for cost saving and improvement in the felt burden of caregiving.

The average output gain is likely to be high given the improved performance of the extreme tail, but to diminish for more widespread improvements

Figure 20.1
Technical efficiency index* for Kosberg carer burden scale

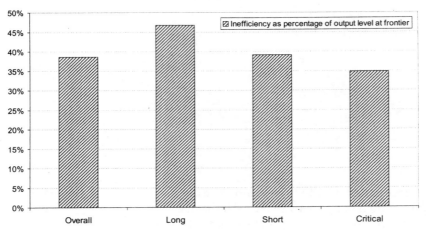

* ratio of difference between outputs achieved given service levels and mix to inputs predicted
for the user and output predicted given maximum technical efficiency given service levels and
mix to the actual output achieved

Figure 20.2
*Average output gain or cost saving from postulated improvement in
technical efficiency in the production of KOSBERG*

*Efficiency improvement strategy: the least efficient are made as efficient as units at a
prescribed higher percentile in the distribution ordered from least to most efficient*

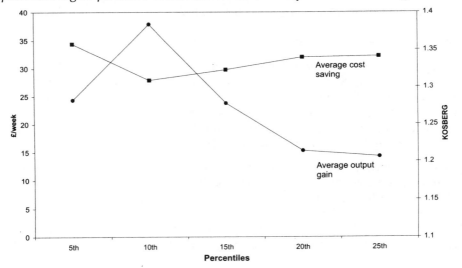

Figure 20.3
Average output gain or cost saving from postulated improvement in technical efficiency in the production of KOSBERG

Efficiency improvement strategy: prescribed percentage increase in efficiency for each of the 33 per cent most inefficient units

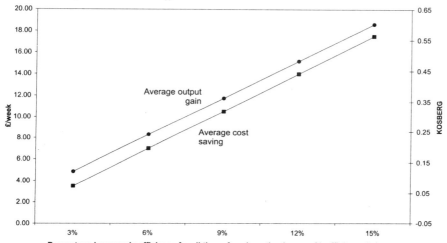

to higher points on the distribution. However, it will be remembered, the higher the floor, the greater the overall gain.

Figure 20.3 shows the results for the strategy by which the 33 per cent of units that are least efficient each improves its performance by the same proportion. The results show a much higher cost saving per percentage point improvement in efficiency than for previous outputs (approximately £1.17 per week).

2. Input mix efficiency

2.1. Assumption (a): Optimisation subject only to the overall budget: 'unconstrained optimisation' (figures 20.4 and 20.5)

2.1.1. Outputs, package costs, service mixes, and analysis group variations

The results are shown in figure 20.4.

Inefficiencies in service balance
Patterns of redistribution due to optimal input mixing are striking.
- The input of home care would be eliminated, but there would be greater use of home-delivered meals. Home care contributes to caregiver welfare, as

Figure 20.4
Input mix efficiency for Kosberg carer burden scale (KOSBERG):
'unconstrained' optimisation

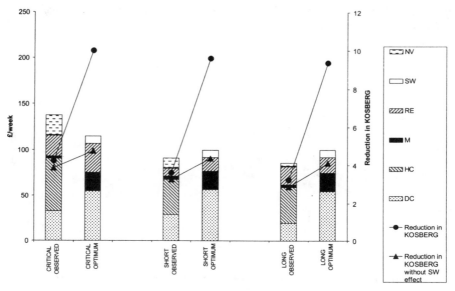

figure 8.25 illustrates. But it would be not as efficient in doing so as combinations of inputs that exclude it.

- Day care would comprise about one half of the average cost of packages for each of the three groups. Figure 8.26 illustrates the high proportion of caregivers who would be beneficially affected by productivity effects of day care.

- Social work and meals would become important package elements.

- There would be greater inputs of respite care for all users, again as would be expected from figure 8.27.

- Nursing visits would be eliminated. No productivity effects were shown for them in the production function in table 8.4.

Differences between user groups

Only three groups are relevant, the others lacking a principal informal caregiver.

The group comparisons also yield striking results.

- Optimisation would more than double the output level for each group, the gains and levels being much the same for each group.

- There would be gains for each group even if the social work effect is discounted. But that the contribution of social work to the gains would be great can be seen from how much less increase in output optimisation attains when the social work effect is ignored.

- The input of day care and meals would be increased to much the same level for each interval need group.
- The allocation of day care would be even given optimisation.
- Respite care would be reduced for users with long interval needs.
- The packages consumed by critical interval cases continue on average to cost more than for other groups, but the cost difference is less in the optimal solution.

2.1.2. *'Collateral outputs': the consequences for other outputs of optimising on KOSBERG*

The results are summarised in figure 20.5.

Actual output compared with the maximum achievable
The unconstrained optimisation of KOSBERG does not imply a redistribution of levels of output between the three groups. On the contrary, all relevant groups would enjoy very substantial relative improvements in KOSBERG.

Collateral compared with actual outputs
- The unconstrained optimisation of KOSBERG would yield more increases than losses in collateral outputs. This is in marked contrast with most of the previous output maximands.
- Most of the gains or losses in collateral outputs would be common for the three user groups.

There would be losses in collateral levels of:
- DAYS for all groups. Although the decreases would not be dramatic, this effect would be important. Indeed, chapter 12 suggested, decreases in the perception of caregiver stress should increase significantly the users' ability for staying in the community for extended periods of time. DAYS and KOSBERG, it follows, are correlated. This result, on the other hand, suggests that despite that interrelationship between the two output measures, the differences in the direct effects of the services are critical and dominate the changes in collateral outputs for DAYS. Hence, the presence in KOSBERG optimum packages of care of significant meals and social work inputs (services that are not effective in extending DAYS) causes the collateral DAYS outputs to be lower than the observed levels.
- IMPIADL for all groups, with greater falls in collateral outputs the higher the users dependency.
- IMPADL for users with long and short interval needs.
- IMPEMP for users with short and critical interval needs.

There are gains in collateral levels of:
- USATISF for all users. This effect is interesting for several reasons:

Figure 20.5
Collateral output levels for optimisation on KOSBERG with 'unconstrained' optimisation

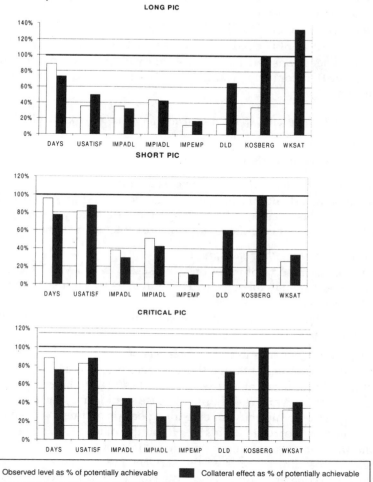

– First, it seems to confirm the association between the two variables depicted by the simultaneous production function model described in chapter 12. As figure 12.2 showed, the model found USATISF (the user level of satisfaction with the level of resources received) to significantly increase the reduction in the PIC's felt burden derived from the caregiving role.

- Second, it establishes that user and PIC related goals need not be in conflict, and that careful designing of care packages might indeed achieve significant improvements for both the user's and the PIC's welfare.

- DLD for all users. This effect should not surprise us, as was mentioned in the previous chapter, because of the strikingly significant effect that social work inputs have on both DLD and KOSBERG.

- WKSAT for all users. This effect is also important, since it represents the voice from the third actor in the triad represented in the study, the care manager. That improving KOSBERG improves WKSAT is therefore a sign of the relevance of KOSBERG as one of the main maximands to consider.

- IMPADL for user with critical interval needs. Of all users, these are probably the ones for whom gains in IMPADL would be most valued.

Collateral outputs compared with the maximum achievable for each output

- There would be approximately equal numbers of high and low collateral output levels.

- Although not quite reaching 80 per cent of their maximum achievable, collateral output levels of DAYS and DLD would be high for the three user groups.

- Collateral output levels of USATISF would be high for users with short and critical interval needs.

- Users with low interval needs enjoy very high collateral levels of WKSAT, above the 100 per cent line.

The outputs with low collateral levels are common to all users. They are the two functioning-related indicators, IMPADL and IMPIADL, and the empowerment indicator IMPEMP.

It is important to compare the results of optimising DAYS and the reduction of caregiver burden to establish the implications of these potentially competing dimensions of output. Competing, because of the potential conflict of interest between users and caregivers, and because of the possibility that the 'joint supply' relationship shown to exist in chapter 11 overall may not apply to all groups.

- For the long and short interval cases, the pattern of variation in figure 20.5 has striking similarities to that in figure 14.4. That is, the pattern when the optimisation is for DAYS would be similar to that when the output optimised is the reduction of caregiver burden, except for DLD and KOSBERG collateral levels.

- The same applies to the critical interval users, for whom the main differences would be for IMPADL and DLD collateral levels.

- The similarities seem to be striking, suggesting the interests of users and caregivers are would not be so differently served whichever of the goals were to be pursued.

2.2.   Assumption (b): Optimisation subject to user group average budgets: 'group-budget-constrained optimisation' (figures 20.6 and 7)

2.2.1.   Outputs, package costs, service mixes, and analysis group variations

The results are shown in figure 20.6.

Figure 20.6
Input mix efficiency for Kosberg carer burden scale (KOSBERG): group-budget-constrained optimisation

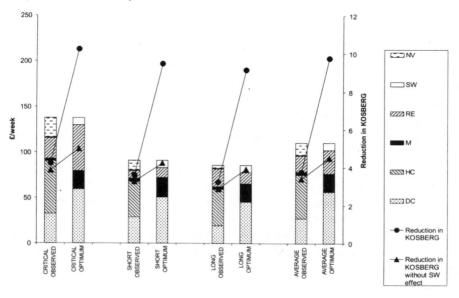

Inefficiencies in service balance
The most efficient input mix in a scenario allowing reallocation over services but not user groups would yield broadly similar results:

- Home care and nursing visits would not be part of packages, but day care, respite care and meals would be increased.

Differences between user groups
- The similarity of the extent of output improvements across groups remains despite the constraint that group budgets stay the same. This is also true when the effects of social work inputs are discounted.
- Optimising subject to keeping group budgets the same results in a strong association of respite care with dependency, and a weaker association of day care input and dependency. There is no such association for meals.
- It follows from the constraint on the optimisation that the cost of packages for critical interval users remains higher to the same degree.

2.2.2. *'Collateral outputs': the consequences for other outputs of optimising on KOSBERG*

Results are summarised in figure 20.7.

The actual output compared with the maximum achievable

As is to be expected, fixing user group budgets allows increases in the maximand variable for all user groups. Hence, the three user groups with PICs en-

Figure 20.7
Collateral output levels for optimisation on KOSBERG with group-budget-constrained optimisation

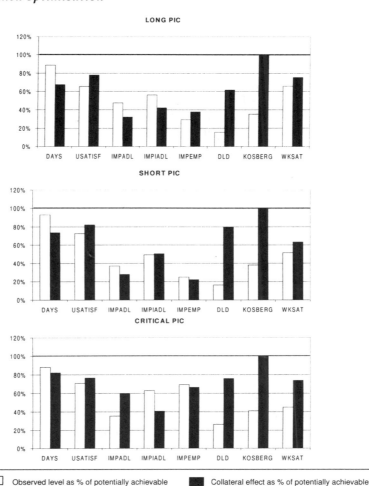

joy significant increases in their KOSBERG levels following optimisation. This was also the case for the unconstrained scenario.

Collateral compared with actual outputs
Since, as noted above, the input mixes implied by the unconstrained and group-budget-constrained optimisations are almost identical, it is not surprising that the patterns for gains and losses are also alike.
- There are still more increases than losses in collateral outputs.
- Again, most of the gains or losses in collateral outputs are common among the three outputs.

There are losses in collateral levels of:
- DAYS for all groups, although the losses for critical interval need users are smaller for the present optimisation.
- IMPIADL for all groups but those with short interval needs.
- IMPADL for users with long and short interval needs.
- IMPEMP for users with short and critical interval needs.

There are gains in collateral levels of:
- USATISF, DLD and WKSAT for all users.
- IMPADL for user with critical interval needs
- IMPIADL for users with short interval need.

Collateral outputs compared with the maximum achievable for each output
Again, the patterns between the unconstrained optimisation and the present one are very similar, except maybe for a slight improvement in the final collateral levels for critical interval need users.

Although not quite reaching 80 per cent of their maximum achievable, the collateral output levels of DAYS, USATISF, DLD and WKSAT are high for the three user groups.

There are fewer outputs with low collateral levels than for the unconstrained case. They are IMPIADL for all users, and IMPADL and IMPEMP for users with long and short interval needs.

2.3. Assumption (c): Budget shares of services are maintained: 'service-budget-constrained optimisation' (figures 20.8 and 9)

2.3.1. Outputs, package costs, service mixes, and analysis group variations

Figure 20.8 summarises the results.

Inefficiencies in service balance
- As for other output maximands, it is the constraint on service budgets that carries the most dramatic changes in the patterns of service and output allocations.
- In the other optimisation scenarios, home care does disappear altogether. In an optimisation that does not allow changes in total service consumed,

Figure 20.8
Input mix efficiency for Kosberg carer burden scale (KOSBERG): service-budget-constrained optimisation

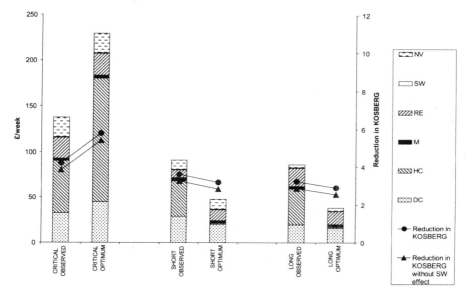

home care is entirely concentrated on critical interval cases. Figure 8.25 suggests that the effect is due substantially to the complementarity with day care, whose utilisation is also increased for the fixed service budget case, though to a lesser extent than the other optimisation scenarios, where day care is increased more. That is, home care is increased greatly because the home and day care reinforce one another's effects, and that complementarity makes this the group for whom its use is most efficient — though day care itself (and other inputs) would have been used in preference to home care were it not a condition of the optimisation that the current actual levels of home care would continue to be consumed.

- Respite care is slightly redistributed towards critical interval cases, though the amount consumed is smaller than when the optimisation is unrestricted.
- Social work is evenly distributed, reflecting its single effect for all groups depicted in figure 8.28.
- There is little redistribution of nursing visits.

Differences between user groups

- The optimisation creates a gain for only one group, those in critical interval need. The gain is much smaller than for any group under the other optimisation scenarios.

- Compared with the other optimisation scenarios, discounting the social work effect makes no difference to the patterns of output gain or loss in this scenario.
- We have observed that home care is concentrated entirely on critical interval cases.
- Total package cost was actually higher for critical interval cases and would be whatever the optimisation scenario. However, in the unconstrained scenario, the differential was reduced. Constraining optimisation to keep the total input of each service the same massively increased the difference between the cost of packages for critical interval and other cases.

2.3.2. 'Collateral outputs': the consequences for other outputs of optimising on KOSBERG

The results are shown in figure 20.9.

As noted above, the solution to the optimisation with fixed service-budgets is conspicuously different from the unconstrained and group-budget-constrained cases.

The actual output compared with the maximum achievable

Contrarily to the first two optimisations, the service budget-constrained optimisation entails the transfer of levels of KOSBERG from users of lower dependency to users with critical interval needs.

Collateral compared with actual outputs

- There are many more losses in collateral outputs in the present optimisation. Moreover, practically the totality of the gains are related to one single group.
- There are losses in collateral levels of all outputs for users with short interval needs, and all outputs but IMPEMP for users with long interval needs.
- There are gains in collateral levels of all outputs for users with critical interval needs and IMPEMP for users with long interval needs.

Collateral outputs compared with the maximum achievable for each output

Measuring the collateral output levels against the maximum attainable gives a very positive view of the effects that optimising KOSBERG with fixed input budgets renders. Indeed, the great majority of them lay above 80 per cent of their potentially attainable levels.

However, it is particularly on the changes in collateral outputs that we should concentrate when analysing KOSBERG, since the three groups that concern it do not account for all the resources utilised in the maximisation of the rest of the outputs, and hence in the calculation of the 'maximum attainable' levels.

Figure 20.9
Collateral output levels for optimisation on KOSBERG with service-budget-constrained optimisation

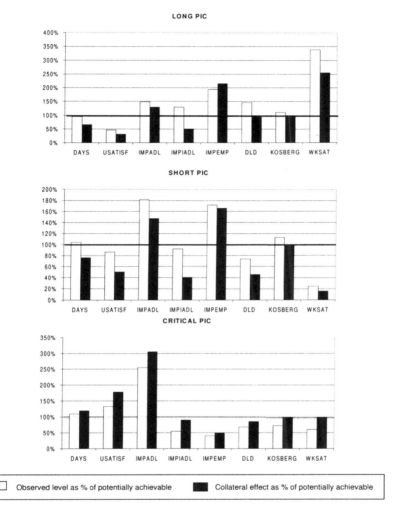

3.　Overview

Technical efficiency

- The level of technical efficiency in the production of KOSBERG is much lower than for the rest of the output variables, with an average of 39 per cent in-efficiency rate.

- The average cost savings or output gains from improvements in the least efficient units are highest when only the 5 per cent least efficient units are included.

Input mix efficiency: the 'unconstrained' optimisation

- The 'unconstrained' optimisation implies the concentration of the resources on four services: day care, meals, respite care and social work.
- Of those four:
  - day care accounts for approximately a half of the total package, with similar (and substantially increased) levels of meals and social work inputs been allocated to all users, and
  - respite care allocated in higher levels to the more dependent.
- The unconstrained optimisation would reduce the association between budgets and levels of dependency.
- Given the optimum input mix, the three groups of users with PICs enjoy higher levels of KOSBERG. In other words, the unconstrained optimisation does not require output transfers between user groups.
- Overall, the unconstrained optimisation increases the levels of KOSBERG above 250 per cent of the observed ones.

The different optimising scenarios: how binding are the constraints?

- As mentioned above, the unconstrained optimisation would not alter the allocation of resources significantly. This was also the case for the DAYS optimisation. Consequently, the optimum allocation of resources and levels of output derived from the group-budget fixed optimisation would be very similar to those obtained from the 'unconstrained' optimising scenario. In that respect, as was the case for DAYS, fixing the user group budgets to their observed levels would not represent a very significant binding constraint for the optimisation of KOSBERG.
- Overall, the group-budget-constrained optimisation would reach 99 per cent of the KOSBERG levels reached by the unconstrained optimisation.
- In contrast, fixing the service supply levels would generate considerable changes to the optimum input mixes and levels of output achieved.
- The optimum solution implies very significant transfers of resources from users with long and short interval needs to critical interval users.
- Consequently, the levels of KOSBERG would rise only for critical interval users and fall for the others.
- Home care would be concentrated on users with critical interval needs.
- The overall gains from the optimisation would be far lower than for the previous optimising scenarios.
- Overall, the service-budget-constrained optimisation reaches only 41 per cent of the gain attained by the unconstrained optimisation.

The collateral effects

- Optimising on KOSBERG would produce high collateral levels for important outcomes, and could therefore be envisaged as a potential maximand for some of the applicable groups.
- However, optimising on KOSBERG would also achieve low collateral levels for functioning-related outputs.

1.   Technical efficiency

Group differences in average inefficiency. The estimates are shown in figure 21.1. They are based on a frontier model.

The results show lower technical efficiency than might have been expected for a variable indicating what is presumably the care managers' judgements

Figure 21.1
Technical efficiency index* for care manager's perception of services' impact on user welfare

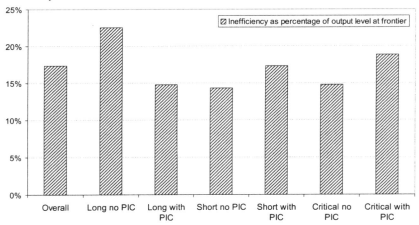

* ratio of difference between outputs achieved given service levels and mix to inputs predicted for the user and output predicted given maximum technical efficiency given service levels and mix to the actual output achieved

Figure 21.2
Average output gain or cost saving from postulated improvement in technical efficiency in the production of WKSAT

Efficiency improvement strategy: the least efficient are made as efficient as units at a prescribed higher percentile in the distribution ordered from least to most efficient

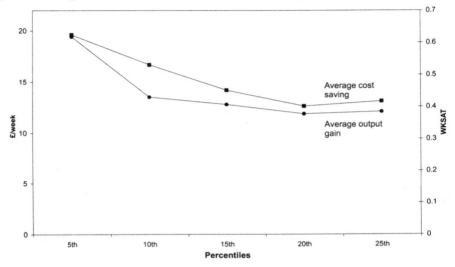

about the degree to which the goals they were aiming at were achieved. One might have expected that the input mixes would have been adjusted to these, and that the workers' goals reflected the dominant cultural assumptions about goals among the in-house providers. Indeed, many of the care managers would also have been the direct field managers of the main form of community service for their users.

There is little variation between analysis groups. Neither are there obvious gradients by interval need or whether there is a PIC.

Gains from alternative strategies for efficiency improvement. Figure 21.2 shows the estimated improvements on average costs and output gains.

- The average output gain is likely to be high given the improved performance of the units of lower efficiency, but to diminish for more widespread improvements to higher points on the distribution.
- Average cost savings would be greatest with the removal of the extreme tail. Again, however, it is the nature of modelling that the predictions for the extreme tail are unreliable.

Figure 21.3 shows the results for the strategy by which the 33 per cent of units which are least efficient each improves its performance by different given proportions.

Figure 21.3

Average output gain or cost saving from postulated improvement in technical efficiency in the production of WKSAT

Efficiency improvement strategy: prescribed percentage increase in efficiency for each of the 33 per cent most inefficient units

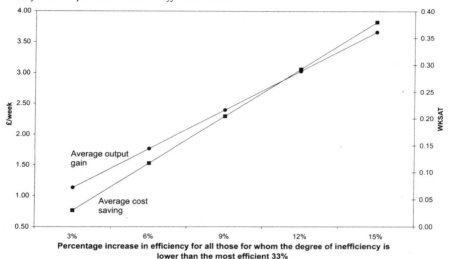

2. Input mix efficiency

2.1. Assumption (a): 'unconstrained optimisation' (figures 21.4 and 21.5)

2.1.1. Outputs, package costs, service mixes, and analysis group variations

The results are shown in figure 21.4.

Inefficiencies in service balance

- The inputs of the oldest-established services, home care and home-delivered meals would be removed. For most groups, the resources released by the removal of home care would be used to increase respite and day care.
- The inputs of community nursing would also disappear.

Group differences in service balance, outputs and package costs

- There would be a large redistribution away from critical interval need users without PICs. The package cost would be much reduced, and so would the output. Similarly, package costs would be greatly cut for long interval cases, though in both cases leaving the level of output much the same. But short interval cases and critical interval cases with PICs would be big gain-

Figure 21.4
Input mix efficiency for care manager's perception of services' impact on user welfare (WKSAT): 'unconstrained' optimisation

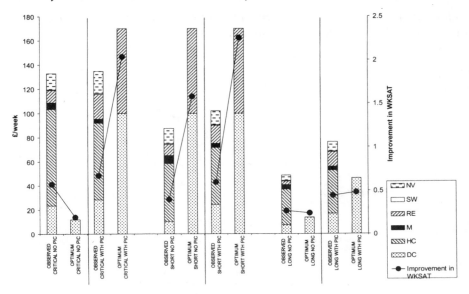

ers. They would be allocated larger packages, and there would be big increases in the output levels.

- The increases in expenditure for the short interval cases, and the critical interval cases without PICs, would be used to provide much more day and respite care. Indeed, these two services would dominate the packages. Likewise the reduction in the package costs for the other case types would squeeze out all but day care.

2.1.2. Collateral outputs

Figure 21.5 outlines the results.

The actual output compared with the maximum achievable

As mentioned above, with unconstrained WKSAT optimisation, some users (long and critical interval needs users without PICs) would lose WKSAT levels, the big gainers (short interval users and critical interval users with PICs) enjoying still bigger gains.

Collateral compared with actual outputs

There are many more collateral outputs below their observed levels than above them.

There would be collateral output losses for:

Figure 21.5
Collateral output levels for optimisation on WKSAT with 'unconstrained' optimisation

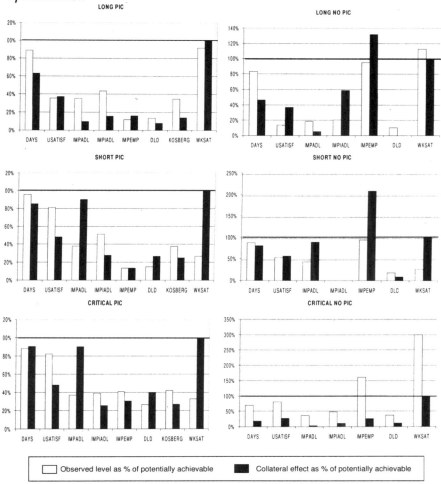

- All outputs for users with critical interval needs and no PICs.
- DAYS for all users except those with critical interval needs and PICs.
- IMPADL for users with long interval needs and users with critical interval needs and no PICs.
- IMPIADL for users with PICs and users with critical interval need without PICs.
- IMPEMP for users with critical interval needs.

- DLD for users without PICs and users with long interval needs.
- KOSBERG for all users with PICs.
- USATISF for users with critical interval needs and users with short interval needs and PICs.

There would be collateral output gains for:
- DAYS for users with critical interval needs and PICs.
- IMPADL for users with short interval needs and users with critical interval needs and PICs.
- IMPIADL for users with long interval need without PICs.
- IMPEMP for users with long and short interval needs.
- DLD for users with short and critical interval needs and PICs.
- USATISF for users with long interval needs and users with short interval needs and no PICs.

Collateral outputs compared with the maximum achievable for each output
There would be many more collateral output levels below 40 per cent than above 80 per cent of their potentially achievable levels. As would be predicted from the optimum budget sizes, the low collateral outputs would be concentrated on users with critical interval needs and no PICs, and on users with long interval needs and PICs. For those two groups, all collateral outputs but one would lie below the 40 per cent threshold.

The high collateral outputs would be enjoyed by four groups and three outputs:
- high DAYS and IMPADL for users with short interval needs and critical interval needs with PICs,
- high IMPEMP for users with long and short interval needs and no PICs.

2.2.   Group-budget-constrained optimisation (figures 21.6 and 7)

2.2.1.   Outputs, package costs, service mixes, and analysis group variations

The results are shown in figure 21.6.

Inefficiencies in service balance: comparing unconstrained with group-budget-constrained optimisations
- As with unconstrained optimisation, group-budget-constrained optimisation would replace the old with the new; home care and meals with day and respite care.
- Again, as with unconstrained optimisation, community nurse visits would be replaced.

Group differences in service balance, outputs and package costs
By definition, there would not be the large cut in the package cost for critical interval users without PICs. The effect would be a substantial increase in WKSAT. Indeed, the effect of maintaining the average budget for the case would be to cause increases in outputs for every case type. They would be

Figure 21.6
Input mix efficiency for care manager's perception of services' impact on
user welfare (WKSAT): group-budget-constrained optimisation

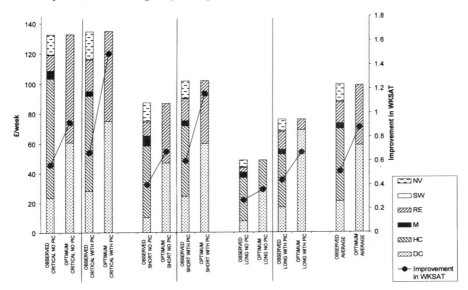

greatest for two of the types gaining most from unconstrained optimisation:
critical and short interval cases with PICs.

2.2.2. Collateral outputs

Results are summarised in figure 21.7.

The actual output compared with the maximum achievable
The group-budget-constrained optimisation of WKSAT, in contrast with the unconstrained case, would increase the levels of WKSAT for the six groups postulated in the analysis.

Collateral compared with actual outputs
Even though there would be still more collateral outputs below their observed
levels, there would be more gains than for the unconstrained case.

There would be collateral output losses for:
- DAYS for all users except those with long and critical interval needs and no
  PICs.
- USATISF for users with short and critical interval needs and PICs.
- IMPADL for users with long interval needs.
- IMPIADL for users with PICs.

Figure 21.7
Collateral output levels for optimisation on WKSAT with group-budget-constrained optimisation

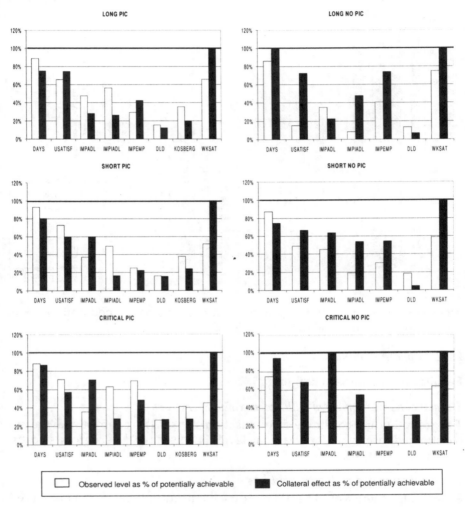

- IMPEMP for users with critical interval needs and users with short interval needs and PICs.
- DLD for users with long and short interval needs.
- KOSBERG for all users with PICs.

  There would be collateral output gains for:
- DAYS for users with long and critical interval needs without PICs.

- IMPADL for users with short and critical interval needs and PICs.
- IMPIADL for users without PICs.
- IMPEMP for users with long interval needs and users with short interval needs and no PICs.
- DLD for users with critical interval needs.
- USATISF for users with long interval needs and users with no PICs.

Collateral outputs compared with the maximum achievable for each output
Again, there would be many more collateral output levels below 40 per cent than above 80 per cent of their potentially achievable levels. Whereas the low collateral outputs are concentrated on users with no PICs, most of the high collateral outputs would be for DAYS.

There would be low collateral levels for:
- DLD and KOSBERG for all applicable users.
- IMPIADL for users with PICs.
- IMPADL for users with long interval needs.
- IMPEMP for users with short interval needs and PICs, and critical interval needs without PICs.

The high collateral outputs are for DAYS for all groups, and for IMPADL for users with critical interval needs and no PICs.

Therefore the mix of collateral outputs produced were WKSAT to be maximised would be unattractive. Indeed, the pattern poses questions about the user and caregiver-sensitivity of care managers.

The setting of group budgets would benefit more groups than would be disadvantaged. It would result in similar or greater collateral outputs for DAYS in all groups. It would result in higher levels of USATISF in all groups. It would improve IMPEMP for users with long interval dependency. But for all analysis groups with PICs, it would reduce the easing of the felt burden of caregiving.

2.3. Assumption (c): service-budget-constrained optimisation (figures 21.8 and 21.9)

2.3.1. Outputs, package costs, service mixes, and analysis group variations

Figure 21.8 summarises the results.

The focus is the comparison of unconstrained with service-budget-constrained optimisations.
- Like unconstrained optimisation, the service-budget-constrained optimisation would reduce package for the typical long interval users and for critical interval users without PICs. But it would also reduce the package cost for the typical short interval case without a PIC. In each case, a substantially lower level of WKSAT would accompany the reduction in package costs.
- The two case types that would gain are critical and short interval users with PICs, particularly the short interval cases. Indeed, respite and day care would be concentrated on the latter. Little of the home care would be allo-

Figure 21.8
*Input mix efficiency for care manager's perception of services' impact on
user welfare (WKSAT): service-budget-constrained optimisation*

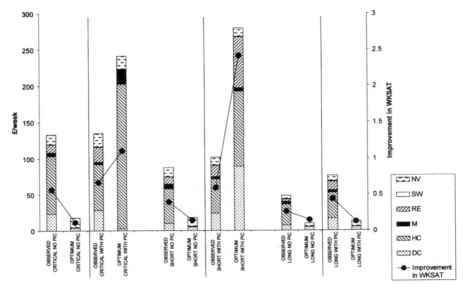

cated to users without PICs and users with long interval needs. Very large
inputs would be made to critical interval users with PICs (who would receive little day care). Moderately large inputs would be made to short interval cases with PICs (who would also receive day care in quantities making
the costs of home and day care for them much the same as the cost of home
care for critical interval users with PICs).

- Community nurses' visits would be no differently allocated than in the current pattern.

There would therefore be a substantial redistribution between case types,
and the mix of services for each type would differ both from the current pattern and the optimum given unconstrained optimisation.

2.3.2. Collateral outputs

The results are shown in figure 21.9.

Collateral compared with the maximum achievable for each output
The patterns would be very different between analysis groups

- For long interval cases, collateral outputs would be low for the main outcome variables save for IMPEMP among the users without PICs. Indeed, they
  would be lower than current levels for all variables.

Figure 21.9
Collateral output levels for optimisation on WKSAT with service-budget-constrained optimisation

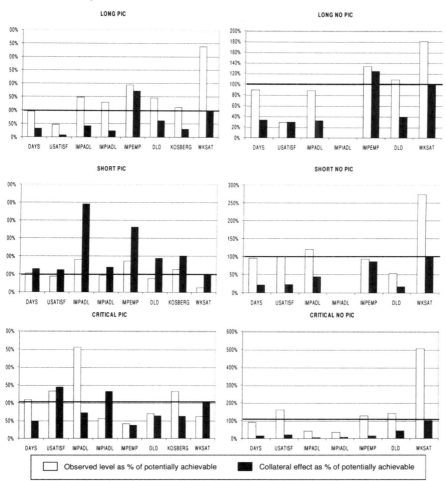

- Similarly there would be low collateral outputs for all variables except IMPEMP for all users without PICs, and the high level for IMPEMP would not occur for critical interval cases.
- Among short interval cases with PICs, the high collateral level for DAYS would be maintained, but the level among critical interval users would be low. However, for users with short interval needs, the reduction in felt care-giver burden would remain high.

Major differences in pattern between optimisations with or without fixed service budgets
The main feature is that optimisation with fixed service budgets would produce lower collateral outcomes for some of the principal dimensions. That would be particularly so for DAYS, for which the collateral output would be lower for all the groups save for short interval cases with PICs. But it would also be the case for USATISF for long interval need users, and users without PICs. (On the other hand, USATISF would be increased for short and critical interval cases with PICs.)

So again, with WKSAT as a maximand, it would be difficult to argue against policy effort to reduce the policies, procedures and assumptions to reduce the degree to which the supply of newer services is insufficiently flexible to capture the superior gains of optimising under the less constrained optimisation conditions.

3.   Overview

Technical efficiency
- The level of technical efficiency in the production of WKSAT would on average be 17 per cent.
- The average cost savings or output gains from improvements in the least efficient units decrease as higher proportions of units are included. Therefore they would be greatest when only the 5 per cent least efficient units are included.

Input mix efficiency: unconstrained optimisation
- The optimisation of WKSAT would imply the concentration of resources among users with short interval needs or critical interval needs and PICs, and on day and respite care inputs.
- As a consequence, those three groups would enjoy the main benefits of the optimisation, leaving the rest of the groups with either similar or lower output levels.
- Overall, the unconstrained optimisation would increase the levels of WKSAT to approximately 230 per cent of their observed levels.

The different optimising scenarios: how binding are the constraints?
- Compared with the unconstrained case, the group-budget constraint optimisation would allocate greater budgets for critical interval need users without PICs and long interval need users, together with a notable reduction in the budget for users with short interval needs and critical interval need users with PICs.
- Input mixes would still consist of exclusively day and respite care, this last providing more intensively for users with higher levels of need.
- In contrast with the unconstrained case, the group-budget-constrained optimisation would produce significant WKSAT gains for all users.

- Overall, the group-budget-constrained optimisation would reach 78 per cent of the output levels achieved in the 'unconstrained' optimisation.
- Compared with the unconstrained case, the service-budget constraint optimisation would imply even greater budgets for users with critical and short interval needs and PICs, and the reduction of the inputs allocated to short interval need users without PICs.
- The optimum allocation would assign all respite and day care inputs to the short interval need with PICs cases, and the majority of meals and home care to the critical interval need and PICs cases.
- Only two user groups would benefit from higher WKSAT levels following optimisation.
- Overall service-budget-constrained optimisation would reach 60 per cent of the levels attained by the unconstrained optimisation.

The collateral effects
- The low levels for some of the key collateral outputs would make WKSAT an unlikely candidate as maximand.
- Given observed budgets, only DAYS would reach levels above 80 per cent of the potentially achievable.

In this chapter, we assume the observed allocations to be perfectly efficient, and interpret the patterns to reflect implicit equity judgements about user groups and outputs made by 'the system'. For instance, the chapter seeks to establish the importance that the system gives to for instance producing DAYS as compared to reduced felt burden of caregiving, and how those priorities change depending on the needs and circumstances of the users.

The rationale is that because it has been demonstrated that the most efficient production of different outputs would require substantially different allocations of resources, the fact that the actual input mixes differ from any of those predicted by the optimisations in chapters 14 to 22 does not necessarily signal inefficiency. The current patterns may conceivably reflect a set of equity patterns balancing the achievement of the different outputs for the different users. And even if we strongly suspect that in their detail they are less the product of policy choice than of inefficiencies, to treat the broad features as if they were the implicit equity choices helps us to consider whether there are equity biases.

This assumption of perfect efficiency is the opposite to that made in the earlier chapters in this part of the book. In effect, each of the chapters has so far made the assumption that improving the production of whatever the output in question is the only system goal, either because of its importance or because of its potential for yielding other collateral outputs. That assumption and the single output optimand assumption we justified on the grounds that the analysis of efficiency requires a clear and authoritative statement of the marginal valuations for each output in each user circumstance. As we argued in chapter 13, there is no such statement now, nor is one a likely product of the policy process in pluralist democracies committed to stakeholder responsiveness. Similarly, without that statement we can neither choose between the perfect efficiency assumption, its opposite, or a third assumption attributing some part of what is observed precisely to equity judgements and the remainder to inefficiency.

1.   Methodology

1.1.   *Reinterpreting the evidence*

The key issue for making deductions about equity patterns in this looking-glass scenario is the pattern of associations of the gap between actual and achievable outputs and need-related circumstances. The closer the actual allocation of resources is to reaching the maximum attainable of the given output, the greater its implicit valuation.

1.1.1.   *Indicators*

The analysis is based on relative performance indicators, rather than absolute ones. This is done in order to achieve some comparability between the different measures of outputs. Otherwise, each output would be expressed in totally different units of measure, and their comparison (such as 'improvement of 2 in KOSBERG score' versus '200 extra DAYS') would be almost impossible. Further, measuring output performance against the maximum attainable allows the analysis to discount for the differences in the system's production capabilities between users. For instance, it is likely to be considered unfair to treat as equivalent the achievement of 100 extra days in the community for users with or without PICs if the presence of PICs alters the effectiveness of services and therefore makes the production of DAYS relatively 'easier' for one of the groups.

However, the simplification achieved by using relative performance indicators is bought at the cost of the risk that the incautious may make some false inferences. The danger of two kinds of false inferences should be remembered. (a) The indicators are likely to exaggerate real gains in welfare for users with low actual output levels, or with very high potential for improvement. For instance, relative increases of several 100 per cent might in fact be describing very small overall changes. To make some allowance for this, the figures reporting the results employ logarithmic scales. (b) More important, embodied in the methodology is the assumption that the maximum levels attainable for the different outputs are equivalent in their contributions to welfare. But it would be absurd to infer that because the system achieves approximately 80 per cent and 40 per cent of their maximum attainable for DAYS and IMPEMP respectively, DAYS is twice as valued. It is therefore important to note how the 100 per cent level, the maximum attainable, does not carry a specific policy meaning, such as for instance the 'desirable' level of output. In fact, whereas inputs might not be capable of yielding the 'socially desirable' levels for some outputs, they might be capable of greatly exceeding them for others.

1.1.2. Output valuations

The importance of each of the outputs is bound to vary between (and within) user types. For instance, decreasing caregiver stress might be judged to be of higher priority than some other outputs in cases in which the user presents very severe cognitive impairment and/or behavioural disturbances. Moreover, users with higher levels of dependency might be allocated higher priority for all measures of output. Wherever possible the analysis tries to distinguish between the system's implicit preferences between outputs, and the system's implicit preferences between users these to the degree possible, though they are frequently inter-related and so impossible to disentangle.

2.   Results

Figures 22.1 and 22.2 reflect the focus on relative outputs.

2.1.   All users (figure 22.1)

Figure 22.1 summarises levels for eight key outputs for each optimisation scenario. The focus is the user group as a whole. The outputs with lowest propor-

Figure 22.1
Proportional gains in overall outputs by optimisation type

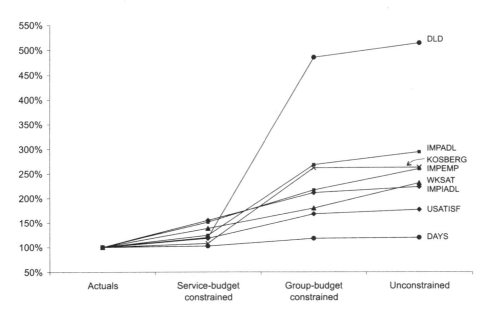

tional gains and therefore closest to their maximum attainable are interpreted to have been allocated the highest priority in the system.

One set of results shows the clearest of patterns:

- Given optimisation in the service-budget-constrained scenario, the outputs in order from the least to most greatly improved (that is, from the highest to lowest priority) would be DAYS (with almost no improvement); KOSBERG; USATISF; DLD; IMPADL; WKSAT; IMPEMP; IMPIADL.
- Given optimisation in group-budget-constrained scenario, the outputs ordered from the least to most greatly improved: DAYS; USATISF; WKSAT; IMPIADL; IMPEMP; KOSBERG; IMPADL, DLD.
- Given optimisation in the unconstrained scenario, the variables ordered from least to most greatly improved would be are: DAYS; USATISF; IMPIADL; WKSAT; IMPEMP; KOSBERG; IMPADL; DLD.

So in all three scenarios, DAYS seems to be by far the most highly prioritised output.[1] In fact, DAYS is hardly increased at all by the service-budget-constrained optimisation, and is increased by only approximately 20 per cent by the group-budget-constrained and unconstrained optimisations. This is a restatement of a finding derived on the other side of the looking glass. It is one of those findings of this book which most clearly relates the assumptive world of the 1989 White Paper to local managers' interpretation of the implicit prioritisations of their authorities (reported in chapter 3) and what the authors of the 1998 White Paper saw to be the greatest changes actually accomplished in the previous decade (quoted below).

Figure 22.1 provides alternative interpretations to other patterns that were well established but differently described by the efficiency chapters.

- The relative position for most outputs would differ little between user-group-budget and unconstrained optimisations. But the implicit valuations for KOSBERG, DLD and IMPADL would differ dramatically between those and the service-budget-constrained scenario of fixed aggregate consumption of each of the services. Indeed, the three outputs would appear to be among the most highly valued in the service-budget-constrained world, though among the least valued in the other scenarios
- After DAYS (and KOSBERG in the service-budget-constrained world), USATISF and DLD are suggested by figure 22.1 to be highly prioritised regardless of the optimisation scenario.
- IMPIADL, arguably one of the main pre-reform traditional objectives of the services does not appear in any of the three optimisation scenarios as highly prioritised.

2.2. *User group patterns (figure 22.2)*

The previous section has looked at the system's performance for users in general by comparing the sum of the actual and optimum output levels for the six user groups. This section focuses on the differences between user groups. In

Figure 22.2
Proportional output gains by optimisation type and user group

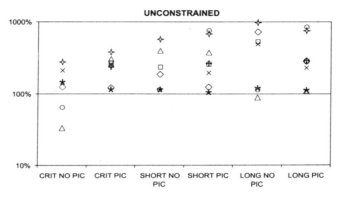

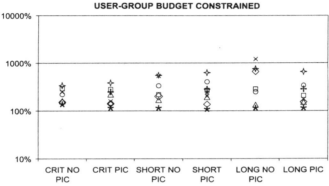

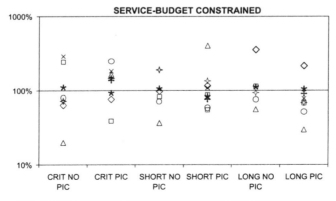

doing so it will try to answer two kinds of related questions:

- Are there particular groups of users that enjoy higher relative levels for most outputs? In other words, is the system biased towards some user groups?
- Does the implicit valuation of outputs change depending on the nature of the users?

The interpretation of each section of figure 22.2 depends on the optimisation to which it refers. This is because whereas the unconstrained and service-budget-constrained cases allow for transfers between the resources allocated to each of the user groups, the user-group-budget-constrained optimisation does not. In other words, the analysis hypothesises a system for the user-group-budget-constrained case in which the mix of outputs to be achieved is 'chosen' subsequently to the allocation of particular budgets to each group. In that sense, the prioritisation between user groups precedes the one between outputs, and is controlled through the relative sizes of the budgets allocated to each of the user groups. Therefore, the analysis of the user-group-budget-constrained scenario illuminate questions defined above; questions about differences in the relative importance of outputs for user groups.

Both the unconstrained and service-budget-constrained optimisations allow for transfers in the resources allocated to each group. In such scenarios, the observed allocation of resources reflects the system's implicit equity judgements about the importance of achieving more of particular outcomes (as for the group-budget case) but as well achieving more of them for particular users. In that sense, the analysis of the diagrams in Figure 22.2 relating to service-group budget constrained and unconstrained optimisations illuminates both questions stated above.

2.2.1. User-group-budget-constrained scenario

For most user groups, the priorities between outputs reflect those described in figure 22.1.

- For all user groups DAYS appears to be the outcome least improved by optimisation. It appears to be the output that most drives the allocation of resources, the most valued output.
- For all user groups DLD is the outcome with greatest potential for improvement, and hence to which least priority is given in the allocation process.
- For users with PICs and users with critical interval needs, USATISF appears to be the second most valued output.
- For each level of dependency, the system reaches levels of WKSAT closer to their maximum achievable for users without PICs.
- KOSBERG appears to have a low priority among all the relevant user groups.
- IMPIADL appears to be given a lower priority for users without PICs. The lower the level of need of the user, the more this is so.

- IMPADL has a low priority compared with the other outputs for users with critical interval needs.
- Generally, there is higher variance in the ratios for the different outputs for users in the lower levels of need. This is particularly so if one considers that the scales in the diagrams are logarithmic. For such users, therefore, the relative trade-offs between outputs seem be to greater.

2.2.2. *Unconstrained optimisation scenario*

In contrast with the user-group constrained scenario, the unconstrained optimisation allows for transfers of resources between the user groups. This explains the presence of some output levels for some users below the 100 per cent line. For such users, the system is achieving greater levels of the given output than the ones justified on efficiency grounds. Whereas this would tend to suggest that the output in question is particularly important for such user group, it may also be that the output is not very important, so that its levels are dictated by the targeting of other outputs.

The results are similar to those for user-group-budget-constrained optimisation in important respects:

- The variance in the gain ratios is significantly greater the lower the users' level of dependency. Again, this is although the patterns are 'smoothed' because of the use of a logarithmic scale.
- As in the previous case, DAYS ratio levels are very close to the 100 per cent levels for all users, indicating the great priority that the system gives to achieving the full potential for the variable.
- Again as in the user group-budget-constrained optimisation, USATISF is produced at levels close to the maximum attainable for most user groups. This is not the case, however, for users in the long interval need category.
- There is a marked contrast between users in the priority given by the system to achieving WKSAT, this being highest for users with long interval needs and critical interval needs without PICs.
- As in the previous case, KOSBERG appears to be accorded a low priority for all the relevant user groups.
- Again, DLD is the outcome with lowest implicit priority for all user groups.

2.2.3. *Service-budget-constrained optimisation scenario*

Figure 22.2 shows the results to differ greatly from those for unconstrained optimisation. It shows many more outputs to be less than 100 per cent.

- Whereas the other two optimisation scenarios showed many affinities, the world with fixed expenditure on each service suggests very different implicit valuations for three outputs:
- For all three applicable user groups, the levels of KOSBERG achieved are much closer to their maximum attainable than for the previous two optimisation scenarios. As was seen in previous chapters, this is due to the limit of

social work input available in the service-budget-constrained optimisation. For users with long and short interval needs, the actual levels of KOSBERG exceed in fact the ones implied by the optimisation. Were the system to be most accurately described by this optimisation scenario, KOSBERG would therefore be the second highest implicitly valued output, its priority being higher for users with low levels of need.

- In total contradiction to what was observed in the first two optimisations, IMPADL would be highly implicitly valued for all groups apart from the critical interval need without PICs. At the expense of that group, the system would achieve higher than optimum levels for all users with PICs.

- Levels of DLD are not valued least for all user groups. Instead, relatively high achievements rates for DLD are reached for users with long interval needs, and users with critical interval needs without PICs. In fact, all such groups enjoy higher levels of DLD than what pure efficiency criteria would allocate to them.

- Although still an important priority for users with short and critical interval needs, USATISF becomes the output with least implicit valuation for users with long interval needs.

- In a world of fixed service budgets, IMPEMP would be much less valued for users with critical interval needs and PICs.

- One of the few similarities between the implicit valuations for the optimisations scenarios, DAYS emerges as the output driving most of the allocation of the resources. Again the levels achieved are almost identical to the optimum ones.

3.   Overview

Previous chapters have suggested the existence of allocative inefficiencies in the production of the different of outputs. Also, optimum allocations have been shown to differ between outputs, so that no single input mix could achieve levels close to the optimum for all the indicators. Assuming the observed allocations to reflect the system's implicit equity balance between goals, the present chapter has tried to determine weights describing priorities between outputs and between users.

Some of the main conclusions are:

- Regardless of the optimisation scenario and for all user groups, DAYS appear to be the most highly valued output.

- The system's implicit priorities for other outputs differ greatly depending on the optimisation scenario. The differences are particularly great for the valuation of KOSBERG and DLD between the service-budget-constrained scenario and the other scenarios. This is mainly because of the effect of social work inputs.

- For scenarios that allow free transfers between services, USATISF generally appear to be the second most valued output.
- Generally, there is greater variance in the implicit priorities allocated to outputs for users of lower disability. Several factors could explain this. First, the pattern could indicate that for users of low disability the system concentrates on particular outputs. More probably, however, this is likely to be the product of a combination of factors. First, the system exhibits marked decreasing returns to scale in the production of most outputs. Taken with the higher allocations of service to users of greater disability, decreasing returns are likely to yield smaller differences for users with higher levels of disability.

Note

1   The results may be partly due to the presence of decreasing returns to scale, which cause marginal improvements in DAYS to be increasingly difficult. However, the clarity of the patterns suggests them to be the product of more than just the nature of the output's production relations.

PART III
EQUITY AND EFFICIENCY
POLICY CHOICES

About Part III

In this part of the book, all but the last chapter illustrate the application of this new technique of policy analysis by using the findings of earlier sections in the discussion of propositions about how to employ the framework created by the new policy structure in *Modernising Social Services*. The first chapter (chapter 23) is about dimensions of 'independence', whose promotion is the central theme of the White Paper. Chapter 24 shows how the findings can illuminate matters that are more a matter of equity than of efficiency. It takes as a case study one of the most pressing issues of equity priorities of current policy discourse in the UK and in several other countries: striking a balance between resource concentration and diffusion. It discusses whether more resources than now should be allocated to less disabled persons on the grounds that it would prevent deterioration and promote rehabilitation. Chapter 25 switches the focus from the user to the other stakeholders; namely the other two members of the triads, informal caregivers and care managers. Chapter 26 turns from propositions about equity and efficiency and allocations to users and caregivers to a proposition that is purely about the supply system: the effects of creating one rather than another scenario for commissioning and decommissioning. Finally there is a chapter which comments on the findings and arguments, and considers their implications for the fundamental assumptions for the design of policy techniques in an outcome-led knowledge-informed policy system.

The policy propositions discussed are a small selection from those that could be illuminated. They are listed under their chapter heads overleaf.

Some policy propositions

Independence: chapter 23

Proposition 1. Make the enhancement of the feeling of enhanced control over life the single maximand

Proposition 2. Make one of the outputs valued by users the single maximand

Proposition 2a. Make the extension of the number of days users are supported in their own homes rather than in institutions for long-term care the single output maximand

Proposition 2b. Make the improvement of user satisfaction with services the single output maximand

Proposition 3. Make compensating for, and improving functioning in, performing the tasks of daily living the output maximand

Proposition 3a(i). Allocate resources so as to maximise the improvement in the performance of PADL tasks

Proposition 3a(ii). Allocate resources so as to maximise the improvement in the performance of IADL tasks

Balancing resource concentration and diffusion: chapter 24

Proposition 4. Allocate more resources to the most dependent, so as to release resources to achieve preventative effects for the least dependent, in this and other ways achieving greater contributions overall to independence

Proposition 4a. Allocate more resources to the less disabled without extending numbers of lower dependency

Proposition 4b. Allocate the same budget to a caseload increased by doubling the numbers in long interval need groups without changing their circumstances

Proposition 4c. Allocate resources to many more persons of lesser disability, targeting the additional resources at persons in circumstances other than those of the current users of low disability

Proposition 4d. Set budget caps on packages and redistribute the purchasing power so released to others

Proposition 4e. Increase or decrease the total budget holding the case-mix constant

Optimising carer burden or workers assessment of impact: chapter 25

Proposition 5. Make reducing the burden from caregiving the maximand

Proposition 6. Maximise what the field care manager interprets to be the greatest beneficial impact

Proposition 7. Control equity by setting average package costs for analysis groups

Flexibility in commissioning: chapter 26

Proposition 8. Improve efficiency by maximising flexibility in commissioning and decommissioning

The reform policy has been interpreted by a leading participant to have been 'highly principled and deeply impregnated by values' (Utting, 1996). The promotion of 'independence' has been the key overarching aim. The White Paper of 1998 made 'promoting independence' the first words of its subtitle and declared it to be the 'guiding principle of adult services' (Department of Health, 1998b, para. 2.5). The White Paper of 1989 defined the function of community care to be to promote independence: 'community care means providing the services and support which people ... need to be able to live as independently as possible in their own homes, or in 'homely' settings in the community' (Department of Health, 1989, para. 1.1). However, 'independence' has many facets. From the principle, the logic of the 1989 White Paper moved to goals, from the goals to 'objectives', and from the objectives to the detail of policy: structures, protocols and guidelines, and the like.

One of the principal contrasts between the post- and pre-reform arrangements is the replacement of fragmented ideational and structural elements by a *policy system*: a dynamic model of inter-related parts, working alone and in combination to achieve the overall goal (Davies, 1993c, 1997a). Central to the system idea is the setting of performance criteria and targets in the light of continuously updated information about needs and outcomes, and the monitoring of their achievement. The setting of performance criteria and the monitoring of performance is at a level of generality which is mostly below that of the objectives in the White Paper. But this is precisely the kind of task that should be most illuminated by such production of welfare studies as this — and of course by many other types of information also.

So the most important of the many complex meanings of 'independence' must be distinguished in order to make the transition from the overarching aim to the specification of operational goals, targets and performance indicators required by the policy process. All the policy propositions discussed below are related to the overarching concept.

1.   **Make the enhancement of the feeling of control over life the single maximand**

The great influence of 'locus of control' on quality of life and psychological and physical health is established in the psychological literature in gerontology, just as it is in the literature for other age groups (Bandura, 1997; Chipperfield, 1993; Herzog et al., 1998; Krause, 1987; Langer and Rodin, 1976; Menec and Chipperfield, 1997a,b; Schultz, 1976; Timko and Moos, 1989). The literature shows direct main effects (by which the sense of control has an effect even in the absence of stressors), stress-buffering effects (reducing the effects of stressors), and mediating effects by which causal agents work through their effects on control to outcomes (Schulz and Heckhausen, 1999). In seeking to enhance the sense of personal control over everyday life, British policy argument fits in with a powerful emphasis of international research-based argument on the determinants of overall quality of life, and how publicly-subsidised care services can contribute to it.

The implementation guidelines telling authorities what to do and how to do it supports the claim that they were deeply imbued with key values. At a high level of generality, the values are common to reforms of community and long-term care in most of the leading countries (Baldock and Evers, 1992; Davies, 1992a,b; Davies et al, 1990; Davies, Fernández and Saunders, 1998; Kraan et al., 1991; Monk and Cox, 1989; van den Heuvel and Schrijvers, 1986). But a closer looks reveals distinct differences whose patterns reflect long-standing cultural and institutional differences and the timing of reform attempts. To the British, the key concept is independence. People were to be enabled to lead 'as normal a life as possible'. They were to be helped to achieve the 'maximum possible independence' and 'their full potential'. They were to have 'a greater individual say in how they live their lives'. These phrases were prominent in the 1989 White Paper, but they could equally have been taken from the current definitive general statement of policy intent, the 1998 White Paper. It is this working through from values to detailed guidance about every aspect of implementation that has created the respect of policy reformers in some other countries, and so enabled the British contribution (to a flattering degree) to the international lexicon and logic in the increasingly globalised network of persons and ideas about community care reform.[1]

The relationship between 'independence' and 'empowerment' depends on the meanings attached to each word; an ambiguity with disadvantages as well as advantages in the policy process. For instance, one combination of meanings makes 'empowerment' principally a means, and 'independence' an end. The meaning that would make 'empowerment' exclusively a means is an implicit assumption that the feeling of being in control of the detail of day-to-day interaction with service is less important than impacts that affect longer term and more general well-being. This seems to be the concept defined by Max Weber: 'the probability that an actor may be able to some degree impose his will in the framework of a social relationship' (1971). However, discussions with users themselves rate the feeling of being in control to be very important, as they did fifteen years ago (Nocon and Qureshi, 1996; Clark et al., 1998; Davies et al., 1990).

The implementation documents have treated 'empowerment' both as a means and as an end. To apply the slogan phrases repeatedly used in the official documents, one of the features of the 'profound cultural change' required was to make services led by user needs and wants, 'needs-led, not service-led'. But the implementation documents put the greater emphasis on the more general and longer-term impacts. And that was what the local managers most clearly prioritised. This was illustrated by the discussion of the interpretation of the 133 managers about their authorities' de facto prioritisation of providing 'a real chance for more users to stay at home rather than enter a care home' reported in chapter 3. This priority of central and local government appears to conform to that of elderly citizens in general and the users of home care services, though the latter tend to over-estimate the degree to which low levels of service reduce the likelihood of entering a home, just as they did fifteen years ago (Clark et al., 1998; Davies et al., 1990). The prioritisation of the scale item 'empowerment as end', 'empowerment, choice and control over their own lives' was second, but mixed the meaning of empowerment as end and means, and so must have captured the priorities given to empowerment both as means and end. One must infer that the way in which local authorities translated the concept of 'independence' into policy prioritisation was to reduce the inappropriate and unwanted utilisation of institutions for long-term care by extending the utilisation of home care, as long as the quality of life was not unacceptably worse.

To summarise the context:
- The central dimension of 'independence' and the fruits of 'empowerment' over what matters to quality of life is what the psychologists call a generalised 'locus of control'.
- Users greatly value a style in which they see themselves as greatly influencing the definition of issues, the nature and content of services, and their day-to-day operation. The reform policy has recognised, and increasingly introduced mechanisms to achieve, the impact of user and carer wishes on assessment, care planning, and service operation and content.

*Implications of the results.*Three indicators were used to measure empowerment aspects of independence: IMPEMP, the indicator of the degree to which users felt that they controlled their own lives; UEMPOW, the degree to which users feel they had an influence, were given choice, and had their concerns addressed during the set-up stage of the care management process; and CEMPOW, the degree to which principal informal carers felt that they had such influence during the set-up stage.

First, the results of table 7.1 show that community care does promote feelings of empowerment. It is conceivable that were the content and style of services to be authoritarian, the greater the service input clients received, the lower would be the level of control which they would feel over their own lives. The opposite is clearly the case. Service variations substantially offset risk factors for IMPEMP in particular, and the effect is widespread. For IMPEMP, the Risk Offset Proportion from Productivity Effect' (ROPP), is a substantial 24 per cent for IMPEMP, and the Cover of Productivity Proportion (COPP) is 54 per cent. The results for UEMPOW suggest a lower but still substantial ROPP of 14 per cent, but a COPP of 74 per cent. The ROPP for CEMPOW was still lower, but still substantial, at 9 per cent, but like UEMPOW, the COPP was a high 74 per cent. These ratios imply that the system is not outrageously ineffective in increasing feelings of empowerment and influence, and that empowerment and influence are not outrageously neglected compared with other outputs. So it would seem misleading to make sweeping generalisations to the effect that the social services do little to give a sense of empowerment of users and caregivers. Harding's statement that 'older people ... have not had a way of voicing their own priorities or discussing how best to meet them' seems not to be valid at the level of individual care management (1999, 43).[2]

At the level of service planning and monitoring for areas, the attempt to empower users has been weaker (Harding, 1999; Phillipson, 1992). Some believe that the effects of doing so would be great.[3] Involvement of users in planning was advocated in the Seebohm Report's chapter on services for elderly people, but it is a measure of the resistance caused by the self-absorption and self-interest of the old civic culture that so little was then achieved (Seebohm Committee, 1968, para. 314). Few authorities followed Birmingham, which employed Tessa Jowell in the Community Care Special Action Project among other things to promote the empowerment of users by securing their participation in process and the articulation of their needs (Jowell and Wistow, 1989). There has been the central government commitment to implementing policies such as user participation in DH inspections only during the last few years. Likewise, the participation of users and carers and representatives of them from user interest groups has been slower to develop in the UK than, for instance, in Australia, and the better American states and programmes.[4]

But Harding's assertion ignores the combined effect of two influences. One is the policy emphasis on putting in place mechanisms for performing the core tasks of care management. Basing their view on the inspections of care management in a large number of authorities, the most substantial collection of evidence yet undertaken of structure and process in care management since the reform, the White Paper commented that the 'focus on individual care management, focused towards helping people to live in their own homes, was the key change to the system' (Department of Health, 1998b, para 2.2).[5] The key importance of the emphasis on the care management process in the context of a single dominant priority, the suggestion of the quotation, is found also in some research-based academic opinion (Davies, 1997a).

That higher rather than lower levels of service contribute to feelings of control over life and to influence over care arrangements does not conclusively prove that we should make the improvement in control over life the main goal of the services. That would only be a valid conclusion were optimising on IMPEMP to result in an arguably better pattern of collateral outputs than alternatives in one or other of the optimisation scenarios.

The patterns of collateral outputs were described in figures 18.5, 18.7 and 18.9. Figure 18.5 shows that in the 'unconstrained optimisation' scenario, making users' feeling of empowerment over their own life the maximand would:

- Actually cause a reduction in the number of additional days in the community currently produced for members of all but one case type, leaving the level of the output low in relation to what could be achieved for some case types. That is so although the current pattern reflects great variations in inefficiency, but the optimisation assumes the removal of inefficiency in combining service inputs.
- Reduce the level of user satisfaction with service for many case types, again leaving the level low for some case types.
- Leave the level of reduction of caregiver stress low, usually lower than currently.
- Create unsatisfactory patterns of some other collateral outputs.
- Leave IMPEMP high for users without principal informal caregivers.

Assuming the 'service-budget-constrained' optimisation scenario, figure 18.9 suggests that to optimise IMPEMP would again result in a substantial reduction in DAYS compared with current levels; again reduce user satisfaction for most groups; and again cause a smaller reduction in felt caregiver burden.

There does not seem to a strong case for selecting IMPEMP as the output maximand for all groups. Fixing user budgets to their observed levels, figure 18.7 suggests there would be no case type for which maximising IMPEMP would simultaneously improve DAYS, USATISF, IMPIADL and WKSAT compared with present levels. The patterns would seem to be all the more unsatisfactory because the estimates assume an unattainable level of efficiency in mixing inputs given their prices and productivities.

2.   Make one of the outputs valued by users the single maximand

The circumstances of many users are such that the performance of what they and others see as the most important tasks would not greatly improve their IMPEMP levels. For them, among others, their sense of control over their lives is likely to be determined by other factors.

So there is a case for maximising those outputs that we know to be most associated with the sense of independence, perhaps a cause or an effect. The extension of stays in their own homes rather than residential institutions might be primarily a cause. Improved user satisfaction with the service might be an effect. The policy papers have associated them with 'independence' in the process of elaborating the meaning of the 'independence' goal.

The discussion of independence requires a consideration of the nature of the association, since it is unlikely to be straightforward, at least for some cases. There is a particular problem in inferring that feelings of satisfaction with (and empowerment in) service processes are a good indicator of 'independence'. The implications of the policy documents are less that each of these goals is independent in its own right, than that they must be interpreted in conjunction with one another. For instance, the maximisation of days spent in their own homes must be evaluated in the context of its implications for feelings of empowerment and the burden felt by informal caregivers. Having little real impact but leaving an impression of responsiveness is hardly a sufficient criterion of effectiveness, though it is arguably a necessary condition for it. Therefore, we have down-played UEMPOW and CEMPOW in this part of the analysis.

For these reasons, the two variants of proposition 2 are:

- make the extension of the number of days users are supported in their own homes rather than in institutions for long-term care the single output maximand; and

- make the improvement of user satisfaction with services the single output maximand.

2.1. Make the extension of the number of days users are supported in their own homes rather than in institutions for long-term care the single output maximand

Context. To users, elderly citizens, central government and local authorities alike, support which reduces the probability of unnecessary stays in residential institutions has the highest priority. Its importance as a policy goal was illustrated by the wording of the 1989 White Paper. This opened with a definition used in the opening paragraph of the chapter. It all but defined community care in terms of support at home to reduce the risk of admission to institutions, and made it the most important aspect of 'independence'.

Findings. The high risk offset and cover proportions for DAYS shown in figure 12.1 fits into a pattern in which not only is diversion from institutions the priority, but is also the output for which the services perform best. So also does the relatively high degree of technical and input mix efficiencies. The relative evenness of this degree between analysis groups suggests the universality of this as a factor underlying care planning. The question about the appropriateness of DAYS as an output maximand is therefore more about what would be its collateral effects on other outputs. The key findings are therefore those in figures 14.4, 14.6 and 14.8.

Figure 14.4 showed collateral output levels assuming optimisation of DAYS given the 'unconstrained' scenario.

- There would be an improvement in collateral outputs compared with current levels for twice as many combinations of output and analysis groups as there would be a deterioration. There would particularly be widespread improvement in the impact of the services on the results of performing personal care tasks compared with currently. The improvements would be greatest for long and short interval users without principal informal caregivers. But the major disadvantage would be a lower reduction in caregiver burden than currently. All user groups with principal informal caregivers would also suffer a deterioration in the impacts of the services on the performance of household care and other instrumental activities of daily living.

- Similar patterns were clear when the collateral levels were compared with their maximum attainable levels were each of the collateral outputs to be the output maximand. The difference would be greatest for groups with principal informal caregivers. There were big gaps for the reduction of caregiver burden and user dissatisfaction with life development.

The effects assuming 'service-budget-constrained' optimisation were shown in figure 14.8.

- The big contrast with 'unconstrained' optimisation is that short and critical interval users with principal informal caregivers would lose substantially compared with their present position. The collaterals for them would be lower for DAYS, user satisfaction with services, the effects of services on the benefits from the performance of personal care and household care and care managers ratings of benefits (USATISF, IMPADL, IMPIADL, and WKSAT).

- As in the other scenario, the reduction in the sense of burden felt by caregivers would be lower than currently for users from each of the three analysis groups.

- Comparing the collateral output levels with those predicted with each of the collateral outputs as the maximand shows that the two levels are close with service-budget-constrained optimisation. That is because the latter offers much lower potential gains in optimisation than the former.

Despite some similarities in the patterns for the two scenarios, it is clear that which scenario is envisaged is of great importance for a choice between output optimands. Again, it is important to note how, for instance, the service-budget-constrained optimisation yields only 86 per cent or less DAYS than the unconstrained optimisation.

The patterns suggest that analysis groups benefit differently. The most striking example is that selecting DAYS as the optimand would reduce the contributions of services to reducing the burden felt by informal caregivers.[6] It is therefore interesting to consider the effects of selecting different optimands for different combinations of analysis groups. Figure 14.6 showed the collateral output levels for the optimisation with the constraint that the budget for each analysis group has the current level. It illustrates how the pattern of collaterals would be particularly favourable for long and short interval cases without principal informal caregivers.

2.2. Make the improvement of user satisfaction with services the single output maximand

In practice, for USATISF, technical efficiency seems less overall, and less even between groups. The results of the unconstrained optimisations shows that treating user satisfaction as the optimand would cause much greater improvements in it than doing the same for DAYS. Both suggest that USATISF is currently much less the implicit aim of the system than DAYS, a finding also of chapter 22. The pattern reflects the focus of the system on those with higher probabilities of admission to institutions for long-term care. So, for instance, figure 15.5 showed that gains in relative improvements resulting from making USATISF the output optimand would be greatest for the groups for whom the probability of admission to institutions is lowest, those with long interval needs. In this respect, the results illustrate how the selection of the output optimand is actually a selection of *cui bono* — who is to benefit, just as it has been shown to be the case for the selection of default options for such elements of the system as care management arrangements or service content (Davies, 1992a; Davies et al., 1990). But figure 15.5 also showed relatively small gains in collateral outputs compared with current provision save for those with long interval needs. That would particularly be the case among users with critical interval needs and/or principal informal caregivers.

With 'service-budget-constrained' optimisation, optimisation would achieve much lower gains. Only long interval need cases would have a better level of USATISF. Figure 15.9 showed that in consequence there would be big losses in welfare for critical interval users, and overall, more collateral losses in outputs for analysis groups than gains; 20 compared with 14. Most of the gains and losses would be concentrated on two groups. The losers would be critical interval users without principal informal caregivers. The gainers would be long interval users without PICs, for whom all the collateral outputs except IMPADL would be above current levels.

2.3. Make improvement in functioning in the performance of the tasks of daily living the maximand

Context. The new policy includes a suite of inter-related performance indicators and performance targets among its key instruments. Several of the currently proposed performance indicators are implicitly targeting-focused — only implicitly, because the data now available do not allow them to be defined in terms of need-related circumstances. International practice and some

British policy proposals make functional deficits central to such definitions. For that reason the context for this proposition has an additional dimension.

Relevant to the discussion is therefore *whether functional deficits should be embodied in targeting criteria, outcome criteria, or both.* However, the embodiment of the goal in the output criterion can be used either to strengthen or replace setting eligibility criteria in terms of 'functional deficits'; in practice the incapacity to perform acts of daily living without help or supervision. Setting targeting criteria is the more usual device.

Using either would lead to the same allocation in a simple uni-factorial world with the reduction of functional deficits as the single goal, with functional incapacity as the sole determinant of productivities, with functional capacity easily and precisely measured at assessment, and with no other equity considerations. But functional deficits are not the only influence on the productivity of services in reducing them, as an earlier chapter has illustrated. Neither are functional deficits the only equity criteria. Their patternings are not simply uni-dimensional (Bebbington 1977; Spector and Fleishman, 1998; Clark and Maddox, 1994; Travis and McCauley, 1985). They are not always easily and precisely measured at assessment (Bauld et al., 2000). Scales for deficits in the performance of personal care activities of daily living tend to be more reliable than those for instrumental activities. But even for the former, scales yield different results depending on the level of difficulty taken, inclusion of the need for supervision or cuing, whether the issue is ability to undertake or whether the tasks are in fact undertaken, and the like (Jette, 1994; Wiener et al., 1990).

The judgement whether to choose targeting criteria defined partly or wholly in terms of functional deficits, the reduction of the deficits as the output goal, or both, should be influenced by among other things some of the empirical relationships described in this study. The case for relying on setting the reduction in deficits as the output criterion is stronger, the greater is the degree to which the production functions predict the decline in functional deficits, and the less important is the influence of functional deficits per se on productivities. In such circumstances, it would be superior to setting the targeting criterion in terms of functional deficits because it allows for the complexity of the production function. To paraphrase, setting the reduction in deficits as the output goal would better allow for the influence of other need-related circumstances; that is, risk factors recognised as a legitimate influence on equity judgements. Conversely, the less well established is the production function and the greater and simpler the productivity effects of functional deficits in relation to other influences, the stronger is the case for relying more on embodying functional deficits into targeting criteria.

Some of the research on the pre-reform system suggested a strong case for ensuring the alignment of targeting criteria with output goals; or, as the manager would see it, with the content and nature of services which would yield the output goal. Evaluations of some intensive home care programmes for persons discharged from hospital are a good illustration. One of the reasons for the failure of one of the most celebrated was that the targeting and the de facto goals of the services provided were not aligned. Targeted at a group of whom many required rehabilitative care, the services provided more intensive inputs of the standard services performing traditional tasks in standard ways (Victor and Vetter, 1988). If what is being considered is a special intervention with a precisely defined rehabilitative goal, perhaps equity and efficiency demand that both output and targeting should focus on the same criterion, functional deficit. But this might be too narrow a goal for community care generally, and it would be difficult to imagine that such narrowness even for some special services would be supportable if the users were to remain users over a long period. The same argument applies here as Rosalie Kane applied to targeting discussion for modes of shelter-with-care (Kane, 1995).

Argument about the situations in which the use of one device, the other, or both devices would most contribute to equity and efficiency is typically far removed from the use of assessed functional deficits in practice. The reason is a particular example of a general problem now well recognised by the principal reform agencies such as the Audit Commission and the Department of Health. The system is excessively driven by process, insufficiently by the achievement of specific outcomes. So also is the balance of the research effort. That inevitably causes opinion about the output effects of process based on only casual evidence to have excessive influence.

Incapacity to perform activities without difficulty and the need for supervision and cueing is everywhere a common factor among the circumstances taken into account. It is the most common element in assessment documentation in British social services departments, Challis et al. show (1996).

Eligibility criteria for targeting defined in terms of functional disability seem often to be found in contexts with two characteristics:

(a) Where 'third party' financing systems are important among the financing mechanisms, but the fiscal intermediary is not required to bear financial risk as in a managed care system. By a third party financing mechanism is meant that there are substantial payments from another agency to local field organisations contingent on the beneficiaries satisfying eligibility requirements. Third party financing systems without managed care arrangements need simple, clear, relevant and reliable criteria for the eligibility requirements. Certain functional deficits appear to have these qualities more than most need-related circumstances. Nevertheless, we have documented how they fail to do so to a degree which make their use problematic in other work (Bebbington and Davies, 1983, 1993; Davies, 1993; Davies and Fernández, 2000a)

(b) Where community-based social care have been developed more as an adjunct of health care systems, adopting a weighting of goals reflecting the role of health professions, and serving the efficiency needs of health agencies. For instance, it often reflects the influence of community nursing; the perception of community care as an extension of home health care. Also, making the most efficient use of the facilities costing most per diem to public funds is a particularly important policy goal in some countries.[7] It has often been as-sumed that community care services can be targeted more effectively on those at high probability of admission to institutions if their eligibility criteria too are based on functional criteria.[8]

The combination of the two circumstances affects the level of deficits built into programme eligibility criteria. Setting the criteria in terms of personal care activities of daily living (PADLs) concentrates resources on the more disabled. Setting them in terms of 'instrumental activities of daily living' (IADLs) — cooking, cleaning, and the like — requires broader coverage, and so forces the thinner spreading of resources. So the dominant programmes in systems that are most focused on replacing hospital and nursing home beds restrict eligibil-ity to persons with incapacity to perform perhaps three of the standard five or six PADLs, and cognitive impairments which reduce their performance unac-ceptably without supervision or cueing. Systems with a broader range of goals tend to set the floor in terms of alternatives that also include IADLs and the as-sociated cognitive impairments and behavioural disturbances.

The relevance is to the British policy discourse in the context of the Royal Commission on Long Term Care and independent long-term care insurance. The introduction of third party financing systems by which central financing agencies pay the care costs of field agencies in whole or in part for users who satisfy eligibility criteria floors presents local recipient agencies with powerful incentives. The incentives are either to change de facto goals of the field or-ganisation, or to attempt to describe those whom they wish to serve in terms that meet the criteria, irrespective of their true circumstances. The former would hardly be desirable if the financing agency set stringent criteria cover-ing a minority of the current recipients. To counteract the latter is technically very difficult, as international experience testifies. Therefore it is useful to use ECCEP data to suggest what might be the implications of a shift to such goals.

Implications of the findings. The analysis is therefore of two variants of the policy proposition:
- 3a(i) Allocate resources so as to maximise the improvement in the perfor-mance of personal care (PADL) tasks.
- 3a(ii) Allocate resources so as to maximise the improvement in the perfor-mance of household and other instrumental (IADL) tasks.

Maximising the improvement in performing PADL tasks. The results of the analy-ses in chapter 16 provide the material for the discussion.
- The results suggest that with unconstrained optimisation, the choice of IMPADL would make little sense as a general maximand. For no less than 26 outputs, the collateral level would be lower than currently enjoyed by the case types concerned. There would be gains (in DAYS and DLD) for only one group. It is not surprising, therefore, that the collateral output levels would

in most cases be below 40 per cent of the level achieved for an output were it
to be the maximand.
- With service-budget-share-constrained optimisation, collateral outputs
  would still be lower for a larger number of cases than for whom they would
  be higher than current outputs. But because the maximum attainable would
  itself be lower, the collateral levels look larger compared with the maximum.

In no scenario would it make sense to choose IMPADL as the general output
to maximise for all case types.

However, it is possible that it could make a suitable maximand for some
case types. Because the other scenarios involve reallocations of package costs
across user types as well as services, the clearest test is for the group-budget-
constrained scenario. Figure 16.7 showed the relevant results. First, collateral
levels must at least approximately equal, if not exceed, actual levels for many
of the key outputs. By this criterion, the most likely groups to qualify would be
the two critical interval case types. For both, the condition would be satisfied
for five out of seven outputs, including DAYS, IMPEMP, DLD and WKSAT as well
as IMPADL — but conspicuously not USATISF and KOSBERG. The second precon-
dition would be that the collateral levels would be higher rather than lower in
relation to the maximum achievable. Only for five outputs (including IMPADL)
would the collateral level approach or exceed 60 per cent of the maximum possible for the critical interval cases with PICs, and the number would be three
for those without PICs.

Maximising improvement in performing IADL tasks. Chapter 17 showed that with
unconstrained optimisation, the choice of IMPIADL as output maximand
would leave most outputs lower than currently for most case types. The same
would be the case with service-budget-share-constrained optimisation for
most types.

Searching the results of the group-budget-constrained optimisation in figure 17.7 does not suggest that IMPIADL would be a strong candidate for maximisation for any group. For several, the number of outputs for which there
would be losses exceeds the numbers for which there would be gains. For all
types, users would have a lower level of DAYS, WKSAT, and KOSBERG (where relevant) than currently. For short interval cases without PICs, the levels of collateral outputs would be approximately 60 per cent of the achievable for three
other outputs, USATISF, IMPEMP and WKSAT, but the output of DAYS would be
only one half that currently obtained. This is not a strong case for its adoption
even for that group.

The conclusion is that the evidence does not clearly support this form of the
independence proposition either.

3.   Conclusions

The chapter has shown first how different would be the consequences of selecting each of the five dimensions of 'independence' discussed. In this way, it has sharpened the choice between systems best for each. It is not just that optimising on felt control over one's own life would fail to deliver other important outcomes; a fact illustrated by the comparison of the results for empowerment with those for the other interpretations of 'independence'. Our findings about the parameters of the production of welfare have revealed a straightforward policy choice. To make the feeling of empowerment over life the central goal would entail foregoing many of the other benefits of community care. The policy-makers must be clear about their priority.

The chapter has also revealed another dilemma requiring a straightforward policy choice. The unconstrained optimisations of DAYS and USATISF imply the concentration of the resources on different user groups. Therefore, achieving the optimum levels of either of the two outputs implies a heavy opportunity cost in terms of the other. The observed concentration of resources on those users with greatest needs suggests that DAYS has been implicitly chosen in preference to USATISF. That might help to explain why many now feel that the concentration of resources has been at the expense of user satisfaction. But perhaps it is impossible to achieve both in the absence of a willingness of users themselves to acknowledge and support one goal as being more important that the other. The reason is that the probabilities of admission to institutions vary so much between users. Experience in some other countries also suggests the same. It may be an inevitable feature of the production parameters of welfare that the maximisation of user satisfaction in a system with a range of users of very different probabilities of admission requires very different distributions than maximising the diversion from unwanted and inappropriate utilisation of institutions for long-term care. One of the key policy choices may be how to balance general empowerment and user satisfaction by diffusing resources among the many, against maximising the diversion from unwanted and avoidable stays in institutions. That is the subject of the next chapter.

Notes

1   Some of the documents have been given almost the status of sacred texts in some countries. For instance, some of the British documents are on the reading lists for the Japanese examinations for potential care managers.

2   The White Paper comment is in contrast too bland: 'sometimes old people and their carers do not appear to have as much influence as they should' (Department of Health, 1998, para. 2.45).

3   The Chair of the Preventative Task Force, the chief executive of the Anchor Trust, was quoted as saying that 'Community care seems to be about finding an economically efficient way of managing the decline and deterioration of old people. For too

long we have been giving them what we thought they should have ... The more we involve older people and other services users in designing service provision the more we are going to have to change.' (Valios, 1999, 3).

4   The 1998 White Paper gives higher priority than ever before to increasing empowerment through user surveys more in the Best Value procedures than in the involvement in the policy process at the middle and higher levels, though it commends the latter. See for instance paragraphs 2.43 and 2.55-7 (Department of Health, 1998)

5   British commentators seem to feel less 'ownership' of care management logic than is visible in the United States. There it is overloaded with expectations about its contributions to functions. However, that may partly be an illusion created because care management is sometimes loosely defined to include systems supports of a kind which in the UK are treated as almost unrelated to care management.

6   It is important to remember that the solutions implied by the optimisations are extreme solutions in the sense that they disregard improvements in outputs other than the output maximand. Given the sizeable effect shown by social work inputs on the levels of carer stress, it may therefore be possible to achieve gains in the two outputs with input mixes based on the optimum solution for DAYS with small increases in social work inputs. As chapter 8 showed, such a compromise would also be likely substantially to affect user morale.

7   That is subtly different from attempting to provide as much opportunity to receive care in home rather than in institutions for long-term care as is judged equitable and efficient. The former is primarily about downward substitution from the acute bed to the chronic bed (in for instance, Canada or France) partly by coping with the last stages of treatment of an episode of care in those cheaper facilities, partly by providing straightforward nursing support there; and from the hospital bed to the nursing home, day care or home care (by offering incentives for the provision of certain treatments previously undertaken in hospitals in those settings). The growth of such activity in American nursing homes is one of the principal features of the last decade (Freiman and Brown, 1999). Another example is the development of 'hospital at home treatment' (Goddard et al., 1999).

8   The argument is fallacious, as the American evidence about predictors of diversion from nursing homes showed during the 1980s. See the reviews in Davies and Challis (1986); Davies et al. (1990); Davies (1992); Kemper et al. (1987); and Weissert et al. (1988).

First formulated clearly in the UK during the late 1970s, this issue re-surfaced from about 1995. To tighten the analysis, we put the issue as a general proposition: *allocate fewer resources to the more dependent, so as to release resources to achieve preventive effects for the least dependent.*

The argument is widely heard in several countries; among them, the UK, Australia, and the USA. Two of these countries share the common experience of policy and resource changes which have concentrated services on fewer recipients; and in the process have excluded persons from services in circumstances in which formerly they would have become users. However, the argument seems always to have been put in a form that is vague with respect to the costs and benefits of alternative policy rules. In the literature from abroad, the precise and admirable research on it by Turvey and Fine (1996) is perhaps the most thorough. It was an investigation of whether there was evidence of substantial effects for those of low disability. But it was not part of its objective to investigate alternative allocation policies.

1. Context

During the pre-reform mid-1980s, many British local authorities paid little attention to the targeting of services, and few targeted with fine discrimination. A higher proportion than now of total resources was allocated to persons of low dependency.[1] There were few high cost and complex service packages. And to the degree that they had been deliberately managed to serve an identified target group, the content of services was geared towards persons of low dependency. The result was that many obtained services without the benefits most stressed in the policy logic of the reforms. Users appreciated the services, and many attributed their continued capacity to continue to live at home to receiving them; 18 per cent of the sample at the second interview with triads in the Domiciliary Care Project sample (Davies et al., 1990, table 4.1).

The increased concentration of resources on users obtaining more substantial care inputs has been widely observed and commented upon since the mid-1980s. It was increasingly clearly documented in the Department of Health statistical reports, and by research results, including research from the ECCEP project (Bauld et al., 2000; Davies, 1997). It is unsurprising that the issue should have been raised in the UK, given the preoccupation of the reform policy with targeting and concentration of resources on those most in need. The care professional discourse on assessment had been moving away from an undue emphasis on 'deficits' and towards user capacities, potential, hopes and expectations. But some of the early argument from policy analytic agencies proposed methodologies that closely identified need with functional disability (Audit Inspectorate, 1983; Audit Commission, 1985, 1986). The methodologies were for more aggregated resource planning rather than individual need assessment. But reviews of assessment criteria as reflected in instrumentation did in fact suggest that the same excessive emphasis on functional deficits existed far later at the field level (Challis et al. 1996).

However, the formulation of the issue remains vague and general. It is argued that failing to provide low levels of support to persons not yet of high dependency fails to allow the services to reduce, slow down, or prevent the deterioration. Those making the case have rarely pointed to losses likely for user types on whom services are concentrated. Neither do they mention the evidence that small service inputs had yielded disappointing preventive impacts during the pre-reform period, the most directly relevant research evidence of that being unreferenced. Therefore, it has been easy for anyone not steeped in that area of scholarship to conclude that there could be no doubt that too high a proportion of the resources has been concentrated on too few users. The conclusion that more of the resources should be put into inexpensive service for the less disabled must seem, and is certainly often stated as if it is, simply a matter of common sense, needing no qualification or justification. That is the tone of propositions in the questions asked by members and answered by witnesses to the House of Commons Health Committee, and the sweeping conclusion in the Committee's report (Tinker, 1996; House of Commons, 1996).

There has been little formal evidence for post-reform care. The assertion has been based on the beliefs and assumptions of managers, of users and their pressure groups. Some of the best grounded evidence describes what users and elderly people at the margin of risk expect and want from services, and value about what they believe to be their impacts, and analyses the local development of preventive strategies (Clark et al., 1998; Lewis et al., 1999).[2] But it still seems to be exceptional for any of the comments to recognise that against a background of limited resources, the issue is of trading benefits of different kinds to different groups, not simply of making a common sense correction to a simple error. In some argument, the issue does not arise because prevention is so defined as to include strategies and approaches which promote the quality of life of older people and engagement with the community (Lewis et al., 1999). Such a definition implies all activities with some small effect to be worth while, and so clearly starts from an assumption of virtually unconstrained resources. The initiatives have indeed been financed partly from many sources other than the local authority rate fund or national taxes.

The response in the 1998 White Paper, subsequent circulars, and the text of a speech by the Secretary of State to a national prevention conference has been more measured, a great advance compared with earlier policy; for instance that in the circular *Better Services for Vulnerable People* (Department of Health, 1997a; 1998a,b; 1999a,b). It places heavier emphasis on the prevention of deterioration, rehabilitation and reablement in all forms than hitherto. However, it avoids creating an alibi for the vague and indiscriminate targeting of services that are often as likely to undermine capacities for independent living as to create them, and that are not tailored to reablement. The focus has been more on specific plans and programmes, with clarity about target groups and the logic linking ends and service means. The same emphasis was evident in a later speech by the Secretary of State. The aim should be to focus on selective targeting and services for prevention: 'by identifying the people who would benefit most from early help, and by offering flexible and imaginative support across services, a crisis can be averted and the need for much greater support and dependence can be prevented' (Dobson, 1999).[3]

It is surprising that much British academic argument has not made as much use of the evidence as some from other countries, and has not been careful in specifying the issues. For instance, the argument often fails to distinguish the case for the subsidisation of 'low level services' to larger numbers of users, from the case for the subsidisation of 'preventative services'. It has not built on the research and analysis of the eighties to investigate who is benefited in what way by what service input or for the performance of what task.

2. Analysis in other countries

The British interest in targeting has its parallels elsewhere. But in no state, except England and Wales of the 1980s, has the discussion been illuminated by evidence about marginal productivities of services of the type presented in this study and its predecessor *Resources, Needs and Outcomes in Community-Based Care* (Davies et al., 1990), or of gain/cost ratios as in Davies, Chesterman and Fernández (1995). The former showed marginal productivities to be invisibly low for most users for most potential outputs in the provision of SSD community services during the mid-80s. The latter implied that the highest productivities in the Kent Community Care Project and its three closest evaluated replications were for those of lower disability (Howe, 1997; Turvey and Fine, 1997). In the USA, researchers found that elderly persons believed home care to have made admissions to institutions unnecessary (Krivo and

Chaatsmith, 1990). Similar results were found in Canada. Evelyn Shapiro, the doyenne of Canadian home health care researchers: 'Since the performance of ... tasks such as shopping, laundry and light housework is essential in meeting the day to day needs of elderly community residents who do not require medical care, a home care program in which eligibility is not restricted to those needing a medical service may be particularly well suited to helping the elderly remain at home' (Shapiro, 1996, 42). There were many American studies 'uring the 1980s showing that in some programmes home care had appeared .o reduce the utilisation of nursing home beds, but also many showing that it had not. There, one issue was perceived to be whether the reduction in utilisation of beds would be great enough to cover the costs of the additional home care inputs, rather than whether the combination of that and other benefits would make the expansion of home care worth while (Greene et al., 1993a,b; Kemper et al., 1987; Weissert, 1988; Weissert et al., 1988). There continues to be a flow of research evidence. Though the conclusions remain that the gains are indisputably worth while only in some programmes, some analyses have shown how more focused targeting or better mixing of inputs could have greatly improved their performance even by the inappropriate criterion chosen (Davies, Baines and Chesterman, 1996; Greene et al., 1993a,b; Ruchlin et al., 1982; Skellie et al., 1982). Another concern was an excessive domination of social care issues by the needs of areas of health policy with narrower fiscal and professional goals (Estes et al., 1993).

Though there is widespread European concern, the issues have been less voluminously elaborated in other countries (Hutton and Kerkstra, 1996). Australia is an interesting example. A committee of the House of Representatives in 1994 recommended the development of clearer eligibility criteria for the matching of resources to needs, and implied the need for more stringent targeting (Morris Committee, 1994). A review confirmed that there was no national guidance about targeting within the Home and Community Care Programme (Fine and Thompson, 1995). In their quasi-experimental study, which also showed a knowledge of outcomes studies in other countries, Turvey and Fine themselves found some positive results, including lower probabilities of admission to hospital and homes in an experimental than a comparison group, but greater recovery of personal care functioning in the latter, though they pointed to methodological problems in the study design and interpretation of the evidence (1996). They concluded that the case for small inputs was neither proved nor disproved (ibid., 70), and argued for a more sophisticated formulation of the questions (ibid., 71).

The conclusion remains in Australia not unlike that for the USA. There was a widespread belief among users that low levels of social care services had made admission to institutions for long-term care unnecessary (Baume et al., 1993).[4] Adherence to the belief may be one of the signs of commitment to the principles of the geriatric revolution that originated in the UK but whose influence is powerful throughout the world, but particularly in former dominions, and it gained support from some of the most powerful research projects from that stream; for instance, Isaacs, Livingstone and Neville (1972).

To summarise: from 1995, opinions implying this proposition have been increasingly expressed. Judgements seemingly based on the views of users and/or professionals have shown a high degree of apparent consensus in supporting the proposition. The small number of authors who have examined evidence on outcomes and successfully found other outcome studies with which to compare their results have been reluctant to reach such general conclusions, and enter many caveats in the interpretation of the evidence.

3. Five variants of the argument

It is important to distinguish between the variants of the argument shown in the list of propositions in the box at the beginning of this Part if the evidence is to clarify choices to best effect. Successive sub-sections first define and explain each variant, if necessary providing a rationale, and then comment on the implications of the findings.

3.1. *Allocate a greater share of the total resources to packages for the less disabled without extending numbers of lower dependency (proposition 4a)*

Context

The analysis investigates whether greater overall outcome for the spend would require more to be allocated to those of lower disability.

Apparent implications of productivities and service contributions. The productivity evidence from ECCEP is directly applicable to the discussion because the range of circumstances in the target population remains the same as that studied. This is one of a set of propositions for which perspectives contributing to our understanding have emerged from different sections of the analysis like clues in a Le Carré novel.

The first clue is from the chapters discussing service productivities. The results strongly suggested that across analysis groups, service inputs are inversely correlated with service productivities: for most outputs, there is a negative correlation between average service contributions to analysis groups and the inputs for them. Inputs of services for the most dependent are more than large enough to compensate for the lower productivities for them and any other influences that work in the same direction. Figure 24.1 confirms the generalisation. Therefore, the results at that stage raised questions about the equity of the allocations. They suggested that aggregates across cases for most outputs would be greater given a redistribution of resources towards those of lower disability. If so, either there must be powerful equity reasons for favouring those of higher disability, or efficiency would apparently be improved by

Figure 24.1
Output gains and average productivities by interval need category

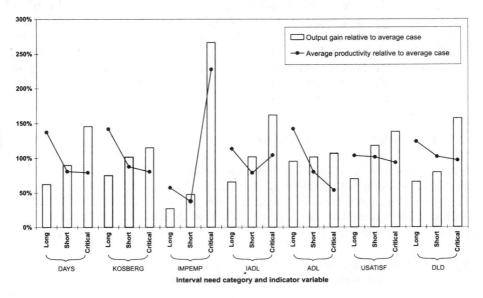

redistributing services towards those of lower disability.

However, quite new perspectives unfolded as the efficiency and optimisation results were described. The negative association between service productivities and service contributions were seen to be only one relevant finding. The mapping of service productivities and service contributions had two informational deficiencies very important for reform discourse.

- First, the mapping reflected current levels of efficiency. Chapters 14 to 21 showed big shortfalls in both technical and input mix efficiencies. The discussion in chapter 13 illustrated how it was a major aim of the reforms to improve efficiencies: to exploit the underlying technologies to better effect as well as to transform those technological relationships described by the productivity curves.

- Secondly, the mapping did not reflect the information contained in the 'policy scenarios': the degree and nature of constraints on supply (distinguishing our 'unconstrained' from our 'service-budget-share-constrained' scenarios) and the imposition of equity controls on the shares of case types (distinguishing our 'unconstrained' from our 'group-budget-constrained' scenarios).

The discussion in Part II (chapters 13 to 21) was dominated by juxtaposing optimisation with each of the scenarios in the context of discussing what output should be chosen to be dominant. Taking into account how efficiency improvements would affect service mixes and final outputs in the different scenarios adds immeasurably greater depth and chiaroscuro to the evidential basis for discussing the policy propositions. It redefines the issue from being a simple problem with a straightforward solution to being a set of dilemmas, whose handling requires a range of policy judgements of value and expert predictions of facts and scenarios.

Implications of the findings

The crucial issues are whether optimisation would:
- increase the package costs of long interval cases more than others, particularly critical interval cases, reducing the share of the total cost of packages received by critical interval cases,
- increase output more for long than critical interval cases, and
- actually reduce the outputs enjoyed by critical interval cases.
  Also important is how these would differ between optimisation scenarios.

First, consider the implications of making the *extension of days in the community* the single output maximised. Figure 14.2 showed that 'unconstrained optimisation' would increase the package cost level of long interval cases without PICs slightly, but there would be no increase for the other long interval group. And the package cost would not be diminished for either critical interval group, though it would decrease slightly for short interval cases. The output would be increased by no more for long interval cases than for the other groups. So with unconstrained optimisation, the proposition would clearly be rejected. With 'group-budget-constrained' optimisation, figure 14.5 similarly showed that outputs would be increased by no more for long interval cases than others, indeed less than for critical interval cases. However, with 'service-budget-share-constrained' optimisation, figure 14.7 showed that package cost would be increased for long interval cases, and that the increase would be financed largely by reducing the package costs of critical interval cases. Also the output level would be increased slightly for both long interval case types, and reduced for critical and short cases without PICs.

So with DAYS as the maximand, the evidence does not support the proposition unless it is assumed that the relative quantities of services commissioned remain much the same. Could it be that the advocates of the redistribution implicitly assume the old inflexibility in commissioning and decommissioning? Certainly many of the British arguments and assertions emerged at the time when the criticisms of inflexibility of commissioning were being increasingly articulated, and were being stated by some of the same analysts as were most promoting advances in commissioning (Nuffield Institute, 1995).

Second, consider the implications of making the *level of satisfaction with services among users* (USATISF) the maximand. Figure 15.4 showed that 'unconstrained' optimisation would indeed cause increases in the package costs for the long interval cases, if only slightly for cases without PICs. Moreover, the large expansion for long interval cases with PICs would be financed by large reductions in package costs for all but long interval cases. The output level for all groups would be increased, but by far the biggest increases would be for long interval cases. A similar picture exists for service-budget-constrained optimisation.

So if USATISF were the output maximand, the proposition would broadly be supported. Again, we see the significance of the fact that where advocates of the proposition have a specific evidential base, they tend to argue for an allocation which would improve USATISF more than most of our other indicators of impact.

Third, consider the implication of making the *reduction in the felt burden of caregiving among PICs* (KOSBERG) the output optimand. Figure 20.4 showed that with unconstrained optimisation, the package cost of long interval cases would be increased by approximately 10 per cent, the increase being financed by a reduction in the package cost of critical interval need cases. The support for the proposition depends on the nature of the optimisation. The service-budget-constrained optimisation would result in the opposite pattern, figure 20.8 suggested.

Fourth, consider the implication of making *users' felt control over their own life score* (IMPEMP) the output maximand. The evidence about the proposition is contradictory, figure 18.4 suggested. With unconstrained optimisation, the package cost of all cases with PICs would be increased, but the package costs of other cases would be reduced, including long interval cases without PICs. The effects on outputs would also be contradictory. With group-budget-constrained optimisation, there would also be big improvements in outputs for all groups. With 'service-budget-share-constrained' optimisation, there would be large reductions in the package costs of long interval users, and small decreases in outputs. The gainers would be critical interval users with PICs, figure 18.8 showed.

Therefore the proposition is not supported by the evidence. Were the costs and benefits of the investments required to make big efficiency improvements to make it economically efficient, the investment alternative would be a better way of improving outcomes for those of low disability than redistributing resources.

Fifth, consider the implications of making *care managers judgements about the degree of success of the intervention* (WKSAT) the maximand. With unconstrained optimisation, figure 21.4 showed, the package cost would be reduced for both long interval case types, output would be reduced compared with current levels for one, and little higher for the other. The beneficiaries from the optimisation would be short interval cases and critical interval users with PICs. Likewise, figure 21.8 showed that with 'service-budget-share-constrained optimisation', there would be big reductions in the budget shares of long interval users, and also big reductions in the levels of output for them. With WKSAT as maximand, the proposition would clearly not be supportable.

To summarise, the results illustrate how the issue is a matter of policy choice.

The choices are of two types: to which outputs to attach the highest priorities, and which optimisation scenario to attempt to create. Assuming unconstrained optimisation, the proposition would clearly be supported were either of two outputs selected as the optimand, clearly rejected if one were selected, and there would be a mixed picture given the choice of another output. But unconstrained optimisation results in greater efficiency than the service-budget-constrained optimisation — for some outputs, dramatically so — and therefore should influence the judgement more if it is judged attainable and maintainable, a topic discussed in the last chapter.

For which output as optimand is the proposition supported is quite as important as for how many and in what scenario. With the unconstrained optimisation scenario, the evidence unambiguously supports the proposition for USATISF and, for those users with PICs, the reduction of caregiver burden. But the proposition would not be supported for DAYS or WKSAT. The redistribution would be more complex for IMPEMP. With the service-budget-constrained optimisation, the proposition would be supported for DAYS and USATISF.

The key importance of DAYS, the indicator of the policy goal of highest priority, has recurred time and again in this analysis. The analysis in chapter 23 suggested that IMPEMP and WKSAT were not good output optimands for community care clients as a whole. The efficiency analyses showed that DAYS would require different input mixes from USATISF and the reduction of caregiver burden, despite the joint supply effects shown in chapter 12. The differences in the productivity curves lead here to different prioritisation of user groups. A major finding of the last few paragraphs is that if we expect to achieve the gains of unconstrained optimisation, the relative prioritisation between DAYS and the other two indicators will be crucial in considering the balance between diffusion and concentration of resources by the direct redistribution of resources between groups. The policy choice looks different if a service-budget-share-constrained scenario is assumed. Whereas the optimisation of DAYS or USATISF would each entail support for the proposition, that would not be so for the optimisation of the reduction in caregiver stress.

The information is available for other outputs. But the summary of the results for these most important outputs suffices to show how what at the end of Part I appeared to be a simple problem is really a set of complex dilemmas of choice.

3.2. Allocate the same overall budget to a caseload increased by doubling the numbers in long interval need groups with the same characteristics as those now served (proposition 4b)

Context

This is less a proposition whose validity is tested than the specification of a scenario whose implications are explored. Paraphrased, the scenario is to leave those of lesser disability using the services the same with respect to risk factors and other need-related circumstances, but substantially increase the numbers. This would be the consequence of the successful provision of such prerequisites as information about eligibility to persons who are not now applying for, or being referred for, service; a concern in the 1998 White Paper (Department of Health, 1998b). It is assumed that the number of users with long interval needs is doubled, the numbers in other need groups remaining as in variant 4(a). Like the other propositions discussed in this chapter, it is assumed that the total budget would remain the same, so that its purchasing power would have to be spread more thinly.

ECCEP evidence is applicable to this scenario also, because the population for which the productivity estimates are made is hypothesised to be similar in range to the extended target population, though different in balance. Again, it is the same features of the analysis group distributions of service inputs and outputs that are relevant: whether optimisation would increase package costs and outputs more for long interval than for critical interval users, and whether the results would be similar for 'unconstrained' and 'service-budget-constrained' scenarios.

The presumption created by the findings in Part I create the same presumption as for proposition 4(a). The relevant finding was that average productivities are inversely correlated with service contributions, because sufficient inputs are made to those of higher disability to more than offset the lower productivities for them. The presumption created is that increasing the caseload in the manner specified by the proposition would inevitably be at the expense of redistribution from the highly dependent. However, this presumption might be false when account is taken of potential efficiency improvement and the nature of the constraints of the scenario for efficiency improvement. We saw how in the discussion of proposition 4(a), taking these into account transformed a straightforward impression of misallocation into a complex set of dilemmas of choice.

Space prevents us from considering the implications of more than one output maximand. We have chosen *length of stay in the community (DAYS)*. Results for the unconstrained optimisation scenario are summarised in figure 24.2. The estimates are given for three situations for each of the case types. The first column shows the current pattern. The second column shows the pattern given the hypothesised situation in which the number of persons with long interval need is doubled. The third column shows the optimal pattern given the current case-mix.

Implications of the findings

The results suggest that:

- Package costs would be lower for all groups with the hypothesised mix than currently or with optimisation with the current mix, as expected. That

Figure 24.2
Comparison of input mix efficiency between actual groups and a
hypothetical group created by doubling the number of users in each long
interval category for length of stay in the community (DAYS):
'unconstrained' optimisation

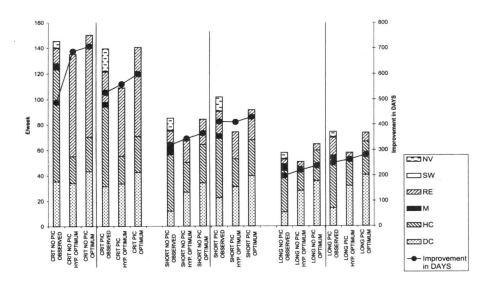

would apply also to long interval users. But the figure shows that resources remain concentrated on critical not long interval cases.

- However, outputs would be higher for all case types but one, and at least as high for all. But they would not be as high as with optimisation given the current case-mix. (That follows from the existence of positive marginal productivities given the range of inputs and outputs under consideration.)
- The biggest increases in output would be for critical interval users without PICs.

The results certainly do not unambiguously support the hypothesis that package costs should be reduced more for critical than long interval cases.[5]

Consider the results for the 'service-budget-constrained' scenario for optimisation, shown in figure 24.3. With this scenario, there would indeed be a much larger cut in the package costs of critical interval cases than of long interval cases, so that the optimum budgets levels across user groups are almost equal. These results suggest that in this scenario with DAYS as output maximand, the optimisation does indeed support proposition 4(b).

However, what would be the effects on collateral outputs? The comparison of 14.4 with 24.4 and 14.8 with 24.5 shows little effect on collateral outputs of

Figure 24.3
*Comparison of input mix efficiency between actual groups and a
hypothetical group created by doubling the number of users in long interval
need categories for length of stay in the community (DAYS): service-budget-
constrained optimisation*

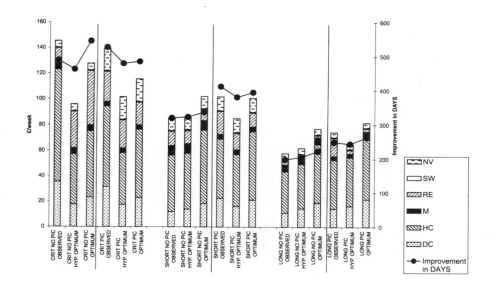

the scenario with more long interval cases.

The conclusion is therefore that the effect of increasing the number of long interval cases depends greatly on what commissioning scenario is predicated. The additional cases would have a large influence on patterns only if the budget shares of services were not easily altered in response to prices and productivities. With unconstrained supply of services, the scenario implies concentration of resources on the most dependent. For both scenarios, the optimisations do not result in much lower collaterals than currently exist.

3.3. Allocate resources to many more persons of lesser disability, in doing so sharing the resources with persons in circumstances other than those of the current low disability types (proposition 4c)

Context

The proposition can be paraphrased: increase numbers of lower disability and change the circumstances of users. Our evidence can be expected to be less informative about this scenario, because the productivity effects are likely to be different for the new cases. Not knowing the productivity effects, we can pro-

Figure 24.4
Collateral output levels for unconstrained optimisation on DAYS with a hypothetical group created by doubling the number of persons in long interval categories

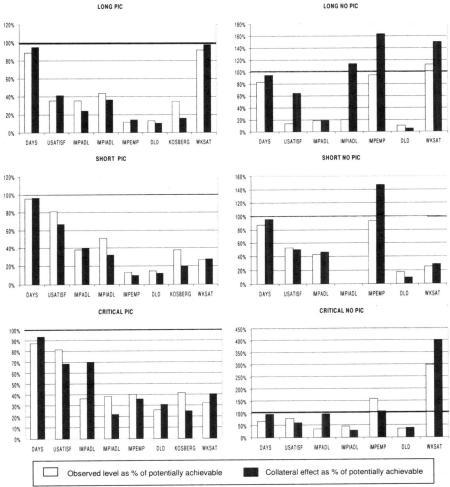

vide little insight into the circumstances of those who should become users, or into what would be the most equitable and efficient mix of resources they should receive. It is a task of innovation and experiment to define these, not the province of the broad study of patterns in mainstream provision. The distinction which is valuably made in the 1998 White Paper's discussion of the Social Services Modernisation programme. That proposed separating the modernisation funds, and the procedures for obtaining them, from mainstream provi-

Figure 24.5
Collateral output levels for service-budget-constrained optimisation on
DAYS with a hypothetical group created by doubling the number of persons
in long interval categories

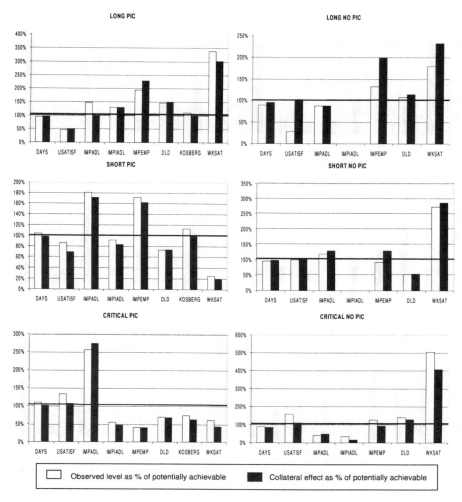

sion and financing (Department of Health, 1999b).

The key issue is whether current productivities would be maintained with the extension of service to not just more persons of lower disability but also to others. The continuing improvement in productivity through targeting and increasing service flexibility is key. Flexibility reduction and target diffusion are deep-rooted features of the cultures of social services departments and local government in general. They make the loss of the productivity improvement created by the reforms a continuing danger.

Many authorities would seek out those for whom productivity could be high in the process of extending cover for the less disabled. That is likely for several reasons:

- The definition of priorities is clearer at the national level. There is a powerful array of weapons to monitor performance and secure improvement. The Best Value initiative and proposals in the 1998 White Paper greatly strengthens them (Department of Health, 1998b, chap. 7).

- The White Paper suggests that the Social Services Modernisation Fund might separate the financing programmes to provide inputs to persons of low disability for preventive purposes from mainstream provision (Department of Health, 1998b, para. 1.16-1.18). That would allow the local performance planning to be used to make the local authorities much more specific in the logics connecting risk factors to the contents of the preventive interventions. For bespoke preventive programmes, the issue is less to recruit users for whom service productivities are high with standard services. It is more to match service nature and content to particular user circumstances in ways that enable the recruitment of those with the risk factors that generate high productivities for that specific programme.

- There is now much greater clarity in the prioritisation of goals by SSDs and the consensus about the priority attached to some of them at all levels of management. It was shown by the evidence from 133 of the interviews with managers at all levels in the departments reviewed in an earlier chapter. Analyses in a parallel ECCEP study shows how the new sense of purpose is associated with patterns and outcomes at the case level (Davies and Fernández, forthcoming, 2000c). And the big improvements in the standards of management have enabled the priorities to be applied more effectively. It is difficult to avoid the judgement that to some degree, this consensus did not pervasively affect policy and practice detail, structures and arrangements at all levels. The contrast with what was reported in earlier studies is striking (Davies and Challis, 1986; Davies et al., 1990; Goldberg and Connelly, 1981).

- Mechanisms have been put in place which make discerning targeting feasible. The reforms have focused field attention on securing better performance of the core tasks of care management. Without the care management mechanisms, there would not have been the processes making the productivity improvements possible. That appears to be the judgements of others also. 'This focus on individual care management ... was the key change to the system', argued the 1998 White Paper (Department of Health, 1998b, following para. 2.2.).

Because the Social Services Modernisation Programme in effect created separate programmes for preventing deterioration among the less disabled, there could be evaluations which could provide the basis for statistically reliable guidelines describing the relationships between circumstances observable at screening and assessment and the preventive effects. With these, it is arguable that in mainstream provision, the loss of productivity caused by broadening the range of low dependency recipients would be reducible. But is it logically and technically feasible to target a larger population of low dependency cases on the basis of high productivity for important outputs?

- ECCEP productivity curves indicate that there are good assessment markers of productivity effects among the existing user population, despite its relative homogeneity, and further refinement (for instance, using standard assessment information alone as predictors) would clarify the limits of the predictability of the productivity effects. However, more analysis is needed.[6]

- Key to effectiveness in prevention is to pick out those users for whom high productivities would require different patterns of coordination between different professions and services at the field level. Coordination is not synonymous with integration. By the former is usually meant function and process. By the latter is usually meant a structure, or the process of creating it. It is the first that is the causal factor of direct impact on the productivities, the second being thought to be of influence by contributing to it. Some may argue that one kind of integration, a straightforward attachment of the care management function with devolved commissioning of social care services to extended primary care teams in the manner of the Down Lisburn arrangements, is an obviously efficient way of achieving requisite coordination for almost all users. Indeed, the Health Committee of the House of Commons came close to arguing this. The argument neglects that creating integrated formal organisations has not always achieved the joint approach and preventive orientation required. In particular, it is arguable that it is more than anything a matter of making the most of the chemistry of those from each profession who have the skills and commitment to make it work, and of expanding the number by example and persuasion. If so, the logic for policy development should be to work from evidence of the relationship between risk factors and the coordination requirements of programmes whose content and resource deployment most raise productivities. Evidence about this could be used to create constellations involving quite different patterns and degrees of coordination for users in different circumstances, based on secondary level teams, as well as a straightforward primary organisation which achieves the degree of coordination required by most. Steps to integration that built mutual confidence, trust, the sharing of perspectives and capacities to observe and understand, would be points on coordination continua (Davies, 1997; Leutz, 1999).

- The effects of extending low level service to a much larger number of users are difficult to estimate. That would require the prediction of the predictors of productivity differences for persons in the broad age group at risk but not yet in contact with the social services and related agencies. The difficulty with testing the predictability from the general population is that databases are thin with respect to subtler assessment-type predictors.[7]

These arguments illustrate both that the issues demand analysis well outside the ECCEP remit, and that there are analyses for which the ECCEP database can be used. What is outside the current remit is the development of services with high preventive and/or rehabilitative productivities and their evaluation. The productivity and efficiency estimates can be no more than background information for this. What is within the ECCEP remit is the demonstration of the implications of simply extending current packaging to users like the less disabled users now receiving services.

3.4 Set budget caps on packages, and use the purchasing power released to buy services for others (proposition 4d)

Context

The purpose is to offset the inequity and inefficiency arising because the opportunity costs of the most expensive home care packages are borne by those of lower disability allocated less or nothing. To explain the role of budget caps in the theory of care management approach, one must discuss (a) their potential incentive effects, (b) the incentive effects that exist in current practice; and (c) international trends in the reform of financing arrangements built around the separation of care from hotel and living costs.

(a) Budget caps and incentives. The budget cap was a classic device of pre-reform argument and experiment, some programmes setting different budget caps for users in different circumstances (Davies and Challis, 1986). In regimes with individual budget caps, packages costing in excess of it would require special managerial review and sanction. The cap focuses incentives on those exceeding the cap, the most expensive to public funds. The budget cap therefore engineers incentives with respect only to some users. The incentive contrasts with a complementary device, setting average budgets per case. Setting an average budget creates an incentive to make the best use of resources across all cases. This incentive makes the average budget an important complement of the budget cap.

Both equity and efficiency issues should be taken into account in setting the level of budget caps. They are typically designed to influence 'modal choice'; triaging towards home care, assisted living, or nursing homes, for example. For some, the care in the alternative mode may be equivalent in its contribution to independence and the quality of life, though the ambivalence, denial, partly irrational fears, and lack of knowledge about the alternative present (and particularly, the alternative future) distort user preferences. For these, the issue is one of efficiency in the use of public funds. For others, it is a matter of equity: the loss of welfare to others outweighs the additional welfare gained from the costs in excess of the hypothetical cap.

There is little information about the true equivalence of the benefits of living with social services support at home and in homes and other forms of shelter-with-care. One way to provide incentives which allow for the expected superiority of the quality of life with support at home is to have higher budget caps for home care than the strict comparison of costs would allow. That is done in the following analysis by setting the caps at various levels.

There is a production of welfare logic for setting up the average service budget and budget cap guidelines for the actual service and the quantity of care management input care management teams in such a way as to balance (Davies et al., 1990, 366-387). Its point is to present a general model of the interrelatedness of influences. One set of influences are outside the control of the community care system, in the short run at least. The other set are key features of a care-managed system in which the care plans brokered by the care managers are the key influences on the commissioning of services. In such a system, the care managers directly and indirectly affect service commissioning, either by direct purchase (spot purchasing) or procuring through time the desired service levels by means of the prescription of commissioned services with their shadow prices charged against their costs.[8] That is, it is a model based on the type of budget-devolved care management developed in the Kent Community Care Project and its replications.

(b) Incentive effects of current arrangements. Perhaps among the ways in which the arguments and experimentation preceding the reforms have been least satisfactorily built on both at national and local levels since 1989 has been the handling of the incentives to balance benefits to one person against another, and one kind of benefit against another kind of benefit.

Currently, the incentives created by local and national financing arrangements and the micro-regulations and procedures influencing care managers and users are variable at the local level. Where there are not budget caps, the current arrangements can allow the creation of home care packages whose total costs much exceed costs in alternative care provision of good standard, causing excessive concentration of public subsidies on too few, at the expense of many others. Approximately 75 per cent of authorities provide care managers with guidance about the cost or expenditure levels above which they would be unwilling to pay for community services for extended periods of time (Challis et al., 1998). There are informal understandings amounting to budget caps in some others. The arbitrariness of the setting of the often implicit budget caps by individual authorities creates perverse incentives. The caps often encourage the triaging to care in homes rather than at home in situations in which that is economically inefficient as well as undesired by the users (Audit Commission, 1996; Department of Health, 1998b). This is in direct opposition to the national policy goal.

Also, as has been consistently argued by the Audit Commission and the Department of Health, authorities have not generally fixed their budget caps on the basis of arithmetic which applies their equity judgements to reliable data and, it may be added, the appropriate concepts for guideline budget caps.[9] One reason has been the failure to develop reliable and relevant costs information for use at the field and higher management levels. Its importance is increasingly recognised. Decision-makers have no evidence about what service packages on average produce what outcomes for persons with different risks and needs. Decision-makers often do not have access to information about the costs of services measured in a way which indicates the opportunity costs - for instance, excluding transfers of finance not corresponding to the flows of real resources, and with realistic allowances for costs which are tied to the activity but actually borne by other budget heads.[10] The economic principle is that the incentives should reflect long run marginal costs of modes, and within them, of service inputs.

Third, the incentives work on users as well as on care managers. The incentive structures based on relative package costs are mediated by the local charging policies.[11]

It must be tempting to fudge the issue at every level of the policy process in many authorities. It is contrary to the care professional values for the field manager to be stressing this opportunity cost in the case supervision and review. It is unattractive for senior policy-makers and managers of field agencies to be articulating guidelines which qualify what is perhaps the main and most popular goal of community care policy for their authority and nationally, the goal which to whose achievement the reform effort has contributed most.

(c) Care costs as the focus. One reason for the practical difficulty of fixing budget caps at the appropriate level is that in residential care modes, elements of care costs are not accounted for separately from the hotel costs.

The Joseph Rowntree Foundation Inquiry (1996) and Royal Commission on Long Term Care for the Elderly (1999) have proposed the correction of incentives by limiting the financial responsibility of social services departments to care costs only, irrespective of the sector providing that service. In this, they are taking into account developments in other countries. Throughout the world, countries are increasingly basing their systems of financing care of frail elderly people on distinctions between care costs, housing and hotel costs, and other income maintenance (OECD, 1996).

Implications of the findings

The analyses investigate the effects of applying caps to populations in the same circumstances as current users. The effects of imposing caps at each of several levels are explored.[12] That procedure is followed because the choice of budget cap could incorporate judgements about the additional value of the benefits of care for persons remaining at home rather than care in a home or other form of shelter-with-care to which the user would move.

The consequences explored for case types are (a) the number of additional days spent by users living in their own homes as a result of inputs of community service packages, indicated by the height of columns in the figures; (b) proportions of current users diverted from community services to residential care modes because they hit the budget ceiling, indicated by percentages within the columns; and (c) average gross costs of packages, indicated by spots connected by broken lines. These consequences are explored for persons with different levels of disability and use of informal care.

Figure 24.6 shows the effects of alternative budget caps without optimisation of input mixes. The effects are shown on the proportion of users affected, package costs and the length of stay in the community (DAYS).

- For users as a whole, the effect on the output average DAYS is predicted to be too small to be visible, as is shown in the first segment of the diagram. That the cap level does not affect the overall output produced makes its selection more a matter of equity than efficiency, given the choice of output optimand. However, the proportion of users affected by caps is predicted to prove sensitive to the level of the budget cap specified. It would be particularly sensitive at low budget cap levels.

- The greatest effects might be expected on the most dependent, because of the association between disability and package cost and the probability of admission to homes. A comparison of the pattern in the segments for each interval group confirms this.

- First, the proportions affected by caps tend to be greater, the greater is the disability. The proportion for critical interval users without PICs is predicted to be 58 per cent. The proportion for long interval users without PICs is predicted to be 16 per cent.

- Second, average package costs are affected substantially only among those of critical interval need. As might be expected, the effect is greatest among those without a PIC, and so without their package-reducing inputs.

- Third, the average number of DAYS is substantially reduced by budget caps only for those of critical interval need. The lower the cap, the greater the fall. The average number rises slightly with progressively more stringent budget caps among other groups, particularly long interval users. This is the result that most clearly shows the equity choices which the level chosen for a budget caps force.

Figure 24.7 shows the effects given unconstrained optimisation. The patterns in the two diagrams have much in common. However, the optimisation mitigates the effects of budget caps.

The most striking conclusion is that setting budget caps would yield little additional benefit in the form of adding to the sum total of the length of stay in the community across all users.[13] But it would shorten the length of stay among substantial proportions of users, particularly some of those with critical interval need. That is, the imposition of caps tend to redistribute benefits without adding to the sum total.

The analysis of average gains to those unaffected by the caps and average

Figure 24.6
Effect of alternative budget caps on user groups' budget levels and length of stay in the community.
Observed patterns of allocation case

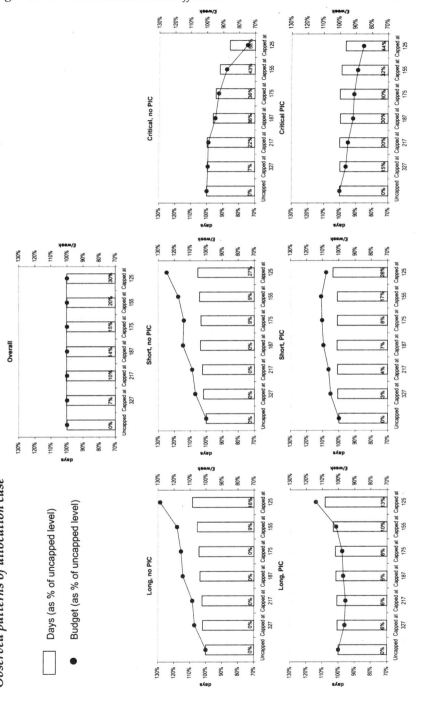

Figure 24.7
Effect of alternative budget caps on user groups' budget levels and length of stay in the community.
Optimised patterns of allocation case

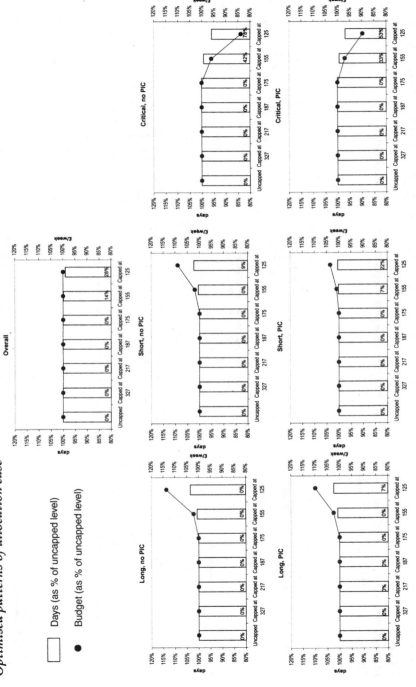

losses to those affected suggest that average losses in outputs and budget are more than 2.5 times the average gain whichever the budget cap taken. The higher the budget cap, the greater is the ratio. The interpretation of these findings depends entirely on an equity judgement.

It would seem important to undertake further analyses to establish whether the same general conclusion would imply for the collateral outputs were DAYS to be the single output optimised, and were the other most important outputs to be the output optimised.

3.5. *Increase or decrease the total budget, holding the case-mix constant (proposition 4e)*

Context

Equity issues like improving the outputs for long interval cases, or increasing their numbers, must be considered in the context of continuous pressure to make the efficiency savings specified in the 1998 White Paper. *Modernising Social Services* specifies a rate of efficiency improvement of 2 per cent for two years rising to 3 per cent in the third, when the Best Value regime will be in operation (Department of Health, 1998b, para. 7.16). Targets for efficiency improvements are presented as a continuing feature of the policy framework. Additionally, the system of triennial Comprehensive Spending Reviews will adjust the rate of increase in total expenditure in relation to needs, demands, and expected efficiency gains. What light do the analyses throw on the consequences of a more or less stringent combination of Treasury settlements and requirements for efficiency improvements?

However, there is a broader case for considering the effects of increases or decreases in the budget, holding case-mix constant. In the logic of needs-based planning, there is little in principle to be said for making the budget level the starting point for target-setting. The targets should ideally be set in terms of the final outputs for users with given need-related circumstances. One aim of the mapping of productivities is to analyse of the consequences of doing so.[14] But in principle also, the choice of target level of outputs for users in different circumstances should be reconciled with the marginal benefits from other users of public funds (Culyer et al., 1971).

The results of this study suggest that marginal productivities are often not constant irrespective of the level of service input. For that reason, a pro rata difference even in the input of one service may not cause a pro rata difference in the level of final outputs. The study has shown that some productivity effects show diminishing returns to scale. That is, the gain in a final output from an additional unit of a service is lower when the addition is to a large amount than when the addition is to a small amount. Some amount to threshold effects, such that the gains are virtually exhausted at a level of inputs that is low compared with the range of current inputs. Indeed, it is a feature of the study that we found evidence of three times as many productivity effects showing threshold effects or diminishing returns than showing increasing returns. There were likewise apparently diminishing returns and threshold effects among the fewer and weaker productivity effects found during the mid-1980s.

Were diminishing returns to dominate, there might be little increase in output were the caseloads to be kept the same but the budget increased even by a substantial proportion. Similarly, it might make little difference to the levels of output for the caseload were the budgets to be reduced. (Because the effects are non-linear, an increase in the budget might lead to improvements of x per cent in outputs, but a reduction in the budget by the same proportion might conceivably cause a fall in outputs by much more than x per cent.)

Whether this would be so cannot be inferred easily simply by looking at the number of productivity effects showing increasing or diminishing returns. It matters less that there is a large number of effects of a certain kind than how big they are, at what levels of inputs the diminishing returns set in, how important are the outputs affected, and how these priorities differ between users of different need-related circumstances. The results reported in Part I suggest that the variations in these are complex.

There would be other influences on the outputs likely given different budget levels. For instance, they would vary depending on whether investments in efficiency improvements had been successfully made, and what scenario exists for the optimisation: the influences investigated in our treatment of efficiency and optimisation in the chapters in Part II above.

In this discussion, we consider the effects for the scenarios in which
- DAYS is the output maximand.
- Efficiencies are assumed to remain as currently.
- Budgets are assumed to be increased or reduced by 10 and 20 per cent.
- Effects on outputs are considered for the average case and for case types.

Results are presented in a set of figures. The figures show the effects of percentage changes in the budget (given the case-mix) for percentage changes in important final output indicators.

Assuming unchanging efficiency. Figures 24.8 to 24.14 summarise the results for the average case and each of the other case types defined by combining need interval with whether they had a PIC.

For the *average case,*
- Figure 24.8 suggests that a large variation in the budget in either direction would make little difference to DAYS in circumstances in which DAYS were the output maximand. It also suggests that the reduction in output accompanying a budget cut by a certain proportion would be little different from the increase in output accompanying a budget increase of the same proportion; a pattern observed for all groups and outputs. However, the effects would be greater on the collateral outputs: greater even for the felt burden of caregiving and users' feelings of control over life (KOSBERG and IMPEMP), and much greater still for care managers' assessment of the impact of the

Figure 24.8

Average case changes in output levels due to changes in budgets:
observed allocations case

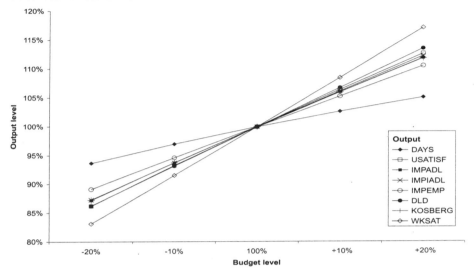

services (WKSAT). For WKSAT, the output most affected, the change in output is almost pro rata with the change in inputs. But in general, the diminishing returns dominate, and output elasticities seem less than unity.

- Figures 24.9 to 24.14 show the results for the *analysis groups*. For cases other than those with (a) long interval needs and PICs and (b) critical interval needs without PICS, the range of differences in the various outputs are much the same for each analysis group. However, analysis groups differ in the outputs most affected.

Assuming input mix efficiency. The results are very similar, save that the variation between groups is greater for some outputs.

To conclude:

- Given DAYS to be the output maximand, it would be likely to be the output least affected by budget variation.
- Generally, the relative changes in output levels are smaller than the changes in overall resources. As noted, this is particularly so for DAYS.
- There are not clear signs of asymmetry in the effects of budget expansion or contraction. The diminishing returns shown in productivity curves have big effects, but with variations in budgets of the scale postulated, their effect is to create a linear relationship between inputs and outputs though with an output elasticity of less than unity.

Figure 24.9
Long interval need with PIC cases. Changes in output levels due to changes in budgets: observed allocations case

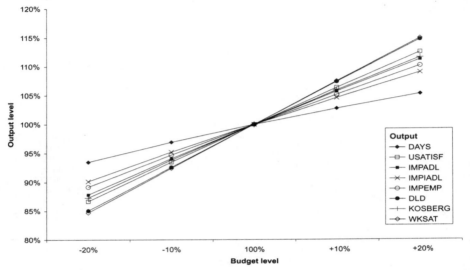

Figure 24.10
Long interval need without PIC cases. Changes in output levels due to changes in budgets: observed allocations case

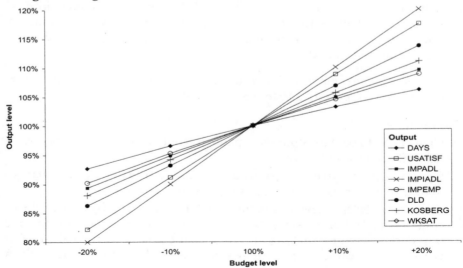

Figure 24.11
Short interval need with PIC cases. Changes in output levels due to changes in budgets: observed allocations case

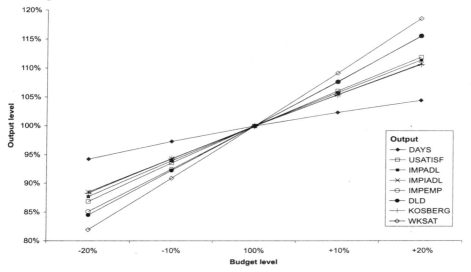

Figure 24.12
Short interval need without PIC cases. Changes in output levels due to changes in budgets: observed allocations case

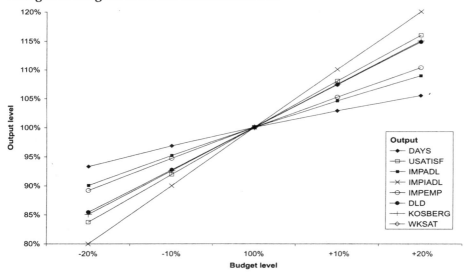

Figure 24.13
Critical interval need with PIC cases. Changes in output levels due to changes in budgets: observed allocations case

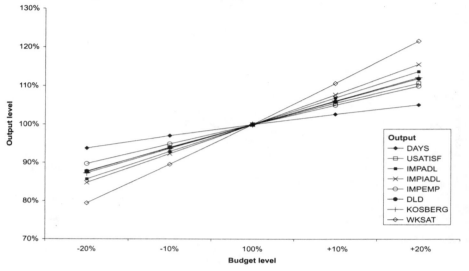

Figure 24.14
Critical interval need without PIC cases. Changes in output levels due to changes in budgets: observed allocations case

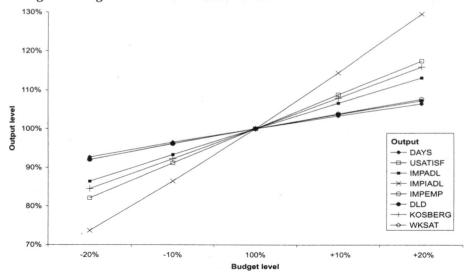

4.   Conclusion

Applying the information from the productivity and efficiency maps, service prices, and the optimisation scenarios illustrates that the issues are more complex than some expressions of expert opinion have suggested.

Section 3.1. considered the case for simply redistributing resources across the existing caseload. Whether the proposition was supportable was shown to depend on priorities and scenario. First, the results remind us of the significance of the large gains from a scenario with great price elasticity, that is a scenario where substantially greater levels of inputs can be provided without great increases in unit prices. These gains make the scenario highly desirable. It supports the policy of investment in efficiency gain associated with investment in market creation and management. But it is in this scenario that the proposition would not be the best basis for policy if the DAYS were to continue to be the highest priority output. However, the proposition would be supported if some of the other important outputs were the optimand. Secondly, the proposed redistribution has high opportunity costs in some of the benefits lost, however accomplished, and whatever the output maximand. Again, the results confirm that the proposition is seen in a different light if the highest priority is given to providing persons with a much reduced expected length of stay in institutions than if some of the other outputs are prioritised. The results help to explain the connection between the beliefs of advocates of the proposition and the nature of the evidence on which they have drawn. Because the predictions from the three scenarios contrast so systematically and clearly whatever the output maximand, a later chapter reviews the evidence about the contrast, and discusses the realism of the scenario offering the best results.

Section 3.2, discussing the implication of increasing the number of less disabled users, reinforced the same general conclusions. The optimum distribution of resources very much depends on the nature of the constraints imposed. The unconstrained scenario, identified with improving the consistency in commissioning and market management, yields the highest gains. In that scenario, there would be little sign of redistributing resources to long interval users. The proposition would not be supported. But again, the proposition would make more sense were the service-budget-constrained scenario to be more realistic.

Section 3.3 suggested confidence about the capacity of the system to take on users with different characteristics from the long interval need cases receiving services without compromising productivity gains — as long as doing so were contained with the framework of centrally approved programmes whose logic connecting targeting, service content and output goals were clear and well-grounded, whose management control ensured the logic's application, and whose monitoring adequately tested the hypotheses on which the logic rested.

Section 3.4 considered the effects of applying budget caps at different levels. The support for the proposition did not vary substantially whether observed or optimum service allocation patterns are assumed.

Generally, the imposition of caps redistributed from the critical to the long interval users. But the gains for the long interval cases were limited when compared to the losses for the critical cases. Package costs were more sensitive to caps in all groups than were DAYS, reflecting the prevalence of diminishing returns to scale. Overall, the use of caps did not translate into higher aggregate levels of DAYS across users.

So there is little evidence for the case that appropriately setting budget caps would lead to a significant increase in the levels of the output. The case for budget caps is different. By achieving consistency in the signals about balancing care for those at home and in homes, it appropriately sets the balance in the total spent on each mode of care. That is, it leads to a more appropriate total budget allocated to care for those at home.[15]

Section 4 showed how the effects of the shapes of the productivity curves and the efficiency distributions is to reduce the sensitivity of outputs to over- or under-shooting in the budgetary process.

Notes

1   There is a related stream of argument about securing the rehabilitation and reablement of persons discharged from hospital and/or who have suffered a health accident from which high proportions can be expected to recover a substantial degree of functioning. The analysis that follows is not primarily directed at this group, but at 'steady decline' cases with progressive chronic disease. The same approach will be applied to all ECCEP cases who used acute hospitals in a forthcoming analysis of the substitution of community care for acute hospital inputs.

2   A more qualified statement is made in an overview of a seminar organised for the Royal Commission on Long Term Care. 'The issue of low level support is controversial. There is clearly no case for providing blanket coverage of low-level support to older people *regardless of their needs* (such as might have been the case with some Home Help services in the past). However, a case can be made for providing particular support for individual service users in order to meet specific preventive needs, or where it will contribute to sustaining independence and promoting social inclusion.' (Henwood and Wistow, 1999, 10).

3   Lewis et al. (1999) find that most evaluation has been concentrated on pilot projects with narrower objectives, and that to obtain mainstream funding, managers felt that they are under pressure to demonstrate effectiveness in narrower and often financial terms. In this respect, local authority behaviour is more in line with national policy, as long as that will in practice require a narrower definition of prevention and tie money from government programmes to their attainment, as well as a targeting and service logic for that.

4   That was a finding in Davies et al. (1990) also.

5   The collateral outputs for other output maximands are presented in the chapters in Part II.

6   Were results of good predictive power not to be forthcoming, it would probably be

for one of three reasons. (a) One is that the population is already selected by the likely risk factors, and so might be too homogeneous for the risks to differ enough to be statistically predicted. (b) The second is that for many, the risks may appear to be inherently random events; that is, unrelated to any of the circumstances which could be observed. The issue is the degree of predictability of strokes, falls causing fractures with permanent handicapping consequences, disease-caused degeneration in function, the death of a spouse, and the like. Reasons (a) and (b) are connected. The incidence of some events and changes in circumstances which might seem to be random in a homogeneous population might be predictable in a more heterogeneous population. (c) The event or change might be very rare, lowering the reliability of prediction (that is, increasing the ratio of standard errors to true proportions and confidence intervals around estimates), other things being equal. Given their intrinsic visibility, rare events may also be less reliably recorded.

7   The appropriate database would have to be for a more general population. Because some of the events and changes it would be necessary to predict are rare, large samples are necessary. Also the nature of the risk factors require a database with a specialised focus. There are examples of such longitudinal databases internationally, with greater scale and depth of cover of relevant variables than in the UK, but there are few of large scale in the UK. For this population, the population would be heterogeneous, and the more events and circumstances might be predicted. But the events and changes might be very rare, lowering that probability.

8   The logic was originally developed as part of an argument with a particular focus. However, its basic feature of showing the logical interconnections between factors in the logic of efficiency-optimising in a budget-devolved care management model is what is important in this context. The original focus was an argument about the implications of area differences. It was argued that there was evidence of big area variations in the relative costs of producing equivalent benefits from home and community services ('home care') on the one hand, and on the other shelter-with-care ('residential'). There was circumstantial evidence that the relative costs varied according to the quantities of each commissioned, with eventually diminishing returns to scale in each care 'mode', home and residential care. Therefore, different combinations of the three parameters would maximise welfare for the costs depending on area, and, it follows, there should be variations in the quantities of each service mode commissioned, and the case-mix of (and so targeting rules for) each service mode.

9   In many authorities, the budget caps apply only to services purchased from independent providers, not to in-house providers. Though they are often intended to be related to the costs of the residential alternative, that is not done precisely. Those who are recommending packages to their managers, or who are responsible for approving them, frequently have only information which is outdated or based on unsuitable accounting conventions about the costs of package elements (Department of Health Social Services Inspectorate and Audit Commission, 1998, chap. 6). Pricing policies are not coordinated across services and packages in a way that balances fairness and efficiency. In these and other ways, incentives to those who allocated services are distorted.

10 *Messages for Managers* comments how financial statistics are often collected in a way which does not force them to complement activity statistics. Because the differences seem to be so large, it implies that the variation in relative costs of services within areas may primarily be due to the differences in accounting conventions (Department of Health Social Services Inspectorate and Audit Commission, 1998, 52). Reli-

able and valid estimates of care as distinct from hotel and living costs have not been estimated by authorities, particularly if by care costs we mean the costs incurred to achieve the specifically community care goals of providing the additions to the costs of meeting all the Maslow needs due to disability: morale and social integration as well as lower level needs. The PSSRU particularly has repeated the principles of costing almost *ad nauseam* (Knapp, 1984; Davies and Knapp, 1988; Netten and Beecham, 1993). With others, the PSSRU has played its part in estimating, collating, and disseminating costs information (Netten and Dennett, 1995, 1996, 1997; Netten et al., 1998, 1999). Yet the best we have is in some important respects only an idea of the broad ranges within which the costs may lie, and only guesswork based on anecdote and unreliable inference based on small-scale observation about beneficial outcomes.

11 The theoretical ideal is a charging system which reconciles clear judgements about what would be a fair contribution given needs and personal finances given different care modes with incentives to care management teams and other allocators to balance opportunity costs against marginal benefits. The ideal is easier to define in principle than in practice.

12 The levels of the caps are chosen to cover costs ranging from the full cost of nursing home care to only the care cost in residential care facilities. Similar estimates were used in the report of the Royal Commission on Long Term Care (1999).

13 The effects of capping on input mixes are negligible and are not reported here.

14 It was attempted in the evaluation of the Kent Community Care Project and in the analysis of community social services during the mid-1980s (Davies and Challis, 1986; Davies et al., 1990).

15 It is possible that it is principally the rate of attrition of cases from the community among those who continue to receive care the longest that would be affected by a policy of diffusion. In that case, the definition of the dependent variable around attrition up to two years would bias the estimates. We shall re-analyse the data for continued care up to five years when the data become available.

25 Listening to the Other Players Instead: Optimising the Reduction of Caregiver Burden or Care Managers' Judged Benefits

One of the key assumptions of this essay is that there is a trio whose field-level appreciations and decisions have particular legitimacy: users, principal informal caregivers, and care managers. The assumption has explained one of the key features of the design of the collection of evidence. It is reflected in the specification of indicators of outputs and risk factors. It is reflected in the foci of other publications from the project, notably the analysis of the 'defensibility' of the pattern of correlation of utilisation levels. So far, the propositions have been focused on one instrument in the trio only. In this chapter, we consider propositions requiring us to listen to the others instead.

1. Make reducing the burden from caregiving the maximand

Explanation. Independence is conceived not just in terms of disabled persons but also of primary family networks. Chapter 12 showed how the reduction of caregiver stress reduces the inputs required to increase DAYS. There are aspects of independence about which there can be conflicts of interest between users and caregivers. In many circumstances, there must therefore be a question of independence for whom: disabled person or caregiver? One of the principal themes of policy statements has been the provision of practical support for caregivers, and responses to their own needs, in order to help them undertake caregiving tasks within limits of what is socially and individually acceptable (Department of Health, 1999b,c). But the local workers have often attempted more: to treat the caregivers more fully as co-clients.

Local policy-makers and practitioners have for long differed greatly in the priority attached to helping caregivers by targeting users with caregivers under strain. *Resources, Needs and Outcomes* (Davies et al., 1990) illustrated these differences. It showed how the pattern of utilisation favoured users with PICs more in one of the London authorities most affected by the new concern for women's interests and the new local politics of using local resources to promote the welfare (and gain the support) of local interest blocs. It could be predicted that local differences in priorities remain. They might be reduced, but are unlikely to disappear in the new context of clear national goal-setting and the new apparatus for ensuring implementation announced in *Modernising Social Care*. The analyses illuminate the degree to which an emphasis on this would improve or detract from performance in delivering other dimensions of independence.

The proposition is relevant to only three of the analysis groups, more than one half of all ECCEP cases.

Implications of the findings. The discussion draws on the results described in chapter 20. The key output was measured by an indicator of the reduction in the felt burden of caregiving, KOSBERG.

With unconstrained optimisation, it was found that:

- There would be more gains than losses in other outputs. Indeed, there would be almost no output for any group for which there would be a substantial loss. In these respects, maximisation on KOSBERG would yield results different from the maximisation of other outputs.
- Despite the joint supply between DAYS and KOSBERG, maximisation of the reduction in caregivers' felt burden does reduce DAYS compared with current levels. That is because the direct effects of inputs on DAYS are in total more powerful than their indirect effect through KOSBERG. That is unsurprising. But the good news is that the levels of DAYS achieved would in all groups remain high in relation to the attainable.
- For all case types, USATISF would also be increased. The cost function model showed KOSBERG and USATISF to be associated, but the simultaneous production function suggested the causal direction to be from USATISF to KOSBERG. But the level compared with the maximum achievable would not be high for long interval users.
- The level of DLD would be greatly increased compared with current levels for all groups. In the background may be the reciprocally reinforcing sense of well-being of users and caregivers.
- The low collateral effects would be for IMPEMP, and in two cases, WKSAT.

Taking into account all groups, the pattern would be less satisfactory given service-budget-share-constrained optimisation. There would be substantial reductions in important outputs like DAYS and USATISF in two groups.

Though with unconstrained optimisation, the pattern would be more satisfactory than most other output maximands, such problems as the low levels of USATISF for long interval cases weaken the case for the application to all three case types. Therefore it is particularly interesting to look at the case for its application only to one or two groups.

Again, we turn to the 'group-budget-constrained' optimisation, whose results were shown in figure 20.7.

- Generally, most collateral levels except for DAYS and IMPIADL are greater than the observed.
- The results are particularly impressive for critical interval cases. The only losses would be small, and leave levels of collateral outputs for most of the important variables high in relation to the maximum attainable. The only truly unsatisfactory result would be for IMPIADL for which the collateral level would be lower than currently and absolutely at a low level.

To conclude, the proposition is one of the more strongly supported by the evidence.

2. Maximise what the field care manager interprets to be the greatest beneficial impact

Explanation. The reforms added new policy and structures to improve the logic for balancing bottom-up and top-down influence in community care.

The contradictions and conflicts between the age-old disjunction between the assumptive worlds of field personnel and what used to be called 'administrators' reflected in conflicting views of how to achieve effective services. Traditionally, the controls on field decisions and activity were by means of resources, procedures, and the appointment of 'professionally' trained staff to the key posts affecting a proportion of users.[1] Organisation theorists described how the dimensions of the Weberian model of organisational control through 'bureaucracy' — not in the pejorative sense — were somewhat adapted to the circumstances of social services departments (Greenwood, 1978; Greenwood and Hining, 1976). But, perhaps what was interesting about Greenwood's results was how small, not how large, were the differences in emphasis between social services and other local authority departments not providing personal, even human, services.

The consequence of excessive (or clumsily-designed) methods of organisational control in service organisations — defined by *cui bono* — was inflexibility in meeting the needs of clients, the consequence for other types of organisation taking different forms, it was argued by Blau and Scott (1956). Subsequent reality flattered theory by imitating it. Inflexibility in meeting user needs became one of the principal themes of the emerging empirical critique which formed the basis of some of the radical experimental models of the 1970s, including the community development projects, patch argument and the experiments in budget-devolved care management (Hadley and McGrath, 1984; Davies and Challis, 1980). Some argued during the late seventies and eighties that the control was not directly focused on the processes and outcomes of most importance to the users. Not only did it fail to engage efficiency well, it also failed to tackle fundamental equity issues of prioritisation. The field staff used their freedom from equity control for at best implicit individual and small team prioritisation of goals. Decision-making in routine services was characterised by service values that had evolved with little managerial goal-setting and monitoring. In social work as elsewhere, the field was characterised by vagueness of ends and means (Goldberg and Warburton, 1976; Stevenson and Parsloe, 1978).

In this context, the finding in *Resources, Needs and Outcomes* that the indicator summarising workers' ratings of the success of an intervention was not highly correlated with outcomes was greeted with some concern but little surprise (Davies et al., 1990). In principle, professionals were among the strongest believers in transforming social services into 'professional organisations' in the Blau and Scott sense of organisations whose beneficiaries were the users. Yet they were not judging their success by the same criteria as the users.

However, one of the objectives of the reforms has been to improve their performance of the certainly paradoxical, apparently contradictory, but crucial effectiveness criterion of the Blau and Scott's ideal-type of the 'service organisation': professional predictability in serving users flexibly and successfully. Again paradoxically, the framework created by new managerialism with its ethic of justification by performance has actually helped the field to satisfy the criterion set for the pure (and, by implication, certainly not new managerialist) professional organisation of the Blau-Scott model. Perhaps the British social services department may be nearer to the latter-day service organisational Utopia dreamt of by social work students of the sixties than we would expect from the agonies of the workers as they face the new harsher dilemmas in what they perceive to be their more constrained working environments.

Our examination of the consequences of making WKSAT, care managers' judgements of success, the single output maximand is an effective test of that hypothesis. The examination amounts to an assessment of the degree to which the post-reform environment has created that validity and reliability of judgements in the context of effective practice and allocations responsive to user needs and wishes that most nearly satisfies the criterion of being an effective service organisation in the sense meant by Blau and Scott (1956).

Implications of the results. The test is what would be the collateral levels of outputs produced given WKSAT to be the maximand. Results were discussed in chapter 21.

With unconstrained optimisation, the pattern of collateral outputs can be used to appraise the consequences for choosing WKSAT as the maximand only for all cases, not for a selection of them, because unconstrained optimisation allows the redistribution of the budget across case types. The results show that the pattern of collateral outputs yielded would not generally be high and even for most groups. That would particularly be the case for users without PICs. The levels of the collateral outcomes for the most important indicators were not in most cases relatively high. So there would not be a strong argument to adopt WKSAT as a general maximand.

Given group-budget-constrained optimisation, the patterns would appear to be more even than with unconstrained optimisation, with the levels of collateral outputs being higher in relation to what would be achieved were the output in question to be the maximand. Given the equity judgement which is assumed to underlie the fixing of group budgets, WKSAT can be evaluated either as the general maximand or as the maximand for one case type alone.

As general maximand,

- DAYS would have high collateral levels in relation to what is achievable for all groups. USATISF would exceed 60 per cent of what would be achieved were USATISF itself to be the maximand for five of the six case types, and would not be far short of that level for the remaining type.
- However, there would be even lower collateral output levels for the relief of caregiver burden than currently achieved. Collateral levels for IMPEMP would be below 60 per cent of what would be attainable for all but one case type.

So the choice of WKSAT as the maximand under these optimisation conditions would require the sacrifice of some important goals to achieve others.

As maximand for one or selection of case types, the types for which WKSAT might be the most credible contender would be long interval cases without PICs. The collateral output levels for the group are shown in figure 21.7. As well as WKSAT, the outputs would be better than currently and also 70 per cent of what would be achievable for DAYS, USATISF, and IMPEMP. This could well be the context where the arrangements for case handling, the care issues, and this particular output criterion might best fit. This is not a context in which users are the object of inputs of large amounts of time for the performance of core care management tasks, far less the time of highly trained professionals. Most inputs are made by what in many areas are virtually if not formally home care organisers by background and task mix. Neither is it the case type where the care management judgements are made in the context of ambivalence and potential conflicting interest with committed but excessively strained caregivers who overestimate their capacity to cope, or in which it is difficult to negotiate the best divisions of labour between informal and formal inputs. Nor is it the case type for which the circumstances of the user have the complexity associated with volatility and unpredictable change, and in which the user would be most likely to be incapable of making and articulating judgements. In these and other ways, it is possible that this is the kind of case in which the judgement of a care manager in goal-setting and outcome evaluation could most be trusted, if faithfully, thoroughly and reliably applying clearly defined value and procedural policies, and trained to recognise the limits of competence and the circumstances in which the help of others would be needed.

With service-budget-constrained optimisation, the levels of the key collateral outputs would not be high enough for WKSAT to be a good general output maximand. For instance, collateral levels for DAYS and USATISF would be low for most groups. Felt caregiver burden would be lower than with current provision. The high levels of collateral outputs for all indicators for short interval cases with PICs do not imply the appropriateness of WKSAT as the criterion variable. The reason is that the pattern for the group would reflect the redistribution across groups suggested by the combination of the choice of maximand and the optimisation scenario — in this case, a redistribution which trebled the budget for the group, as can be seen from figure 21.8.

3.   Matching the output prioritisation to the analysis group: the role of analysis group budget-setting

Explanation. The chapter has so far shown that for the analysis groups to which it is relevant, the optimisation of the reduction of caregiver stress has much to commend it. Were it to be the choice for these groups, other optimands would be required for the other groups. Fixed analysis group budgets would be a device for allowing the matching of the output maximand to the group. They would anyhow be a potentially valuable device for the control of equity. The technique, it was argued in chapter 13, balances top-down control of broad equity patterns with an arrangement allowing field level responses to the complex patterns of individual variations in the circumstances, including wishes, of users and caregivers.

Proposition 4d in chapter 13 focused on the application of budget caps to limit the degree to which the most expensive packages would consume resources which might add more to the sum of user well-being if redistributed among other users. Reflecting the logic which underlay the family of experiments based on the Kent Community Care Project, and reflected in *Matching Resources to Needs*, it was argued that budget caps focused on providing a framework of information and incentives to combine home-based care and residential facilities of various kinds in ways which would maximise the output given the budget, while fixing an average budget for the targeted case-mix was a tool for creating incentives to allocate the community service budget for home-based care in the way which would maximise the output generated given the budget.

The group budget belongs to the same suite of devices. Its point, it was argued, was to provide a tool for controlling equity. Were it to reflect understanding of the average costs of outputs for users of different broad case types, the group budgets could be so fixed that on average the relative benefits enjoyed by groups would be fair by the criteria of the higher managers and policy-makers as long as each of the groups in the area covered by the budget had enough cases for random variations within them to cancel out between areas.[2] Since the care managers would be able to vary package costs between cases in each group, they could also respond to the big individual cost-influencing variations in circumstances within groups, thus exercising professional judgements within a broad organisational framework for equity control.

The implications of setting different combinations of average group budgets have not yet been simulated. However, the results reported above usefully indicate the degree to which constraining optimisation by setting budgets for case types reduces the gains from 'unconstrained' optimisation. A constrained optimisation is likely to improve outputs less given the overall size of the budget. The difference in the magnitude of the output gain given group-budget-constrained optimisation rather than unconstrained optimisation therefore indicates the likely trade-off between improving equity by setting group budgets and the loss of output by foregoing redistribution across case types.

Implications of the results. Figure 22.1 showed the percentage gains for each of the most important outputs given the different optimisation scenarios. The comparison required for the analysis of this proposition is between the last two categories on the graph. The results clearly show that:

- As compared with current levels of outputs, the high proportions of the output gains which would be made given perfect input mix efficiency with unconstrained optimisation would also be made with perfect input mix efficiency given group-budget-constrained optimisation. Very large improvements could be achieved by improving input mix efficiency given either unconstrained or group-budget-constrained optimisation.
- The output for which the gains from improving input mix efficiency would be greatest would be DLD. A high proportion of the improvement in it given an unconstrained optimisation scenario would be achieved with group-budget-constrained optimisation.
- The association also exists for some of the other outputs for which the improvements in input mix efficiency offers great gains given an unconstrained optimisation scenario: notably, IMPADL, the reduction in the felt burden of caregiving (KOSBERG), IMPIADL, and DLD. But this is less the case for one of the important outputs for which the gains from improved input mix efficiency would be great: IMPEMP. But even for IMPEMP, four-fifths of the gains given the unconstrained optimisation scenario would also be made given group-budget-constrained scenario.
- The potential gains of optimisation are least for DAYS. It will be remembered from chapter 3 that providing users with more chance of being cared for at home was interpreted by the 133 managers as having been their authorities' top priority in all areas. Authorities seem to be performing in ways in which improvements in input mix would not have dramatic effects.[3]

Therefore what figure 22.1 showed is that with respect to most of the outputs for which improving output gains would generate large increases in outputs from the same overall budget, one can use group budgets to gain greater policy control over broad equity patterns without paying a high price in terms of losses in efficiency in terms of the greatest good of the user group as a whole. Of course, like all the results of studies using designs and analysis techniques of the kind applied in ECCEP, the conclusion has greater validity for smaller than for larger adjustments to the present pattern.

4.   Conclusion

The chapter first showed that maximisation of the reduction in caregiver burden was a credible option as output maximand for the groups to which it has relevance. In its second section, it showed how there was one group, users with long interval needs but no PICs. So the policy-maker might wish to set different output goals for combinations of output groups. The third section showed how this could be done by using analysis group budgets. Such group budgets could anyhow be used to reconcile responsiveness to individual circumstances with overall organisational control of equity patterns in a way which complemented the other devices of performance management in budget-devolved care-managed community care.

Notes

1   That was an uneasy combination of the bureaucratic devices traditional in the organisational control of Beatrice Webb's English local government with those used in free-standing, professionally-governed service organisations. The latter was often an implicit goal of the professional social workers in the age immediately preceding and following the Seebohm Report.

2   The same effect would be more efficiently achieved when the average budget is used in conjunction with one or more budget caps, special arrangements for special cases, for redistribution given an exceptional pattern of bombardment, and the like. The reason for this is the positive skew in the predicted costs of outputs within each broad case type. The skew makes the predicted average cost highly sensitive to relatively few cases at the upper end of the cost distribution. The system in Kent implemented from 1980 to 1987 for the selected recipients of the care management programmes based on the earlier Kent Community Care Project had mechanisms allowing for adjustments for special cases and changes in caseload.

3   Additionally, chapter 14 described how the observed user group budgets coincided with those implied by the unconstrained optimisation of DAYS.

26 Flexibility in Commissioning and Decommissioning

In this chapter, the policy proposition discussed is that investments should be undertaken to reduce the price elasticity of supply of services by making commissioning and decommissioning flexible and by market creation and management.

Aspects of post-reform arrangements and the aspirations and fears of many councillors and officers create a bias towards incrementalism in budgeting, it was argued in chapter 13. For that and other reasons, the Department of Health, the Audit Commission and others have heavily emphasised increasing the flexibility in commissioning and decommissioning, 'business planning to drive change', and the use of other weapons in the arsenal authorities have to adjust the content of services to needs and demands (Audit Commission, 1997; Department of Health Social Services Inspectorate and Audit Commission, 1998, 38).

This chapter focuses on only one feature of the complex issues relating to flexibility in commissioning and decommissioning: the contrast between the hypothetical worlds postulated by two of the scenarios. In one, substantial changes in amounts of services can be made without affecting unit costs. In the other, substantial changes in amounts of services cannot quickly be made.

1. Implications of the optimisations

The key issue is the degree to which the gains achievable from greater output mix efficiency are diminished given a service-budget-constrained optimisation scenario compared with an unconstrained optimisation scenario. Figure 22.1 summarises this evidence also. The comparison is between the actual output levels at the left-hand side of the graph with the levels given service-budget constrained optimisation, and with unconstrained optimisation.

The results are clear.

- The gains from perfect input mix efficiency would be small given a service-budget-constrained optimisation scenario. They would be a small proportion of the gains given unconstrained optimisation.
- The relative scale of the gain from unconstrained optimisation compared with the service-budget-constrained optimisation differs greatly between output types. It is smallest — that is, the handicap imposed by the service-budget-constrained scenario is greatest — for most of the outputs for which the gains from optimisation are greatest: DLD, IMPADL, and the reduction in the felt burden of caregivers (KOSBERG). The latter is a particularly important output. The effect of optimising in the service-budget-constrained scenario is smaller for DAYS, USATISF, WKSAT, and IMPEMP. The second group includes important variables. But it the magnitude of the handicap is large for most of them also; a difference between 150 and 250 per cent increase for IMPEMP at one extreme, more modestly between 120 and 175 per cent for USATISF.

The nature of these results will not be surprising to the readers of earlier chapters. The same general feature appeared there when we considered the implications for each of the six case types. But the summarisation in the figure illustrates just how great are the differences between the scenarios. It is clear the proposition gains strong support from our evidence. The questions posed are whether it would be feasible to create circumstances approximating to the unconstrained optimisation scenario, and if so, what would be the investment costs of doing so. The first question is the subject of the next section. The second cannot be answered from our evidence.

2.   Could the unconstrained optimisation scenario be created?

It will be remembered from chapter 13 that the scenario has two important features.

2.1   *Flexibility of substitution in the search for best value*

To anticipate, the discussion concludes that this unconstrained scenario is based on assumptions that seem to be less far-fetched than may appear at first sight, partly because the translation of this scenario into reality is already in effect a reform goal. The key topic is whether, with policy effort, the quantity of home care supplied can be increased without substantial increases in price: the assumption that in the discussion of alternative investment strategies for efficiency improvement over years, we can think as of the supply curve as perfectly elastic.

2.2. *Apparent elasticity of supply*

This feature of the scenario deserves discussion for three reasons. First, an assumption that supply can be substantially increased at no higher cost is counter-intuitive under most conditions, particularly for well-indoctrinated economists. Second, one of the most important though implicit steps in several strands of pre-reform and reform argument is increasing the elasticity of supply. Indeed, unless the elasticity of supply could be made sufficiently high, some of the chains of logic of the argument would be invalid. Third, the importance of the consequences of exogenous local influences and local social services policy and behaviour for the degree of elasticity of supply has not been systematically explored either in the policy or academic literature: its importance, as one of the general and over-arching goals, has not been recognised.

2.2.1. *Difficulty of the assumption of perfect elasticity*

The assumption seems vaguely counter-intuitive because the elementary texts tell us that supply curves slope upwards. And, argue the theoreticians, they slope upwards most steeply, the shorter the time period over which one is considering the relationship (Alchian and Allen, 1959).

2.2.2. *Implicit role of increasing elasticity in pre-reform argument*

There were two distinct streams of pre-reform argument with respect to supply elasticities and supply curve shifts: (a) optimisation through field level resource mobilisation and substitution, and (b) reaping the substitution advantages of a more mixed supply economy. They should be distinguished because there are strands of (a) which have been lost in the formation of national policy. Supply might be made more elastic with them.

Optimisation through field level resource mobilisation and substitution. Pre-reform argument suggested that the way in which care management tasks are performed could for some types of service, make supply curves more elastic. This strand of pre-reform argument was focused at the field level. It was particularly about the performance of care management tasks, and community development in small areas. Some was about practice reflecting incentives to 'optimise'[1] the role of informal caregiving from informal caregivers, and to mobilise community resources to the optimum degree.[2] That strand of reform argument built directly on the classic argument of the sixties and early seventies.

It was argued that there were potentially many more sources for the supply of the care of the broad types whose productivities are analysed in this study. The reason for the potentially great substitutability of inputs of the same type from different sources is that typically, the greatest social services expenditure is not on input based on elaborate technologies or persons with abstruse technical training in short supply. High proportions of the populations have the personality and basic skills which make them able to undertake the task given modest training and an adequate framework of supervision and management. Moreover, there is great potential variation in the relative costliness of the substitutable inputs, and great variation in the relative costliness of similar inputs obtained from different sources, making substitution beneficial in many circumstances (Davies, 1995; Davies and Challis, 1986). An important corollary is that curves for a system based on reform ideas would be flatter than those in the pre-reform system.

Pre-reform developments provided evidence compatible with this logic. That was illustrated in some of the pre-reform programmes that most reflected the analysis later to be incorporated into the critique. Examples were the Kent Community Care Project and those of its descendants which most built on its idea of creating incentives for, and expectations among, case managers that they should resourcefully seek more cost-effective ways of matching resources to needs.[3] The Kent Community Care Project and those that resembled it in this respect found new, more effective, as well as less costly ways of providing day care, home care, and respite care; all of them tapping community resources. Increasingly, social services departments, too, were tapping inputs from an extended range of community sources. The case management stream was not alone in working on increasing the flexibility of community sources of care inputs. Other argument pointed in the same direction, incorporating Michael Bayley's concept of 'interweaving', adding to it a communautarian thrust, as can be seen in some of the discussions of the Barclay Committee (1982).

Price effects of inter-sectoral competition. The strand of reform argument focused on creating a more competitive supply economy was unsatisfactorily reconciled with the argument about optimisation through field level resource mobilisation and substitution. Seeing how each could best be mutually reinforcing was difficult because one was about policy, process and practice at the field level, and traditionally the concerns of practitioners, lower level managers, and some specialist middle managers; while the other was a concern of senior and other specialists in middle management.[4]

Using competition to keep down the price and cost of services was transparently important in pre-reform argument about developing independent supply. The phrase used by Griffiths, the manager who had overseen the transformation at Sainsbury's from multiple grocer in which each branch carried a narrow range of goods to supermarket chain offering enormous variety, was 'variety and choice through competition': more Austrian than Marshallian (Griffiths, 1988; Davies et al., 1990).[5] But the initial appreciation of top and middle managers in local authorities was the opposite: more about taking short-term opportunities for lower prices, less about securing technical change and diversity. The Audit Commission Handbook quotes how in the context of fiscal pressures, SSDs were tempted to 'drive prices down and squeeze as much as possible from providers in the short term. In the longer term, this approach will prevent the development of the higher quality services authorities want, and will remain expensive in terms of the high transaction and monitoring costs' (Audit Commission, 1997, para. 116). The authorities which responded most to national guidance were also more concerned to establish distance between purchasers and providers imagined to be almost part of the definition of a market, than about establishing partnerships and more complex fiduciary relationships (Wistow et al., 1994). The Audit Commission suggested the need for the better communication of commissioning opportunities to providers (Audit Commission, 1997, para. 149). The Management Handbook contrasts present behaviour with presumed good practice. It argues for 'relational' management styles: 'accountability, openness, sustainability and trust' in 'all relationships between purchasers and providers'. Social services departments typically have adversarial relationships with the independent sector but a lack of accountability in arrangements with in-house providers. They argue that social service forms have not learned from the right examples in other markets, quoting the features of good modern contracts from the Latham Report on the construction industry and the DTI-CBI Partnership Sourcing Initiative.

Corresponding to these differences in emphasis were different elements in the argument about policy influences on price. One was the substitution of service produced by lower cost independent providers, partly in response to more efficient management in systems which were too new to have fixed inputs reflecting obsolescent technologies, and partly reflecting the lower unit costs of labour from secondary labour markets. The other was that supply curves of providers from both in-house and independent sectors could be made flatter by policy action. The supply side of the market would have to be proactively managed to do so.

Whatever forms of competition the local managers of the mixed economy have been seeking to promote, and will be seeking to promote during the next few years, the central proposition of importance to the argument here holds: unit costs of some of the important community and other services could conceivably remain constant, or even fall. That could be so even if it were a period during which the quantities commissioned and supplied increased greatly, at least for a few years; and even when allowance is made for the introduction of the minimum wage, EU requirements, and the Baumol effect (the higher rate of inflation in labour-intensive industries than others).

The preconditions for the trends in prices to make the supply seem very elastic are assumed to be infrequently met. The gap in the supply price of sectors must be large enough for the increase in the price from the cheaper sector (due the degree of inelasticity of supply in that sector), accompanied by perhaps a fall in the price in the more expensive sector (due to crawling down an upward-sloping supply curve), to result in an average price across the sectors no higher than when the level of demand was lower. Viewed from another perspective, the sum of the elasticities of supply in the two sectors must be low enough to accommodate the increase in the demand without increasing the average price.[7]

2.2.3. Elasticity of the 'pseudo-supply curve': current evidence

Though perhaps unexpected, it seems that the preconditions may have been satisfied in many areas. Indeed, between financial years 1996 and 1997, the gap between home care prices from in-house services and independent providers in England and Wales as a whole might have widened both absolutely and relatively, despite an increase in the proportion of hours provided by the independent sector of 28 per cent. In FY1996, the cost of in-house services was reported to be 8.7 per cent greater than the standard price quoted for independent sector provision, a difference of 94 pence per hour. In FY1997, the estimated figures were 21.6 per cent and £1.79 respectively. In that year, the pseudo-supply curve actually had a strong negative slope. The combined effect of market development and substitution had greatly outweighed any positive elasticity of supply in the two sectors.[8] The increase in provision was actually associated with a fall in the price of independent provision: from £8.10 to £7.33.

The patterns are stronger for some classes of authority. They strongly suggest that the norm was only small increases in prices of independent provision during a year in which there were large increases in the quantities of independent residential and home care commissioned. This suggests that very flat pseudo-supply curves may be general.

Area differences. The unconstrained scenario is more likely in some than other areas. And although the general framework of priorities and objectives is national, objectives are to be set, achieved, and nationally monitored at the level of the individual authority (Department of Health, 1998b, paras 7.15, 7.17, 7.18-22). For some applications of our analysis, the scenario can be chosen authority by authority.

It is likely that for some authorities the unconstrained optimisation scenario will be credible. For others, the opposing scenario might be more realistic. Standard costs and prices of in-house and independent provision vary greatly between authorities. The size and variation is reflected among ECCEP authorities. The differences in FY1996 were 36 per cent in Area 4, a home county; 25 per cent for Area 10, a northern shire county; and 13 per cent for Area 3, a unitary authority in the midlands. The authority with the biggest relative difference in the standard prices in the two sectors was the one which obtained the highest proportion of the home care hours from independent providers; no less than 46 per cent in 1996. In this authority, at any rate, the increased utilisation of independent care had certainly not reduced the cost differential — by driving up its price and reducing unit costs of in-house provision — to a degree which had exhausted the substitution opportunities. However, it was an authority which during the preceding two years had not been expanding the number of hours purchased, but had been contracting it.[9]

The pre-reform logic did not suggest that the supply curves would be equally flat everywhere, given equal effort and skill of the SSDs in market development and management. There would be variations due to differences in the potential for existing agencies to enter the market in an area, in the likely supply of locally-generated entrepreneurship, and in the supply of labour.

Consider two examples:

- One example is the scale of the local market. Recruitment is more difficult in areas of dispersed populations, as illustrated by reports from inspections and joint reviews as well as in research studies (Audit Commission and Social Services Inspectorate, 1998a; Clark, 1994; Oldman and Field, 1997). The labour market may be a pool with clear edges, a finite size, given the incentives that the purchasers are willing to provide. Economies of concentration are relatively greater in dispersed areas, as is reflected in the greater reliance on shelter-with-care observed in many countries.

- A second example is the degree of competition in the labour market for personnel with the most suitable characteristics. The proportion of women in paid employment continues to vary greatly between areas, and has been recognised as a key indicator for both the demand and supply side of care since the earliest studies of territorial variations in need and provision. Truisms of labour market studies include that the degree of competition affects the suitability of persons, the need and nature of supervision, labour turnover, and the length of time posts remain unfilled, as well as the supply price. Larger organisations are argued to have greater recruitment difficulties. That is presumably because they lack the flexibility, the local knowledge and capacity to tap into local networks, given what seems to be a dependence on recruitment methods which reflect the localism of labour markets for activities which are not recognised as a 'trade' or 'profession' (Ford et al., 1998). The differences in the mix of motivations and rewards of paid and volunteer helpers in the Kent Community Care Project replications illustrate great area variations in some motivational features, but not others, a main source of variation being the need to be paid because of low household income: the more affluent might undertake voluntary activity, the poor with otherwise similar motivations and personality traits may attempt to achieve the same rewards by seeking a care job (Davies and Challis, 1986; Davies and Chesterman, forthcoming; Qureshi, Challis and Davies, 1989).

The supply of personal care provided by agencies may have been particularly sensitive to local competition because the terms and conditions offered by for-profit agencies have been so unattractive. Many workers may be highly sensitive to remuneration because of their low household incomes, but at the same time be sufficiently vulnerable to be have a low 'withdrawal price' in the labour market. Qureshi et al. (1989, table 1.1) summarised the range of estimates of wage elasticities for men and women in British and American studies, showing higher elasticities among women, and Dilnot and Kell (1987) found great sensitivity of the labour market behaviour to poverty trap incentives when husbands were unemployed.

The general economics of labour markets shows how the nature of product markets influences the markets for the labour whose demand is derived from those product markets. The market for the service is the product market. The derived demand is for the staff and management of those services. The product market has two characteristics. First, SSDs have great influence on the terms and conditions of demand in it, often with their values in conflict with the increasing pressure to keep down increases in spending. Secondly, great flexibility of supply is required to fit around user needs and preferences: for example, winter pressures, tasks performed well outside the office day and week, tasks adjusted to daily variation in user circumstances, frequent visits to perform tasks requiring inputs of short duration, a high proportion of users requiring inputs for only a short episode altogether. Passing the costs of such flexibility to the worker keeps down the bid price of contracts. So with the possible exception of home care agencies providing more specialised care or care for niche markets, the independent providers have created a text-book example of a 'secondary' labour market: casualisation, low wages, little training, few benefits (Doeringer and Piore, 1975; Ford et al., 1998). Local authorities' in-house services had since time immemorial offered employment in a primary labour market; and government, employers and unions had together ensured that the terms and conditions in that primary labour market had been massively improved during the period of lesser fiscal stress and higher levels of employment. That was exactly what would have been predicted from the pre-reform argument about the potential range of sources for the essential labour input. Geographical variations in labour market influences within a period are likely to have similar consequences. Generally, the harder the labour market for workers of the circumstances and characteristics in which they are likely to be recruitable to care jobs, the more likely the agencies are to offer terms and conditions more similar to a primary labour market.

However, in the independent sector, supply-side institutions have been adopted which open local areas to national entrepreneurial and service-providing expertise, notably the spread of national enterprises and franchising. These increase the credibility of what seems now to be the dominant assumption: that there are few areas of the scale of whole authorities where independent provision cannot expand provision from the independent sector for their more populous districts at similar or lower costs than in-house provision, as long as the SSD market management applies the right principles with expertise and efficiency.

2.2.4. *Elasticity of supply: future prospects*

During the next perhaps three to five years, a number of factors make the reduction in the differential between in-house and independent provision likely: the minimum wage and European regulations, in particular. But the current scale of the differences is large enough to allow a substantial reduction over time without exhausting the potential for cost-reducing substitution. Over the longer run, the interpretation of the scenario should be more influenced by judgements about the market conditions than by the historical experience of the late 1990s. During the longer run, there are those who see demographic trends, with the changing dependency ratio as an important facet, transforming excess supply by excess demand in the labour market, perhaps by the second decade of the new millennium.[11] On the other hand, there are authorities that have barely begun to help to develop independently-provided supply, and perhaps in most, policy and practice has either not reflected the current principles sufficiently or have been attempting to do so for an insufficiently long time for the effects to have worked through to independent supply.[12]

Conclusion

It is clear is that there are big gains to be made from adopting policies that encourage supply in the independent sector to be developed without excessively increasing costs for new providers. Appendix 26.1 provides further empirical evidence about the pseudo-supply curves currently.

Notes

1   Optimising, that is taking into account ethical constraints, certainly not crudely maximising without them, *pace* the suggestions to the contrary in some of the academic literatures.

2   A person from Pluto conscientiously reading the academic literature would infer much greater variety in the value assumptions and repertoires of assumed interventive technique than actually existed. The reason is that perceptions of what one another were doing in the twilight underworld of micro-projects and programmes were interpreted by some as more reflecting the rhetoric of the macro-ideological battles of the Gods than was actually the case. Some who saw themselves as defenders of civilisation against the new barbarism of those high level arguments accused the most successful experiments in this strand of crude maximisation of caregiver and volunteer inputs, and so exploitation (Parker, 1990; Challis and Davies, 1991; Walker and Warren, 1996; Davies, 2000, forthcoming). Oddly, the programmes attacked had the fullest of the available accounts of process, and the process accounts carefully explained the procedural and value protection against what was feared. It is as if some wrote as if they neither grasped the logic nor mastered the evidence; that they wrote before they had absorbed what had been written, or wrote before they had attempted to read what was available.

3   This was more the case in the Dover, Tonbridge and Malling, and perhaps the Gwynedd cases than in the Gateshead, Darlington and Lewisham cases. The policy culture and political ethos of Gateshead moulded the project in the direction of giving quasi-employee status and terms and conditions to persons whose tasks were undertaken by volunteers and quasi-volunteers in the KCCP, Dover and Tonbridge projects (Saunders, 1982). That changed price ratios. The Darlington project was conceived by the local agencies and was not in its original concept a reflection of

PSSRU ideas. It was an interesting example of a more common model of its period, the mid 1980s, the intensive domiciliary care project. The case management principles were appended as a condition for selection for the DH funding under the Care in the Community Initiative, but were immediately abandoned after the event. It was conceived and analysed as an intensive domiciliary care project by some members of its advisory committee who have written about it (Wright, 1998), was referred to thus by some of its leading professionals throughout its history, and that became its formal name at the end of the externally-subsidised evaluation period (Carr and Selby, 1998). What made the original concept interesting were the care assistants who would undertake a broader range of personal care as well as the conventional home help tasks undertaken at that time. The PSSRU then worked to clarify the arrangements and accountabilities. Fixed in relation to the high unit costs of long-stay hospital beds, budget caps were high enough, and the supply of the care assistants was sufficient, to create little incentive to be resourceful in finding new more cost-effective sources for the performance of tasks, and that was reflected in patterns (Challis et al., 1980, 1995).

4   That was although there were managers and academics who did not see the difference in the nature of the arguments, finding, for instance, the acceptance of some of the streams of the former more difficult because they were adopted in reforms in which the latter was so greatly emphasised.

5   Among the middle managers and others struggling with the early stages of creating and managing the mixed economy, there was some confusion initially about the competitive mechanism being promoted by the proponents of reform. Was it to be primarily price competition, allowing quality to settle at a level that would be as adequate as could be assured with the mechanisms being put in place? Or was it to be strongly quality competition for the benefit of the users and carers who received the service in question, balancing long-run improvement against immediate economy and the provision of a larger quantity of service which the economy would allow? The Audit Commission's Management Handbook still finds a variant of this to be a question worth putting to local managers in joint reviews (Audit Commission, 1997, 32). Was it to be competition within an existing technology, or competition aimed to find new ways of doing things, the mechanisms discussed by the Austrian than by the English economists — though not with the 'gales of creative destruction' envisaged by Schumpeter, judging from the protection given by authorities to their in-house community services, and the caution of the DH in giving market freedom in the health services when allocation be market was considered to be a key policy instrument (Davies et al., 1990; Le Grand, 1999)?

6   The explanation depends on differentiating the slope of the supply curves at a point in time from the marginal overall supply price of services over time given substitution between sectors. A positive supply elasticity for the provision of one sector might be more than offset by trends in the sectoral mix. Within each sector, there might be a positively sloping supply curve. But the absolute level of the curves might be much lower in one than the other sector, and the expansion in quantities commissioned might be entirely supplied by the lower cost sector, with the higher cost sector providing a progressively smaller share of the market. In that case, the downward shifts in the overall supply curves for each service might be sufficient and fast enough for an expansion path to the accompanied by a falling or almost constant price.

7   The supply of in-house provision is likely to be influenced by the fact that it carries heavy overhead costs. The terms and conditions of employment are those of a pri-

mary not secondary labour market. So crawling down the supply curve might not greatly reduce unit costs. Where that is the case, it is the elasticity of supply in the independent sector that is crucial.

8 There are more signs of positive supply elasticity for in-house provision, the standard price having risen from £9.04 to £9.12. This could well have been due to a spreading of costs, which in the short run is inescapable over a smaller number of units of service.

9 The data on which these comparisons are based are less than entirely reliable. They compare figures based on actual history with estimates for the following year published before the year to which the estimates relate is over. Also many authorities do not provide these data elements in the returns to CIPFA, the data source. Again, it is not obvious exactly how unique figures are chosen to represent what must be price schedules in each authority.

10 In one study of three areas, the average length of time taken to fill vacant posts in the relevant category of the Standard Occupational Classification was 12 weeks in the area of greatest labour market pressure, and seven weeks in another area (Ford et al., 1998, 34). The same study also suggested high degrees of labour turnover.

11 Some groups in the Commissariat générale du plan believe this to be the case even for the French economy, with its much higher rates of visible and concealed unemployment among those of middle age (Bézat, 1999).

12 The findings of the joint reviews suggest why authorities differ so much in their achievements in that respect, though, being careful not to infer more than the evidence would demonstrate, the argument does not assert the causal link. One authority is described as relying excessively on residential institutions. In that authority, services were not adjusted to user needs and packages were not well co-ordinated, users being allocated service on the basis of eligibility rather than because they would contribute greatly in that particular case. Yet again, we see what was demonstrated in some early experiments in intensive home care: intensive provision of what, for the cases, have low productivities, does little to allow diversion from care in institutions to care in the community, despite high cost community packages (Audit Commission and Department of Health Social Services Inspectorate, 1999).

27 Conclusions:
Production of Welfare Analysis and the Convenient Assumption of Technological Determinacy

Part III has redefined the policy questions outlined at the beginning of the book with greater precision than is often found in contemporary policy argument, has mapped some of the dilemmas they raise, and has drawn some policy conclusions. Its generality makes this more an epilogue than a chapter like the others. First, section 1 below comments on the broad pattern of the findings. Its most important argument is the basis for section 2, which suggests that the findings imply, and to some degree reflect, a profound but largely unacknowledged change in the assumptions on which we should base policy analysis. They imply an unimaginably higher degree of technological determinacy than existed fifteen years ago, when the possibility of making the system more determinate was first discussed in the context of British community care. Is this really the case? If so, what are its implications? Section 3 reminds us of some caveats and needed advances yet to be made.

1. Some general patterns

The results described in Part II of this book are not what was expected when the analysis commenced. The analyses of our meagre and narrower data sets (like the comparisons between the experimental and comparison groups in the PSSRU community care experiments) had suggested, and *Resources, Needs and Outcomes* had confirmed, that low marginal productivities were a major challenge to the validity of the logic of the new community care policy of 1989 and later. We had become accustomed to an entropic system that attached little value to what is now called Best Value. It was not positively managed to achieve clearly-defined goals and to respond to change. It seemed least anarchic in the respects in which it was most bound by tradition. Usually it was insufficiently imaginative, weak, too accommodating to shibboleths and autonomy-preserving defensiveness about modus operandi and turf. It had developed most quickly during an era when efficiency was not a high priority. Following the same research strategy that had led from the Kent Community Care Project to its replications and the Domiciliary Care Project, we had researched the patterns of potentially efficiency-improving innovations. They were almost always geographically localised, short-lived and ill-concerted. The innovations were almost always too disjointed, bounded and incremental, too geographically localised, too isolated, and insufficiently evaluated and promulgated among others by those with the power. Some of those based on broader thinking were caught in assumptive time warps, and had features that would be counter-productive in the new world. Even if the rate of such innovation accelerated, they could not have achieved the profound, pervasive and systemic change required (Davies, 1981; Davies and Ferlie, 1982, 1984; Ferlie, Challis and Davies, 1989).

Improvement could reasonably have been expected for a cohort recruited two years after the reforms came fully into operation. But we anticipated the improvements to have been substantial only in departments whose approach to reform had been most coherent. Instead, what the analysis has discovered is a large number of service productivity effects for the entire group of authorities. That provides one part of the answer to the most general of the questions posed at the opening of the book. We should at least maintain the investment ratio because the investments of the past decade have had powerful and pervasive effects on productivities in the production of highly valued outputs. A decade ago, the argument was that the investment ratio had to be raised or the new policy would face disaster (Davies et al., 1990, 399). Today, the case is that investment ratio should be high because the rate of return on investment has been shown to be great. The other part of the answer is given by the complex story about how the best policy strategy depends on circumstances, but how investment would have a good chance of success in creating those circumstances that would continue to transform equity and efficiency.

Together, the service productivity effects have what appears to be a substantial if not large impact on seventeen user- and carer-focused outputs that between them cover the most important reform goals. We assess the impact of service productivities by comparing them with the effects of risk factors in a new performance indicator, the Risk Offset of Productivity Proportion (ROPP). The ROPPs were shown in figure 12.1. For fourteen of the outputs, the ROPP value exceeded 9 per cent. The group of seven for whom ROPP values were in excess of 18 per cent included the indicators of such important outputs as the number of additional days cared for while living at home due to social services input, reduction in principal carers' felt burden of care-giving, users' satisfaction with the services, and users' feeling of empowerment. And the overall impact of the productivity effects for each output affected a high proportion of users. The proportion impacted by the productivity effects for each output was measured by another new performance indicator, the Cover of Productivity Proportion (COPP). Figure 12.1 showed the COPPs to vary between 40 and 100 per cent.[1]

That is not to argue that the productivity effects are simple and general. The pattern is what would be predicted from the 'weak' form of the fundamental proposition of the production of welfare approach: it is only over certain ranges that there are powerful productivity effects, and these productivity effects are contingent on the presence of risk factors, and cannot be estimated without bias unless these risk factors affects are taken into account, a perception reinforced by the history of the long attempts to study differences in school resource inputs on educational outputs.

Likewise the patterns of substitutability between service inputs confirms what had been argued to be one of the key characteristics of community social care when designing the Kent Community Care Project more than a quarter of a century ago. Over a wide range, many service mixes can potentially produce any one of a wide range of mixes of outputs. Individual services can do likewise. The same applies to 'inputs' from many other sources than formal services. Limitations there are, as the study of family care has shown. But it is important to start with the assumption that inputs of many kinds can be made substitutable for one another in important ways, rather than the opposite. The reason is that the first assumption liberates the imagination of field and other managers. The latter constrains such imagination, and so tends to reinforce the belief in what now exists, in a system in which a closed and narrow conservatism, smug both about impacts and user satisfaction, is one of the greatest obstacles to achieving betterment.

Relatively few broad kinds of risk factor influence productivities. The basic simplicity is encouraging for more reasons than our preference for simplicity, for reasons touched on in the opening chapter. Nevertheless the pattern is best described with a substantial number of indicators. However, that is what we see in the more sophisticated gerontological studies too. Each study adapts the precise specification of the indicator of the risk factor to the theoretical framework, the precise causal argument, to the outputs studied, and to the context, though many will use few. Also some of the variants reflect differences in the thresholds above which productivity effects are important, or the ranges within which they operate. For instance, some productivity effects operate powerfully among those above the threshold of disability indicated by the inability to perform a particular task of daily living, or the difficulty with that task is a marker for the syndrome which is common at that level or above. Also, whether just markers (and so possibly to some degree causally epiphenomenal), or causally the factor of importance, what best predicts empirically may in part reflect such influences as the case-mix, so that the apparent variety of indicators may exaggerate the true variety of the risk factors.

However, if the results in Part II are better than was expected, the mapping of efficiencies in Part III shows great variations in both technical and input mix efficiencies. And Part II and Part III alike demonstrate that the system has been applied to producing some outputs more than others, and so to producing the benefits of more value to some users than to others. There are some impressive associations when one juxtaposes evidence of various kinds: what was clearly the main function of community care as implied by the assumptions, goals and objectives of the statement of the 1989 policy; the interpretation of managers at all levels about what the behaviour of their authority implied to be the highest priority (reported in chapter 3); evidence from ECCEP as well as other research about what the users most fear and what effects that they hope and believe the services to have; and the pattern of the results in Parts II and III. The allocations of resources and how these relate to productivity variations between users and the patterns of efficiency variation alike demonstrate the prioritisation of extending lengths of the stay of persons in their own homes. Again, the coherence of the British system in this respect would not have been predicted from the results of the pre-reform stage of the study.

The results imply trade-offs between benefits. They emerge from the mapping of productivities, service contributions and efficiencies; and still more clearly in their application to the discussion of the policy propositions of chapters 23 to 25. They apply with current efficiency patterns, or the patterns which the modelling suggest to be optimal. Perhaps the message is clearest in the contrasting patterns of input mixes required to produce outputs, and the patterns of collateral outputs produced from optimisations for outputs. For instance, chapter 24 shows how optimising on the most general indicator of improved independence fails to deliver high collateral outputs for user and caregiver influence on the set-up stages of community care. More generally, optimising on that general indicator of empowerment fails to deliver on several of the other important outputs. For instance, optimisation for extending days in the community does not lead to the highest levels of user satisfaction feasible. Optimising on extending days does not mix inputs in a way that yields the greatest reductions in caregiving burden compatible with the system. That is so although chapter 11 showed that achieving a high level of user satisfaction improved service productivities for reducing caregivers' felt sense of burden, and achieving a high level of reduction in caregivers' felt burden improved productivities in extending days; not the reverse. So these results help to map the dilemmas faced by policy-makers, assuming the continuation of present productivities.

One question is the degree to which the prioritisation of outputs can be matched to the needs of different user types. Part II suggested that group budgets could be a useful instrument for this. But space has not allowed us to investigate their full potential. To do that, we should explore the effects of alternative definitions of analysis groups, among other things. Another question is how far the productivity and efficiency patterns can be so changed as to make more similar the inputs required to produce different high priority outputs. Already, the patterns show high substitutability of some inputs for the production of some outputs, at least over some ranges. Could not the pattern of substitutability be further changed by policy action? Since underlying the dilemmas created by the trade-offs is that users need different outputs, the two questions are related. Would it be useful to use the group budget device associated with group-specific output optimands for tailoring service development, as well as mixing to the needs and wishes of the group in question? That is not greatly different in principle to what the policy of providing grants under the Modernisation Fund for schemes promoting rehabilitation, reablement and prevention. Should the field agencies in each area be applying the same techniques for improving the relations between resources and outcomes for user groups?

However, it would be optimistic to assume that even the most successful policies can reform away all dilemmas. One reason is that a successful group-focused intervention development strategy of the kind outlined in the previous paragraph would require judgements about the size of the budgets for each group. Again, ECCEP evidence helps to suggest what dilemmas are least tractable. In a fifth of cases, the ECCEP care managers thought that the interests of users and their principal informal caregivers were in conflict (Davies, 1997, 350). In many such cases, interests cannot simply be reconciled. There must either be a choice, or the interests balanced. For instance, the ECCEP care managers expected that one case in ten, the caregiver would be the sole beneficiary of the care plan (Davies, 1997a, 341). Again, we should recall the fundamental trade-off formulated by the new administration in Wisconsin in the late 1980s. They postulated an opposition between the interests of the most disabled, all of whom satisfied the disability criteria for entry to institutions for long-term care, and the less disabled, for whom the issue was more the quality of life and perhaps prevention of deterioration. Then they sought to develop an informed basis for balancing the priorities by stimulating a dialogue with interest and user groups, using this postulated trade-off as part of their framework (Davies et al., 1990). Our review in chapter 24 of the nature of the argument supporting the opinions expressed about the benefits of the provision of low level inputs invites the question whether the Wisconsin experience in creating a constructive politics of community care could be useful to us in the UK at a time when we are feeling our way to developing the polity of community care as well as the formulation of the main equity issues.

Throughout Parts III and IV, we have seen the importance of what scenario we assume about the feasibility and price consequences of commissioning and decommissioning. One of three reports on commissioning published in mid-1999 illustrated the slow and uneven transition from the incrementalist world (Department of Health, 1999a). The Chief Inspector of Social Services repeated one of its criticisms: that 'commissioning plans lacked clarity about the services SSDs sought to run down or decommission' (Department of Health SSI,

1999b, 2). The results of this study suggest that which scenario to assume, or rather, which scenario to use our investment effort to create to a greater or lesser degree, proves to be of key importance to finding the best balance between diffusing resources to more low cost cases of low disability and concentration on those for whom the risk of admission to institutions is greatest and most imminent. This is the second part of the answer to the most general question posed at the beginning of the first chapter: whether the returns from investment would make it worth while at least to maintain the current investment ratio.

The argument shows that the policy judgements required are complex, qualified and contingent; from the ambiguous world of George Smiley not the clear world of Sherlock Holmes. If we assume the continuation of the traditional vices of incrementalist and rigid budgeting of pre-reform authorities, optimisations for several outputs imply a redistribution towards users of lower disability. If one assumes supply elasticity and flexibility, optimisations imply the opposite. The overview provided by chapter 26 shows the enormous efficiency — and so output or cost — gains possible given supply flexibility at the same price compared with the opposing scenario. The question is how far the unconstrained optimisation scenario with its supply flexibility and elasticity can be achieved and maintained by policy means against the background of changes in the supply. We have anecdotal evidence that there are already shortages of care personnel in some areas not noted for their high levels of economic activity. Suppliers of residential and nursing homes are currently predicting large cost increases because of the European directives.[2] However, the effects of the introduction of the minimum wage and European working time regulations will be concentrated on only a few years. The changing demographics of those of working age will have longer-term importance.

2.   Is the technology more determinate, and if so, what are the consequences?

By the degree of technologically determinacy we mean the extent to which the relationships between service inputs and outputs for users in different circumstances can be statistically estimated with useful precision, and whether they are stable for long enough to be applied in policy-making. That the estimates presented above can yield quite new kinds of policy argument, and can be used for other purposes also, are two reasons why it is of some importance for management and policy analysis. The argument has shown that it matters greatly partly because, to paraphrase Marx, the point is not to describe the system of 1995, but to guide the changes to it intended by the policy-makers. We have shown how most elements of the reforms combine improving the consistency in making the best of current production of welfare relationships with improving them in ways which make them inseparable in practice.[3]

The degree of technological determinacy suggested by the results has implications for how we conceive the nature of the policy world and so what we assume in our policy analysis. Even fifteen years ago, the description of current technological relationships would have seemed a venture unlikely to succeed to those most steeped in the study of field service and organisational analysis of social services as bureaucracies. It was even more so when the first suggestions of new reformist argument emerged during the 1970s.

The reasons are important to understand if the messages of this essay are to be understood.

- One was the nature of the world at that time. The critique of effectiveness and efficiency of services heavily emphasised a general vagueness about ends and means (Davies, 1981; Davies and Challis, 1986; Goldberg and Connelly, 1982; Goldberg and Warburton, 1976). Among some, this was a critical reaction to the argument of the Seebohm Committee and the writings of that time. Discourse during the era of the Barclay Committee did nothing to lessen this reaction. One of the implications of the unsuccessful hunt for productivities during the mid-1980s reported in *Resources, Needs and Outcomes* was that the vagueness lay not just in the eyes of workers, managers, policy-makers and policy analysts. It was a reality reflected in inconsistent targeting and low productivities. The management of what most counted for impacts, and what most counted for equity and efficiency, were not highly developed fields of policy or practice during the years between Seebohm and the early 1980s. That was the biggest contrast with some of the better American field agencies. The executive directors of organisations like ACCESS seemed to be characterised by a restless search for improving effectiveness and efficiency rare in the UK, no doubt in part reflecting the role of the PhD based on project evaluation in promotion in policy and service agencies. Formal evaluation played an incomparably larger part in shaping ideas about how to so design programmes that they would achieve improved efficiency and effectiveness.[4] Research suggested that supervision was inconsistent, and reflected the same absence of incentives to seek efficiency improvement as practice itself (Parsloe and Stevenson, 1979).

- The second is that there was a general belief that such vagueness was almost an inevitable and defining characteristic of human services. It was assumed to arise partly from the nature of the enterprise. Field workers were seen to be archetypically street-level bureaucrats. Like Starsky and Hutch, they not only saw the policies and structures created by the bureaucracies which employed them to be irrelevant or obstructive, but considered that to be a technological inevitability. Such effectiveness as was achieved was believed often to be in spite of the policies and structures, not because of them. So successful operation demanded adroitness at bucking the system. Related was the idea that performance in achieving goals of the subtlety assumed in social work could never be measured with sufficient validity and reliability. For many clients, the goals should change quickly and unpredictably in the elusive pursuit of the more general welfare. How services and many of the more obvious user circumstances affect outcomes were of the nature of things unstable, and variable between users in ways which it was impossible to predict. And so on. Technological indeterminacy was an inescapable feature of human services. It was positively wrong-headed to imagine that it could be greatly reduced.

Writing about the assumption of technological determinacy fifteen years ago, some PSSRU argument contrasted how assumptions about the degree of technological determinacy by the Barclay Committee (on social work) and the Serpell Report (on the finance of railways) led to contrasting biases: an unnecessary vagueness in the formulation of ends and means in the former; in the latter, commendable precision, but some spurious estimation of the unquantifiable. It showed how wrong-headed the Department of Health and Social Services thought new members of the Select Committee on Social Services were in expecting the Department to aim for quantitative predictability in the consequences of policy changes in 1979 and 1980[5] despite the long and slow development of opposing assumptions in central administration since the days of the Plowden Report; and how the prevailing paradigm assuming the inevitability of technological indeterminacy eventually prevailed in the sense that the questions by these new members increasingly came to assume it (Davies and Challis, 1986, 514-9).

This process of absorption and re-education of outsiders is familiar at the local level also. Nearer the beginning of the modern policy analysis of local government, Minns described how the result could be cognitive dissonance. Councillors belonging to both housing and social services committees applied the assumptions about the consequences of family problems and the expectations about the consequences of interventions from the dominant paradigm of local housing policy in the deliberations of the Housing Committee, but applied different and incompatible assumptions and expectations from the social services paradigm in the deliberations of the Social Services Committee (Minns, 1972). Similarly, Dearlove compared processes by which the assumptions and orientations of new council members were altered to demonstrate conformity to similar processes when joining a club (Dearlove, 1973). Examples could be multiplied. A joint review allusion to the fact that in one authority the policy process was 'closed', making it also slow to respond to users' needs has already been quoted as far from rare, a proposition supported by research in general (Barnes et al., 1999; Craig and Manthorpe, 1999).

What was implicit in policy and action has changed faster than the starting assumption of the theorists of social services policy-making. The theme is how the assumptions and tools of new public sector managerialism were developed in community care, and how they came to affect both the degree of technological determinacy at a point in time and to affect innovation and change through time. Some of the tools of new public sector managerialism and proactive central enforcement of its policies make sense only if one assumes a degree of technological determinacy, though neither has relied only on instruments which make that assumption for all purposes and in all circumstances.[6]

Thatcherite dirigisme launched initiatives which promoted techniques that could work only assuming a higher degree of determinism than was previously assumed. In particular, the Department's response to the Financial Management Initiative, with its new mantra, 'value for money', created structures which promoted techniques whose validity depended on a degree of technological determinacy: in community care, the replacement of the Social Work Service by the SSI with a recognition of efficiency as well as effectiveness in its remit, the establishment of the Audit Commission, and the like. It was the beginnings of a shift from a preoccupation with traditional service to a preoccupation with managing performance in the production of outcomes directly valued in their own right. The logical underpinnings of new managerialism are economistic in their separation of final outputs from means, and so focused on them, the equity of their incidence, and efficiency in their production (Self, 1975). The course has been neither direct nor smooth,[7] but future historians will be able to chart it. It is unnecessary to describe the ways in which current policies are both themselves based on the assumption of technological determinacy, and promote that assumption.

The importance is that the more strongly technological determinacy becomes a dominant assumption, the more useful it will be to invest in the kinds of collection and analysis of evidence undertaken in and for this essay, but also the more useful it will be to incorporate it into the routines of management and policy-making. One example will suffice. Simply asking some simple questions of users in each area is only a first step. How far might the periodic reviews of performance in each authority go towards collecting a simplified version of the evidence used in this essay, and how far might the analyses use simplified versions of those used here?

In fact, there are obvious and unquestionably correct reasons why technologies can only be partially determinate. Technological determinacy is such a convenient assumption during the era of new managerialist hegemony that there will be an inevitable tendency sometimes to exaggerate its degree — though less in statistical modelling, which provides estimates of the goodness of fit of models to the reality reflected in the data. But the point is whether starting from that assumption better helps to advance equity and efficiency than the reverse. The findings of this essay and of the ECCEP project in general are that, compared with the assumptions of fifteen years ago, assuming technological determinacy is better.

3. Mapping and optimisation: the potential and limits of social science

We hope that the essay may be of interest as much for the type of knowledge and analysis generated as for its substantive results. We have attempted to combine different purposes, each requiring a different degree of specificity of knowledge. At the one level, it is an attempt to map productivities. This is partly to generate hypotheses. Only replications of the collection can show how many of these effects will prove to have been stable and correctly described. At another level, it is to describe equity and efficiency around some crude and standard analysis groups. At a third, it is an attempt to develop argument about the directions of policy change. We hope that in the performance of each task, we have suggested new questions and provided new devices and techniques that others will find useful and illuminating: for example, the reduced form productivity curves; the diagrammatic description of service contributions to outputs; the new performance indicators like ROPPs and COPPs; the concept and diagrammatic description of collateral effects. This has been a study in the substitution of diagrams for tables and equations. We hope that readers think that the approach as a whole contributes to the methodology of policy analysis as well as to knowledge about community care. And also we hope that readers think that the innovations to policy analysis like the use of the triadic design combined with longitudinal information add sufficient power to make their additional cost in effort and complexity worth while repeating.

Social scientists untrained in quantitative skills are deeply suspicious of the apparent precision of statistical modelling. Often this is because they focus on the results outside their context in theoretical and policy argument. For instance, they do not see that whereas a particular estimate or test might be biased or erroneous, what is of interest is the accumulation of results, the general pattern, the direction to set for policy change. They therefore fail to see the potential contribution of such techniques for sharpening questions and suggesting conclusions at an altogether higher level than the results themselves.

Nothing could be more ambitious than to attempt to map the relationships between basic building blocks of social service care. It tackles one of the most fundamental of scientific issues, particularly when this analysis is linked with planned analyses of the same database aiming to explain the production relations, the production function providing a framework of questions for the systematic analysis of process. The questions asked in a production function study with associated explanatory analysis of process are a social science equivalent of those of a genome project. But the very importance of the question, and the apparent power of the approach makes it attractive enough for it to be necessary to make sure that caveats are understood.

The philosophers of knowledge tell us that social science can never be like natural science. Human molecules have motives, observe, learn and adapt, so that the systems are unstable and fast-changing. Those who study society can usually only observe, not conduct fully controlled experiments, so that inference is less certain. We can never be certain that we are measuring the causes and effects rather than merely the epiphenomena.[8] We are still at a stage at which few indicators of final outputs have known properties and have been shown to be interval scale measures of basic concepts with some externally valid meaning. We must not attempt too much lest our academic colleagues think that we have forgotten Icarus, that we risk bringing respectable academe into disrepute, or that we risk misleading those in the outside world, for instance, politicians and other policy-makers, respectful innocents of inferior sense and scepticism as some of these fellow academics presumably assume policy-makers to be.

Alas, all except the last reason have much validity. For a moment, cast an envious glance at natural science. The front pages of some newspapers in mid-December 1998 gave news of a breakthrough in biological science. Scientists had produced the complete genetic blueprint of Caenorhabditis Elegans: not a nattily-togad Roman aristocrat, but a species of roundworm — though perhaps not so humble after making it to the front page. ('Please call me Elegans, not Squidgy, my good fellow', he was suspected of saying when squirming with his wiggling admirers that day.) 'This is a watershed in the history of biology,' said the director of the National Institutes of Health. The achievement seemed to rival the greatest in the Human Genome Project in its ten years of impressive (and vastly expensive) activity. Not that the scientists had yet figured out how the genes worked. That would be the leading challenge of the next decade, said one of the leaders of the happy research team, perhaps already thinking of how they would use the next tranche of Nobel prize money.

That is indeed a different world. The shift in assumptive world towards technological determinacy, so convenient for new managerialists and politicians, will not beam us up to it. But also it arguable that the philosophers have made us too pessimistic. Mapping ends-means relationships and using them to think about destination and routes has proved more interesting than could have been expected. Perhaps we can hope that our crude and unreliable sketches are understood for what they are, but may nevertheless be of service in deepening and sharpening our discourse. Again, the test is usefulness. Which assumption most contributes most to the advancement of useful knowledge? A paralysing belief that we should not try to map the fundamental production of welfare parameters that determine equity and efficiency? Or the belief that the attempts should be made in spite of the risks that some of the relations will not stand the test of replication?

Notes

1 Not all the productivity effects have been described in this study. For instance, as yet unreported parallel analyses by the authors show the productivities of home care to be high in the reduction of utilitisation of acute hospital beds, an important result because some suggest that as many as 20 per cent of bed-days are occupied by persons whose medical condition make less expensive forms of appropriate (particularly by elderly persons) and because the gap between costs of an acute bed day and care in other settings continues its long-term growth.

2 The National Care Homes Association estimates that the combination of the minimum wage with European working time regulations will increase wage costs by between 8 and 12 per cent during 1999 (Chadda, 1999, 8).

3   Other publications from the ECCEP projects are more illuminating about the improvability of the productivities. For instance, the work for the forthcoming ECCEP monograph on case management and outcomes illustrates that few of the cases had truly multidisciplinary assessments, and that and other work in other ways describes weaknesses in the coordination of health and social care. So that work is more informative about issues like the circumstances of users for whom the productivity of inputs in producing outputs depends on coordination of the speed and mutual understanding that can be achieved only by successful integration at the field level. That will also be where the evidence from this country and abroad will be used to inform other aspects of the general issue of the potential benefits for different user groups of 'horizontalising' the vertical hierarchies which divide up our policy space; that is, joining up the government at the individual level.

4   See the accounts of the evolution of programmes and the part played in the process by externally-funded evaluated programmes in ACCESS and other agencies in Davies (1986a,b), and Davies and Challis (1986).

5   One focus was the effect of shortening lengths of stays in acute hospital beds for the demand for community care inputs, and the effects of community care provision on the length of hospital stays. The Department doubted the estimability and stability of the relationship for a wide range of reasons, but in particular the relevance of estimates based on national average to local contexts. ECCEP shows such substitutability to exist currently, and is investigating the local variations.

6   The current range of social services modernisation policies is an example.

7   As an example, take this confession from government. 'During the past two and half years, the major structural change of the introduction of the community care reforms made it necessary to spend a lot of time concentrating on processes and systems. It is now time to move on, and consciously to remind ourselves that process and systems are not an end in themselves, but only a means to achieving our objective. That objective must be to secure at a local level the best achievable practice to ensure the most positive outcome for users and carers.' Departments of Health and for the Environment (1995), para 1.14.

8   For instance, should we be redefining what constitutes the inputs so that they are about the nature of the services rendered and reflect the supply circumstances as well as service consequences; that is import the qualitative and process nature of services into the measures of resource inputs? Equating resource inputs as service inputs neglects the history of economic theory. The classification of inputs reflected contrasting propositions about the nature of their supply curves: in classical economics, the inelasticity of supply of land, the differences between labour and capital; and later the addition of 'organisation' as company management emerged as a separate focus. Might not a classification of service inputs in a way that both reflected supply theory and characteristics argued produce more illuminating production functions? Examples might be to distinguish inputs from personnel with different training levels as in the analysis for *Needs Led or Resource Driven*, the forthcoming ECCEP work on utilisation. Another example would be to measure types of organisational inputs. That was considered in the design stages of the analysis of the Domiciliary Care Project. Such an approach would better reflect the theoretical argument about the nature of the substitutability of resource inputs put forward in *Matching Resources to Needs* and argument based on a retrospective view of the KCCP and its descendants (Davies, 1995; Davies and Challis, 1986). The difficulty is that it would so multiply the number of resource inputs, and so the complexity of the modelling. The authors are considering some reanalysis of the database testing out such models when higher priority work has been completed.

Appendix Table 2.1
Output variables used in production functions

Variable	Description	Question asked	No.	Mean	s.d.	Min	Max	Percentiles 25	50	75
DAYS	Number of days living at home prior to admission to institutions for long term care	Number of days spent in the community. Starts from assessment until admission to residential care facility. If the user is still in the community, number of days is the count of days between the assessment and the day of interview (these are truncated observations). For those who are still in the community the 25th percentile is 637 days (21 months), 50th percentile is 676 days (22 months) and the 75th percentile is 702 days (23 months). 42 per cent of the users who were assessed had left the community.	274	517	226	1	1114	334	621	689
IMPADL	Improvement in number of personal care functions of daily living ascribed by user to the social services	SQ16A: Thinking back over the last 6 months, how much would you say the help you received from social services has improved your personal cleanliness and hygiene, including your ability to use the toilet?	143	6.8	3.3	1.0	10.0	5.0	8.0	10.0
IMPIADL	User satisfaction from improved IADLs	SQ16B: and SQ16C: Thinking back over the last 6 months, how much would you say the help you received from social services has improved the cleanliness of your house and room and the quality and quantity of food and drink?	152	13.1	6.1	1.0	20.0	9.0	14.0	19.0
USATISF	Degree of satisfaction of user with level of services received	SP4a: How satisfied are you (user) with the service you are receiving?	195	2.1	0.7	1.0	3.0	2.0	2.0	3.0
NSF	Count of unmet needs for help with function areas covered by community social services	@SP1329: Which, if any, of the services on this list do you (user) think you need more of, or is there anything that you don't receive that you need? Help at home, meals, dc, etc.	191	0.6	1.3	0.0	8.0	0.0	0.0	1.0

Appendix Table 2.1 (continued)

Variable	Description	Question asked	No.	Mean	s.d.	Min	Max	Percentiles 25	Percentiles 50	Percentiles 75
SATAMSUP	Caregiver's degree of satisfaction with amount and type of support PIC had from services to look after user		97	2.8	0.8	1.0	4.0	2.0	3.0	3.0
PICSEXP	Degree to which PIC experience with the social services was favourable during last six months	RQ23b: How would you describe your experience with social services over the last 6 months? Favourable, mixed or unfavourable?	105	2.5	0.6	1.0	3.0	2.0	3.0	3.0
PGC	Overall lack of morale; PGC score	SH1-SH19	241	8.4	4.7	0.0	19.0	4.0	8.0	12.0
GDL	General dissatisfaction with life score; GDL	SH4: Do you see enough of your friends and relatives? SH6: As you get older do you feel less useful? SH8: As you get older are things better than expected? SH15 Is life hard for you most of the time? SH16: Are you satisfied with your life today? SH17: When things go wrong does it affect you a lot?	236	2.7	1.7	0.0	6.0	1.0	3.0	4.0
DLD	Dissatisfaction with life development score; DLD	SH1: Do you (user) have as much energy as you did, last six months? SH2: Does life seem to get worse as you get older? SH6: As you get older do you feel less useful? SH10: Are you as happy as you were when you were young?	238	1.2	0.8	0.0	2.0	1.0	2.0	2.0
KOSBERG	Kosberg carer burden scale RJ35a-RJ35t		163	3.9	3.9	0.0	16.0	1.0	2.0	6.0

Appendix Table 2.1 (continued)

Variable	Description	Question asked	No.	Mean	s.d.	Min	Max	Percentiles 25	Percentiles 50	Percentiles 75
IMPEMP	User felt control over own life score	SH13: Do you (user) feel free to run your life the way you want? SK20: Do you often feel helpless? SH20@6: Do you ever worry about losing your independence and other people making decisions for you?	195	1.5	1.9	0.0	3.0	1.0	1.0	2.0
UEMPOW	User felt empowerment/ influence during set-up stage of care management scale	UO3: Did it feel as though you had a say in plans being made? UO5: Did you feel sw was in charge, telling what was needed, someone to discuss different alternatives, or someone to get the services you want? UO29: Overall would you say sw offered you any choice in help you received? UO30: Overall how satisfied are you with the way ss have assessed and tried to help you with your recent problems?	217	5.7	2.0	0.0	4.7	4.1	5.9	7.6
CEMPOW	PIC felt empowerment/ influence during set-up stage of care management	CO3: Were you involved in separate discussions with social worker (sw) about user? CO7: Was sw interested in hearing from you about problems with caring? CO8: Did it feel as though you had a say in plans being made? CO12: Did you feel sw was in charge of telling what was needed, someone to discuss different alternatives, or someone to get the services you want? CO49: Overall how satisfied are you with the way social services have assessed and tried to help user with recent problems? CO50: Overall how satisfied are you ss took account of your needs in your own right? CO51: Overall how satisfied are you ss took account of your need in support in caring for user?	152	25.4	4.0	6.3	31.0	24.3	26.7	27.7

Appendix Table 2.1 (continued)

Variable	Description	Question asked	No.	Mean	s.d.	Min	Max	Percentiles 25	Percentiles 50	Percentiles 75
IMPREL	Degree to which user considered social services to have improved how well user gets on with family and friends	SQ16E: Thinking back over the six months how much the user says the help s/he has received from social services has improved how well s/he gets on with family and friends.	181	7.5	3.0	1.0	10.0	6.0	9.0	10.0
SATSOC	Degree of satisfaction of user with chances to meet people	SQ13: How satisfied are you with your chances to meet people and socialise?	209	3.8	1.0	1.0	5.0	3.0	4.0	5.0
WKSAT	Worker rating of degree to which social services improved the welfare of the user	KG18: To what extent has all the help the user received significantly improved or maintained his/her welfare?	319	2.8	0.8	0.0	4.0	2.0	3.0	3.0

Appendix Table 2.2
Explanatory variables used in the modelling

Variable	Description	Mean	s.d.	Min	Percentile 25	Median	Percentile 75	Max	Valid No.
Need-related circumstances									
Physical disability									
CANTBED	User cannot go to bed by him/herself	0.186	0.39	0	0	0	0	1	290
CANTEAT	User cannot eat by him/herself	0.114	0.318	0	0	0	0	1	290
CANTGROC	User cannot buy groceries by him/herself	0.824	0.381	0	1	1	1	1	290
CANTHHWK	User can't do heavy housework by him/herself	0.903	0.296	0	1	1	1	1	289
CANTLHWK	User can't do light housework by him/herself	0.564	0.497	0	0	1	1	1	289
CANTMEAL	User can't prepare meals by him/herself	0.58	0.494	0	0	1	1	1	288
CANTTOIL	User cannot go to toilet by him/herself	0.163	0.37	0	0	1	0	1	289
CANTWASH	User cannot wash him/herself	0.517	0.501	0	0	1	1	1	288
CANTWHND	User cannot wash hands by him/herself	0.138	0.345	0	0	0	0	1	290
INTNEED	Isaacs and Neville interval need level	1.084	0.869	0	0	1	2	2	308
INTLNG	User in long interval need category	0.42	0.49	0	0	0	1	1	308
INTSHT	User in short interval need category	0.24	0.43	0	0	0	0	1	308
INTCRIT	User in critical interval need category	0.34	0.47	0	0	0	1	1	308
UADLS	Count of problems with ADLs (user perception)	1.328	1.572	0	0	1	2	5	290
UIADLS	Count of problems with IADLs (user perception)	4.007	2.155	0	2	4	6	7	290
WADLS	Count of problems with ADLs (CM perception)	1.722	1.495	0	0	2	3	4	306
WIADLS	Count of problems with IADLs (CM perception)	2.454	1.551	0	1	2	4	5	306
Mental health									
KATSCORE	Katzman cognitive impairment score	11.013	9.981	0	2	6	20	28	306
KATZMAN	Katzman cognitive impairment level	0.624	0.821	0	0	0	1	2	306
PGC	PGC lack of morale score	8.804	4.678	0	5	8	12	19	285
WBEHAV	User perceived by CM to present behavioural difficulties	0.102	0.304	0	0	0	0	1	303

Appendix Table 2.2 (continued)

Variable	Description	Mean	s.d.	Min	Percentile 25	Median	Percentile 75	Max	Valid No.
WCOGIMP	User is perceived by CM to be cognitively impaired	0.287	0.453	0	0	0	1	1	307
WDEPR	User is perceived by CM to be depressed	0.134	0.341	0	0	0	0	1	307
WLOWMORAL	User is perceived by CM to have low morale	0.512	0.501	0	0	1	1	1	303
Other health problems									
WCANCER	User suffers from cancer	0.046	0.209	0	0	0	0	1	307
WCORONAR	User has coronary problems	0.218	0.414	0	0	0	0	1	307
WHEALTH	Count of number of health problems	2.798	1.563	0	2	3	4	9	307
WINCONT	User presents incontinence of urine or faeces	0.16	0.367	0	0	0	0	1	307
WSKEL	Count of muscular and skeletal problems	0.502	0.628	0	0	0	1	3	307
WSTROKE	User had stroke	0.205	0.405	0	0	0	0	1	307
WULCER	User has ulcerated legs or pressure sores	0.072	0.258	0	0	0	0	1	307
Informal care related factors									
CAGE	PIC age	51.29	25.37	0	43	57	70	90	214
CCPBEAR	Problem felt by PIC during caring: loss of earnings	0.03	0.18	0	0	0	0	1	182
CCPBEMB	Problem felt by PIC during caring: embarrassment	0.02	0.15	0	0	0	0	1	182
CCPBFAM	Problem felt by PIC during caring: not enough time for family	0.09	0.29	0	0	0	0	1	182
CCPBFIN	Problem felt by PIC during caring: financial cost	0.03	0.18	0	0	0	0	1	182
CCPBFRI	Problem felt by PIC during caring: do not see enough of friends	0.09	0.28	0	0	0	0	1	182
CCPBHLP	Problem felt by PIC during caring: unable to help other dependent	0.03	0.18	0	0	0	0	1	182
CCPBJOB	Problem felt by PIC during caring: loss of job	0.03	0.16	0	0	0	0	1	182
CCPBLEI	Problem felt by PIC during caring: loss of leisure	0.18	0.39	0	0	0	0	1	182
CCPBNB	Problem felt by PIC during caring: count	1.14	2.14	0	0	0	1	11	182
CCPBPHY	Problem felt by PIC during caring: physical effort	0.15	0.36	0	0	0	0	1	182
CCPBREL	Problem felt by PIC during caring: strain on relationship	0.10	0.30	0	0	0	0	1	182

Appendix Table 2.2 (continued)

Variable	Description	Mean	s.d.	Min	Percentile 25	Median	Percentile 75	Max	Valid No.
CCPBSTR	Problem felt by PIC during caring: stress	0.19	0.39	0	0	0	0	1	182
CCPBWOR	Problem felt by PIC during caring: loss of sleep due to worry	0.09	0.29	0	0	0	0	1	182
CCPPBSLE	Problem felt by PIC during caring: loss of sleep due to attention required by user	0.09	0.28	0	0	0	0	1	182
CEMPLOY	PIC is employed or a student	0.33	0.47	0	0	0	1	1	214
CHADHLPB	PIC had health problems at time of user's referral to SSD	0.48	0.50	0	0	0	1	1	214
CHAFFECT	PIC health affects caring	0.38	0.49	0	0	0	1	1	132
CLOVE	PIC cares because of love	0.81	0.40	0	1	1	1	1	182
CUPBBUR	Problem felt by user during caring: user feels a burden on others	0.08	0.27	0	0	0	0	1	182
CUPBEMB	Problem felt by user during caring: user feels embarrassment	0.03	0.16	0	0	0	0	1	182
CUPBIND	Problem felt by user during caring: user complains from loss of independence	0.09	0.28	0	0	0	0	1	182
CUPBNB	Problem felt by user during caring: count	0.36	0.91	0	0	0	0	5	182
CUPBPRI	Problem felt by user during caring: user complains from loss of privacy	0.04	0.21	0	0	0	0	1	182
CUPBSTR	Problem felt by user during caring: user is stressed	0.09	0.28	0	0	0	0	1	182
INFCOMP	Companionship informal help (hrs/wk)	9.51	17.71	0	1	3	8	83	151
INFHWK	Housework informal help (hrs/wk)	2.16	4.79	0	0	0	2	35	165
INFMED	Medical informal help (hrs/wk)	2.17	9.90	0	0	0	0	83	176
INFPCP	Personal care informal help (hrs/wk)	3.02	9.39	0	0	0	2	83	165
KOSBERG	Kosberg PIC stress score	4.09	4.30	0	0	3	7	17	214
MCMEAL	Main PIC does meals	0.43	0.50	0	0	0	1	1	277
OCMEAL	Other informal carer than PIC prepares meals	0.11	0.32	0	0	0	0	1	277
UPIC	Presence of informal PIC (user perception)	0.90	0.30	0	1	1	1	1	279

Appendix Table 2.2 (continued)

Variable	Description	Mean	s.d.	Min	Percen-tile 25	Median	Percen-tile 75	Max	Valid No.
USERBEN	Help provided for users benefit	0.84	0.36	0	1	1	1	1	193
WCARISK	Number of risks PIC is subject to	1.51	1.34	0	0	1	2	6	168
WCASERVI	Count of number of services aimed at helping PIC	1.76	1.66	0	0	1	3	6	224
WCBALANC	Caregiver is perceived to be balanced (by CM)	0.50	0.50	0	0	1	1	1	138
WCENGULF	Caregiver is perceived to be engulfed (by CM)	0.19	0.39	0	0	0	0	1	138
WCLOFEM	PIC is a close female relative	0.50	0.50	0	0	1	1	1	260
WCSTRESS	PIC is perceived to be stressed by CM	0.53	0.50	0	0	1	1	1	276
WCUCONFL	Interests of user and caregiver are perceived by CM to be in conflict	0.24	0.43	0	0	0	0	1	110
WCUPOOR	PIC and user have a poor relationship	0.06	0.24	0	0	0	0	1	274
WPIC	Presence of an informal PIC (CM perception)	0.89	0.32	0	1	1	1	1	279
WPICLIVI	PIC lives with user	0.41	0.49	0	0	0	1	1	256
WSPOUSE	is spouse	0.13	0.33	0	0	0	0	1	260
Poverty and material environment factors									
HOUSBEN	User receives housing benefit	0.2	0.4	0	0	0	0	1	306
INCOME	User income level	1.96	0.44	1	2	2	2	4	238
INCSUPP	User receives income support	0.22	0.42	0	0	0	0	1	306
PENSION	User receives pension	0.7	0.46	0	0	1	1	1	306
UOWNSHS	User owns house (alone or with others)	0.34	0.48	0	0	0	1	1	177
VEXED	User is vexed by charging	0.15	0.36	0	0	0	0	1	107
WFINPB	User has financial problems	0.13	0.34	0	0	0	0	1	297
WHEATPB	Presence of heating problems	0.03	0.17	0	0	0	0	1	297
WHOUSPB	Presence of housing problems	0.269	0.444	0	0	0	1	1	297
WPERSENV	Number of personal environmental problems	0.481	0.784	0	0	0	1	4	297
WWIDENV	Number of wider environmental problems	0.209	0.549	0	0	0	0	4	297

Appendix Table 2.2 (continued)

Variable	Description	Mean	s.d.	Min	Percentile 25	Median	Percentile 75	Max	Valid No.
Other									
AGE	User's age	80.58	7.246	65	75	81	86	97	286
ATTALL	User receives attendance allowance	0.3	0.46	0	0	0	1	1	306
CATARISK	Number of cataclysmic risks with at least 50 per cent chance of happening	1.3	1.16	0	1	1	2	6	148
CURRENT	Case known to SSD before present major review	0.49	0.5	0	0	0	1	1	307
DETERISK	Number of risks with more than 50 per cent probability of deterioration	1.828	1.817	0	0	1	3	8	198
FROMHOSP	Whether referral to SSD straight from hospital.	0.27	0.44	0	0	0	1	1	308
KEEPHOME	CM perception of extent to which help will keep user at home in future	1.63	0.56	0	1	2	2	2	196
MALE	User is male	0.252	0.435	0	0	0	1	1	306
PALLCARE	Formal help intended as palliative care	0	0	0	0	0	0	0	218
SHORTINT	Care plan designed as a short intervention	0.16	0.37	0	0	0	0	1	136
STILSET	CM still setting up care plan at moment of T1 interview	0.05	0.21	0	0	0	0	1	213
UALONE	User lives alone	0.61	0.49	0	0	1	1	1	308
UCONFIDE	User has confidant	0.83	0.38	0	1	1	1	1	235
UFEARS	Count of users fears	1.62	1.76	0	0	1	3	7	306
UMARRIED	User is married	0.18	0.39	0	0	0	0	1	274
UPERCENT	User level of reaction against placement in residential or nursing care facility	3.97	1.06	1	3	4	5	5	247
WPERSREL	Number of personal relationship problems	2.09	1.62	0	1	2	3	8	303
WURELIAN	User over-reliant on others compared with users in similar circumstances	-0.41	0.83	-1	-1	-1	0	1	135
WUSERISK	Number of risks to user	3.33	2.52	0	1	3	5	14	216

Appendix Table 2.2 (continued)

Variable	Description	Mean	s.d.	Min	Percentile 25	Median	Percentile 75	Max	Valid No.
Services									
DC_WCOST	Weekly cost, day care	21.41	36.48	0	0	0	33	165	299
HC_	Weekly cost, home care	45.79	51.18	0	8	29	64	354	302
MWCOST	Weekly cost, delivered meals	3.54	6.29	0	0	0	6	20	300
NV_WCOST	Weekly cost, nursing visits	11.76	33.15	0	0	0	6	225	269
RE_WCOST	Weekly cost, respite care	14.27	36.07	0	0	0	7	244	293
SW_WCOST	Weekly cost, social worker input	0.42	1.14	0	0	0	0	7	90

Appendix 26.1 Commissioning Responses to Relative Prices and Costs of In-House and Independent Provision

Chapter 26 showed that two issues were key to the content and implementation of equity and efficiency policy: (a) whether current reality approximates better to the 'unconstrained' optimisation scenario (with flexible supply at current price levels) or the 'service-budget-constrained' optimisation (with inflexible aggregate service shares); and (b) whether the unconstrained optimisation scenario is generally attainable by British authorities. The chapter asserted that there exists circumstantial evidence of differences in costs between sectors, and argued that this made the unconstrained optimisation scenario nearer to reality and more attainable.

1. Theoretical logic

Keys to the analysis of commissioning are the supply curves for each kind of service in each area, and the relative position of supply curves for each sector for each service. There is no reason why supply curves for each sector should be identical across areas. Indeed, there is evidence suggesting that they would not be: Audit Commission (1996, 25) for independent provision, and Davies et al. (1990) for in-house provision. Neither has it been proved that the supply curve for in-house provision is steeper and further to the left than that of independent provision. But the description of supply circumstances and technologies in the text of the chapter suggest that to be likely.[1]

The model implicit in figure A26.1.1 describes how a benefit-maximising authority would behave were the two sets of supply curves to be as envisaged above. (Substitution and complementarity are ignored.) With unchanging total demand, an authority facing these supply curves would increase its consumption from the cheaper sector, and diminish it from the more expensive sector, until the prices of the marginal unit commissioned were the same in the

Figure A26.1.1
Supply curves for in-house and independent provision

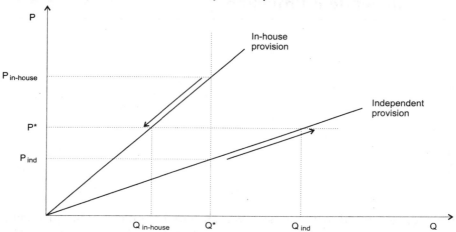

two sectors. That is, the authority would crawl up the supply curve for independent provision, and down the supply curve for in-house provision, until the price was p*, with the result that the quantities consumed would be $OQ_{in\text{-}house}$ and OQ_{ind}. It would be tempting to use the data available for standard prices and unit costs for areas to estimate the supply curves under the assumption of broad similarity of area supply curves. Given identical area supply curves, the estimates could then be used to analyse the behaviour of each authority, as well the national average position. But the nature of the data suggests this to be too ambitious. So this appendix presents some evidence about (a) inter-sectoral differences in prices, (b) whether commissioning responded to the gap between marginal prices in the two sectors, and whether (c) year-on-year changes in the quantities consumed in each sector were associated with the changes in the differences between prices implied by the model in figure A26.1.1.

2.   Data

The evidence is from a special count of the DH community care returns, the disk editions of the Social Services Statistics for financial years 1996 and 1997 published by the Chartered Institute of Public Finance and Accountancy. The CIPFA data are unreliable for various reasons. They do not cover all authorities, many authorities objecting to supplying the data as a matter of principle. The number of authorities for which data are not provided is large enough to risk making the remainder a biased sample of the total. Data for successive years in some other authorities cannot be compared because of local government reorganisation. There is terminological imprecision about concepts which anyhow require those supplying the data to simplify a complex world. The data take no account of intersectoral differences in transactions costs to the authority arising from regulative responsibilities.

3. Results

3.1. *Price differences and changes in price differences between FY1996 and FY1997*

*Differences between sectors.*Table A26.1.1 is compatible with the descriptions provided in chapter 26:

- In-house prices were much higher than independent sector standard prices in the vast majority of cases for home care and residential care. This was also true in one half of authorities for day care, and only in approximately a quarter of them for meals.

- In-house home care and residential care unit costs were on average approximately 40 per cent above the independent sector prices, 20 per cent above for meals, and were practically equal to the independent sector prices for day care. The pattern was similar in both years, with if anything an increase in the price-gap in favour of the independent sector.

Table A26.1.1
Intersectoral price gaps

	Home care	Meals	Day care	Resid. care
Price levels FY1996				
Average absolute service price gap	2.73	.34	-1.27	85.37
Average in-house to independent sector price ratio	1.38	1.20	1.04	1.39
In-house price above independent sector price (%)	85	25	48	95
Price levels FY1997 and changes FY1996-FY1997				
Average absolute service price gap (£)	2.98	.82	-.54	104.74
Average rate of change in-house price (%)	10	27	22	11
Average rate of change independent sector price (%)	10	17	16	9
Average in-house to independent sector price ratio	1.40	1.40	1.11	1.43
Authorities with reduction in price gap (%)	28	0	32	38
Number of authorities	47	8	25	63

The frequency distributions of intersectoral price gaps for each of the two years are summarised in table A26.1.2. It shows practically no local authorities with in-house costs below independent sector prices for home care and residential care services. This was so neither for meals nor day care services. The pattern is similar for both years.

Table A26.1.2
Distribution of absolute service price gaps*

Percentiles and averages	10th	25th	Median	75th	90th	Mean	N
FY1996							
Home care (hour)	0	1.2	2.83	4.00	5.89	2.72	47
Day care (session)	-12.5	-4.64	0	3.51	10.18	-1.27	25
Residential care (week)	15.56	49.23	75.2	105.00	144.79	85.37	63
FY1997							
Home care (hour)	0	0.58	3.41	5.08	6.47	2.98	47
Day care (session)	-14.65	-4.21	0	6.03	15.13	-0.54	25
Residential care (week)	15.8	37.00	73.03	120.00	222.80	104.74	63

* In-house price minus independent sector price

3.2.   *Intersectoral quantities demanded FY1996 and FY1997*

The price evidence should be interpreted in the context of the relative consumption of services between sectors. Table A26.1.3 shows the levels of the services provided by the two sectors for FY1996, and the changes between FY1996 and FY1997.

Table A26.1.2 shows an important contrast in the proportion of services contracted from the two sectors between community and residential services.

- Contrary to what the model hypothesised, local authorities appear to have purchased community services much more heavily from in-house providers, despite their higher costs. Overall, the level of community based services purchased from in-house providers exceeds the level contracted from the independent sector in approximately three-quarters of the local authorities.

- The picture for residential care services is in total contrast. Only in 35 per cent of local authorities did the levels of services commissioned from in-house providers exceed the level purchased from the independent sector. On average, the volume of the service contracted to independent providers exceeded in approximately 10 per cent of the authorities the volume of services provided in-house. In terms of residential care, therefore, local authorities seem to have been exploiting the cost saving opportunities of lower independent sector prices.

- Most levels of inputs increased from FY1996 to FY1997. However, the rate of increase in the level of services contracted from the independent sector exceeded that from in-house providers for home care, day care and residential care services, the opposite being the case for meals. The average share of services contracted from independent sector providers increased particularly significantly for home care and residential care services.

Table A26.1.3
Intersectoral service levels provided

	Home care	Meals	Day care	Resid. care
Service levels FY1996				
Average in-house to independent sector service level ratios				
10th percentile	0.56	0.14	0.52	0.16
25th percentile	1.03	1.23	0.95	0.38
Median	1.89	2.80	1.78	0.71
75th percentile	4.14	7.61	4.27	1.19
90th percentile	7.04	12.71	9.62	1.62
Average	3.09	4.91	3.57	0.93
In-house level above independent sector level (%)	76	77	75	35
Service levels FY1997 and changes FY1996-97				
Average increase in level of service from in-house providers (%)	-4	35	5	4
Average increase in level of service from independent providers (%)	18	26	38	9
Average in-house to independent sector service level ratio	2.89	4.69	3.63	0.81
Authorities showing increase in independent sector's share (per cent)	63	46	53	75
Number of authorities	74	24	50	84

3.3. Relationship between price gaps and changes in purchasing

The models reported in this section explore whether the data suggests local authorities set their allocation policies in view of the intersectoral price gap, that is, examine the degree to which the intersectoral price gap is reflected in the changes in quantities demanded, and vice versa. In order to do so, the models postulate as dependent variable the share of services purchased from the independent sector in FY1997, and as explanatory variables the absolute intersectoral price gap, and the share of services purchased from the independent sector in FY1996. This model is not estimated for meals, given the small numbers of observations. The results are summarised in Table A26.1.4.

Table A26.1.4 shows important similarities across services in the way local authorities set the share of services they purchase from independent providers.

- The relative share of services commissioned in FY1997 from independent providers was negatively correlated with the share of services commissioned in-house in FY1996. This confirms that the change in commissioning patterns was greatest where in-house services were most dominant.

Table A26.1.4

Share of provision of independent sector FY1997 by service type

	Home care		Day care		Residential care	
	B	Sig	B	Sig	B	Sig
Constant	0.486	0.000	0.399	0.000	0.740	0.000
Ratio of in-house to independent provision, 1996	-0.055	0.000	-0.014	0.055	-0.137	0.000
Absolute inter-sectoral price gap 1996	0.021	0.013	0.006	0.167	0.001	0.800
Significance level	0.000		0.000		0.000	
Adjusted R^2	0.559		0.197		0.590	
Number of authorities	47		25		63	

- More important, there was a positive correlation for the three services explored between the share of services provided by the independent sector and the size of the price gap between the two sectors. Although the effect is only significant at the 5 per cent level for home care, it suggests that some action was being taken by local authorities to exploit the cost saving opportunities of significantly cheaper services from the independent sector.

4.   Conclusion

The evidence is partial and unreliable. However, for what it is worth, it is compatible with:

- Substantial price gaps between unit costs of in-house provision and the standard price for services purchased from the independent sector in many authorities. This suggests that the substitution of independently-provided services would allow expansion in service at little or no additional cost: the essence of the 'unconstrained' scenario. It still more strongly suggests that a situation approaching the unconstrained optimisation scenario is not an impossible goal for many, perhaps most, authorities to achieve.

- Statistically significant responses of authorities to the price gaps: the greater the price gap, the greater the increase in the share of the independent sector between years.

Note

1   It would be tempting to use the data available for standard prices and unit costs for areas to estimate the supply curves under the assumption of broad similarity of area supply curves. Given identical area supply curves, the estimates could then be used to analyse the behaviour of each authority, as well the national average position. But the nature of the data suggests this to be too ambitious.

References

Abrams, P. (1977) Community care: some research problems and priorities, *Policy and Politics*, 6, 2, 125-152.

Albert, M.S. (1994) Brief assessments of cognitive function in the elderly, in M.P. Lawton and J.E. Teresi (eds) *Annual Review of Gerontology and Geriatrics, 14*, Springer Publishing Company, New York, 93-106.

Alberta Health (1993) *Alberta Assessment and Placement Instrument for Long-Term Care (AAPI): Reference Manual*, Home and Community Long-term Care, Edmonton, Alberta.

Alchian, A.A. and Allen, W.R. (1967) *University Economics*, 2nd edition, Wadsworth Publishing Co., Belmont, California.

Attias-Donfut, C. and Rozenkier, A. (1981) *Etudes et recherche: Vieillir chez soi: I Les bénéficiaires*, Caisse nationale de l'assurance vieillesse, Paris.

Audit Commission for England and Wales (1985) *Managing Social Services for the Elderly More Effectively*, HMSO, London.

Audit Commission for England and Wales (1986) *Making a Reality of Community Care*, HMSO, London.

Audit Commission (1996) *Balancing the Care Equation: Progress with Community Care, Community Care Bulletin 3*, HMSO, London.

Audit Commission for England and Wales (1997) *Take Your Choice: A Commissioning Framework for Community Care*, Management Handbook, Audit Commission, London.

Audit Commission for England and Wales and Department of Health Social Services Inspectorate (1997) *Oxfordshire: A Report of the Review of Social Services in Oxfordshire County Council*, Audit Commission, London.

Audit Commission for England and Wales and Department of Health Social Services Inspectorate (1998a) *Messages for Managers: Learning the Lessons from Joint Reviews of Social Services*, Audit Commission, London.

Audit Commission for England and Wales and Department of Health Social Services Inspectorate (1998b) *North Yorkshire: A Report of the Review of Social Services in North Yorkshire County Council*, Audit Commission, London.

Audit Commission and Department of Health Social Services Inspectorate (1999) *A Report of the Joint Review of Social Services in Gateshead Metropolitan Borough*, Audit Commission, London.

Audit Commission for England and Wales, Department of Health Social Services Inspectorate, and National Assembly for Wales (1999) *Making Connections: Learning from Joint Reviews, 1998/9*, Audit Commission, London.

Audit Inspectorate (1983) *Social Services: Provision of Care for the Elderly*, HMSO, London.

Auditor General (1988) *First Triennial Review of the Home and Community Care Program: Final Report of the Home and Community Care Working Group*, Australian Government Publication Service, Canberra, ACT.

Baldock, J. and Evers, A. (1992) Innovations and care of the elderly: the cutting edge of change for social welfare systems. Examples from Sweden, the Netherlands and the United Kingdom, *Ageing and Society*, 12, 3, 289-312.

Bandura, A. (1997) *Self-Efficacy: The Exercise of Control*, Freeman, New York.

Banerjee, S. (1993) Prevalence and recognition rates of psychiatric disorder in the elderly clients of a local authority community care service, *International Journal of Geriatric Psychiatry*, 8, 125-131.

Banerjee, S. and MacDonald, A. (1996) Mental disorder in an elderly home care population: associations with health and social service use, *British Journal of Psychiatry*, 168, 750-756.

Banerjee, S., Shamash, K., Macdonald, A., and Mann A. H. (1996) Randomised controlled trial of effect of intervention by psychogeriatric team on depression in frail elderly people at home, *British Medical Journal*, 313, 1058-1061.

Barclay Committee (1982) *The Role and Task of Social Workers*, Bedford Square Press, London.

Barnes, M., Harrison, S., Mort, M. and Shardlow, P. (1999) *Unequal Partners: User Groups and Community Care*, The Policy Press, Bristol.

Bauld, L., Chesterman, J., Davies, B., Judge, K. and Mangalore, R. (1998) Informal and formal inputs for older people: services and costs in post-reform community care, Discussion Paper 1449, PSSRU, University of Kent at Canterbury.

Bauld, L., Chesterman, J., Davies, B., Judge, K. and Mangalore, R. (2000) *Caring for Older People: An Assessment of Community Care in the 1990s*, Ashgate, Aldershot.

Baume, P., Isaacson, B. and Hunt, J. (1993) Perceptions of unmet need in four community services for elderly people, *Australian Journal of Public Health*, 17, 3, 267-8.

Bebbington, A.C. (1977) Scaling indices of disablement, *British Journal of Preventive and Social Medicine*, 31, 122-126.

Bebbington, A. and Davies, B. (1983) Equity and efficiency in the allocation of the personal social services, *Journal of Social Policy*, 12, 3, 309-330.

Bebbington, A. and Davies, B. (1993) Efficient targeting of community care: the case of home help service, *Journal of Social Policy*, 22, 3, 373-391.

Bebbington, A. and Quine, L. (1986) A Comment on Hirst's Evaluating the Malaise Inventory, *Social Psychiatry*, 22, 5-7.

Bebbington, A., Brown, P., Darton, R. and Netten, A. (1996) Survey of admissions to residential care: SSA analysis report, Discussion Paper 1217/3, PSSRU, University of Kent at Canterbury.

Becker, G. (1964) *Human Capital*, Columbia University Press, New York.

Beecham, J. and Netten, A. (1993) *Community Care in Action: The Role of Costs*, PSSRU, University of Kent at Canterbury.

Benjamin, A.E., Doty, P., Matthias, R., Franks, T., Mills, L., Hasenfeld, Y., Matras, L., Park, E., Stoddard, S. and Kraus, L. (1998) *Comparing Client-Directed and Agency Models for Providing Supportive Services at Home*, Department of Social Welfare, UCLA, Los Angeles.

Bézat, J-M. (1999) M. Jospin n'exclut pas de faire tomber le tabou de la retraite à 60 ans, *Le Monde*, 29 January 1999, 8.

Blau, P.M. and Scott, W.R. (1956) *Formal Organisations: A Comparative Approach*, Routledge, London.

Bocquet, H., Berthier, F. and Grand, A. (1994). L'aide apportée aux personnes âgées dépendantes par les épouses, les filles et les belles-filles, *Santé Publique*, 235-248.

Bocquet, H., Berthier, F., and Pous, J. (1996). Rôle et charge des aidants de personnes âgées dépendantes, in Henrard, J.-C., Clément and Derrienic, F., *Vieillissement, Santé, Société*, INSERM, Paris, 125-148.

Bonoli, G. and Palier, B. (1996) Reclaiming welfare: politics of reform of social protection in France, in M. Rhodes (ed.) *Southern European Welfare States: Between Crisis and Reform*, Francis Cass, London.

Bouget, D., Tartarin, R., Frossard, M., and Tripier, P. (eds) (1990) *Le prix de la dépendance: comparaison des dépenses des personnes âgées selon leurs modes d'hébergement*, La Documentation Française, Paris.

Boulding, K.E. (1973) *The Economy of Love and Fear*, Wandsworth, California.

Brody, E.M. and Schoonover, C.B. (1986) Patterns of parent-care when adult daughters work and when they do not, *The Gerontologist*, 26, 372-381.

Brown, R. and Phillips, B. (1986) *The Effects of Case Management and Community Services on the Impaired Elderly*, Mathematica Policy Research, Princeton, New Jersey.

Carr, P. and Selby, S.A. (1998) The Darlington service: past, present and future, in D. Challis, R. Darton and K. Stewart (eds) *Community Care, Secondary Health Care and Care Management*, PSSRU Studies, Ashgate, Aldershot, 57-72.

Chadda, D. (1999) Rising costs closing care homes, *Community Care*, 15-21 July, 8-9.

Challis, D. (1994) Case management: a review of UK developments and issues, in M. Titterton (ed.) *Caring for People in the Community: The New Welfare*, Jessica Kingsley, London.

Challis, D., Carpenter, I. and Traske, K. (1996) *Assessment in Continuing Care Homes: Towards a National Standard Instrument*, PSSRU, University of Kent at Canterbury.

Challis, D., Darton, R., Hughes, J., Stewart, K. and Weiner, K. (1998) Care management study: report on national data, mapping and evaluation of care management arrangements for older people and those with mental health problems, Department of Health, London.

Challis, D., Chessum, R., Chesterman, J., Luckett, R. and Traske, K. (1990) *Case Management in Social and Health Care: the Gateshead Community Care Scheme*, PSSRU, University of Kent at Canterbury.

Challis, D., Darton, R. and Stewart, K. (1998) *Community Care, Secondary Health Care and Care Management*, Ashgate, Aldershot.

Challis, D., Darton, R., Johnson, L., Stone, M. and Traske, K. (1995) *Care Management and Health Care of Older People: The Darlington Community Care Project*, Arena, Aldershot.

Challis, D. and Davies, B. (1991) Improving support to carers: A response, *Ageing and Society*, 11, 69-73.

Challis, D. and Davies, B.P. (1986) *Case Management in Community Care*, Gower, Aldershot.

Chipperfield, J.G. (1993) Perceived barriers in coping with health problems: a twelve-year longitudinal study of survival among elderly individuals, *Journal of Aging and Health*, 5, 123-139.

Clark, D. (1994) *Supported Housing in Rural Areas*, HACT, London.

Clark, D. and Maddox, G. (1994) *A Replication of Dimensions of ADL Functioning and Application to Estimating Prevalence*, Long-Term Care Resources Program, Duke University, Durham, NC.

Clark, H., Dyer, S. and Horwood, J. (1998) *That Bit of Help: The High Value of Low Level Preventative Services for Older People*, Policy Press, Clifton.

Cohen, C.A., Gold, D.P., Shulman, K., Wortley, J., MacDonald, G. and Wargon, M. (1993) Factors determining the decision to institutionalise dementing individuals, *The Gerontologist*, 33, 6, 714-720.

Coopers and Lybrand Consulting Group (1994) *Alberta Health: Home Care Classification (HCCC) System: Final Report*, Alberta Health, Home Care, Community Long-Term Care, Edmonton, Alberta.

Craig, G. and Manthorpe, J. (1999) Unequal partners? Local government reorganisation and the voluntary sector, *Social Policy and Administration*, 33, 55-72.

Craig, G. and Mayo, M. (eds) (1995) *Community Empowerment: a Reader in Participation and Development*, Zed Books, London.

Culyer, A.J., Lavers, R. and Williams, A. (1971) Social indicators: health, *Social Trends*, 2, 31-42.

Davies, B.P. (1968) *Social Needs and Resources in Local Services*, Michael Joseph, London.

Davies, B.P. (1971) *Planning Resources for Personal Social Services: the James Seth Memorial Lecture*, Department of Social Administration, University of Edinburgh, Edinburgh.

Davies, B.P. (1976) The measurement of needs and the allocation of grant, in *Local Government Finance:* Appendix 10 to the Report of the Committee of Inquiry under the Chairmanship of Frank Layfield, Cm 6543, HMSO, London.

Davies, B.P. (1977) Needs and outputs, in H. Heisler (ed.) *Fundamentals of Social Administration*, Macmillan, London.

Davies, B.P. (1978) *Universality, Selectivity and Effectiveness in Social Policy*, Heinemann, London.

Davies, B.P. (1981a) A Policy accident and the regulatory response: an historical study of the developement of policy, procedures, tools, and practice in the the reimbursement and regulation of nursing and rest homes in the US 1966-1980, Discussion Paper 165, PSSRU, University of Kent at Canterbury.

Davies, B.P. (1981b) Strategic goals and piecemeal innovations: adjusting to the new balance of needs and resources, in E.M. Goldberg and S. Hatch (eds) *A New Look at the Personal Social Services*, Policy Studies Institute, London.

Davies, B.P. (1985) The production of welfare approach: state of the art and future directions, Discussion Paper 400, PSSRU, University of Kent at Canterbury.

Davies, B.P. (1986a) American lessons for British policy research on long-term care of the elderly, *Quarterly Journal of Social Affairs*, 2, 3, 321-355.

Davies, B.P. (1986b) American experiments to substitute home for institutional long-term care: policy logic and evaluation, in C. Phillipson, M. Bernard and P. Strang (eds) *Dependency and Interdependency in Old Age: Theoretical Perspectives and Policy Alternatives*, Croom Helm, Beckenham, Kent.

Davies, B.P. (1987a) Equity and efficiency in community care: supply and financing in an age of fiscal austerity, *Ageing and Society*, 7, 2, 161-174.

Davies, B.P (1987b) Allocation of services in England: facts and myths and the equity and efficiency of social care services, *Revue d'Epidemiologie et de Santé Publique*, 35, 17-26.

Davies, B.P. (1988) Making a reality of community care: a critique of the Audit Commission Report, *British Journal of Social Work*, 18, supplement, 173-188.

Davies, B.P. (1989) Why we must fight the eighth deadly sin: parochialism, *Journal of Aging and Social Policy*, 1, 217-236.

Davies, B.P. (1992a) *Care Management, Equity and Efficiency: The International Experience*, PSSRU, University of Kent at Canterbury.

Davies, B.P. (1992b) Case management and the social services: on breeding the best chameleons, *Generations Review*, 2, 2, 18-22.

Davies, B.P. (1992c) On resources, needs and outcomes: why academic caution is practically useful, in K. Morgan (ed.) *Gerontology: Responding to an Ageing Society*, Jessica Kingsley, London.

Davies, B.P. (1993a) On the sensitivity of needs estimates to targeting criteria, *International Journal of Health Sciences*, 4, 4, 15-25.

Davies, B.P. (1993b) Division of labour and home care in England, in J. Rogers Hollingsworth and E.J. Hollingsworth (eds) *Care of the Chronically and Severely Ill: Comparative Social Policies*, Aldine de Gruyter, New York.

Davies, B.P. (1993c) La réforme des soins communautaires: création et mise en oeuvre d'une politique nationale, *Gérontologie et Société*, 67, 113-126.

Davies, B.P. (1994) Maintaining the pressure in community care reform, *Social Policy and Administration*, 28, 197-205.

Davies, B.P. (1995) Case management for elderly people: the Kent community care project [the 'KCCP'] and its descendants in their international context, *Hong Kong Journal of Gerontology*, 9, 1, 33-43.

Davies, B.P. (1997a) Equity and efficiency in community care: from muddle to model: from model to ?, *Policy and Politics*, 25, 4, 337-359.

Davies, B.P. (1997b) On the reduction in efficiency and effectiveness due to missed rehabilitative opportunities among users of community social services for elderly people, Discussion Paper 1348, PSSRU, University of Kent at Canterbury.

Davies, B.P. (1998) Shelter with care and community reforms, in R. Jack (ed.) *Residential Versus Community Care: The Role of Institutions in Welfare Provision*, Macmillan, London.

Davies, B.P. (1999) Social welfare and economics: lessons of the reforms of British community care for elderly people, *Journal of the [Japanese] Institute of Health Administrators*, 1999, 1, 87-95. (In Japanese)

Davies, B.P. and Baines, B.J. (1991a) On life-time costs and targeting: effects of current case management practice on future resource commitments with entropic assumptions about productivities, Discussion Paper 738, PSSRU, University of Kent of Canterbury.

Davies, B.P. and Baines, B.J. (1991b) Discounted present values of costs to social services departments through time of home care and residential care of persons admitted from home care, Discussion Paper 739, PSSRU, University of Kent at Canterbury.

Davies, B.P. and Baines, B.J. (1992) On the silting up of SSD resources and the stability of need states in a cohort of new recipients of community-based social services, Discussion paper 815, PSSRU, University of Kent at Canterbury.

Davies, B.P. and Baines, B. (1994) Attitudes to residential care and the subsequent probability of admission: experience of a cohort of new users of community-based social services, in D. Challis, B.P. Davies and K. Traske (eds) *Community Care in the UK and Overseas: New Agendas and Challenges*, Ashgate, Aldershot.

Davies, B.P. and Challis, D. (1980) Experimenting with new roles in domiciliary service: the Kent Community Care Project, *The Gerontologist*, 20, 288-299.

Davies, B.P. and Challis, D. (1986) *Matching Resources to Needs in Community Care: An Evaluated Demonstration of a Long-Term Care Model*, PSSRU Studies, Gower, Aldershot.

Davies, B.P. and Chesterman, J. (2000) *Budget-Devolved Care Management in Two Routine Programmes*, Ashgate, Aldershot, forthcoming.

Davies, B.P. and Ferlie, E.B. (1982) Efficiency promoting innovations in social care, SSDs and the elderly, *Policy and Politics*, 10, 181-205.

Davies, B.P. and Ferlie, E.B. (1984) Patterns of efficiency improving innovations: Social care and the elderly, *Policy and Politics*, 12, 3, 281-95.

Davies, B.P. and Fernández, J.L. (1997) On the sensitivity of proportions of SSD recipients of community social services excluded and cost to variations in qualifying levels of eligibility, Discussion Paper 1341, PSSRU, London School of Economics and University of Kent at Canterbury.

Davies, B.P., Fernández, J.L. and Saunders, R. (1998) *Community Care in England and France: Reforms and the Improvement of Equity and Efficiency*, Ashgate, Aldershot.

Davies, B.P. and Knapp, M. (1979) *Old People's Homes and the Production of Welfare*, Routledge, London.

Davies, B.P. and Knapp, M. (1988) Costs and residential social care, in I. Sinclair (ed.) *Residential Care: The Research Reviewed*, HMSO, London.

Davies, B.P. and Fernández, J.L. (2000) *Needs-Led or Resource-Driven*, Ashgate, Aldershot, forthcoming.

Davies, B.P., Baines, B.J. and Chesterman, J.F. (1996) The effects of care management on efficiency in long-term care: a new evaluation model applied to British and American data, pages 87-101 in J. Phillips and B. Penhale (eds) *Reviewing Care Management for Older People*, Jessica Kingsley, London.

Davies, B.P., Bebbington, A., Charnley, H. with Baines, B., Ferlie, E., Hughes, M. and Twigg, J. (1990) *Resources, Needs and Outcomes in Community-Based Care: a Comparative Study of the Production of Welfare for Elderly People in Ten Local Authorities in England and Wales*, PSSRU Studies, Gower, Aldershot

Davies, B.P., Chesterman, J. and Fernández, J.L. (1995) Implications of unmet need (UM), welfare gains, (G) and gain/cost (G/C) bases for targeting criteria, Discussion paper 1167, PSSRU, University of Kent at Canterbury.

Davies, B.P., Fernández, J.L. and Nomer, B. (2000) *Needs, Processes and Service Packages: Post-Reform Community Care at the Case Management Level*, PSSRU, University of Kent at Canterbury, forthcoming.

Davies, B.P., Fernández, J.L., and Saunders, R. (1998) *Community Care in England and France: Reforms and the Improvement of Equity and Efficiency*, PSSRU Studies, Arena, Aldershot.

Davies, B., and Warburton, R. (1996) Post-reform community care for elderly people: who gets how much of what service, *Care Plan*, 3, 2, 25-30.

Davies, B., Fernández, J-L., Milne, A. and Warburton, R. (1995) Do different case management approaches affect who gets what? Preliminary results from a comparative British study, *Care Plan*, 2, 2, 26-30.

Dearlove, J. (1973) *The Politics of Policy in Local Government*, Cambridge University Press, Cambridge.

Dechaux, J.-H. (1994) Les échanges dans la parenté accentuent-ils les inégalités? *Sociétés contemporaines*, 17, 75-90.

Department of the Environment, Transport and Regions (1998) *Modernising Local Government: In Touch with People, Cm 4014*, TSO, London.

Department of Health (1989) *Caring for People: Community Care in the Next Decade and Beyond, Cm 849*, HMSO, London.

Department of Health (1997a) *Better Services for Vulnerable People, EL(97)62, CI(97)24*, Department of Health, London.

Department of Health (1997b) *The New NHS: Modern, Dependable, Cm 380*, TSO, London.

Department of Health (1998a) *Modernising Health and Social Services: National Priorities Guidance 1999/00-2001/02*, Department of Health, London.

Department of Health (1998b) *Modernising Social Services, Cm 4169*, TSO, London.

Department of Health (1999a) *Caring about Carers: A National Strategy for Carers*, TSO, London.

Department of Health (1999b) *Promoting Independence: Partnership, Prevention and Carers Grants: Conditions and Allocations 1999/2000; LAC (99)13*, Department of Health, London.

Department of Health (1999c) *Promoting Independence: Preventative Strategies and Support for Adults: LAC (99)14*, Department of Health, London.

Department of Health and for the Environment (1995) *Building Partnerships for Success: Community Care Development Programmes*, Department of Health, London.

Department of Health and Social Security (1987) *From Home Help to Home Care: An Analysis of Policy, Resourcing and Service Management*, Social Services Inspectorate, DHSS, London.

Department of Health and Social Security (1991) *Care Management and Assessment: Managers' Guide*, HMSO, London.

Department of Health Social Services Inspectorate (1996) *Progress through Change: Fifth Annual Report of the Chief Inspector of Social Services*, HMSO, London.

Department of Health Social Services Inspectorate (1997) *Facing the Future: Seventh Annual Report of the Chief Inspector of Social Services*, TSO, London.

Department of Health Social Services Inspectorate (1999a) *That's the Way the Money Goes: Inspection of Commissioning Arrangements for Community Care Services*, Department of Health, London.

Department of Health Social Services Inspectorate (1999b) *Modern Social Services: A Commitment to Improve: Eighth Annual Report of the Chief Inspector Social Services Inspectorate 1998/99*, TSO, London.

Department of Health Social Services Inspectorate and Audit Commission (1998) *Messages for Managers: Learning the Lessons from Joint Reviews of Social Services*, Audit Commission Publications, Abingdon.

Department of Health, Education and Welfare (1980) *Request for Proposals RFP-74-80-HEW-OS: National Long-Term Care Channeling Demonstration*, Division of Contract and Grant Operations, Department of Health, Education and Welfare, Washington, DC.

Department of Health, Housing and Community Services, Aged and Community Care Division (1992) *It's Your Choice: National Evaluation of the Community Options Projects*, Aged and Community Care Evaluation Series number 2, AGPS, Canberra.

Dilnot, A. and Kell, M. (1987) Male unemployment and women's work, *Fiscal Studies*, 8, 1-16.

Dobson, F. (1999) Frank Dobson sets out long-run vision promoting independence, Press release 1999/0338, 8 June, Department of Health, London.

Doeringer, P.B. and Piore, M.J. (1975) Unemployment and the 'dual labour market', *Public Interest*, 38, 67-79.

Doty, P., Jackson, M.E., and Crown, W. (1998) The impact of female caregivers' employment status on patterns of formal and informal eldercare, *The Gerontologist*, 38, 3, 331-341.

Doty, P., Kasper, J. and Litvak, S. (1996) Consumer-directed models of personal care: lessons from Medicaid, *The Milbank Quarterly*, 74, 3, 377-409.

Eggert, G.M. (1990) *The ACCESS Experience: What we Have Learned*, MLTCP, Rochester, New York.

Eggert, G.M., Bowlyow, J.E. and Nichols, C.W. (1980) Gaining control of the long-term care system: first returns from the ACCESS experiment, *The Gerontologist*, 20, 3, 356-363.

Estes, C.L., Swan, J.H. and associates (1993) *The Long-Term Care Crisis: Elders Trapped in the No-Care Zone*, Sage, London.

Farrell, M. (1957) The measurement of productive efficiency, *Journal of the Royal Statistical Society*, A, 120.

Ferlie, E.B., Challis, D.J. and Davies, B. (1989) *Efficiency-Improving Innovations in Social Care of the Elderly*, Gower, Aldershot.

Fernández, J.L. (1997) Results of tests of bias in the ECCEP sample, Discussion paper 1362, PSSRU, University of Kent at Canterbury.

Fillenbaum, G. (1978) *Validity and Reliability of the Mulitdimensional Functional Assessment Questionnaire: the OARS Methodology*, Duke University, North Carolina.

Finch, J. (1995) *Family Obligations and Social Change*, Polity, Cambridge.

Fine, M. and Thompson, C. (1995) *Factors Affecting the Outcomes of Community Care Service Interventions: a Literature Review*, Service Development and Evaluation Reports, Aged and Community Care Division, DHSS, AGPS, Canberra.

Ford, J., Quilgars, D. and Rugg, J. (1998) *Creating Jobs: The Employment Potential of Domiciliary Care*, Joseph Rowntree Foundation, York.

Freedman, V.A. (1996) Family structure and the risk of nursing home admission, *Journal of Gerontology: Social Sciences*, 51B, 2, S61-9.

Freiman, M. and Brown, E. (1999) *Special Care Units in Nursing Homes: Selected Characteristics 1996*, Agency for Health Care Policy and Research MEPS Research Findings 6, AHCPR, Rockville, Maryland.

Frossard, M. and Boitard, A. (1995) *Evaluations économique de la coordination gérontologique*, Fondation de France, Paris.

Fuss, M. and McFadden D. (1978) *Production Economics: A Dual Approach to Theory and Applications*, North Holland Publishing, Amsterdam.

Glass, T.A. (1998) Conjugating the 'tenses' of function: discordance, among hypothetical, experimental and enacted function in older adults, *The Gerontologist*, 38, 1, 101-112.

Goddard, M., McDonagh, M., and Smith, D. (1999) *Acute Hospital Care: Final Report*, Centre for Health Economics, University of York, York.

Goldberg, E.M. (1970) *Helping the Aged*, George Allen and Unwin, London.

Goldberg, E.M. and Connelly, N. (1982) *The Effectiveness of Social Care of the Elderly: An Overview of Recent and Current Evaluative Research*, Heinemann, London.

Goldberg, E.M. and Warburton, R.W. (1976) *Ends and Means in Social Work*, Allen and Unwin, London.

Gostick, C., Davies, B., Lawson, R. and Salter, C. (1997) *From Vision to Reality in Community Care: Changing Direction at the Local Level*, Arena, Aldershot.

Gouldner, A. (1960) The norm of reciprocity: a preliminary statement, *American Sociological Review*, 25, 161-178.

Graaf, J.V. (1957)*Theoretical Welfare Economics*, Cambridge University Press, Cambridge.

Grand, A. (1991) Modes de socialisation et handicap dans une population âgée en milieu rural, *Cahiers du CTNERHI*, 55-6, 73-85.

Grannemann, T.W., Grossman, J.B., Dunstan, S.M. (1986) *Differential Impacts among Subgroups of Early Channeling Enrollees*, Mathematica Policy Research, Princeton, New Jersey.

Greene, V., Lovely, M.E. and Ondrich, J.I. (1993a) Do community-based, long-term care services reduce nursing home use? A transition probability analysis, *Journal of Human Resources*, 28, 297-318.

Greene, V., Lovely, M.E., and Ondrich, J.I. (1993b) The cost-effectiveness of community services in a frail elderly population, *The Gerontologist*, 33, 177-190.

Greene, V.L., Lovely, M.E., Miller, M. and Ondrich, J.I. (1989) *Reducing Nursing Home Use Through Community-Based Long-Term Care: An Optimisation Analysis*, Maxwell School of Citizenship and Public Affairs, Syracruse University, Syracruse, New York.

Greene, W. (1993) *Econometric Analysis*, Prentice Hall, New Jersey.

Greenwood, R. (1978) Politics and public bureaucracies: a reconsideration, *Policy and Politics*, 6, 403-420.

Greenwood, R. and Hining, C. (1976) Contingency theory and public bureaucracies, *Policy and Politics*, 5, 159-180.

Greenwood, R., Hining, C.R. and Ranson, S. (1977) The politics of budgetary process in English local government, *Political Studies*, 25, 1, 25-47.

Griffiths, R. (1988) *Community Care: Agenda for Action*, HMSO, London.

Hadley, R. and McGrath, M. (1984) *When Social Services are Local*, Allen and Unwin, London.

Harding, T. (1999) Enabling older people to live in their own homes, in M. Henwood and G. Wistow (eds) *With Respect to Old Age: Long Term Care — Rights and Responsibilities: Community Care and Informal Care; Research Volume III*, a report of the Royal Commission on Long Term Care, Cm 4192-II, TSO, London.

Harris, A. (1971) *Handicapped and Impaired in Great Britain*, HMSO, London.

Hasenfeld, Y. (1983) *Human Service Organisations*, Prentice Hall, Englewood Cliffs, New Jersey.

Henderson, J.M. and Quandt, R.E. (1971) *Micro-Economic Theory: a Mathematical Approach*, McGraw Hill Kogakusha, Tokyo.

Henrard, J.C. (1992) *Les systèmes d'aides aux personnes âgées*, Documentation Française, Paris.

Henrard, J.C., Cassou, B. and Le Disert, D. (1990) The effects of system characteristics on policy implementation and functioning of care for the elderly in France, *International Journal of Health Services*, 20, 1, 125-139.

Henwood, M. and Wistow, G. (1999) Evaluating the impact of caring for people, in Royal Commission on Long Term Care, *With Respect to Old Age: Long Term Care — Rights and Responsibilities: Community Care and Informal Care*, Cm 4192-II/3, Research Volume III, TSO, London.

Herzog, A.R., Franks, M.M., Markus, H.R. and Holmberg, D. (1998) Activities and well-being in older age: effects of self-concept and educational attainment, *Psychology and Aging*, 13, 179-185.

HM Treasury and Cabinet Office (1998) *Modern Public Services for Britain: Investing in Reform, Cm 4011*, TSO, London.

Horowitz, A. (1985) Sons and daughters as caregivers to older people, *The Gerontologist*, 25, 6, 612-617.

House of Commons Health Committee (1996) *Third Report: Long-Term Care: Future Provision and Funding*, HC 1995-96 59-II, Q352, TSO, London.

Hutton, J.B.F. and Kerkstra, A. (1996) *Home care in Europe: a Country-Specific Guide to its Organisation and Financing*, Arena, Aldershot.

Intrator, O., Castle, N.G. and Mor, V. (1999) Facility characteristics associated with hospitalization of nursing home residents, *Medical Care*, 37, 228-237.

Intriligator, M., Bodkin, R. and Hsiao, C. (1996) *Econometric Models, Techniques, and Applications*, 2nd ed., Prentice Hall International, London.

Isaacs, B., Livingstone, M. and Neville, Y. (1972) *Survival of the Unfittest*, Routledge and Kegan Paul, London.

Jette, A. (1994) How measurement techniques influence estimates of disability in older populations, *Social Science and Medicine*, 38, 937-942.

Jette, A.M., Tennstedt, S.L. and Branch, L.G. (1992) Stability of informal long-term care, *Journal of Aging and Health*, 4, 193-211.

Johnston, J. (1963) *Econometric Methods*, McGraw Hill, New York.

Joseph Rowntree Foundation Inquiry (1996) *Meeting the Cost of Continuing Care: Report and Recommendations*, Joseph Rowntree Foundation, York.

Jowell, T. and Wistow, G. (1989) Consumers: give them a voice, *Insight*, 28, February, 22-24.

Kane, R.A. (1995) Expanding the home care concept: blurring distinctions among home care, institutional care and other long-term care services, *The Milbank Quarterly*, 73, 2, 161-186.

Katzman, R., Brown, T., Fuld, P., Peck, A, Schechter, R. and Schimmel, H. (1983) Validation of a short orientation-memory-concentration test of cognitive impairment, *American Journal of Psychiatry*, 140, 734-739.

Kelly, A. (1989) An end to incrementalism? The impact of expenditure restraints on social services budgets 1979-86, *Journal of Social Policy*, 18, 2, 187-210.

Kelly-Hayes, M., Jette, A.M., Wolf, P.A., D'Agostino, R.B. and Odell, P.M. (1992) Functional limitations and disability among elders in the Framingham study, *American Journal of Public Health*, 82, 841-45.

Kemper, P., Applebaum, R. and Harrigan, M. (1987) Community care demonstrations: what have we learned?, *Health Care Financing Review*, 8, 87-100.

Killingsworth, M.R. (1983) *Labour Supply*, Cambridge University Press, London.

Klein, R. (1995) Self-inventing institutions: institutional design and the UK welfare state, in R.E. Goodin (ed.) *The Theory of Institutional Design*, Cambridge University Press.

Knapp, M. (1984) *The Economics of Social Care*, Macmillan, London.

Koutsoyannis, A. (1979) *Modern Microeconomics*, 2nd ed., Macmillan, London.

Kosberg, J.I. (1996) *The Consequence of Care Index: Form A*, School of Social Work, Florida International University, North Miami, Florida.

Kosberg, J.I. and Cairl, R.E. (1986) The Cost of Care Index, *The Gerontologist*, 26, 273-278.

Kosberg, J.I., Cairl, R.E., and Keller, D.M. (1990) Components of burden: interventive implications, *The Gerontologist*, 30, 236-242.

Kraan, R.J., Baldock, J., Davies, B., Evers, A., Johansson, L., Knapen, M., Thorslund (1991) *Care for the Elderly: Significant Innovations in Three European Countries*, Campus Westview, Frankfurt and New York.

Krause, N. (1987) Chronic strain, locus of control and distress in older adults, *Psychology and Aging*, 2, 375-382.

Krivo, L.J. and Chaatsmith, M.L. (1990) Social services impact on elderly independent living, *Social Science Quarterly*, 71, 3, 474-491.

Langer, E.J. and Rodin, J. (1976) The effects of choice and enhanced personal responsibility for the aged: a field experiment in an institutional setting, *Journal of Personality and Social Psychology*, 34, 191-8.

Latham, M. (1994) *Constructing the Team: Final Report of the Government/Industry Review of Procurement and Contractual Arrangements in the UK Construction Industry*, HMSO, London.

Lawton, M. (1975) The Philadelphia Geriatric Center Morale Scale: a revision, *Journal of Gerontology*, 30, 85-9.

Lawton, M.P., Moss, M., Hoffman, C., Grant, R., Have, T.T. and Kleban, M. (1999) Health, valuation and the wish to live, *The Gerontologist*, 39, 406-416.

Le Grand, J. (1999) Britain: competition, cooperation or control?, *Health Affairs*, 18, 3, 27-39.

Leibenstein, H. (1966) Allocative efficiency versus x-efficiency, *American Economic Review*, 56, 3, 392-415.

Leibenstein, H. (1976) *Beyond Economic Man: A New Foundation for Microeconomics*, Harvard University Press, Cambridge, Massachusetts.

Leibenstein, H. (1979) A branch of economics is missing: micro-macro theory, *Journal of Economic Literature*, 17, 2, 477-502.

Leontief, W.W. (1951) *The Structure of the American Economy, 1919-1939*, Oxford University Press, New York.

Leutz, W.N. (1999) Five laws for integrating medical and social services: lessons from the United States and the United Kingdom, *The Milbank Quarterly*, 77, 77-110.

Levin, E., Moriarty, J. and Gorbach, P. (1994) *Better for the Break*, HMSO, London.

Levin, E., Sinclair, I. and Gorbach, P. (1989) *Families, Services and Confusion in Old Age*, Avebury, Aldershot.

Lewis, H., Fletcher, P., Hardy, B., Milne, A. and Waddington, E. (1999) *Promoting Well-Being: Developing a Preventative Approach with Older People*, Anchor Trust, Oxford.

Lewis, J. and Glennerster, H. (1996) *Implementing the New Community Care*, Open University Press, Buckingham.

Lieberman, M.A. and Fisher, L. (1995) The impact of chronic illness on the health and well being of family members, *The Gerontologist*, 35, 1, 94-102.

Lindblom, C.E. (1965) *The Intelligence of Democracy: Decision-making through Mutual Adjustment*, The Free Press, New York.

Litwak, E. (1965) Extended kin relations in an industrial society, in E. Shanas and G. Streib (eds) *Social Structure and the Family: Generational Relations*, Prentice-Hall, Englewood Cliffs, New Jersey.

Liu, K. and Manton, K.G. (1984) The characteristics and utilization pattern of an admission cohort of nursing home patients: II, *The Gerontologist*, 24, 70-76.

Liu, K., Manton, K.G. and Liu, B.M. (1990) Morbidity, disability, and long-term care of the elderly: implications for insurance financing, *The Milbank Quarterly*, 68, 445-492.

Manton, K. (1988) A longitudinal study of functional change and mortality in the United States, *The Journal of Gerontology*, 43, S153-S161.

Manton, K., Corder, L. and Stallard, E. (1993a) Estimates of change in chronic disability and institutional incidence and prevalence rates in the U.S. elderly population from the 1982, 1984, and 1989 National Long Term Care Survey, *Journal of Gerontology*, 48, 4, S153-S166.

Manton, K., Vertrees, J. and Clark, R. (1993b) A multivariate analysis of disability and health and its change over time in the National Channeling Demonstration Data, *The Gerontologist*, 33, 610-618.

Mathematica Policy Research (1980) *A Proposal to Conduct an Evaluation of the National Long-term Care Channeling Demonstration*, Mathematica Policy Research, Princeton, New Jersey.

Mathematica Policy Research (1982a) *National Long-Term Care Demonstration: Clinical Assessment and Research Baseline Instrument*, Mathematica Policy Research, Princeton, New Jersey.

Mathematica Policy Research (1982b) *National Long-Term Care Demonstration: Follow-up Instrument*, Mathematica Policy Research, Princeton, New Jersey.

Means, R. (1997) Home independence and community care: time for a wider vision, *Policy and Politics*, 25, 405-419.

Menec, V.H. and Chipperfield, J.G. (1997a) The interactive effect of perceived control and functional status on health and mortality among young-old and old-old adults, *Journal of Gerontology: Social Sciences*, 52B, S118-S126.

Menec, V.H. and Chipperfield, J.G. (1997b) Remaining active in later life: the role of locus of control in seniors' leisure activity participation, health and life satisfaction, *Journal of Aging and Health*, 9, 105-125.

Miller, B. and Cafasso, L. (1992) Gender differences in caregiving: fact or artifact?, *The Gerontologist*, 32, 498-507.

Monk, A. and Cox, C. (1989) International innovations in home care, *Ageing International*, December, 11-19.

Morris Committee (1994) *Home but not Alone: Report on the Home and Community Care Program*, Australian Parliament, House of Representatives, Standing Committee on Community Affairs, Morris, A. (Chair), AGPS, Canberra.

Morris, J.N. and Sherwood, S. (1975) A re-testing and modification of the PGC Morale Scale, *Journal of Gerontology* , 30, 78-84.

Mukamel, D.B. (1997) Risk-adjusted outcome measures and quality of care in nursing homes, *Medical Care*, 35, 6, 804-816.

Neal, M.B., Ingersoll-Dayton, B. and Starrells, M.E. (1997) Gender relationship differences in caregiving patterns and consequences among employed caregivers, *The Gerontologist*, 37, 6, 804-816.

Netten, A. and Beecham, J. (1993) *Costing Community Care: Theory and Practice*, PSSSRU Studies, Ashgate, Aldershot.

Netten, A. and Davies, B. (1991) The social production of welfare and the consumption of social services, *Journal of Public Policy*, 10, 331-347.

Netten, A. and Dennett, J. (1995) *Unit Costs of Community Care 1995*, PSSRU, University of Kent at Canterbury.

Netten, A. and Dennett, J. (1996) *Unit Costs of Health and Social Care 1996*, PSSRU, University of Kent at Canterbury.

Netten, A. and Dennett, J. (1997) *Unit Costs of Health and Social Care 1997*, PSSRU, University of Kent at Canterbury.

Netten, A., Dennett, J. and Knight, J. (1998) *Unit Costs of Health and Social Care 1998*, PSSRU, University of Kent at Canterbury.

Netten, A., Dennett, J. and Knight, J. (1999) *Unit Costs of Health and Social Care 1999*, PSSRU, University of Kent at Canterbury.

Nocon, A. and Baldwin, S. (1998) *Trends in Rehabilitation Policy: A Review of the Literature*, King's Fund, London.

Nocon, A. and Qureshi, H. (1996) *Outcomes of Community Care for Users and Carers. A Social Services Perspective*, Open University Press, Buckingham.

Noonan, A.E and Tennstedt, S.L. (1997) Meaning in caregiving and its contribution to caregiving wellbeing, *The Gerontologist*, 30, 5, 583-594.

Oldman, C. and Field, J. (1997) *The Provision of Housing and Community Care in Rural Scotland*, Scottish Office, Edinburgh.

Pareto, V. (1971) *Manual of Political Economy*, Kelly, New York.

Parker, G. (1990) Whose care? Whose costs? Whose benefit? A critical review of research on case management and informal care, *Ageing and Society*, 10, 459-467.

Parsloe, P. and Stevenson, O. (1978) *Social Services Teams: the Practitioners' View*, HMSO, London.

Partnership Sourcing Limited (1992) *Partnership Sourcing*, London.

Patrick, D.L., Darby, S.C., Green, S., Horton, G., Locker, D. and Wiggins, R.D. (1981) Screening for disability in the inner city, *Journal of Epidemiology and Community Health*, 36, 65-70.

Peace, S., Kellaher, L. and Wilcocks, D. (1997) *Re-evaluating Residential Care*, Open University Press, Buckingham.

Pearlin, L.I., Mullan, J.T., Semple, S.J. and Skaff, M.M. (1990) Caregiving and the stress process: an overview of concepts and their measures, *The Gerontologist*, 30, 5, 583-594.

Phillipson, C. (1992) Challenging 'the spectre of old age': community care for older people in the 1990's, in N. Manning and R. Page (eds) *Social Policy Yearbook*, Plenum Press, London.

Pruchno, R.A., Michaels, J.E. and Potashnic, S.L. (1990) Predictors of institutionalisation among Alzheimer disease victims with caregiving spouses, *Journal of Gerontology, Social Sciences*, 45B, 6, 259-266.

Pruger, R. (1977) *Making Information Work: The Story of the Equity Project*, School of Social Welfare, University of California, Berkeley, California.

Pruger, R., Miller, L., Clark, M., Helme, M. and Jew, J. (1977) *Final Report of the Homemaker Study of the Bay Area Welfare University Consortium*, School of Social Welfare, University of California, Berkeley, California.

Qureshi, H. and Walker, A. (1989) *The Caring Relationship: Elderly People and their Families*, Macmillan, London.

Qureshi, H., Challis, D. and Davies, B. (1989) *Helpers in Case-Managed Community Care*, Gower, Aldershot.

Robinson, J. (1933) *The Economics of Imperfect Competition*, Macmillan, London.

Royal Commission on Long Term Care (1999) *With Respect to Old Age: Long Term Care — Rights and Responsibilities*, Cm 4192-I, TSO, London.

Ruchlin, H.S., Morris, J.N. and Eggert, G.M. (1982) Financing long-term care: a reply, *New England Journal of Medicine*, 306, 1494-5.

Rutter, M., Tizard, J. and Whitmore, K. (1970) *Education, Health and Behaviour*, Longman, London.

Saunders, R. (1982) A community care scheme for the elderly using the voluntary agencies, Discussion Paper 200, PSSRU, University of Kent at Canterbury.

Schultz, R. (1976) Effects of control and predictability on the physical and psychological well-being of the institutionalized elderly, *Journal of Personality and Social Psychology*, 33, 563-573.

Schulz, R. and Heckhausen, J. (1999) Aging, culture and control: setting a new research agenda, *Journal of Gerontology: Psychological Sciences*, 54b, 139-145.

Seebohm Committee (1968) *Report of the Committee on Local Authority and Allied Personal Social Services*, HMSO, London.

Self, P. (1975) *Econocrats and the Policy Process*, Macmillan, London.

Shapiro, E. (1996) Patterns and predictors of home care use by the elderly when need is the sole basis for admission, *Home Health Care Services Quarterly*, 7, 1, 29-44.

Sheppard, R. (1970) *Theory of Cost and Production Functions*, Princeton University Press, Princeton, New Jersey.

Simon, H.A. (1955) A behavioural model of rational choice, *Quarterly Journal of Economics*, 69, 1, 99-118.

Sinclair, A. and Dickinson, E. (1998) *Effective Practice in Rehabilitation: The Evidence of Systematic Reviews*, King's Fund, London.

Skellie, A., Dennis, L., Favor, F., Tudor, C. and Strauss, R. (1982) *Alternative Health Services: Final Report*, Department of Medical Assistance, Atlanta, Georgia.

Soldo, B.J., Wolf, D.A. and Agree, E.M. (1990) Family, households and care arrangements of frail elder women: a structural analysis, *Journal of Gerontology: Social Sciences*, 45B, 6, S238-249.

Spector, W.D. and Fleishman, J.A. (1998) Combining activities of daily living with instrumental activities of daily living to measure functional disability, *Journal of Gerontology: Social Sciences*, 53B, 1, S46-S57.

Stevenson, O. and Parsloe, P. (1978) *Social Services Teams: the Practitioners' View*, HMSO, London.

Stoller, E.P. (1983) Parental caregiving by adult children, *Journal of Marriage and the Family*, 45, 851-858.

Stone, R.I. and Short, P.F. (1990) The competing demands of employment and informal caregiving to disabled elders, *Medical Care*, 28, 513-526.

Strawbridge, W.J., Shema, S.J., Balfour, J.L., Higby, H.R. and Kaplan, G.A. (1998) Antecedents of frailty over three decades in an older cohort, *Journal of Gerontology*, 53B, 1, S9-S16.

Thurow, L.C. (1975) *Generating Inequality* , Basic Books, New York.

Timko, C. and Moos, R.H. (1989) Choice, control and adaptation among elderly residents of sheltered care settings, *Journal of Applied Social Psychology*, 19, 636-655.

Tinker, A. (1996) Oral evidence in House of Commons Health Committee. *Third Report: Long-Term Care: Future Provision and Funding: HC 1995-96 59-II*, Q352, TSO, London.

Titmuss, R. (1970) *The Gift Relationship*, Allen and Unwin, London.

Townsend, P. (1962) *The Last Refuge*, Routledge and Kegan Paul, London.

Townsend, P. and Wedderburn, D. (1965) *The Aged in the Welfare State*, Bell, London.

Travis, S. and McCauley, W. (1985) Deviance from the ADL hierarchy in a long-term care population, *The Gerontologist*, 25, 26-30.

Tukey, J.W. and Wild, M.B. (1971) Data analysis and statistics: techniques and approaches, in E.R. Tufte (ed.) *The Quantitative Analysis of Social Problems*, Addison Wesley, Reading, Massachusetts.

Turvey, K. and Fine, M. (1996) *Community Care: The Effects of Low Levels of Service Use*, Report No. 130, November 1996, Social Policy Research Centre, University of New South Wales, Sydney.

Twigg, J. (ed.) (1992) *Carers Research and Practice*, HMSO, London.

Twigg, J. (1996) Issues in informal care, *Caring for Frail Elderly People: Policies in Evolution*, OECD, Paris.

Twigg, J. (1998) Review of S. Peace, L. Kellaher, and D. Wilcocks (1997) *Re-evaluating Residential Care, Journal of Social Policy*, 27, 295-6.

Twigg, J. and Atkin, K. (1994) *Carers Perceived, Policy and Practice in Informal Care*, Open University Press, Buckingham.

Twigg, J., and Atkin, K. (1995) Carers and services: factors mediating service provision, *Journal of Social Policy*, 24, 1, 5-30.

Utting, W. (1996) The case for reforming social services law, in T. Harding (ed.) *Social Services Law: the Case for Reform*, National Institute for Social Work, London.

Vachon, J. (1994) Coordinations gérontologique: un nouveau départ?, *Actualités Sociales Hebdomadaires*, 1868, 9-10.

Valios, N. (1999) Targeted community care harms prevention, *Community Care*, 17-23 June.

Van den Heuvel, W. and Schrijvers, G. (eds) (1986) *Innovations in Care for the Elderly: European Experiences*, Uitgeversmaatschappij de Tijdstroom Lochem – Gent.

Verbrugge L.M. and Jette, A.M. (1994) The disablement process, *Social Science and Medicine*, 38, 1-14.

Verry, D. and Davies, B. (1976) *University Costs and Outputs*, Elsevier, Amsterdam.

Veysset-Puijalon, B. (1992) *La coordinations gérontologique: démarche d'hier, enjeu pour demain*, Fondation de France, Paris.

Victor, C. and Vetter, N. (1988) Rearranging the deckchairs on the Titanic: failure of an augmented home help scheme after discharge to reduce the length of stay in hospital, *Archives of Gerontology and Geriatrics*, 7, 83-91.

Walker, A. and Warren, L. (1996) *Changing Services for Older People*, Open University Press, Buckingham.

Weber, M. (1971) *Economie et société*, Plon, Paris, 650.

Weissert, W. (1988) The National Channeling Demonstration: What we knew, know now and still need to know, *Health Services Research*, 23, 1, 175-198.

Weissert, W., Cready, C. and Pawelak, J. (1998) The past and future of home and community-based long-term care, *The Milbank Quarterly*, 66, 309-88.

Wenger, C. (1992) *Help in Old Age: Facing up to Change: A Longitudinal Network Study*, Liverpool University Press, Liverpool.

Wiener, J., Hanley, R., Clark, R. and Van Nostrand, J. (1990) Measuring the activities of daily living: comparisons across national surveys, *Journal of Gerontology: Social Sciences*, 45, 229-237.

Williams, A. (1974) Need as a demand concept, in A.J. Culyer (ed.) *Economic Policies and Social Goals*, Martin Robertson, London.

Wistow, G., Knapp, M., Hardy, B. and Allen, C. (1994) *Social Care in a Mixed Economy*, Open University Press, Buckingham.

Wistow, G., Knapp, M., Hardy, B., Forder, J., Kendall, J. and Manning, R. (1996) *Social Care Markets: Progress and Prospects*, Open University Press, Buckingham.

Wittenberg, R., Pickard, L., Comas, A., Davies, B. and Darton, R. (1998) Demand for Long-Term Care: Projections of Long-Term Care Finance for Elderly People, PSSRU monograph, PSSRU, University of Kent at Canterbury.

Wright, K. (1998) Cost opportunities and constraints in developing secondary health care in the community, in D. Challis, R. Darton and K. Stewart (eds) *Community Care, Secondary Health Care and Care Management*, PSSRU Studies, Ashgate, Aldershot, 137-148.

Yates, M.E., Tennstedt, S. and Chang, B.-H. (1999) Contributors to and mediators of psychological well-being for informal caregivers, *Journal of Gerontology*, January.

Yesavage, J.A., Brink, T.L., Rose, T.L., Lum, O., Huang, V., Adey, M. and Leirer, V.O. (1983) Development and validation of a geriatric depression screening scale: a preliminary report, *Journal of Psychiatric Research*, 17, 1, 37-49.

Young, K. and Kramer, J. (1978) *Strategy and Conflict in Metropolitan Housing*, Heinemann, London.

Zarit, S.H. (1997) Brief measures of depression and cognitive function, *Generations*, 21, 1, 41-43.

Ziebland, S., Fitzpatrick, R. and Jenkinson, C. (1993) Tacit models of disability underlying health status instruments, *Social Science and Medicine*, 37, 69-75.

Author Index

Subject Index